# THESE
# AMERICAN
# LANDS

# THESE
# AMERICAN
# LANDS

## Parks, Wilderness, and the Public Lands

DYAN ZASLOWSKY AND
THE WILDERNESS SOCIETY

HENRY HOLT AND COMPANY
NEW YORK

TO T. H. WATKINS

LIBRARY OF CONGRESS CATALOGING-IN-PUBLICATION DATA
Zaslowsky, Dyan.
These American lands.
"Portions of this book first appeared in *Wilderness* magazine"—T.p. verso.
Bibliography: p.
Includes index.
1. National park and reserves—United States—History.
2. Wilderness areas—United States—History.
3. United States—Public lands—History.
I. Wilderness Society. II. Title.
E160.Z37     1986     973          86–3156
ISBN 0-8050-0084-4

First Edition

Designer: Ann Gold
Maps copyright © 1986 by David Lindroth
Printed in the United States of America

1   3   5   7   9   10   8   6   4   2

ISBN 0-8050-0084-4

# CONTENTS

# CONTENTS

# FOREWORD

The substantial and impressive document you hold in your hands was launched, I'm happy to report, as the result of a long-standing complaint of mine that there was no single source to which interested Americans (conservationists included) could turn that would tell them everything it was important to know about the most magnificent natural inheritance enjoyed by any nation on earth—the more than 600 million acres of America's public lands. One could find individual books about the national parks, or the national forests, or Alaska, or wildlife refuges, and even a couple that dealt with the national resource lands of the Bureau of Land Management. Few such books, however, combined the past and present in a coherent narrative, fewer still discussed with sufficient detail and authority the manifold problems afflicting the nation's public lands, and none addressed itself to presenting a blueprint for the future management and expansion of this splendid legacy. I suggested that The Wilderness Society produce a modest series of reports—we dubbed them the "white papers"—that would satisfy the needs outlined above and do so in a manner palatable to the general reader.

Well, those "white papers" have since become a good deal more ambitious and useful (as well as more attractive). In the skilled hands of author Dyan Zaslowsky and The Wilderness Society's diligent staff of resource specialists, they have been transformed into a volume that not only meets all those specifications in fine style but does so within a single set of covers.

No man's complaint ever had a happier ending. It is all here in one comprehensive package: the history, problems, and prospects of America's national parks, national forests, national resource lands, wildlife refuges, designated wildernesses, Alaska lands, wild and scenic rivers, and national trails. Each chapter outlines in a lively fashion the history of the unit of public lands under discussion, clarifies the resource use and policy conflicts that are currently besetting it, then follows with a detailed "agenda" that sets forth the management, expansion, and preservation goals that The Wilderness Society believes the conservation community, Congress, and the federal land-managing agencies will need to meet to ensure the future health of the United States' most precious resource. Finally, an appendix offers—for the first time in a single place—all relevant statistical information regarding these lands (including the only existing comprehensive list of the names, locations, and acreage of the entire current National Wilderness Preservation System), together with a handy chronological history of all major public land legislation.

There is no other book like it anywhere, and I believe that it is destined to become one of the most relied-upon tools available to the conservation community, Congress, policymakers, land managers, and, indeed, any citizen in search of a true and solid understanding of our national patrimony of lands.

That such an understanding is needed now and will be needed even more profoundly in the future should go without saying. That it does not illustrates the dimensions of the problems facing us today. A little over twenty years ago, the modern conservation movement appeared to have gained an impetus that would ensure its permanent and continuing influence on the shaping of public land policies. The Wilderness Act of 1964—unique among the nations of the world— seemed to mark the beginning of a national shift away from the tradition of exploitation to that respect for the whole community of life which Aldo Leopold called the Land Ethic. In the next sixteen years, more wilderness areas, parks, wildlife refuges, lakeshores, and seashores were established than in any other period of our nation's history. During this same period, dramatic gains were made in controlling air and water pollution, in regulating strip mining and other environmentally damaging activities, and in managing solid wastes and recycling resources. We even made a start, albeit a small one, in controlling hazardous wastes and toxic substances, and in regulating the use of dangerous herbicides and pesticides. From politicians to businessmen, all Americans seemed to agree that no domestic issue was more important to the nation in the long run than the conservation and wise use of our natural resources.

Tragically, at the precise moment in history when circumstances demanded not just a continuation of past policies but a vigorous expansion of them, we received a presidential administration that launched its own shortsighted campaign to turn the clock back. More and more frequently we began to hear the argument that we cannot afford environmental goals—that it costs too much to protect the integrity of the air, water, and soil; that it is a misappropriation of the taxpayers' hard-earned money to buy new parklands and wildlife refuges; that wilderness designation "locks up" oil, gas, timber, and other resources necessary to the continued health and growth of the economy. We have to choose, it was argued, between the environment and the economy.

This is an old argument, and as wrong now as when it was being used to oppose the conservation movement when it was young; it is the lineal descendant of the argument used to destroy the Hetch Hetchy Valley more than seventy years ago. Those who hold such beliefs miss the vital point that the economy and the environment are inextricably intertwined; while you can have a country rich in resources with a poor economy, you cannot have a rich economy in a country poor in its resources or its access to them—and if we continue to degrade and destroy our own, in the end we will have invented our own poverty. When it is asked how much it will cost to protect the environment, one more question should be asked: How much will it cost our civilization if we do not?

This book can help to answer that question—and I am convinced that it can also delineate a path by which we may not only avoid the worst but achieve the best.

Gaylord Nelson
Counselor, The Wilderness Society
Washington, D.C.

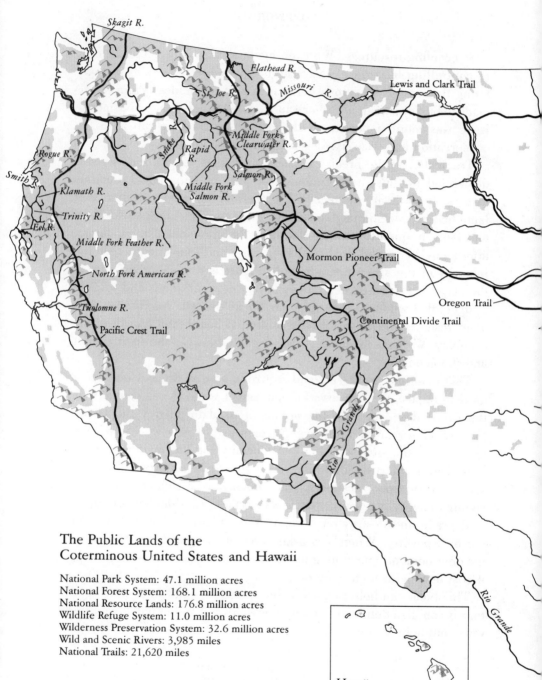

Skagit R.

Flathead R.

Lewis and Clark Trail

St. Joe R.

Missouri R.

Middle Fork
Clearwater R.

Snake

Rapid
R.

Rogue R.

Salmon R.

Smith R.

Klamath R.

Middle Fork
Salmon R.

Trinity R.

Eel R.

Middle Fork Feather R.

Mormon Pioneer Trail

North Fork American R.

Oregon Trail

Tuolomne R.

Continental Divide Trail

Pacific Crest Trail

Rio Grande

Rio Grande

## The Public Lands of the
## Coterminous United States and Hawaii

National Park System: 47.1 million acres
National Forest System: 168.1 million acres
National Resource Lands: 176.8 million acres
Wildlife Refuge System: 11.0 million acres
Wilderness Preservation System: 32.6 million acres
Wild and Scenic Rivers: 3,985 miles
National Trails: 21,620 miles

Hawaii

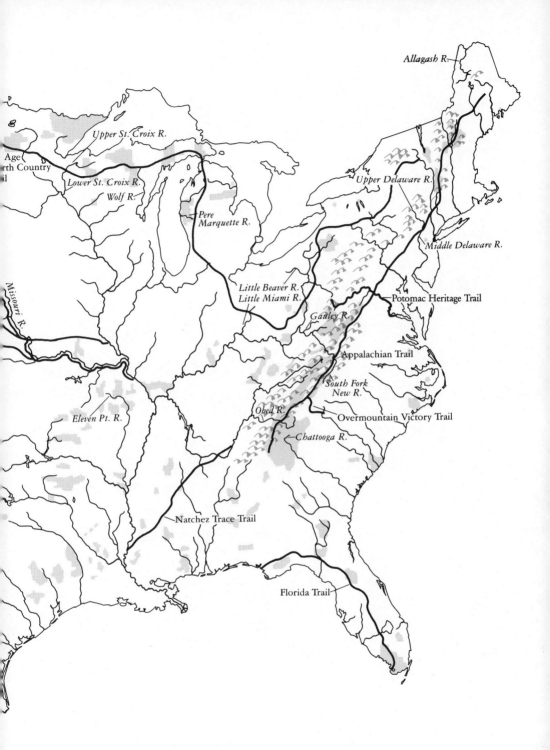

Allagash R.

Upper St. Croix R.

Age
rth Country
l

Lower St. Croix R.
Wolf R.

Pere
Marquette R.

Upper Delaware R.

Middle Delaware R.

Missouri R.

Little Beaver R.
Little Miami R.

Potomac Heritage Trail

Gauley R.

Appalachian Trail

South Fork
New R.

Obed R.

Overmountain Victory Trail

Eleven Pt. R.

Chattooga R.

Natchez Trace Trail

Florida Trail

# THE VIEW
# FROM HOME

From my house and neighborhood I can see the difference between private and public land. In this mountain suburb the privately owned lots are two acres or more, and the houses built on them are large. The yards are decorated with swings and redwood decks. There are hot tubs, and dog runs slant down the sunny slope. Some residents have fenced out others. I can see that more and more people are installing satellite dishes to pick up cable-television programs, and one of our neighbors has planted an orange windsock on his roof to guide his helicopter onto a landing pad. A llama farm occupies the valley below. Our property expresses ourselves; we do what we like with the land we own.

The houses are oriented to achieve the best views, which lie beyond the llama farm, to the south and west. A forest of pine, fir, and spruce drapes one million acres of rugged country, and depending on the season, the higher elevations are streaked with the pale green, gold, or silver of aspen. All the trees play out at twelve thousand feet. The Continental Divide, outstretched like an eagle's wing, soars another 2,400 feet above the treeline. At night the forest is as black and concentrated as pitch, making the sky light by comparison. This is all national forestland, all belonging to that portion of the continent that will never be subdivided and subjected to impulse. Such is our

1

understanding as, with a hypocritical sense of relief, we welcome the knowledge that limitations have been imposed on the spread of the sort of temporal pleasures that confuse even our own yards. The exercise of free choice on private property has resulted in a patchwork of development, raising our living standards possibly, yet leaving us unsatisfied. Where we live, the value of our property is mostly determined by the permanence of the big, raw reach of public land. We have bought proximity to a national forest, and with it a view that astonishes us every morning. But it is hard to forget that the land, the source of our astonishment, is commonly owned. The land beyond the llama farm is our shared patrimony and, as long as major distinctions are enforced, our greatest material bequest.

One-third of the nation's land is publicly owned, and managed by various bureaus of the federal government for the perpetuation of America's natural resources. The public land systems compensate for the chief shortcoming of free enterprise—which is its inability to respond to any but its own pressing demands, all of them originating, understandably, in the need to maximize profits as quickly as possible. "On the evidence of several generations of exploitative freedom no one could guarantee the future its share of the American earth except the American government," wrote Wallace Stegner in *Beyond the Hundredth Meridian.* Despite the accumulating evidence of land abused through economic incentives, the federal government did not assume the role of conservator easily, or in one bold leap forward. Congress dispensed federal assistance only as a last resort— approaching, then avoiding, matters that questioned the ultimate wisdom of unchecked private initiative.

Consider the 1872 debate surrounding the reservation of Yellowstone, the first national park. "I have grave doubts about the propriety of passing this bill," said Senator Cornelius Cole of California in 1872. "The geysers will remain, no matter where the ownership of the land may be, and I do not know why settlers should be excluded from a tract of land forty miles square. . . . I can't see how the natural curiosities can be interfered with if settlers are allowed to appropriate them." The park was finally set aside after assurances from the politically savvy geographer Ferdinand V. Hayden that the Yellowstone region was as worthless as it was magnificent, and hence of no use

2

to future settlers. From that time to this, nature preservation has always been submitted to an economic calculus for which it is poorly suited. Ironically, the national parks were quickly accepted as the embodiment of democracy. They were, in fact, "a predictable response to despoliation and avarice," noted Joseph L. Sax, a law professor and public-land theorist. National parks, according to Sax's *Mountains Without Handrails*,

> harmonized with a principle that was at the very crest of its influence in American land policy. The Yellowstone era was also the time of the Homestead and Desert Land Acts, when every American family was to have its share of the public domain free of monopolization by the rich. The application of that principle to the great scenic wonders could not be realized by granting a sequoia grove or Grand Canyon to each citizen. But it was possible to preserve the spectacular sites for the average citizen by holding them as public places to be enjoyed by all.

The same principle logically extends to the public land systems that followed the establishment of national parks.

Apart from the politically understandable desire to avoid restraining the Great White Hope of free enterprise, there was another, more deeply seated reason why a broad consensus in favor of nature conservation and appreciation took longer than necessary to take root. To the earliest European arrivals, land that had not been subdued to man's ends was wilderness, and the word had only terrifying connotations. Pioneer concepts of wilderness had been shaped by the Bible, and, according to those who have counted, the Old and New Testaments contain some three hundred disparaging references to it. The ancestral memory of Europe's frontier during the Dark and Middle Ages bound the meaning of wilderness even more closely to brutish existence. "Successive waves of frontiersmen had to contend with wilderness as uncontrolled and terrifying as that which primitive man confronted," wrote Roderick Nash, a historian of the American wilderness movement, in *Wilderness and the American Mind*.

> Safety and comfort, even necessities like food and shelter, depended on overcoming the wild environment. For the first Americans, as for

3

medieval Europeans, the forest's darkness hid savage men, wild beasts and still stranger creatures of the imagination. In addition civilized man faced the danger of succumbing to the wilderness of his surroundings and reverting to savagery himself. The pioneer, in short, lived too close to wilderness for appreciation.

Americans had to become more citified before they could abide wildness in their world.

Possibly too much has been blamed on the Judeo-Christian teachings calling for the subjugation of the earth. Often cited in this argument is Genesis 1:28, in which man is given dominion over nature and is divinely blessed. But environmental degradation occurred long before many civilizations had any contact with biblical writings. China, for instance, was deforested years before the first Christian missionaries arrived. Besides, the early teachers in almost all religions instructed their adherents on how to take care of the land. Hebrews were commanded to let fields lie fallow every seventh year so that soil nutrients would be restored. "Woe unto them that join house to house, that lay field to field, till there is no place where one may be alone in the midst of the earth," Isaiah admonished. Noticing the disparity between the preaching and the practice, the scientist René Dubos said that "the professed ideals of a culture, like those of its politicians, are rarely translated into actual practice, but this is at least as true of Orientals as of Western peoples." According to Dubos, deforestation, combined with ignorance of the long-range effects of intensive agriculture, is the main reason for the deterioration of land, rather than a conscious effort to destroy it.

While no single culture holds the patent for land abuse, the newly formed United States was gifted with more wild land than any other modern nation in the world. The land was wasted at an appalling rate, accelerated further still by such improved axes, saws, and firearms as the colonists could acquire. Nineteenth-century artists and authors recorded numerous instances of profligacy. James Fenimore Cooper's Leatherstocking novels, glorifying the noble savage, warned of excess. Richard Jones, a fool in Cooper's *The Pioneers*, scoffs when he is told not to burn too much wood. "Why, you might as well predict that the fish will die for want of water in the lake!" he retorts. Actually, by the 1820s, wood shortages were severe in many New England towns, and poorer families froze to death in winter. In Vermont alone, so much of the forest cover had been cut or burned that the land was good only for grazing sheep, which made the situation worse.

A reckless attitude toward natural resources had quickly become a national trait, just as Europeans were beginning to curse their own habit of waste. For them it was too late; hardly any open land remained. In America, the critics were rising. Among them was an odd man named Henry David Thoreau, observed in his native Concord, Massachusetts, standing in downpours for hours, or staring at mallards on a pond long after his neighbors deemed there was any purpose in it. He won national acclaim for *Walden, or, Life in the Woods*, published in 1854. *Walden* recorded Thoreau's experiment of living in the woods alone, in a cabin he built himself. "If a man walks in the woods for love of them half of each day, he is in danger of being regarded as a loafer, but if he spends his whole day as a speculator shearing off those woods and making the earth bald before her time, he is esteemed as an industrious and enterprising citizen," he wrote. In an essay for *The Atlantic Monthly* four years later, Thoreau wrote, "The pine is no more lumber than man is, and to be made into boards and houses is no more its true and highest use than the truest use of a man is to be cut down and made into manure. There is a higher law affecting our relation to pines as well as to men." To Thoreau, who died in 1862 at the age of forty-five, the perfect man in the perfect place would permit civilization into no more than half his life, letting nature rule the other half.

And that portion was hardly enough for bearded, peripatetic John Muir, who had come from Scotland when still a boy. Temporarily blinded in an accident while working in a wheel factory, Muir vowed that once he regained his eyesight he would live only in wild places. Light returned, and Muir set out, wandering for years, studying the earth, botanizing, and dodging the draft that had been instituted during the Civil War. Before his explorations led him into the remotest pockets of the North American continent, including Alaska, Muir greatly admired Thoreau, and Thoreau's own mentor, Ralph Waldo Emerson. But Muir was as fervently committed to making changes as these men were to talking and writing about them. Eventually Muir dismissed Thoreau as "the captain of a huckleberry party."

Muir's accounts of his travels and opinions on man's role in nature were published in the widely read *Century Magazine* and elsewhere. "The world, we are told, was made for man, a presumption that is totally unsupported by facts," Muir wrote, repudiating his Calvinist upbringing. "Nature's object in making animals and plants might possibly be first of all the happiness of each of them, not the creation of all for the happiness of one. Why ought man to value himself as more than an infinitely small composing unit of the great unit of creation, and what creature of all the Lord has taken the pains to make it less essential to the grand completeness of the unit?"

And Muir acted: he vigorously championed the nascent national park movement, and the addition of Yosemite was his almost exclusive contribution to the system. Muir knew the valley better than any man, having debunked the prevailing theories of its geological origins. Before most people could accept the idea, Muir knew that the only hope for nature's preservation lay with the U.S. government. Decisive protection was needed desperately in all the national parks, although Frederick Law Olmsted, the principal planner of New York's Central Park, had beaten Muir to that conclusion before there even were national parks. Muir also believed forests needed to be nationalized, and he applied himself to that end. Being famous in his own right made the famous seek him out. He became nature's most eloquent spokesman, a man who knew the language of both trees and Americans, and initiated a vital communication between them. In one of those delightful instances of historical convergence, President Theodore Roosevelt invited Muir to meet him in Yosemite and to tell him more about government's duties in preservation. During their time together, Roosevelt asked only that they "keep away from civilization." Then, for three nights, "two major figures in American history enacted in microcosm the culture's persistent dream: creative truancy in the wild heart of the New World," wrote Frederick Turner in *Rediscovering America*, his biography of Muir.

Although the federal role in land preservation did not evolve exactly as Muir had advised, there is no doubt that many of his opinions influenced Roosevelt, the first chief executive to put conservation on the national agenda. Even with Roosevelt's great strides, however, public land management has, since the beginning of the century, withstood the various thrusts and parries of the political system. Until the last twenty years or so, public lands lacked a unifying theme: units of land for the many aspects of preservation were added piecemeal; false hopes lingered. Some administrations have been more mistrustful than others of public lands' purpose and of those directed to fulfill it, believing, as Senator Cole did in 1872, that the private sector can do everything right, given a chance. Any slippage away from the slowly emerged ideal can have serious long-range consequences. A friend of mine from the Soviet Union asserts that U.S. preservation policies still make too many concessions to private enterprise to do any good. Wilderness areas for public recreation? Air-conditioned hotels in national parks? What message is being sent to the people? he asks. Such lenience will lead to failure, he predicts, resulting in weakened nature and soft people. This friend, who is in private a harsh critic of his own regime in most matters, praises the strict Soviet approach to preservation. "Nature must be left completely alone somewhere," he insists. Armed guards are posted around nature reserves in the USSR, and access to the reserves is limited to approved scientists.

These are unacceptable measures in the United States, where effective perpetuation of all publicly held resources must begin with the recognition that public land is not an anomaly in American life, but an integral part of it. Side-by-side systems of private and public land can function symbiotically. Maintaining a large base of land in its natural, healthy condition makes it possible for us to prosper. Meanwhile, the material indications that the nation is very well off also suggest that the United States can afford to protect its landed estate. As Israel's prime minister, David Ben-Gurion, remarked when he flew over the West in the early 1960s, "Who but America can afford to keep such deserts?" Nature, wrote Professor Sax, "is also a successful model of many things that human communities seek: continuity, stability, and sustenance, adaptation, sustained productivity, diversity and evolutionary change. . . . Natural systems renew themselves without any exhaustion of resources . . . they thrive on tolerance of diversity and [they] resist the arrogance of the conquerors. . . ." Natural systems are good ones to emulate, but at this point in our cultural evolution, government must show us how, by emphasizing always that health, beauty, and permanence are the only

7

important goods, and by educating us to the fact that productivity, measured longitudinally, is the by-product, and not the overriding commitment. Wrote Wallace Stegner:

> If that government contained quarreling and jealous bureaus, that was too bad. If it sheltered grafters . . . too bad. If it was too far from the resources in question to make every decision right, too bad.
>
> Too bad. But the alternative was worse. The alternative was creeping deserts, flooded river valleys, dusty miles of unused and unusable land, feeble or partial or monopolistic utilization of the available land and water. The alternative was great power and great wealth to a few and for a brief time rather than competence and independence for the communities of small freeholders on which [the] political economy unchangeably rested.

As this book will relate, America's history is rife with such grim alternatives. America's future, with regard to its parks, forests, wildlife, rivers, and nonrenewable resources, can tell another story.

Dyan Zaslowsky
Evergreen, Colorado

# 1

# THE PLEASURING GROUNDS

## The National Park System

By moonbeam and the bagged yellow light of two hundred glowing *farolitos*, fifty foreign guests steered their way down a tight passage into the Cliff Palace Ruin at Mesa Verde National Park in southern Colorado. Out on the far edge of candlelight, in the back of an Anasazi chamber, a Ute Indian sat cross-legged and played the oboe. "I have wanted to come here for a thousand years," murmured a man from Kupang, Indonesia, cradling himself against a slick-rock pillow. In the gently orchestrated darkness of this late summer's night in 1984, he and the others must have felt the truth in the fact that the world would be poorer without such places as Mesa Verde—without, on a grand scale, the whole national park system of the United States.

Along with free public education and private philanthropy, the creation of natural national parks ranks among the few thoroughly American contributions to world culture. And the success of the United States' venture has encouraged the establishment of more than 1,200 national parks in over one hundred countries. The 334 units of our own national park system, encompassing 89 million acres, are the portion of federally retained lands that Americans encounter soonest, understand best, and cherish most. Touching affirmation of this is evident in letters written to National Park Service officials by battle-worn soldiers during several wars. A soldier wrote from Europe during World War II:

I had no conception of how much the national parks could mean in wartime until I came here. If you could hear the men talk of our parks and forests, you know how great a part they play in the American scene. When the talk turns to "before the war," it is invariably . . . the hours spent with rod and reel on lake and stream, the camping trips, the quiet nights in the pine woods . . . and it is those things that these men are fighting for, as well as for their homes, sweethearts, wives and families.

The forty-eight national parks cover about 47 million acres. Many of these—Yosemite, Yellowstone, Olympic, for example—are considered the "crown jewels" of the system by virtue of their extraordinary natural beauty and wildness, but the system has grown well beyond its original and revolutionary purpose of preserving spectacular landscapes for the pleasure of the public. In the past century it has sprouted numerous monuments, preserves, lakeshores, rivers, seashores, historic sites, memorials, military parks, battlefield parks, historical parks, recreation areas, parkways, and other additions—all preceded by the word "national" in official usages, and all intended to inspire or edify the public. The diversity of the group commemorates not only the continent's natural gifts, but the course of its human events as well. This combination has at times strained the National Park Service's ability to cover all bases. The jurisdiction of the Park Service, with its billion-dollar annual budget and more than eight thousand full-time employees, ranges from the 8.3-million-acre Wrangell–St. Elias National Park and Preserve in Alaska to the one-third-acre Ford's Theatre National Historic Site in the District of Columbia. The agency must perpetuate the backwoods solitude of Wyoming's Grand Tetons, and accommodate an audience of 9,500 on the rolling lawn of the Wolf Trap Farm Park for the Performing Arts in Virginia.

Such diverse responsibilities have aroused the complaint that the mission of the National Park Service has been muddied. Rather than concentrate on administering a few things very well, some critics charge, the Service diffuses its energies and talents among too many duties of a contradictory nature. If so, it is symptomatic of a paradox that has haunted the agency ever since 1916 and the Organic Act that created it. The Service's mission in regard to the national parks, that act stated, was "to conserve the scenery and the natural and historic objects and wildlife therein and to provide for the enjoyment of the same in such manner and by such means as will leave them unimpaired for the enjoyment of future generations." But at no point did the act define precisely how this delicate balance between preservation and public pleasure was to be accomplished or maintained— and there still are no precise guidelines to solve one of the Park Service's most persistent modern dilemmas, as succinctly outlined by Ronald A. Foresta in *America's National Parks and Their Keepers*: "If use destroys, how can a management policy both accommodate use and preserve the natural area? A mandate which is inherently contradictory must, by logical extension, become a management dilemma—a problem for which there is no solution that does not violate a restraint."

Ironically, contradictions in American society itself once provided the national park system with its greatest support. As Joseph L. Sax wrote in *Mountains Without Handrails: Reflections on the National Parks*:

> The happy convergence of many disparate interests permitted Congress and the public to sustain contradictory, but compatible beliefs that permitted a park system to flourish: On one side the repugnance of the seemingly boundless materialism that infused American life, a spiritual attachment to untrammeled nature, and a self-congratulatory attitude toward the preservation of nature's bounty; and on the other a commitment to economic progress wherever it could be exacted, nationalistic pride, and the practical uses of nature as a commodity supportive of tourism and commercial recreation.

## TOWARD A "NATION'S PARK"

It was a long journey from the happy condition described by Sax to the frustrations of today. It began in 1832, but not, as one might expect, because that was the year that Congress withdrew the region of Hot Springs, Arkansas, from appropriation by the various land laws and declared it the first natural federal preserve. Hot Springs was valued not for its scenic grandeur or even its claim as a natural

11

wonder, but for its perceived medicinal value; this was the great age of hydrotherapy, and Congress believed that all Americans should have access to the curative waters that bubbled up in that part of the Ozarks (Hot Springs, in fact, did not formally enter the modern national park system until 1921). The real beginning that year took place a thousand miles to the northwest, at the confluence of the Missouri and Yellowstone rivers, where a young artist stood amazed at the beauty of the country all around him. His name was George Catlin. His specialty was painting Indians, and to find them he had gone aboard the first steamboat to ascend the Missouri as far as the mouth of the Yellowstone. He surveyed the untamed landscape along the river and wrote in his journal that that place, or some other place in the West, ought to be set aside as a "nation's park, containing man and beast, in all the freshness of their nature's beauty." Catlin added that "I would ask no other monument to my memory, nor any enrollment of my name among the famous dead, than the reputation of having been the founder of such an institution."

As an artist who used nature as the backdrop of his paintings, Catlin was more sensitive to natural beauty than were many of his countrymen. Yet he may also have been reacting to the sense of cultural inferiority that penetrated the young, entrepreneurial nation. National park historian Alfred Runte maintains that the park movement sprang originally from America's desire to appear as refined as the older nations of Europe. But the United States, barely emerged from the cleared forests, had no cathedrals, no Roman ruins, and no intricate gardens that bespoke human triumph and national greatness. Writing in his *Sketch Book* in 1819, Washington Irving shared a common view when he said he preferred to "wander over the scenes of renowned achievement—to tread, as it were, in the footsteps of antiquity—to loiter about the ruined castle—to meditate on the falling tower—to escape, in short, from commonplace reality of the present, and lose myself among the shadowy grandeurs of the past." At about the same time, James Fenimore Cooper acknowledged that Europe contained the "sublimer views," unless the United States resorted to "the Rocky mountains and the ranges of California and Mexico"— which at that time were as foreign to the United States as was Europe.

Aggravating this sense of cultural anxiety was the fact that Americans had generally left their most scenic areas in a shambles. Niagara Falls had been recognized as the nation's greatest natural spectacle, but by the 1830s its cliffs were combed by rogues and unscrupulous operators, who laid claim to the best overlooks and then charged tourists exorbitantly for the view. Fly-by-night enterprise cluttered the area, turning the place into a cheap circus. The setting had become so tawdry that when Alexis de Tocqueville visited the Falls in 1831, he urged an American friend to "hasten" to see the place before all its grandeur was lost. Delay, Tocqueville warned, would mean that "your Niagara will have been spoiled for you. Already the forest round about is being cleared. I don't give the Americans ten years to establish a saw or flour mill at the base of the cataract."

The fact that some Americans were beginning to see the disgrace for themselves and realize (as Catlin did) that symbols of national greatness lay in another direction was not sufficient to make Congress try to protect "scenery," not even in 1864, when it turned the Yosemite Valley over to the state of California for operation as a park. This casual gesture, made by a Congress preoccupied with the Civil War, hardly preserved the valley. Since the state did not mind commercial enterprise—but, indeed, encouraged it—the valley was soon victimized by the same kind of exploitation (including grazing and logging this time) that had made such a mess of Niagara Falls.

Yosemite was sublime even in disgrace, but little known outside its own state. In Wyoming Territory, however, a few hundred miles southwest of the spot where Catlin had discerned his vision of a "nation's park," lay the Yellowstone country, the subject of widespread if sometimes incredulous fascination almost from the beginning of the nation's expansion into the trans-Mississippi West. It lay untouched by anything but wonder, and had for a long time.

First word of the Yellowstone region was brought to civilization in 1807, when John Colter returned from a solo trip. Colter had been a member of the Lewis and Clark expedition, but, in 1805, enticed by the possibilities of fur trapping, he asked to take his leave. He was released, and Lewis's journal makes this note: "The example of this man shows us how easily men may be weaned from the habits of civilized life to the ruder but scarcely less fascinating manners of the woods. Just at the moment when he is approaching the frontiers,

13

he is tempted by a hunting scheme to give up those delightful prospects and goes back without the least reluctance to the solitude of the woods."

The solitude of the woods led Colter to Yellowstone Lake, the land of geysers and of falls higher than those of Niagara. He returned to St. Louis with rich pelts and richer tales of boiling springs and towers of water that rose one hundred feet. Apparently he "saw too much for his reputation as a man of veracity," wrote the historian Hiram Martin Chittenden. No one believed him. The place he described was jeeringly known as "Colter's Hell." It did not help matters that Jim Bridger, a mountain man, was apparently the next English-speaking person to return from the area with breathless descriptions. Bridger was well-known as a man who played fast and loose with the truth. He confirmed Colter's sighting of geysers and hot springs, but he embellished these realities with glittering reports of petrified birds that sang petrified songs, of mountains made entirely of glass that had the property of telescopes and so transparent that a person could walk right into them if he wasn't watchful. And so the region of the Yellowstone remained little more than a fantasy land for most of the busiest years of the westward movement. Between 1804 and 1870 there were 110 scientific explorations west of the Mississippi River, but only one of them was assigned to the Yellowstone region, and that was not until 1859. In that year, Captain W. F. Raynolds was ordered to report his findings around Yellowstone, so that the stories of nature's opulence could be either confirmed or denied. At one point Captain Raynolds stood where he could see the entire region of the park. But he got no closer. News that the Civil War had erupted reached him, along with orders that sent him back to the States. In his wistful report, Captain Raynolds noted that duty compelled him to content himself with "listening to marvelous tales of burning plains and immense lakes without verifying these wonders."

Finally, in 1870, an exploration party of nineteen men from the Montana Territory organized a trip that would once and for all set the record straight. Cornelius Hedges, the member of the party who usually receives credit for coming up with the national park idea, noted that "a more confirmed set of skeptics never went out into the wilderness than those who composed our party, and never was a party more completely surprised and captivated with the wonders of nature." Even Old Faithful cooperated. When the party came within several hundred feet of the geyser, a massive flume of water shot 150 feet into the air. The popular story is that while Hedges, Nathaniel P. Langford, and other expedition members sat around their campfire at the junction of the Gibbon and Firehold rivers one night, they discussed Yellowstone's possibilities. Once their reports were published, Yellowstone would, of course, be exploited to the fullest. Hedges, with Langford supporting him, rejected this scenario and decided that the Yellowstone country should be set aside as a national park, preserved in its natural state. Whether or not such a conversation took place is debatable. Historians now believe an employee of the Northern Pacific Railroad by the name of A. B. Nettleson first passed this suggestion on to his superiors in Washington, D.C. Moreover, even if Hedges did bring up the subject of a national park, he did not originate the idea, because a few years earlier he had heard a Jesuit missionary make the same suggestion while giving a talk on Yellowstone in Helena, Montana. And as early as 1865, Montana Territorial Governor Thomas E. Meagher had voiced a similar proposal. Whoever originated the notion, it was clearly an idea whose time was near. In 1871, Ferdinand Vandiveer Hayden took his Geological and Geographical Survey of the Territories into Yellowstone with artist Thomas Moran and photographer William Henry Jackson. Moran's paintings and Jackson's photographs were added to the support material of a growing number of park promoters. By now, these included no less than Jay Cooke of the Northern Pacific Railroad, who backed the idea on the quite proper assumption that anything that promoted the wonders of the West could do wonders for his railroad.

The promotional flurry paid off on March 1, 1872, when Congress created Yellowstone National Park as "a public park or pleasuring ground for the benefit and enjoyment of the people." With the easy establishment of Yellowstone, Congress inaugurated the dubious tradition of creating a park without appropriating money for its protection. The government operated under the delusion that the park would pay its own way once visitors started streaming in. The delusion was a fortunate one insofar as it led to the establishment of the park; once it was created, however, there was no money to operate it. For the first five years Superintendent Nathaniel Langford donated his time and services. For the next twenty-two years no superintendent had the legal authority to detain or discipline the countless vandals and poachers who infiltrated the park once its fame spread. A superintendent could do no more than evict an offender from the park; the closest seat of justice lay 250 mountainous miles away, in the town of Evanston. Moreover, Yellowstone's enabling act contained no provision for the protection of wildlife, leaving game vulnerable to slaughter. The buffalo in the park constituted one of the few wild herds left in the country, but poaching reduced their number from 541 to twenty-two before Congress finally appropriated funds to buy domesticated specimens to breed with the remaining wild ones.

Tourists, rare as they were at first, added to the headaches. Visitors painted their names on any surface they could reach, and threw boots and small trees into the geysers and hot springs. Anyone who visited the park in its earliest years deserved some credit, however, because getting there was no weekend excursion. Congress had sternly rejected the railroads' frequent bid to lay track right through the park, and it was many years before even a branch line served it. Consequently the best route to Yellowstone was the northern one, from Bismarck in Dakota Territory. But first the traveler would have to take a steamboat up the Missouri River 400 miles to the Yellowstone River, up that another 360 miles to the mouth of the Bighorn, then another 60 miles up the Bighorn to Clark's Fork. At this point a coach would take travelers the last 72 miles to the park's border. The distance from Bismarck was 1,050 miles, and the round trip took from three to four weeks. This was not only the shortest route—in terms of mileage—it was the cheapest, although the $100 it cost was a princely sum at the time.

And the hardships were just beginning. Lodging was unreliable—unbuilt, in fact, for several years after its predicted completion. Food could be downright poisonous. From the outset, Congress had intended preservation to go hand in hand with use, and in 1882 it made the first concession agreement with a pair of businessmen from Dakota Territory. In exchange for the free use of 4,400 acres of prime scenic land, Carroll T. Hobart and Henry F. Douglas would feed and shelter park visitors via their Yellowstone Improvement Company. Unfortunately, the company's "improvements" included a planned luxury hotel, the killing and consumption of wild game ostensibly under park protection, and the stripping of timber for construction of the Mammoth Hot Springs Hotel. The agreement was canceled, and in its aftermath Congress decided that certain standards had to be established and enforced. For example, no longer could forests be logged arbitrarily, nor could construction take place within one-quarter of a mile of the park's most important wonders. Still, the word "improvement" continued to be used in reference to levels of accommodation, ranging from tents on platforms and a zealous effort to produce hot meals to more palatial appointments. The term was vague enough to inspire one European-trained landscape artist to devise a plan that would have placed an observatory, a rowing club, a forest institute, a swimming pool, a racetrack, and health spas throughout the park. He also recommended setting aside "thousands of acres for private villas."

Congress may not have been at all sure of what it meant by "improvement," but it made great strides in defining it after a commission visited Yellowstone in 1885 and made some important suggestions. The park, commission members agreed, should be "spared the vandalism of improvement" as much as possible. Yellowstone's "great and only charms are in the display of wonderful forms of nature, the ever-varying beauty of the rugged landscape, and the sublimity of the scenery. Art cannot embellish them," the report stated. Nevertheless, anarchy continued in Yellowstone, while Congress continued to refuse to empower or adequately fund a park supervisory staff. Desperate for assistance, the Secretary of the Interior had only one avenue open to him. He could, at his discretion, ask the Secretary of War to station troops in the park, which is exactly what Lieutenant General Philip Sheridan had suggested years earlier. And so, late on the evening of August 17, 1886, Troop M of the United States Cavalry rode into Yellowstone and relieved the civilian superintendent of his duties. The cavalry's presence was assumed to be temporary. It remained there, however, for thirty-two years, and by all accounts did an excellent job. Army supervision was later established in Yosemite, Sequoia, and General Grant parks as well, and in the performance of their duties the military park rangers even earned the praise of John Muir. "In pleasing contrast to the noisy, ever-changing management or mismanagement of blustering, blundering, plundering, moneymaking vote sellers . . . the soldiers do their duty so quietly that the traveler is scarcely aware of their presence," Muir wrote. "Blessings on Uncle Sam's soldiers. They have done their job well, and every pine tree is waving its arms for joy."

## A SYSTEM WITHOUT SYSTEM

In the eighteen years following the establishment of Yellowstone, only one other national park was created, and that temporarily: Mackinac Island National Park in Michigan, established in 1875, and twenty years later turned over to Michigan to be conserved as that state saw fit. The next flurry of park creation came in 1890, when Yosemite, Sequoia, and General Grant (later incorporated into Sequoia) national parks were established within days of one another.

On the flanks of the Sierras surrounding the Yosemite Valley, sheep had stripped the grass down to the soil, which, once exposed, quickly eroded away. John Muir—"Muir of the Mountains," as he was known even then—called the sheep "hoofed locusts," and campaigned hard for the creation of a federal reserve in the high country above the valley. The resulting national park, called Yosemite, was a peculiar place for the first fifteen years of its existence. It was shaped like an enormous doughnut, the hole being the state-owned and woefully abused valley in its center, with fenced ranges, houses, hotels, stores, and saloons; the last advertised such corrosive beverages as "corpse revivers" and "Samsons with the hair on." In 1905, again largely through the efforts of Muir and his Sierra Club, the state returned the valley to the federal government and it was added to the national park.

Sequoia and General Grant were known primarily as "tree parks," and were reserved to stop the vandalism of the world's largest tree— *Sequoiadendron giganteum.* Acres of the great trees had been logged for the sheer wonder of them. They were hard to cut down and their wood was too brittle to be of much use, but they were up to four thousand years old and the novelty of their age and size attracted attention. A tree would be felled just so a section of it could be displayed in sideshows back East and in Europe. (At least one such enterprise went bankrupt because the public refused to believe a tree that large could be real, and crowds stayed away.) Some of the most impressive groves remained in private hands after the parks were created, and it took a funding drive initiated by the National Geographic Society to purchase the best of these and add them to the federal reserve.

Slowly, in such piecemeal fashion, and with varying degrees of opposition and confusion, the system grew: Mount Rainier, 1899 (but only after the Northern Pacific won a right-of-way as the price of its support); Crater Lake, 1902 (the vision of a single individual, Judge William Gladstone Steel, who then had to fund the park's care himself and serve as its superintendent without pay); Mesa Verde, 1906; Petrified Forest, 1906 (generally attributed to the efforts of John Muir); Grand Canyon, 1908; Zion, 1909; Olympic, 1909; Glacier, 1910; Rocky Mountain, 1915; Hawaii Volcanoes, 1916. Growth of the system had been accelerated (however inadvertently) in 1906, when Congress responded to the gross vandalism and theft of Anasazi relics among ancient Indian cliff dwellings in the Southwest by passing the Antiquities Act, which authorized the preservation as national monuments of sites containing scientific, historic, or scenic treasures and gave the President the power to designate them without first seeking congressional approval. By 1916, twenty national monuments had been declared by Presidents Roosevelt, Taft, and Wilson. The ability to create national monuments by executive order strengthened the national park movement enormously because it circumvented long debates and the possible rejection, for political reasons, of important sites. About one-quarter of today's national parks started out as national monuments.

By 1916, then, one might charitably say that a national park system was in place—but if so, it was a system without system. It was, first of all, headless; nowhere in official Washington could "an inquirer find an office of the national parks or a single desk devoted solely to their management," remembered J. Horace McFarland, president of the American Civic Association and one of the best friends the national parks ever had. "If the national parks were to meet the demands of the motor age," he recalled, "if they were ever to have enough

19

money, enough publicity and enough protection, they had to be administered by a bureau of their own. They could not go on as the responsibility of a few clerks freighted with a superabundance of other matters classed as more important." In 1912, McFarland and other park supporters persuaded President Taft to send a special message to Congress. "I earnestly recommend," the President said, "the establishment of a Bureau of National Parks." But opposition from the Department of Agriculture's powerful Forest Service lobby, which was convinced that the parks should be folded into the national forest system, managed to forestall action over the next four years.

Nothing demonstrated the need for a protective agency for the parks more than the conflict over Hetch Hetchy, a valley in the northwest corner of Yosemite National Park whose beauty John Muir considered second only to that of Yosemite Valley itself. San Franciscans had wanted to build a dam on the Tuolumne River since before 1900, largely for the generation of municipally owned hydroelectric power. But since the dam would have flooded the Hetch Hetchy Valley, the city petitioned Congress in 1901 to grant the necessary permission. Congress gave its assent, but Interior Secretary Ethan Allen Hitchcock refused to authorize the reservoir, as did his successor, James Garfield. To President Theodore Roosevelt, Muir wrote that the Hetch Hetchy dam promoters demonstrated "the proud sort of confidence that comes of good sound irrefragable ignorance," and for eight years preservationists successfully fought the project. But in 1913 Franklin K. Lane, former city attorney of San Francisco and a firm believer in the city's dam, became Secretary of the Interior and began promoting it himself. In the final vote on enabling legislation that year, Congress backed Lane and the dam proponents, and within a few years the Hetch Hetchy Valley had disappeared beneath the waters behind the O'Shaughnessy Dam.

"I'll be relieved when it's settled," Muir had said earlier that year, "for it's killing me." After the dam's approval, friends noticed that he was sick quite often; a little more than a year after his greatest defeat, he died of pneumonia at the age of seventy-six.

## STEPHEN MATHER: PRESSURE AND PROMOTION

With the loss of Hetch Hetchy, efforts to create a park service heated up again. The first step in this resurgence was taken in 1914 when

Interior Secretary Lane himself, ironically enough, hired an old class-mate of his named Stephen Tyng Mather to be his assistant in charge of the parks. Mather, a forty-seven-year-old millionaire who had spent twenty-two years in the borax business, had made the mistake of writing Lane to complain about the horrid food and lodging in Yo-semite Valley. Lane, not completely insensitive to the meaning of parks, wrote back: "Dear Steve, If you don't like the way the parks are being run, come on down to Washington and run them yourself." Mather decided to try, if just for a year.

Mather, who traced his lineage back to Cotton Mather, turned out to be precisely what the ailing parks needed. He was dynamic and tireless and, it seemed, could sell anything. He had promoted his 20-Mule Team Borax into the American household, and he gave the national parks the same frenzied devotion, determined to make the parks something Americans simply could not live without. In the year he was allowing for the job, Mather planned to sweep the superfluous and tacky concessions from the parks, prevent further commercial intrusions, add worthy units to the system but keep out what he called the "dead cats" that were too often the pork-barrel pets of congress-men, and, above all, increase both the friends and the funds of the parks. To help achieve these high-minded goals, he selected as his assistant Horace Albright, an idealistic and very able young lawyer who was working elsewhere within the Interior Department.

It took him thirteen years, not one, but Mather accomplished much of what he set out to do. The first order of business was to get a National Park Service bill through Congress, and he immediately began drumming up support for the idea. To the argument that the Forest Service was the proper custodian of natural wonders, he re-plied, with some justification, that in the care of the Forest Service natural beauty would always be measured against utilitarian values and beauty would come out the loser. Trees on national forest land, he said, were viewed as a crop. They required cultivation and har-vesting, like cotton or corn, and preservation was a slim prospect under such conditions. To counter congressional apathy, he organized a media blitz of respectable dimensions. First, he financed, out of his own pocket, extravagant park tours and invited along congressmen and carefully chosen men of influence, such as George Horace Lor-imer of *The Saturday Evening Post* and Gilbert Grosvenor of *National*

21

*Geographic.* Next, again out of his own pocket, he hired journalist Robert Sterling Yard (a former editor of *Century Magazine*) to write and place magazine articles, generate news stories, and produce descriptive booklets concerning the glories of the parks. Finally, he persuaded such railroads as the Southern Pacific and the Santa Fe to finance the publication of an elegant book, the *National Parks Portfolio*, which was then distributed free of charge to 250,000 people by the General Federation of Women's Clubs. This frenzied effort came to fruition in 1916, when Congress passed and President Woodrow Wilson signed the act creating the National Park Service with its noble (and later difficult) adjuration "to conserve the scenery and the natural and historic objects and the wildlife therein, and to provide for the enjoyment of the same in such manner and by such means as will leave them unimpaired for the enjoyment of future generations."

The imprimatur of Congress had little behind it in the way of practical aid. "The Service was a small agency with a limited charge," Ronald A. Foresta notes in *America's National Parks and Their Keepers.* "It ran a mere fifteen parks. Its field staff numbered a few hundred and its Washington staff, consisting of Mather, Albright, a draftsman, a few clerks, messengers, and secretaries, could be housed in a couple of offices." This situation slowed Mather down hardly at all. Before illness forced his retirement in 1929 (he died in 1930), he doubled the size of the park domain from 7,500 to 15,846 square miles by adding seven new parks and thirteen new monuments to the system, carved increasingly larger appropriations out of Congress, and built the agency into an institution comparable in public estimation—if never in size—to the Forest Service.

For the most part, he did it with the same methods that he had used in creating the Park Service: pressure and promotion. Until Mather's affection for tourist development—particularly the building of roads—estranged the two men permanently, Yard continued to publish scores of magazine articles, hundreds of news features, and thousands of copies of booklets, maps, and pamphlets, and together they gave lectures in churches, clubs, and schools all over the country, accompanied by Mather's amateurish but enthusiastic home movies of his own edifying park experiences.

Mather often infused the National Park Service with his own money in other ways, the propriety of which might be called into question in these more modern times. He bought the old Tioga Road into Yosemite and financed part of its improvement, for example. He also purchased the ranger headquarters at Glacier National Park for $8,000 and donated it to the service. (In this instance the property was a privately owned parcel within the park, which had been foreclosed upon when Mather bought it. The only condition was that the owner had the option to buy back the property within a year of its sale. And the owner would have done so, had he not fallen down and died on the steps of the courthouse where he was going to file for possession.) In yet another burst of goodwill and generosity, Mather lent $200,000 to a park concessioner to make necessary additions and improvements to a hotel. He also lobbied businessmen for financial support, and among his earliest allies were, as noted, railroad executives.

Promoting the parks fit in well with the railroads' own "See America First" campaign, which depended on good train transportation before the proliferation of the automobile. "Every passenger that goes to the national parks, wherever they may be, represents practically a net earning," said Louis W. Hill, head of the Great Northern Railroad. Mather particularly encouraged sizable railroad investment in the form of luxury hotels. The Great Northern underwrote Glacier, the Northern Pacific built hotels in Yellowstone, and the Union Pacific took care of Bryce, Zion, and the north rim of the Grand Canyon. Since the railroads expected to earn their greatest profits on passenger service to and from the parks, hotel prices were kept at reasonable levels. Mather assured the companies that sponsored the hotels that they would be allowed a controlled monopoly of the parks they served. Uncontrolled free enterprise had merely cluttered and degraded the parks before his tenure, and Mather believed monopoly was the answer, so long as profits and the manner in which they were made were closely scrutinized by the Park Service. In return for the guaranteed monopoly, licensed concessioners financed capital improvements to serve their captive audience.

Mather was no primitivist when it came to park accommodations. Having toured Switzerland, he believed that comfortable lodgings and good food enhanced the travelers' admiration of the landscape. In America's parks he ordered a range of services from the luxurious to the spartan. Scenery, Mather maintained, "is a hollow enjoyment to a tourist who sets out in the morning after an indigestible breakfast and fitful sleep on an impossible bed." He was a man of decent tastes, however, and was very firm about how far commercialism should be allowed to venture. One day he visited Coney Island in New York with park landscape architect Gilbert Stanley Underwood for "an object lesson." The two men spent the day wandering through the crowds, stuffing themselves with hot dogs and raw onions, and washing it all down with orange pop. At one point Mather turned to Underwood and said, "This is exactly what we don't want in the national parks. Lots of people seem to like it and if they do, they ought to have it, but not in the national parks. Our job in the National Park Service is to keep the national parks as close to what God made them and as far as we can from a horror like this."

Perhaps the most famous story about Mather's insistence upon refinement in the parks took place at Glacier one August. On his arrival he noticed that a sawmill used to build the Great Northern Railroad's hotel at the Many Glacier site had not been dismantled as he had repeatedly ordered. Furious with this disobedience, he assembled a group of visitors to watch as he lit the fuse to thirteen charges of dynamite and blasted the sawmill to flinders. When asked by amazed onlookers why he had done this, Mather replied that he was merely celebrating his daughter's nineteenth birthday.

The most far-reaching decision Mather made during his directorship was to allow automobiles into the parks. Shortly after he took charge, he gave support to Western automobile enthusiasts who were demanding a park-to-park road system. To Mather, the plan was one more way to promote the parks and increase their visitations—easily translated into more money and prestige. At the dedication of Rocky Mountain National Park, over which Mather presided in 1916, three hundred cars and their drivers attended, forming "the greatest automobile demonstration ever seen in Colorado." Even without adequate roads, automobiles in great numbers were soon rumbling through most of the parks—only some ten thousand vehicles a year at first, but by 1919 the number had soared to 98,000. People were happy to shed that "horrid fiend, the railroad timetable," as the Lincoln Highway Association called it, and those who arrived by car outnumbered by four to one those who arrived by train. Few people realized then that the automobile would also be the parks' great undoing. One who did was James Bryce, the percipient British ambassador to the United States, who, after a visit to Yosemite in 1913, said, "If Adam had known what harm the serpent was going to work he would have tried to prevent him from finding lodgement in Eden; and if you were to realize what the result of the automobile will be in that wonderful, incomparable valley, you will keep it out." No one was listening, least of all Steve Mather.

## "IN ABSOLUTELY UNIMPAIRED FORM"

Looking for park friends wherever he could find them, Mather realized that his greatest need was to get support east of the Mississippi River. All national parks lay to the west, and it was easy for Eastern congressmen to argue that they were not "national parks" at all, and should therefore be the responsibility of the states in which they were located. For the sake of the parks in the West, then, Mather and Albright embarked on a park-hunting expedition in the East. The big problem here was that nearly all the land had passed into private or state hands, and most of what remained was under the administration of the Forest Service. Nevertheless, a search committee scoured the Eastern and Southern regions in the early 1920s and finally came up with two worthy possibilities in the Appalachian Mountains: the Shenandoah Valley in Virginia, and the Great Smoky Mountains in Tennessee and North Carolina.

While the Great Smokies were fairly remote by the standards of their part of the country, the Shenandoah was a place where you could feel the "nearness of mankind," the first park to broaden the basic dictum that "a national park is where you find it" to "a national park is where the people are." In 1925 Congress stated its intent to establish these two parks in the East, provided that the states involved could raise the money to purchase the necessary private lands. It was a messy, drawn-out business. The Shenandoah, which covers about 195,000 acres along the crest of the Blue Ridge Mountains, was authorized by Congress in 1926 but was not fully established until 1935, by which time the state of Virginia had bought some seven hundred private land holdings in the area. The money for the purchases came from donations large and small. Schoolchildren gave their allowances to the cause. "I ain't so crazy 'bout leavin' these hills," said historian Freeman Tilden, an eighty-three-year-old lifetime resident, "but I never believed in bein' agin the government . . . besides, I always said these hills would be the heart of the world." Authorization to dedication of Great Smoky Mountains National Park took almost fourteen years, even though its half-million acres of private land were acquired with the help of John D. Rockefeller, Jr., through the Laura Spelman Rockefeller Memorial. Rockefeller offered $5 million in honor of his mother, and his donation was matched by smaller contributions from the states of North Carolina and Tennessee.

In addition to finding new parks and expanding old ones so that such things as elk and deer habitats would be protected (and the elk and deer along with them), Mather was frequently confronted with the threat of inappropriate uses. During World War I the parks, supposedly off-limit to most grazing, were open to stockmen who maintained that it was an act of patriotism to increase the nation's food supply. Several of the national parks had private landowners in their midst, which complicated management of the parks. On some private lands, logging continued, as did hunting and other activities outlawed in the parks. The number of private properties in Glacier, Mount Rainier, and Rocky Mountain National Park increased the fire hazards in those places, since private owners could not be required to take the same precautions the federal government took. To this day, private inholdings, which account for about 600,000 acres in the park system, create a major headache for park officials striving for uniform management over a large area.

In the wake of the Hetch Hetchy debacle, which he inherited and could do nothing to stop, Mather had a number of other in-park development projects he could and did fend off. Recurrent among these were plans to dam Yellowstone and other lakes as part of irrigation projects designed to help Idaho farmers. One plan given initial approval would have submerged ten thousand acres of prime meadows and forests. Secretary Lane, who tended to favor reclamation over preservation, gave his tentative permission for the park to be used in this fashion. This bestirred Mather to tender a letter of

26

resignation. "Every plan to exploit Yellowstone has failed to receive the consideration of Congress," he wrote. "Mighty railroad projects have gone down to everlasting defeat. Must all the victories of the past now become hollow memories by the granting of reservoir rights that will desecrate its biggest and most beautiful lakes and form the precedent for commercial exploitation of all scenic reservoirs?"

Lane did not accept Mather's resignation, and he himself resigned before giving the final go-ahead on the project. Interestingly, before Lane stepped down he issued an important policy statement—perhaps dictated by Mather—that has remained one of the guiding lights of park management.

The statement declared, first, that national parks "must be maintained in absolutely unimpaired form for the use of future generations as well as those of our own time"; second, that "they are set aside for the use, observation, health and pleasure of the people"; and third, that "the national interest must dictate all decisions affecting parks."

This final assertion, unfortunately, allowed consideration of hundreds of projects that might otherwise have been considered detrimental and contradictory to the park ethic from the outset. Dams in Yellowstone, for instance, looked like a sure thing when Albert Fall, a devotee of schemes promoting oil, mineral, and even livestock exploitation of public resources, was appointed Secretary of the Interior in 1921. When Mather pleaded with him to disavow the dam project, Fall was noncommittal. "Every generation since Adam and Eve has lived better than the generation before," said Fall. "I don't know how they'll do it—maybe they'll use energy of the sun or the sea waves—but those boys will live better than we do. I stand for opening up every resource." Yet for some unknown reason he never did sanction the Yellowstone dams before the Teapot Dome scandal drove him from office, and for that he remains a kind of strange bedfellow in the preservationists' camp.

## THE BATTLE OF JACKSON HOLE

After Mather's departure in 1929, the directorship fell to his colleague and protégé, Horace Albright, who brought to the position the same enthusiasm Mather had shown, and accomplished a great deal during his own four-year term. At the beginning he stated that his job was "to consolidate our gains, finish up the rounding out of the park system, go rather heavily into the historical park field, and get such legislation as is necessary to guarantee the future of the system on a sound permanent basis, where the power and the personality of the Director may no longer have to be controlling factors in operating the Service." American history was Albright's pet interest, and he made it an important part of Park Service administration, beginning in 1930, when Congress appropriated funds for the reconstruction of George Washington's birthplace on the Wakefield Plantation in Virginia. Under Albright, the Park Service also advanced its unique program of "interpretation" of sites, through which a park ranger might not merely guide visitors, but make them *feel* the essence of a particular park.

Albright's goals prepared the way for a major reorganization of the Park Service in 1933. After a brief conversation during an automobile ride with Albright, it is said, President Franklin Roosevelt transferred jurisdiction of all memorials, military cemeteries, battlefields, and numerous other sites to the National Park Service. From then on, the guardians of Yosemite looked after the Statue of Liberty and Antietam as well. One residual effect of reorganization was to exacerbate relations with the Forest Service, which had never been very good, by transferring the administration of Mount Olympus and Bandolier national monuments from the Forest Service to the Park Service. (Relations grew even worse when New Deal economist Rexford G. Tugwell suggested moving forests out of the Department of Agriculture and into the Department of the Interior; Harold L. Ickes, Interior Secretary, liked this idea and pursued it, unsuccessfully, for the next thirteen years.)

In 1931, at Albright's instigation, Senator George Nye had introduced a bill that would rid the national parks of some of the destructive practices that had plagued them from the beginning. Mineral prospecting in Mesa Verde and Grand Canyon was prohibited; summer home permits were rescinded at Glacier; all provisions that had previously authorized the Secretary of the Interior to grant railroad rights-of-way through parks were finally and fully revoked. Another precedent-setting expansion of Park Service authority under Albright had to do with roadbuilding. Before 1931, Park Service funds were to be used for in-park road construction and maintenance only. After that year, the Park Service was authorized to spend part of its appropriation on "approach roads" outside the parks. The new practice was supported by the states, which felt that the burden of building roads into the parks from major highways was excessive.

The question of roads had catapulted Albright into the middle of one of the fiercest and longest Park Service controversies ever. The conflict concerned Grand Teton National Park, created shortly after he became Park Service director. Albright had loved Jackson Hole, the valley out of which the Tetons rose some seven thousand feet, as much as any scene in America. However, the park he had been given did not include the valley, but only the east side of the mountains. It was a "stingy, skimpy, niggardly little park" in some estimations, and Albright itched to expand it. Jackson Hole was filled with dude ranches, gas stations, hot dog stands, and a few working ranches where cattle were intensively grazed, and Jackson Lake had been dammed for irrigation. Albright thought that perhaps the people of Wyoming would be happy to trade the valley for a good road system through the area—which was precisely what the powerful coalition of dude ranchers did not want, since their business depended on the attraction of unroaded wilderness to guests. For their part, the working ranchers feared restrictions and cutbacks on their grazing habits.

Amid a flurry of abuse, the Park Service withdrew its suggestion. Albright kept his hopes for Jackson Hole to himself, for he had already set a plan in motion. In 1924, while accompanying John D. Rockefeller, Jr., on a tour of the Tetons, Albright had maneuvered Rockefeller into a place where the whole valley spread out before him, and with this vista in sight, he began to talk about how wonderful it would be if the place could be restored to its natural condition. Rockefeller agreed. He told Albright he would buy the valley from its private owners and turn it over to the Park Service. But the work had to be done slowly and surreptitiously, lest prices increase with the knowledge of a Rockefeller on the loose.

Throughout the years of his tenure as Park Service director, and for years after Albright left the service at the end of 1933 to head the American Civic Association, Rockefeller's dummy corporation, the Snake River Land & Cattle Company, managed to buy up most of the private land in Jackson Hole—spending more than a million dollars in the end.

But Rockefeller couldn't give it away. Congress, bowing to pressure from delegations from most of the Rocky Mountain and some other Western states, made it clear that it had no intention of adding Jackson Hole to Grand Teton National Park, and under those circumstances the Interior Department could not accept the gift of land. Finally, in 1942, after fifteen years of paying taxes on land he had entertained no notion of owning for so long, Rockefeller gave Interior Secretary Harold Ickes an ultimatum: Take the land now or Rockefeller's people would start selling it off. Ickes turned to President Roosevelt and persuaded him to declare Jackson Hole a national monument, incorporating the Rockefeller holdings within it. Roosevelt did so on March 5, 1943.

The ensuing uproar was predictable, though fruitless. Wyoming's congressman Frank Barrett compared Roosevelt's action to those of Adolf Hitler and immediately introduced a bill rescinding Jackson Hole's national monument status. It failed to move during that session, the session that followed, and in fact through all of the several congressional sessions in which he presented it until he left Congress. By 1950, public sentiment even in the region of Jackson Hole had shifted, and that year the monument was incorporated into Grand Teton National Park—just as Albright and Rockefeller had intended.

## A LEGACY IN TRANSITION

One residual effect of the Jackson Hole controversy was a certain presidential hesitancy about invoking the Antiquities Act as a means of reserving land for park purposes; not until the 1970s would any large-scale national monuments be created again. In the meantime, the National Park Service had plenty with which to occupy itself.

The legacy of promotion and expansion established by Mather and Albright held strong even during the Depression, when the new Park Service director, Arno Cammerer, was forced to cut his budget to $5 million—half that of previous years. Physically, the system was markedly improved through the efforts of the Civilian Conservation Corps, which did an enormous amount of fix-up work in both the national forests and the national parks. By some estimates the 118 camps operating in the parks did the work of fifty years in only ten. The CCC built roads, trails, and campgrounds. It cleared trees and planted them. The CCC boys performed hard, clean work under a program considered one of Roosevelt's greatest New Deal successes.

But the CCC work also tended to widen the gap between strict preservationists like Robert Sterling Yard, first president of the militant National Parks Association and later cofounder of the equally militant Wilderness Society, and development-minded officials like Cammerer. CCC roadbuilding was offensive to many preservationists, but not to national park officials, who stood by their ambitions to have roads constructed to and through as many parks as possible. Disappointment with the Park Service's emphasis was part of the sentiment that led to the formation of The Wilderness Society in 1935 (see chapter 5). Ironically, four of the eight founders of The Society were either employed by or had close ties to the Forest Service, once the nemesis of preservation, and the new conservation organization threw much of its support to the Agriculture Department's agency, while aiming most of its barbs at the Park Service, no longer considered by like-minded conservationists the true savior of primitive America.

In spite of criticism from conservation groups, the Park Service continued to steer an expansionist course. Beginning with Lake Mead in 1935, when the reservoir began filling up behind the newly built Hoover Dam, the Park Service was assigned responsibility for the administration of such man-made recreation areas. Under Cammerer, the Park Service also became more interested in adding seashores to its domain. In 1937, Cape Hatteras National Seashore, in North Carolina, was the first to be authorized, with the slow and costly job of private land acquisition left up to the state. In 1938, Interior Secretary Ickes stated the case eloquently for seashore reservations:

When we look up and down the ocean fronts of America, we find that everywhere they are passing behind the fences of private ownership. The people can no longer get to the ocean. When we have reached the point that a nation of 125 million people cannot set foot upon the

31

thousands of miles of beaches that border the Atlantic and Pacific Oceans, except by permission of those who monopolize the ocean front, then I say it is the prerogative and the duty of the Federal and State Governments to step in and acquire, not a swimming beach here and there, but solid blocks of ocean front hundreds of miles in length. Call this ocean front a national park, or a national seashore, or a state park or anything you please—I say that the people have a right to a fair share of it.

Cammerer retired in 1940, his health broken by six years of work without a day off in the first five. When Newton Drury assumed the directorship, the parks were in better shape than they had ever been, but now they faced a new set of challenges. World War II placed severe demands on the parks, and Drury, the most preservation-minded of the early directors (he was a close friend of Robert Sterling Yard, for one thing), staved off assaults from stockmen and other commercial interests. The pressures of war did force him to relent on some mining intrusions in the parks: copper was extracted from the Grand Canyon, manganese came out of Shenandoah, and Yosemite was opened to yield a meager fifty-five tons of tungsten. But nothing was as serious as the threat to Olympic National Park's Sitka spruce. It was because of the spruce that timber interests had fought the designation of the park in the 1930s, but the onset of war imbued their sentiments with patriotism. The Sitka spruce were essential for building airplanes, they said. The War Production Board agreed, and recommended that the Sitka spruce be cut and used for defense. In so dark a time, the use seemed legitimate and unavoidable. Drury resisted, however, and Secretary Ickes supported him, with the statement that "the virgin forests in the national parks should not be cut unless the trees are absolutely essential to the prosecution of the war, with no alternative, and only as a last resort. Critical necessity rather than convenience should be the governing reason for sacrifice of an important part of our federal estate." Lending a helping hand, the Park Service then found healthy stands of spruce in Canada and Alaska, shortly after which aluminum replaced wood in most aircraft construction anyway.

## THE PITFALLS OF PEACE

Efforts to exploit national park commodities did not lessen after the war. If anything, they increased, for the demands of peacetime growth were more pervasive and lasting than the focused exigencies of war. In 1950, while Director Drury was thumbing through the *Federal Register*, he noticed that the Bureau of Reclamation was planning to build two dams in Dinosaur National Monument as part of its comprehensive Colorado River Basin Storage project. Drury assumed there had to have been a mistake. After all, he had never even been consulted about the dam proposals. But it was not a mistake. Drury protested. Interior Secretary Oscar Chapman believed in the project and gave it his endorsement. According to the historian John Ise, "The traditional, bureaucratic thing would have been for Drury to agree that dams in Dinosaur were absolutely necessary and good and holy." Drury did not do the bureaucratic thing, and Chapman pressured him to resign.

On his way out of the Park Service, Drury spoke from his heart:

No resources should be consumed or features destroyed through lumbering, grazing, mining, hunting, water control developments or other industrial uses. This is a cardinal point, which park agencies and executives have learned they must adhere to as closely as possible. Nearly always there is arrayed against it the multiple-use philosophy of public resource management which holds that scenic and recreational resources may be used for numerous other reasons without sacrificing the scenic and recreational values; that grazing will reduce the fire hazard; that damming of lakes and streams for irrigation and power will make them more useful for recreation, will do little harm, and will bring economic benefits. This is an attractive argument to the utilitarians but it misses the point. . . . If we are going to succeed in preserving the greatness of the national parks, they must be held inviolate. They represent the last stand of primitive America. If we are going to whittle away at them we should recognize at the very beginning that all such whittlings are cumulative and that the end result will be mediocrity. Greatness will be gone.

Public opinion persuaded Congress to kill the Dinosaur dams in 1956. Publicity against the project was powerfully mounted by a coalition of conservation groups, chief among them The Wilderness Society, the Sierra Club, and the Izaak Walton League, a combination unprecedented in conservation history and one with enough visible and vocal public support to make any future attempts to violate park sanctity increasingly difficult to engineer. It was this coalition, more than any other factor, that managed to block immense dams at Bridge Canyon and Marble Canyon that would have inundated major portions of Grand Canyon National Monument and even parts of Grand Canyon National Park in the 1960s, and it was this coalition that formed the core of the modern environmental movement.

Meanwhile, when the parks were not in danger of injury from megadams and other resource development, they were in danger of being loved to death. After the war, the public returned to the parks by the millions—30 million a year by 1950. But roads and services had remained at 1940 levels. Buildings, trails, and campgrounds were dilapidated, and more of everything seemed to be needed. In 1956, Conrad Wirth, Drury's replacement, presented a "wish list" for the parks to Congress—and for the first time in the history of its dealings with the parks, Congress approved a major financial commitment: an $800 million to $1 billion appropriation for a program of improvement and expansion. Wirth dubbed the project "Mission 66" in honor of the year it was scheduled to be completed—not coincidentally, also the fiftieth anniversary year of the creation of the Park Service—by which time the parks would be equipped to handle as many as 80 million visitors a year. Or so the projections said.

However ambitious, Mission 66 simply could not keep up with the numbers; in just four years, visitation had jumped to 72 million a year and the projected figure of 80 million visits was reached and passed long before the anniversary year of 1966. Fifteen new recreation areas were designated in this period, and in 1961, 27,000 acres of the Cape Cod shore were added to the park system, closely followed by significant additions at Point Reyes in California and Padre Island in the Gulf of Mexico, just off the coast of Texas. All of this did little to relieve the population pressure. As early as 1958 the problem was so obvious that Congress had established an Outdoor Recreation Resources Review Commission (ORRRC) to look into the situation nationwide. In 1962 it issued its report, which declared that there was nothing less than "a crisis in outdoor recreation." Secretary of the Interior Stewart Udall responded by creating the Bureau of Outdoor Recreation, designed to advise and administer the development of recreation facilities on public lands under the Interior Department's aegis—and answerable directly to his office.

Park Service Director Wirth resented both the Review Commission and the bureau that followed it, both of which were out of the control of his department. His cooperation with both was minimal, and Udall became so disenchanted with him that he forced Wirth's resignation in 1964. As Udall explained it in a letter to Horace Albright, who retained his strong interest in and influence on park policy all his life, "We have sometimes been critical, even strongly critical, of the stiff-necked attitude of the National Park Service. When it stands like Horatius at the bridge, patience runs low." Wirth was replaced by George Hartzog, a former Park Service official who had returned to private law practice before being rehired as director by Udall. Hartzog, like Mather before him, was an idiosyncratic type who did not often stand on protocol; among other legends that grew up around his tenure was the reported time when he grew so frustrated at the swollen mass of rules, regulations, and guidelines that had grown up around Park Service management over the years that he cleared off of the bookshelves of his office all but three volumes: one covering administrative policies for natural areas, one for historic areas, and one for recreational areas. More than a yearning for simplicity, however, commended him to Udall. Hartzog was a devoted supporter of what Udall called the "New Conservation," one of whose principal tenets was that the Park Service could no longer function in isolation from the needs of the larger society, that it was far more than just a caretaker of natural beauty, and that recreation as one of its administrative functions could not be viewed as something merely incidental in American life. Rather, it was an utter necessity to the spiritual and emotional well-being of each and every citizen. That said, the Park Service must move to provide recreational opportunities over a broad spectrum of the nation—including its cities.

While Udall and Hartzog fine-tuned park policy, Congress moved to build up the system itself—or at least make such an expansion possible. Except for those minor additions noted earlier, not much along these lines had been done within recent memory. Of the 23.8 million acres of national park natural areas in existence in 1964, 22.9 million had been reserved before World War II. Realizing that park acquisition might remain at a standstill—while visitations could only continue to soar—Congress broke with its long-standing tradition of not appropriating funds for land acquisition and, in 1964, passed an act creating the Land and Water Conservation Fund (LWCF) to ensure that money always would be available for such purchases; funding would come from the sale of excess federal property, from park entrance and permit fees, from a tax on motorboat fuel, and, after 1968, from receipts for oil and gas leases on the outer continental shelf. (These last receipts now amount to about 90 percent of the total of $900 million in annual income to the fund.) Since 1964 the LWCF has served as the source for nearly all parkland purchases—including those necessary for the creation of Redwood National Park in 1968, the largest addition to the system since the Great Smoky Mountains in the 1930s. The fund has been so successful that James Watt, while head of the Bureau of Outdoor Recreation during the Nixon administration, called it "one of the most effective conservation programs in America."

## THE URBAN EXPLOSION

Among the most enduring legacies of Udall's New Conservation was to bring life to the concept of urban parks. There had been urban parks, of a sort, in the system for years—Rock Creek Park and the smaller parks in the District of Columbia were paramount among these—and with some park planners there had always been a mild conviction that there should be more. But it was the 1962 report of the ORRRC that brought the idea out of the realm of speculation and into the light of urgency. "Over a quarter-billion acres are public designated outdoor recreation areas," the report noted, "however, either the location of the land, or restrictive management policies, or both, greatly reduce the effectiveness of the land for recreation use by the bulk of the population." This land, then, the report continued, was "of little use to most Americans looking for a place in the sun for their families on a weekend, when the demand is overwhelming. The problem is not one of total acres but of effective acres."

The most effective acres, clearly, would be in or near major metropolitan centers. "The new conservation," President Lyndon B. Johnson said, "is built on a new promise—to bring parks closer to the people." Udall and his park director, George Hartzog, put their minds and hearts behind this goal, but it was easier said in a speech than done in the field. Any significant move in the direction of urban park development would encounter a whole new system of problems outside the Park Service's experience, problems tied inextricably to those afflicting every aspect of life in urban America—including poverty, crime, racial turmoil, and congestion. Moreover, as Ronald A. Foresta points out,

> the agency had no proven criteria for urban park selection. It did not have a good idea of which parks would be good ones from the standpoints of management ease or political support. It did not even know which ones would be able to meet their stated objectives. One thing was certain, however; the urban parks would require large staffs, large development outlays, and large budgets, perhaps large enough to starve the other parks in the system. These questions and facts meant that a major urban commitment would be a very large gamble at unknown odds.

Still, the commitment was made, albeit haltingly and on a generally piecemeal basis. By the time Hartzog left office in 1972, only a few major additions had been made to the system that qualified—by proximity if sometimes little else—as urban parks, among them Delaware Water Gap National Recreation Area, Fire Island National Seashore, and Indiana Dunes National Lakeshore. But under subsequent directors, and with an increasingly active role from Congress, the urban park system expanded dramatically through the seventies, with the addition of Golden Gate National Recreation Area, around San Francisco; Gateway, in the environs of New York City; Cuyahoga Valley, between Cleveland and Akron; Chattahoochie River, near Atlanta; Santa Monica Mountains, near Los Angeles; and Jean Lafitte National Historical Park and Recreation Area, scattered in and around New Orleans.

## THE WATT INTERLUDE

If the 1970s saw a major shift in emphasis away from the traditionalist view of the national parks as a collection of scenic jewels, and the Park Service as little more than their custodian, it was a situation largely confined to the lower forty-eight states. In Alaska, it was quite a different matter. As will be discussed in chapter 6, controversy surrounding the construction of the Trans-Alaskan Pipeline had accelerated concern over the future of the Alaska lands, including the preservation and expansion of the state's own park and monument system. That concern ultimately would be expressed in passage of the Alaska National Interest Lands Conservation Act (ANILCA) in 1980—but even before then, President Jimmy Carter had evoked memories of earlier presidential actions when he moved in 1978 to create, by executive fiat, millions of acres of national monuments in Alaska as an interim measure to protect them while their ultimate fate was decided by Congress. This was park-making on a grand scale, and very much within the traditions of the past, a fact given even greater reality when ANILCA firmly embedded more than 43 million acres in the national park and monument system.

Passage of ANILCA was a watershed in another, less benign fashion. It stood squarely at the end of the only administration of President Carter, the most conservation-minded President since Franklin Roosevelt, and at the beginning of the first administration of Ronald Reagan, whom most environmentalists would characterize as the *least* conservation-minded President since Dwight D. Eisenhower. At issue, almost immediately, was future policy regarding the national park system, a question put into focus by Reagan's first Interior Secretary, James Watt, early in 1981. Less than ten years before, Watt had praised the virtues of the Land and Water Conservation Fund, but now he no longer believed it should be used for park expansion; in fact, he did not think the parks needed expansion at all. They needed fixing, and LWCF money should be used for that and that alone. The crown jewels, he asserted, were in a "shameful condition." In truth, some of the parks *were* looking as bedraggled as they had before the Mission 66 project had refurbished them. Visitations had increased to more than 300 million a year, with the heaviest use concentrated in such Eastern parks as Shenandoah, which in 1980 received 7.5

38

million visitors, while Yellowstone and Yosemite each received about two million. In some of the parks, roads and sewage systems needed repair, and Watt declared many park buildings "hazards." He said that it would cost $1.6 billion to make the necessary capital improvements, and acquiring new lands would be irresponsible if the old ones were not repaired first. Watt's estimate was too high by more than half a billion dollars, according to a later estimate by the Park Service, and in any case Congress refused to permit LWCF money to be used in any way other than for acquisition.

The conservation community tended to look upon Watt's assertions skeptically, contending that his lament over the sorry condition of the national parks was nothing more than an act to camouflage his ingrained antagonism toward park expansion. During the first four years of the Reagan administration, the Interior Department consistently proposed spending millions of dollars less in LWCF acquisition money than Congress just as consistently appropriated—and even with more money than it had requested, the Interior Department, after Watt declared a "moratorium" on parkland acquisitions, spent very little of it. In the end, the Park Service launched a massive rehabilitation effort with separate funding. Before the budget crunch of 1985 brought it nearly to a halt, the agency managed to spend $800 million or so of what was billed as a "billion-dollar program."

## THE THREATS WITHIN

The Reagan administration's reluctance to expand the system significantly—or even to buy out private inholdings in order to "expand" parks from within—exacerbated a problem that had been steadily growing even as the parks grew in the seventies: the ironic fact that many of the original parks were in some ways becoming quite as "urban" as the urban parks. In an interview in 1980, Park Service Director Russell Dickenson conceded the problem: "Any time that you take a park like Yosemite or Grand Canyon that handles up to 25,000 cars a day, you have an impacted situation. You have an urban situation." One park planner voiced the still-heretical opinion that the superintendents of many parks ought not to be chosen from the rank and file of the Service but from the administrative offices of cities with a population of about 150,000.

As early as 1968, Edward Abbey, the iconoclastic author of *Desert Solitaire*, had spoken for many who felt that the Park Service had only itself to blame, and that the trouble stemmed primarily from the agency's affection for roads and elaborate visitor centers. Abbey wrote:

"Parks are for people" is the public relations slogan. Which decoded means that parks are for people-in-automobiles. Behind the slogan is the assumption that the majority of Americans, exactly like the managers of the tourist industry, expect and demand to see their national parks from the comfort, security and convenience of their automobiles. . . . So long as they are unwilling to crawl out of their cars they will not discover the treasures of the national parks and will never escape the stress and turmoil of the urban-suburban complexes they had hoped, presumably, to leave behind.

Referring perhaps to the consequences of Mission 66, Abbey, a seasonal ranger during the years of improvement, wrote that "old foot trails may be neglected, back-country ranger stations left unmanned, and interpretive and protective services inadequately staffed, but the [park] administrators know from long experience that millions for asphalt can always be found. Congress is always willing to appropriate money for more and bigger paved roads anywhere—particularly if they are loops." James Watt's own improvement program—"Mission Fixit," some conservationists called it—included many road projects that could be accused of merely substantiating Abbey's indictment for the 1980s.

But it was not just elaborately engineered roads that threatened to change the face of the national parks. Some concessioners also had a suspect influence. Ever since Mather's time, concessions had worked as closely supervised monopolies in the parks. In the beginning, business was risky because of the unpredictable number of visitors and the brief season in which to make a profit. As a result, concessioners often had to be prodded to make improvements. Even Horace Albright had called the most reluctant of them "soulless corporations," because their concern for the public's health and safety was so clearly second to their concern for their own balance sheets.

Other concessioners, however, were as keen on the parks as the rangers were. Given their low profit margins and the problems of providing full services in remote, rugged places, some behaved lovingly and loyally. The Curry Company, for instance, was a family-run concession in Yosemite that served the park for three generations. But in the 1960s and 1970s, concession management began to change, particularly in the major parks, where small family operations such as the Currys' were bought out by conglomerates. Music Corporation of America, a subsidiary of Universal Studios, acquired the Curry Company in 1973. Amfac, a sugar conglomerate, became the concessioner for most of Grand Canyon National Park, and Trans World Corporation took over operations in Bryce Canyon, Zion, and part of Grand Canyon. Large concessioners gained more control over the parks by the passage of the Concessioners Policy Act in 1965, which permitted operators to have "possessory interest" in all facilities within the parks.

In a sense there was little difference between "possessory interest" and outright ownership, since if Park Service administrators were dissatisfied with a concessioner, the agency could not cancel the agreement without simultaneously buying out all concessioner-owned capital improvements at current market value. The act was intended to protect concessioners from capricious rule changes, but instead made it much more difficult and expensive to rid the parks of genuinely bad management. The most dramatic example of a forced buyout took place in Yellowstone in 1979. General Host, a concessioner for eleven years, had let conditions deteriorate because it did not want to spend the $10 million on improvements it had previously promised to make. The return on corporate investment, company executives asserted, would not be high enough to warrant any added expenditure. Conditions in the parks were too deplorable to be ignored, and staff morale was so low it could not be missed by park visitors. The Park Service had no choice but to terminate the contract, paying General Host almost $20 million for that privilege.

MCA's control of Yosemite had also gotten out of hand. From the moment the entertainment company assumed control of visitor facilities in the seven-mile-long, one-mile-wide Yosemite Valley, things began to change—just as MCA officials had promised. New brochures proclaimed the park as "Nature's eloquent answer to convention city."

Management devoted itself to the task of putting something in the park for everyone. Bars. Beauty parlors. Swimming pools and tennis courts. A bank. A kennel. Assorted boutiques. "This Isn't No Man's Land. Or Primitive Wilderness," one brochure boasted. "This Is Civilization." Rustic cabins were replaced by modern motel rooms, and a campaign to attract convention business displaced many more traditional park visitors. The park continued to suffer insult upon injury until an MCA television production called "Sierra" inadvertently came to its rescue. Intended as a serious adventure series about park rangers, with Yosemite National Park as the setting, it was so badly done that it ended up making both the park and the rangers look foolish. The final indignity came when the director of the series, hoping to improve the park's appearance for television audiences, ordered some of the rocks painted.

Outrage over this cosmetic tampering with nature was widespread and vehement. It offered a convenient focal point for conservationists all over the country to emphasize the need for a truly noble master plan to govern future administration of the park. The Park Service, in cooperation with a thoroughly chastised MCA and under the scrutiny of 63,000 people who submitted criticisms and commentaries, completed such a plan in 1980. While there was still much to be done, Yosemite's prospects for intelligent management improved enormously. Not as much could be said for the rest of the parks.

## THE THREATS WITHOUT

Park critic Joseph L. Sax once remarked that the Park Service has succumbed to an "enclave mentality," meaning it has lost the ability to influence, and the desire to try to influence, what happens beyond the parks' boundaries. While all federal land management agencies are restricted by the territory they administer, a sheltered state of mind has flourished more easily within the Park Service. For one thing, the nature of its mission emphasized the difference between parks and the rest of the country. For another, the first parks themselves were sheltered, situated deep within unexploited regions of public domain, hundreds of miles from society's most debilitating characteristics. People came to visit, perhaps even behaved disrespectfully, but when the season was over the crowds left, usually giving flora and fauna time to recover. Private landholders entrenched within the parks (there were still 24,000 of them) caused their share of headaches to park managers, but the scale of these intrusions was of a size that could be comprehended.

This is not the case anymore. Civilization in all its forms has advanced to the gates of the national parks, and has laid a formidable siege. In 1984, for example, bulldozers were poised at an overlook into the Black Canyon of the Gunnison National Monument in Colorado, prepared to break ground for a large housing subdivision. The views from the subdivision would have been spectacular; the views from the Black Canyon would have been something other than that. At the last moment, arrangements were made through The Nature Conservancy so that the National Park Service could eventually acquire the critical piece of land from the developer and furnish it with permanent protection. Even then, some bulldozing for subdivision preparation had occurred. Far more drastic was the possible fate that awaited Canyonlands National Park in Utah, for five years a leading candidate to have a nuclear-waste disposal site for a neighbor. Four thousand feet from the park's boundary, waste that would have remained lethally radioactive for twenty thousand years was to be buried. Canyonlands administrators, not at all trained in the field of nuclear-waste disposal, were forced to spend most of their time for several years contemplating the construction, traffic, intense security, and high-powered floodlights that such a decision would entail. After much public indignation, the Department of Energy subsequently eliminated the Canyonlands site as a prime candidate—although a final, firm decision has yet to be made regarding the location of a resting place for the dregs of nuclear energy.

There has been talk of the need for buffer zones around the parks, so that they will not have to rub directly against the world from which they offer escape. But even with LWCF money, sufficient funds to cushion every sensitive place do not exist. Besides, there is resistance within the agency as well as without it to own, in fee simple title, land that is not of national park stature. One of the ways the Park Service is considering expanding the system is through the development of "greenline parks," which are mixtures of public and private land ownership covered by a single comprehensive plan aimed at preserving significant sites. The establishment of the Pinelands National Reserve in New Jersey was strongly influenced by the greenline concept, although the Park Service is not the head administrative agency. Some critics argue that the proliferation of such quasi-parks might dilute Park Service dedication to natural area preservation even more than has the growth of urban parks, which calls into question once again what the proper role of the Park Service should be.

In any case, greenline parks are no protection from smoke, acid rain, particulates, and dust that ride in on the wind from hundreds of miles away, befouling the air and water of America's most pristine places. The alarming truth is that many parks are being degraded most severely by distant offenders. The region known as the Golden Circle of the Southwest encompasses Grand Canyon, Canyonlands, Bryce Canyon, Capitol Reef, and Arches national parks, and Lake Mead and Glen Canyon national recreation areas. Visibility within the Golden Circle has been reduced from sixty to forty miles, largely because of all the power plants in the area. The Four Corners power plant at Farmington, New Mexico, has been called "the stacks of death," because it disperses about 80,000 tons of sulfur dioxide a year into the Colorado Plateau area. "For many individuals, smog, haze, or plumes over the Grand Canyon destroy the value of the wilderness experience," wrote Gundars Rudzitis and Jeffrey Schwartz in a 1982 issue of *Environment.* "Unfortunately, emissions from the Navajo Power Plant near Page, Arizona, have on occasion filled the Grand Canyon with a layer of haze, reducing visibility to less than fifteen miles and obscuring the opposite rim." The presence of the Four Corners plant is so pronounced that when astronauts orbited the earth in 1965 aboard the Gemini III capsule, they reported that the only signs of human life they could detect were plumes of smoke from its towering stacks.

The Everglades, more than two thousand miles from the Golden Circle, was described by the late California congressman Phillip Burton as the "most overwhelmingly threatened national park in the entire system." The increasing use of Florida's water for agriculture and urban and industrial development has dramatically altered the park's water cycle, vital to the maintenance of the Everglades ecosystem. The populations of some wading birds have decreased by 90 percent in the last fifty years. "The natural variation in the water tables is what makes the Everglades so great," park superintendent Jack Moorhead told conservation writer Robert Cahn in 1982. "But if this keeps up, the people coming to Everglades in the year 2000 might see a cover of Brazilian pepper instead of sawgrass, and few birds and no gators or any of the eleven species that are endangered or threatened and need the park habitat."

The list of parks threatened by things beyond their control goes on. Nothing made this more abundantly clear than *State of the Parks*, a report published by the National Park Service itself in 1980. An investigation into the condition of the national park system had been prompted by a bipartisan congressional request. Although the Park Service was at first reluctant to comply, pleading a lack of time and manpower, it finally produced a fairly startling document. Identified were 4,345 threats to park integrity, more than half of which originated outside the parks. "No area is immune," the report stated. "Although some impacts are subtle and not immediately obvious, long-term consequences can be disastrous," it concluded. Threats were divided into seven categories: aesthetic degradation, air pollution, extraction of resources, encroachment of exotic animal and plant species, visitor impacts, water-quality pollution, and park operations, including the use of biocides. "Very few park units possess the baseline natural and cultural resource information needed to permit identification of incremental changes that may be caused by a threat," the report stated. "The priority assigned to the development of sound resource information has been very low compared to the priority assigned to meet construction and maintenance needs. . . . Simply stated, the current levels of science and resource management activities are completely inadequate to cope effectively with the broad spectrum of threats and problems." The report also said that Park Service personnel seemed "frightened and frustrated" by their inability to protect the parks.

To help the Park Service feel less inadequate in this regard, the National Park System Protection and Resources Management Act was introduced in Congress shortly after *State of the Parks* was published. The bill, which has since passed the House in two different Congresses, only to be blocked in the Senate, seeks to establish ways park administrators can keep track of the condition of the natural and cultural resources—precisely those attributes for which the parks were created in the first place. Concern for the rate and nature of change in these resources would be of primary importance, differentiating it from concern about buildings and sewer systems. The Park Protection Act, as it is called for short, also attempts to give the Park Service more clout in determining how other federal agencies can use or abuse the parks, the Canyonlands dump-site proposal being a perfect case in point. So far, however, Park Service officials have opposed the protection bill because of the extra work they believe it would require of them—and because of their conviction that they are already doing the best possible job. The Reagan administration has been dead set against the bill from the beginning.

The national park system, then, after a noble history, stands at a crossroads where decisions must be made. Author John G. Mitchell's words about the Everglades, written more than fifteen years ago, bear both a symbolic and a very real significance for the entire system today:

> Now you are in an altogether different world, a world that is pressing hard against the outer limits of the natural one next-door. The sign in the visitor center in the national park does not acknowledge the presence of this larger world of people. Thus it can claim enduring preservation of an area that in fact is too fragile to endure the circumstances—and the excesses—of encroaching development. . . . So the myth of permanence is shattered. Yet the challenge to save what is left . . . still remains.

## AN AGENDA FOR THE NATIONAL PARKS

Born of simple, justifiable pride in the abundance of natural grandeur this country had to offer the world, the national park system has grown far too complex for it to be comfortably taken for granted. It faces the need for major changes in policy and management if it is going to survive "unimpaired, for the enjoyment of future generations." The pride remains, but for many it is now accompanied by a rising sense of urgency.

Congressman Phillip Burton of California was one of the most vigorous supporters of the national parks in their history. As chairman of the National Parks and Insular Affairs Subcommittee of the House Interior and Insular Affairs Committee from 1977 to 1980, he established a notable record in the making and protecting of parks—especially with the Omnibus Parks Act of 1978, which brought such enclaves as the Santa Monica Mountains into the fold of the national park system. Shortly before his death in the spring of 1983, he penned a lengthy description of the threats facing the system for *Wilderness* magazine, and concluded with a statement few conservationists would oppose today: "All of these and many, many more are either chipping away right now at the security of the national park system or may soon be doing so. And they are not long-term threats awaiting us some distance down the road to the twenty-first century; they face us now—today, tomorrow, the day after tomorrow. Our response must be geared to that imminence."

We must begin the process of making a genuine, long-term commitment to a shift in emphasis in the administration of the national parks. For a generation now, that emphasis has clearly been on the concept of use, of ready accommodation to the pressures of society, all of which inevitably has led to the degradation of the system. We can no longer afford this policy. As William Penn Mott, appointed director of the National Park Service early in 1985, remarked shortly after taking office, from now on, "we must err on the side of preservation." The National Park Service should make its highest priority the elimination, reduction, and mitigation of all present and potential threats to the integrity of park resources. The best immediate way of setting that idea in motion is passage of a Park Protection Act. As noted earlier in this chapter, two versions of just such an act have already been introduced and passed by the House, only to come to a halt in the Senate. Another version must be introduced and carried through as soon as it can be accomplished, and among its strongest elements should be the following major provisions:

*A biennial "State of the Parks" report.* To ensure the continued monitoring of resource threats and problems, the Secretary of the Interior should be required to prepare and present to Congress and the President every two years a comprehensive report on the condition of all natural and cultural resources in the national park system, together with steps made or being made to ameliorate harmful impacts. The report should analyze in specific detail the status of each unit in the system, and a preliminary draft should be made available to the public for comment and criticism no less than three months before official submission.

*An annual report on critical resource threats.* In addition to a biennial report, the Secretary should be required to submit to the appropriate committees of Congress an annual statement identifying and describing the fifty most critical threats to the natural and cultural resources of the parks, together with an estimate of the cost for the mitigation or elimination of such threats. Such costs should be incorporated into the congressional budget appropriations process for each year.

*Scientific support and advice.* To aid in a major, continuing program of data collection, research, monitoring, analysis, and documentation of national park conditions, the Secretary should contract with the National Academy of Sciences for the creation of a plan by which the National Park Service can best acquire and maintain a fund of scientific knowledge necessary to the preparation of both biennial and annual reports.

*Individual management plans.* Just as the National Forest Management Act (see chapter 2) required the U.S. Forest Service to issue individual management plans for each unit of the national forests, a National Park Protection Act should mandate similar plans for each unit of the national park system. Unlike the forest management plans, which are to be updated every ten years, the extraordinary nature of the various threats to the national parks dictates that park management plans should be revised every two years. They should include an inventory of park resources, long-range plans to deal with identified problems, and a summary of work done in the past, and should be offered for public scrutiny in draft form before final submission and acceptance.

*Limitations on agency actions*. Since many federal agencies have the capability of inflicting damage on the national parks through various management decisions, any National Park Protection Act must include stipulations designed to prevent and modify agency actions that may have adverse impacts. This includes the Department of the Interior itself. The Secretary of the Interior, for example, has the authority to issue directives regarding leasing, development, and other disposal of various national park properties. A Park Protection Act should require that the Secretary be allowed to make such orders only after it has been clearly determined that any resulting action would not impair any of the values for which any national park unit was established—and further, that any such determination should not be made without public notice and the full opportunity for a hearing on the record. Similar limitations on the Secretary's actions should be imposed for any lands adjacent to any national park unit on which the Secretary has authority to make such management decisions (for example, through the Bureau of Land Management or the Bureau of Reclamation, both under the aegis of the Secretary of the Interior).

Agencies outside of the Department of the Interior—the U.S. Forest Service and the U.S. Army Corps of Engineers, for instance—also are often in a position to make administrative decisions that have the potential for impairing the natural or cultural resources of park units, and some means must be established to control and monitor such actions. A National Park Protection Act therefore should encompass the following specific provisions:

1. Any agency that is contemplating an action on lands or waters within a national park boundary must not take such action without the concurrence of the Secretary of the Interior.
2. The Secretary of the Interior must be informed, in writing, of any action contemplated by any federal agency on any lands or waters adjacent to any national park unit that may have measurable impact on that unit.
3. The Secretary must be told of any such contemplated action in sufficient time for him to make comments and recommendations regarding it, and if for any reason he does not do so, the

49

Secretary must inform, in writing, the appropriate committees of Congress.

4. The agency contemplating the action must then notify the Secretary of decisions reached in response to his comments and recommendations, and the appropriate committees of Congress must be told of both the decision and the Secretary's original suggestions.

Among its other virtues, a National Park Protection Act that included the stipulations described above would go a long way toward establishing administrative lines of communication—contact that has too often in the past been blocked by bureaucratic tradition and sometimes interagency antagonisms. As well, it would assure that the oversight role of Congress, too frequently evaded or simply left unexercised, would become a more viable and continuing part of the administrative process. Congress can move in other ways to protect the integrity of the park experience. It should, for example, direct the Federal Aviation Administration to work with the National Park Service to formulate such regulations as may be necessary to establish minimum flight altitudes over any area of the national park system for both military and civilian aircraft. Sightseeing flights over such parks as Grand Canyon have long been an offense to the eyes and ears of park visitors, and attention should be paid to this growing problem immediately.

Similarly, Congress should move to amend the 1965 Concessioners Policy Act so as to give the National Park Service firmer control over park concessioners. Amendments should eliminate the administrative concept of "possessory interest," should place limits on the length of concessioner contracts, and should provide for the removal or relocation of any nonessential visitor facilities—it should, in fact, be the stated policy of Congress that all such facilities are to be kept to an absolute minimum now and in the future.

With protection must come expansion of the national park system— and the need is quite as crucial. There is every indication that the American people will be seeking what the parks have to offer in the way of recreation and kinship with nature in greater and greater numbers as our world becomes increasingly urbanized. Park visitation has risen tenfold since 1950, and within the next decade the national parks will very likely be subjected to as many as 400 million total visits every year. If we are to prevent significant damage to the physical and recreational value of the resource from the kind of overcrowding that already characterizes such parks as Yosemite and Great Smoky Mountains, we must move to meet the challenge immediately.

To implement this effort, the Land and Water Conservation Fund (LWCF), authorized at a ceiling of $900 million annually, must be fully funded every year until all necessary purchases have been made to expand and "fill in" the system. There are two major categories of need where this funding should be applied:

*Inholdings.* There are approximately 24,000 privately owned "inholdings" now checkerboarding the national park system. Many thousands of these have already been authorized for purchase, yet remain unacquired, and many thousands more should be acquired—both to fully integrate land holdings within individual parks and to prevent inappropriate uses. The National Park Service should develop a package program to eliminate all of the current backlog within three years, so as to be able to put all future parkland acquisitions on a "pay as you authorize" basis, to avoid such backlogs in the future. If outright purchase is impossible in some cases, then the full spectrum of alternatives should be applied wherever appropriate. Such alternatives would include "life estate" purchases, in which the current resident of the property is allowed to live on the land until death; scenic and conservation easements, in which the land is preserved from any sort of development that will degrade the resource in any way, even while remaining in private ownership; and restrictive zoning in cooperation with state and local governments. Purchase is always to be preferred, however, and when necessary this can be accomplished through a declaration of taking.

*New park units.* There are a number of areas left in the lower forty-eight states that are deserving of park status, both for their value as unique ecosystems and for the natural grandeur they encompass.

The Park Service should revise and submit to Congress—as the law already requires it to do—a national park system plan designed to make significant immediate additions to the system. Candidate areas would include a Grasslands National Park in Montana, a Tallgrass Prairie National Park in Kansas/Missouri, a Great Basin National Park in Utah/Nevada, a Big Sur National Seashore or National Park in California, and a Bioluminescent Bay National Park in Washington.

There are three additional programs that should be set in motion immediately, either administratively or by legislation. Chief among these is wilderness designation for many parks, a program that has been allowed to stagnate over several years. As well, the professionalism with which wilderness lands are now managed within the National Park System needs serious attention, in particular the review and upgrading of administrative policies. The entire wilderness program needs to be given much higher priority—and the process should begin with the designation of the greater part of Great Smoky Mountains National Park as wilderness, a project that has been "on the books" ever since passage of the Wilderness Act in 1964.

Second, a moratorium should be placed on all national park road construction and reconstruction. Ever since the passage of the Surface Transportation Assistance Act of 1982, there has been an uncommonly extensive amount of road work done in many parks; some roads have been widened, regraded, and otherwise improved to the point that the reconstruction has significantly degraded the park environment and the park experience. A system-wide moratorium should be put into effect by the Park Service on all such activities, and a thorough review—with public involvement—should be conducted. Of special concern here are Olympic, Crater Lake, and Shenandoah national parks.

Finally, the National Park Service should move to expand and restructure its interpretive and public information programs. The national parks, with their high visitation representing a broad spectrum of the American public, offer one of the best opportunities we have to educate people properly in those basic ecological principles essential to a true understanding of the natural world and the place of all living things within it. With such principles demonstrated "on the ground," so to speak, there is some hope that we can eventually make a Land Ethic a viable functioning part of American society.

ABOVE: Stephen T. Mather *(third from left)*, the first director of the National Park Service, and Horace M. Albright *(far right)*, the second director, join other early national park enthusiasts in Rocky Mountain National Park, 1915. *The Wilderness Society*

RIGHT: President Theodore Roosevelt and John Muir, Sierra Club founder and staunch defender of the national park idea, at Yosemite National Park, 1903. *Underwood & Underwood*

OPPOSITE: The Hetch Hetchy Valley in 1910, scene of an early battle over land use, before utilitarian values led to its conversion to a reservoir. *Bancroft Library, University of California, Berkeley*

ABOVE: The Teton Range from the valley of Jackson Hole, Grand Teton National Park, Wyoming. *Dale Schicketanz*

OPPOSITE, TOP: Winter view from the head of Bright Angel Trail, Grand Canyon National Park. *Philip Hyde*

OPPOSITE, BOTTOM: Echo Park, Dinosaur National Monument. *Philip Hyde*

OVERLEAF: Bryce Canyon National Park, Utah. *Philip Hyde*

OPPOSITE: Half Dome, Yosemite National Park, California. *Dale Schicketanz*
ABOVE: Yosemite Valley, Yosemite National Park, California. *Dale Schicketanz*

Otter Cliffs, Acadia National Park, Maine. *Read D. Brugger*

# 2

# A HEART OF WOOD

## The National Forest System

When Bill Kreutzer went to work on the White River Plateau Timber Reserve in Colorado, he soon grew accustomed to being ambushed and beaten, even shot at. The year was 1905 and Kreutzer was a forest ranger, one of the first in a tiny new agency called the U.S. Forest Service. His story, matter-of-factly told in the reports and other documents of what is now White River National Forest, was typical. Day or night, on horseback or on foot, he patrolled the Delaware-sized forest reserve alone, watching for fires and putting them out when he could, keeping an eye out for illegally cut timber, making sure the number of grazing cattle and sheep did not exceed the number allowed on government land, and sometimes risking his life in defense of an idea—though he would not have been likely to couch it in such a high-toned manner.

For Kreutzer and a handful of other sturdy young foresters were representative of something utterly new in American history: the first serious challenge by the government of the United States to those who, for at least two generations, had been using and abusing federal lands almost entirely without hindrance. President Theodore Roosevelt had bluntly stated the case against such traditional practices shortly after taking the oath of office a second time. "In the past we have admitted the right of the individual to injure the future of the Republic for his present profit. The time," Roosevelt declared, "has come for a change."

The national forest system is the embodiment of that change. Now

191 million acres in size, it comprises about 18 percent of the remaining commercial forestland in the country, with 153 individual national forests and eighteen grassland units in forty states. The national forests cloak the slopes of nearly every major mountain range in the nation in a chevron pattern of tree and shadow: Alaska's Chugach and Tongass; the Far West's Cascades, Coast Range, Sierra Nevadas, and Siskiyous; the arid West's Rockies; the central region's Black Hills, Ozarks, and Ouachitas; the Northeast's White Mountains and Green Mountains; the South's Appalachians. Among their rocky pinnacles, rivers are born of rain and snowmelt, metamorphosing at lower elevations into white flumes of crashing power or placid skeins of muddy water that are, in either form, the lifeblood of hundreds of small towns and large cites. In the Intermontane West, where rainfall is scarce, 85 percent of all water originates on 25 percent of the land—land that is located, not accidentally, within the boundaries of national forests.

Water and earth, along with trees and grass, are only the most visible resources of national forests. Additionally, they contain deposits of nonreplenishables such as gold, silver, chromium, molybdenum, nickel, tungsten, copper, and zinc, along with reserves of oil and natural gas. Drive through any national forest, and at its perimeter you will see a faintly rhomboidal sign in brown and ivory, proclaiming that here is the "Land of Many Uses," these being outdoor recreation, range, timber, watershed, and wildlife and fish habitat. Since 1964, wilderness preservation has also received official sanction. "Many uses" means that there are many users. There are loggers who come to cut timber, and recreationists who crave rugged beauty and solitude, in numbers surpassing those who visit national parks. Fourteen thousand ranchers graze 7 million sheep and cattle on the forest ranges, while more than 70,000 individuals or groups have been granted special-use permits for their television transmission stations, ski slopes, reservoirs, lodges, camps, and even public schools where land in adjacent towns is in short supply.

This multiple-use orientation is the most distinct characteristic of the national forest system. It is also the watchword of the United States Forest Service, the bureau in the Department of Agriculture that manages and protects forestlands on behalf of the public interest.

In a letter signed by Agriculture Secretary James Wilson on February 1, 1905, and disseminated for all to read, the Forest Service's guiding principle was first elegantly proclaimed: "Where conflicting interests must be reconciled the question will always be decided from the standpoint of the greatest good of the greatest number in the long run." William Greeley, who served as chief forester in the 1920s, explained in his autobiography that the phrase "multiple use" expressed "our zeal for the utmost public service from a section of land. We had the thrill of building Utopia and were a bit starry-eyed over it."

Perhaps too starry-eyed. Today, multiple use does not mean that every activity must be allowed on every acre in the national forests. It means instead that there must be a sense of balance throughout the entire system. The point at which this balance has been achieved, however, can be arguable. Thousands of times a year, Forest Service officials have the chance to upset or stabilize the national forests' equilibrium. Whether to permit clear-cutting on one thousand acres of Gunnison National Forest in Colorado, whether to build logging roads through de facto wilderness in Flathead National Forest in Montana, whether to chemically treat an infestation of spruce budworm, whether to approve a new ski slope, whether to add trails, whether to close campsites, whether to proceed with all of these things or none of them right now entails the making of numerous decisions that affect balance. And each is a decision that cuts to the heart of America's resource choices. This is the way Teddy Roosevelt might have seen it. "As a people," he said, "we have the right and duty, second to none other but the right and duty of obeying the moral law, of requiring and doing justice, to protect ourselves and our children against the wasteful development of our natural resources, whether that waste is caused by the actual destruction of such resources or by making them impossible of development hereafter."

Roosevelt spoke, of course, from his knowledge of what had gone before.

## THE ANCESTRAL FOREST

To those who set eyes upon it first, the American forest—the largest and most varied in the world outside of the tropics—seemed utterly indomitable. Pilgrims considered the scene before them with dread. The bravest among the early arrivals ventured out, according to Pilgrim chronicler William Bradford in the 1620s, "for a view of a more goodly country to feed their hopes; for which way soever they turned their eyes (save upward to the heavens) they could have little solace or content in respect of any outward objects." The forest washed inland over the continent far beyond a Pilgrim's ability to imagine it, clear to the Mississippi River he did not know existed, and was bounded on its outer edge by a pale hem of shore the length of which he could only guess. Yet the sense of human defeat was momentary. It gave way to the conviction that the industriousness of the people was as boundless as the forest. And neither, it seemed, would ever give out.

"Unlike Europe, the wooded continent was prediction, not chronicles, it was dreams, not traditions," wrote Richard Lillard in *The Great Forest*. "It implied new chapters in the history of commerce and agriculture and politics and statesmanship." Forests were cleared for settlements and fields and pastures. Wood was fashioned into houses and fences and fuel at so rapid a pace that the effects of deforestation were felt in the most populous regions within fifty years of settlement. In 1681, William Penn attempted to prevent widespread clear-cutting when he established the colony of "Penn's Woods." He decreed that for every four acres of trees cut, one acre was to be left standing. Nevertheless, an astute Pennsylvanian observed in 1753 that "our Runs dry up apace, several which formerly wou'd turn a fulling Mill, are now scarce sufficient for the Use of a Farm, the Reason of which is this, when the Country was cover'd with Woods & the Swamps with Brush, the Rain that fell was detain'd by These Interruptions." Yet such commentary was rare in that age, the more common view being one expressed by Isaac Weld, Jr., a tourist from England, who remarked that the man who could cut down the most trees was "looked upon as the most industrious citizen, and one that is making the greatest improvements in the country." By unanimous consent, the forest was only as good as what was made of it.

A capable settler learned to read his patch of forest like a treasure map, for the kind of trees that grew in a place told him what crops might thrive in their stead, explained Rutherford Platt in *The Great*

*American Forest*. In Virginia, for example, land bearing the largest oaks was known to be good for yielding fine tobacco; in Georgia, hickory land was cleared for corn; everywhere, soft maple and birch were not worth the trouble of clearing, since these breeds grew in places considered too cold and wet for proper cultivation. And certain trees themselves could be a useful treasure. Oak and hickory were hard to split and so made the sturdiest wagon parts. Oak, along with maple and walnut, was turned into furniture that lasted generations. Supple ash made the best bows and arrows, while birch, maple, and cherry burned very hot, and the small, tight fires kindled from them were ideal for cooking. Chestnut, with its long, ropy grain, could be split the length of an eight-foot log, and so lent itself to the ubiquitous split-rail fence. Favoring one tree over another did not mean that only the desired specimen was cut. Sometimes it was easier to clear the whole stand as though trees were weeds, and leave it barren for future use.

Life in the broadleaf interior of the East was different from life amid the evergreens farther north and west, and the standard equipage of each made this plain. In the deciduous forest a settler was associated with "the ax, the cornpatch, the split rail fence, a dog, a cow, a woman in the cabin and children," wrote Rutherford Platt. "In the conifer forest the symbols were the canoe, snowshoes, fur-bearing animal traps, the spoor of bear and moose, a trading post and lonely campsite." The trees of the conifer forest offered shelter and fuel, but no special services like those of the deciduous forest. In both forests profligacy flourished, perhaps unavoidably, according to the forest historian Samuel Trask Dana. He wrote in *Forest and Range Policy*:

Labor and capital, being scarce and therefore expensive, were used as sparingly and intensively as possible. In modern terminology, they were "conserved." Natural resources, being abundant and therefore cheap, were used as liberally and extensively as possible. In other words, they were exploited. There was nothing "ruthless" or reprehensible about this procedure. It was merely the application of sound common sense to the economic problem of making the most effective use of the productive factors at the disposal of the colonists.

## THE GREAT ASSAULT

Colonial expedience became a national industry in the years of growth that followed the War of Revolution, and in a continuing climate of abundance, the forests fell as the industry moved. First through New England, then into the Adirondacks and Catskills of New York and Pennsylvania, south into the Appalachians, through the Blue Ridge Mountains and the Great Smoky Mountains, clear to the edge of Florida. Up into the old Northwest, where Michigan lost its original forest in a single lifetime, where the old forests of Wisconsin were cut, rough-sawn into billions of board feet of unfinished lumber, packed together into rafts the size of football fields, and floated down the rivers to market. By the turn of the century the industry had jumped the continent to the West Coast, first to California, where the coast redwoods and the sugar pine of the Sierras fell to the saw and the donkey engine; then to Oregon and Washington, where spruce and Douglas fir disappeared into the holds of coastwise lumber schooners; then back into the interior of the continent, to the Rocky Mountains, through Colorado, Wyoming, Montana, and Idaho, where another industry consumed wood to timber its mines and to build its boom cities.

In its scope, in the amount of wood taken, and in the swiftness of its passage, there was nothing in human history to compare with the decades of this astonishing assault on the natural world. And there was precious little done to stop it. By some accounts, Congress passed more than one thousand land laws in the century following the Revolution, but only five of these up to 1873 dealt specifically with forests, or with the keeping of them in that condition. All five, the first of which was passed in 1799, affirmed the government's right to reserve timber on the public domain for shipbuilding and its intent to prosecute those caught taking wood for unauthorized use. "Trespass" became the polite word for what amounted to stealing timber from naval timber reserves, although it applied quite well to the pilfering of any sort of timber from the public domain at large. Not that the laws had much effect. The American attitude then toward government reserves was about the same as it had been toward those reserves established under King George III. Great Britain's "broad arrow" reserves of colonial white pine for the Royal Navy's masts had been branded a form of tyranny, period. There had even been a "Pine Tree Riot" in 1772, during which more than twenty rebellious Down-Easters crossed out, with switches and clubs on the British sheriff's bare back, "the account against them of all logs cut, drawn and forfeited," making the sheriff "wish he had never heard of pine trees fit for masting the royal navy."

Throughout most of the century following the Revolution, such attitudes fostered a tradition of laissez-faire, the conscious policy not to defend seriously against trespass or to prosecute those suspected of depredations. This represented a major reversal of President Thomas Jefferson's assertion that lands to which the government held title would be protected from exploitation. From the moment Jefferson left government office, his dictate was ignored. "In its place was tacitly substituted the rule that the public domain is a vast commons on which all may freely go and take," wrote Thomas LeDuc in 1964. "By continuous refusal of adequate appropriations for police protection, Congress expressed its clear intent that federal power should not be used to protect public property." The timber barons understood this fully, and it was with clear consciences that they not only took the trees they wanted where law did not prevent them, but ignored and subverted those laws that did finally evolve—as we shall see in chapter 4.

A few government officials did make the mistake of trying to enforce the law in spite of laissez-faire tradition. Carl Schurz, Secretary of the Interior from 1877 to 1881, took timber depredation very seriously. He had been born and raised in Germany, where the science of forestry was commonly practiced and plundering had long since fallen out of favor. He fired land agents who had gained their positions through patronage or who had developed a knack for looking in the other direction when corruption approached. Schurz replaced them with tougher, independent men. He also lobbied for the novel idea of selling timber-cutting privileges while retaining the land to prevent its mistreatment. These efforts got him nowhere, for Congress grew uneasy about his burst of enforcement and in 1880 responded by passing a law that actually excused timber violators on public lands from civil or criminal prosecution, if they paid $1.25 an acre for the land they had unlawfully cleared. Critics of the measure, who were mostly in the East and the Lake States, where gutting the landscape had such destructive consequences, sarcastically called it "the bill to license thieves on the public domain," or "the bill to condone crime and invite trespass and encourage theft."

Frustrated in his efforts to restore sanity to public land matters, Schurz resigned. Almost immediately his successor backed off from Schurz's reforms. He even apologized to Congress, stating that "extenuating circumstances surrounding the acts of trespass" would always be dug up to avoid further prosecution of wrongdoers. But the appointment of William Andrew Jackson Sparks, a former congressman, to the post of General Land Office commissioner in 1885 brought yet another crusader for land reform. For frauds involving various land laws, particularly the Timber and Stone Act of 1878, Sparks suspended all entries in the regions where the flimflam had been uncovered: in Dakota, Idaho, Utah, Washington, Colorado, and Wyoming—in other words, in the greater part of the public domain. Sparks's campaign to end "widespread, persistent public land robbery committed under the guise of various forms of public land entry" impressed Congress as little as had the Schurz crackdown, and he did not remain on the job for long. Soon after he was dismissed, Interior Secretary Lucius Q. C. Lamar revoked his program, even though Sparks had reported, before leaving his position in 1887, that more than 41 million acres of fraudulently claimed land had been restored to the public domain for honest disposition.

Unfortunately, reformers within the government, like Schurz and Sparks, were so rare as to be easily identified—and gotten rid of. For the most part, during that period of the nineteenth century, which the social historian Vernon L. Parrington called "the Great Barbecue," the timber industry did its cooking unencumbered by federal sanctions or concern.

## THE PRESCIENCE OF GEORGE PERKINS MARSH

Even as the timber industry went about its business, however, a body of sentiment for the protection of the forests was slowly coalescing. Some of it, remarkably, developed out of studies commissioned by the government itself. In 1876, Congress had established a Division of Forestry in the Agriculture Department, and had placed Franklin

B. Hough, a physician and amateur forester, at its head. Hough, who had served as superintendent of the 1870 U.S. Census, won his appointment by conducting his own study of American forests, using census data, and submitting independent reports to Congress. His studies revealed that timber-cutting had dropped off entirely in some areas but was accelerating dramatically in others. The emerging pattern revealed forests in various stages of depletion. Congress gave Hough $2,000 to conduct further investigations into "the annual amount of consumption, importation, and exportation of timber and other forest products, the probable future supply for future wants," and "the means best adapted to their preservation and renewal." Almost all of this, however, was confined to private lands; try as he might, Hough could not convince Congress that his studies ought to be applied to the lands of the public domain as well. In 1880 another government study, this one conducted by Harvard botanist Charles Sargent, predicted that if the present rate of timber-cutting continued, the remaining American forests would be gone in ten years. Sargent's forecast may have been too pessimistic, but few who studied the situation could believe that the forests would hold out much more than thirty years. In the course of a Victorian lifetime, an area the size of Europe already had been deforested in the United States.

In the face of such investigations, agitation for federal protection of forests was growing among the ranks of amateur foresters who had joined to form the American Forestry Association in 1875. Many of them had been profoundly affected by one of the most prescient books in the nation's history: George Perkins Marsh's *Man and Nature*, first published in 1864. A renowned polymath, Marsh had much besides this book to occupy him. He was, at the beginning of his public life, an impoverished Vermont statesman who had served as the state's railroad commissioner and fish commissioner. As an architectural authority, Marsh had designed the Vermont capitol building and determined the final proportions of the Washington Monument. After the deaths of his wife and young son and a second marriage to a woman who was bedridden the rest of her life, Marsh immersed himself in Scandinavian history, compiled Icelandic folklore, and popularized the travels of the Vikings. His reputation as a historian and linguist caught Abraham Lincoln's attention, and Marsh was appointed minister plenipotentiary to the Kingdom of Italy in 1861. He served in this capacity until his death in 1882, making his term one of the longest in American diplomacy. The undemanding duties of the post gave him the leisure to research and write his most famous work.

*Man and Nature*, entitled *Man, the Disturber of Nature's Harmonies* until the publisher objected on the grounds that it simply could not be so (Marsh retitled the 1874 edition *The Earth as Modified by Human Action*), surveyed the decline of ancient civilizations through the decline of the lands they occupied. For example, Marsh said, the Fertile Crescent, which had spawned some of mankind's brighter cultural achievements, had been turned into "an assemblage of bald mountains, barren, treeless hills and Swampy and malarious plains"; the abused land of ancient Greece and Rome revealed "a desolation almost as complete as the moon," and parts of China were hardly better. All of this, he made clear, was the direct consequence of deforestation, and he did not neglect his own native land: "Man has too long forgotten that the earth was given to him for usufruct alone, not for consumption, still less for profligate waste," he wrote. In the United States "we are, even now, breaking up the floor and wainscoting and doors and window frames of our dwelling, for fuel to warm our bodies and seethe our pottage, and the world cannot afford to wait till the slow and sure progress of exact science has taught it a better economy."

## RUIN AND REDEMPTION

In Michigan, for instance, science and economy were progressing in a different direction. This was just one of the states where the lumber industry was running full-tilt in the last half of the nineteenth century. By the 1870s more than one hundred sawmills were operating in the Saginaw–Bay City area alone—six days a week, twelve hours a day. In 1882, the peak year, these mills turned out more than one billion board feet of lumber. By 1897, Michigan sawmills had produced more than 160 billion board feet of white pine, leaving only 6 billion board feet in the entire state. To reach this point had taken less than fifty years.

In more pedestrian terms, 160 billion board feet of timber can be translated into about 10 million six-room houses, or enough planks to build a pine floor over Michigan and Rhode Island together. Much of it actually did go into the construction of houses and barns between the Lake States and the Rockies. But public demand alone did not push Michigan, or any other state, to the brink of deforestation. Technology had developed beyond the ability of the resource to regenerate. Mills that had once peaked at 10 million board feet a year were, by the end of the nineteenth century, cutting 40, 50, even 200 million feet a year. In his memoirs the Civil War historian Bruce Catton, who grew up on the far side of Michigan's timber boom, described the recurring circumstances: "One of the baffling factors of the age of improved technology now made its appearance. The cost of production became lower but only on the condition that the producer was able to put more and more money into it . . . big operators had to invest a lot of money and they could not get it back unless they operated at capacity."

Fire was another big consumer of wood, much of it the result of wasteful timber practices. Until the later days of the era, timbermen could afford to take only the best trees, stripping logs of their crowns and branches before hauling them out. The residue was left on the forest floor beneath the remaining "undesirable" trees. After years of accumulation and drying, such detritus made living tinderboxes out of many forests—imminent fires waiting for the strike of lightning, the spark from a passing locomotive, the flames from a runaway cookfire. The results were often horrific. So it was with the Peshtigo Fire of Wisconsin in 1871, when 1,280,000 acres were burned and more than 1,500 people were killed; so it was in Michigan in 1881, when fire killed a million acres of trees and 138 people; so it was in Minnesota in 1894, when the Hinckley Fire destroyed 160,000 acres of forest, twelve towns, and 418 people. After fire, quite often came flood—an inadvertent demonstration of watershed ecology. Hillsides with little left but black snags and soot could not hold the water during seasons of rain. Rivers swelled with runoff and debris and carried it all into downstream towns with devastating effects.

As the forests went, so did the economy they had directly supported. Catton described the sound of ruin he heard as a boy:

When the buzz saws and the edgers and the jolting game saws and the clattering conveyers at last fell idle for good, the boss would pull

73

the whistle cord, tie it down, and let the steam go up to join the clouds. One long haunting blast—the same that had been rousing the townspeople and calling men to work for a generation or more— would go echoing across the plains, slowly losing its pitch and its volume as the pressure died, falling at last to a dispirited moan and at last fading out altogether . . . and that mill was out of action forever, and possibly the town along with it, and people would begin to wonder what they were going to do next.

It was too late to help Michigan, but when Congress passed the General Revision Act of 1891, relief from the perils of unchecked deforestation was on the way. Not that Congress intended any such thing, for the act brought succor in a form most of the legislators had never seriously contemplated, and certainly would not have condoned if they had. The only thing they had meant to do on March 3, 1891, was rescind some of the most ill-suited and flagrantly abused of the land laws. Instead, owing to vigorous arm-twisting by Interior Secretary John W. Noble, a conference committee attached a rider to the bill (later called the Forest Reserve Act) that altered the course of public land history. The rider authorized the President to "set apart and reserve . . . any part of the public lands wholly or in part covered with timber or undergrowth whether of commercial value or not, as public reservations." Noble had been convinced of this measure's urgency by Bernard Fernow, who had succeeded Hough at the Division of Forestry.

Fernow and others had tried for about two years to convince Congress of the need for federally protected forests, but had not even been able to get a serious hearing. Yet once Noble's rider slipped through, a "long chain of peculiar circumstances" kept most congressmen from noticing its presence, according to the historian John Ise. The only notable criticism was voiced by Arkansas Senator Thomas C. McRae, who denounced the rider as "an extraordinary and dangerous" power to give a President. The bill with its provocative rider nevertheless passed, "not through the initiative of Congress," Ise wrote, "but rather because Congress had no good opportunity to act on the provision." Exercising his new authority, President Benjamin Harrison proclaimed the Yellowstone Timberland Reserve next to the park, and the White River Plateau reserve in Colorado. He soon added four more, encompassing 13 million acres.

At first it seemed as though no one had noticed, and those few who did cautiously praised Harrison's proclamations on the grounds they would prevent carelessly set fires and floods. No one was exactly sure what else the reserves might be for. Naturalist John Muir convinced himself that they were another form of national park, and rejoiced at the advancement of preservation. Others were not so sure. People in Meeker, Colorado, a town near the White River reserve, did not share Muir's joy, feeling that any such thing would stifle their economic development. The *Meeker Herald* suggested that local communities join hands "in a solid phalanx against the dude design for an outdoor museum and menagerie." The uncertainty irritated President Grover Cleveland. He added another 20 million acres of reserves, but refused to set aside any more until Congress defined their purpose. Congress obliged on June 4, 1897 (again in an amendment to a larger bill), by passing the Forest Organic Act.

The act stated that reserves were established "to improve and protect the forest within the boundaries for the purpose of securing favorable conditions of water flow, and to furnish a continuous supply of timber for the use and necessities of citizens of the United States." The act also specified what kind of timber could be removed from the forests—and required each tree to be "marked and designated" before it was cut and sold. Administration of the forest reserves was handed over to the General Land Office in the Department of the Interior. Perhaps the most far-reaching provision in the act was its authorization of the Interior Secretary to "regulate the occupancy and use" of the forests without providing a clue as to what was meant by this term. Charles Wilkinson, a professor of natural resource law, has labeled the Organic Act "a blank check" because of this. Gifford Pinchot, who assumed control of the Division of Forestry in 1898, called it "the milk in the coconut."

### THE FIRST CHIEF FORESTER

Pinchot, a hatchet-faced Yale graduate belonging to a well-to-do family of French extraction, began to figure prominently in forestry matters shortly after completing his silvicultural studies in France.

75

The neat rows of commercial timber there, with the ground swept as clean of clutter as a living room floor, and with roads and paths intersecting at regular intervals, was a vision he wanted to transplant into the unruly forests of America. It was time, he felt, to introduce the European tradition of growing trees like a crop to the United States. On his return from Europe in 1891 at age twenty-six, Pinchot opened a forestry consulting office. Demand for his services was predictably light, but he did find a few opportunities to demonstrate the practicability of the European system. At the 1893 World's Fair in Chicago, Pinchot exhibited his impressive results from managing the seven-thousand-acre forest on the Biltmore estate of multimillionaire George Vanderbilt.

In 1896, Pinchot tagged along with the National Academy of Science's Forestry Commission on a tour of Western forests. The commission's recommendations led to the passage of the Organic Act the following year, and to the addition of another 21 million acres of reserves. Fernow, who did not believe that forestry could be practiced on a grand scale under the American political system, was replaced in 1898 by Pinchot, who with all his heart believed precisely this. But with no control over the federal forests, still in Interior, Pinchot and his small staff in Agriculture's Division of Forestry could do little more than provide individuals and lumber companies with silvicultural advice regarding their own private forests. He called his first year at the division a "halcyon and vociferous time," but it was not enough. He wanted those Western forest reserves, and, not a man to keep his opinions to himself, he lashed out at the General Land Office, for its "executive incompetence and political toad-eating." When Land Office Commissioner Binger Hermann asserted that his office was "fully competent to deal with forestry," Pinchot retorted that not only was the land office "incompetent to deal with it, but it understood so little about forestry even to know that it was incompetent."

"Obviously to bring Uncle Sam's forests and foresters together was nothing more than common sense," Pinchot stated in his autobiography, *Breaking New Ground*. "Brought together they were going to be, if I had any luck, and when they were I proposed to be the forester in charge." Luck had little to do with it; determination and a firmly

76

developed friendship with Theodore Roosevelt did. After struggling for seven years, Pinchot finally achieved his heart's desire. With the prodding of Roosevelt after he assumed the presidency, Congress eventually transferred all the reserves over to the Department of Agriculture for safekeeping in 1905. Soon afterward, the reserves were renamed national forests and the Division of Forestry became the Forest Service, reflecting the more active role the agency would assume. Immediately, Pinchot set his program into motion, clarifying it first in a letter of instruction that bore Agriculture Secretary James Wilson's signature, but was pure Pinchot. "It must be clearly borne in mind that all land is to be devoted to its most productive use for the permanent good of the whole people and not for the temporary benefit of the individuals or companies," the instructions began. "All the resources of the Forest Reserves are for *use* and this use must be brought about in a thoroughly prompt and businesslike manner, under such restrictions only as will insure the permanence of these resources. . . ." Pinchot had learned in Europe that the success of any forestry effort depended on community support. Therefore, in his agency he promised that "local questions will be decided on local grounds," with first consideration being given to the dominant industry.

## INVENTING CONSERVATION

To promote the gospel of wise use, Pinchot replaced the timber agents of the General Land Office, most of them political appointees, with men of his own, civil service people all. According to one of Pinchot's first employees, the newcomers formed "a corps of inspectors Pinchot knew he could trust; men who knew the West and how to get around; men who would go, look, see and not take anybody's word for nothing; men who couldn't be bribed or bluffed." Pinchot was considered a "tough hombre" to work for, but those who were selected from the hundreds of applicants considered their time well spent. Most, in fact, felt there was no better way to spend it. The Forest Service's esprit de corps was unmatched by any other government bureau. Its men were respected for their courage and efficiency. It operated as though it were oblivious to the existence of political expediency.

Those who worked in the Washington office were regularly invited to Pinchot's mansion for gingerbread and baked apples, served with long discussions of forestry. To these soirees Pinchot also invited illustrious guests to mingle with his staff. In the backcountry, things were different. "It was a world of strings of packhorses or men who walked alone—a world of hoof and foot and the rest done by hand," Norman Maclean wrote in *A River Runs Through It*. Rangers never went without a .45 revolver, with which they could "hit a postage stamp stuck to an aspen tree at fifty feet," and, after 1907, a forty-two-page book entitled *The Use of the National Forests*, which fit into a shirt pocket. The *Use* book was Pinchot's way of preaching to his men when there was no one around to tell them what to do. "The man who skins the land and moves on does the country more harm than good," was one of the book's pronouncements. "He may enrich himself and a few others for a very brief time, but he kills the land." Despite the Forest Service's righteous attitude and the unshakable conviction that foresters knew what was best, the agency made peace with those it regulated. Before too long, men like F. E. Weyerhaeuser, the son of the lumber company's founder, were talking in a way that signified Pinchot's effectiveness. At one timber convention Weyerhaeuser asserted that "practical forestry ought to be of more interest and importance to lumbermen than to any other class of men."

Even though Pinchot's doctrine of utility was an inspiring and highly commendable departure from the profligacy that had gone before, it had some shortcomings from the outset. It bound the forest to materialism. If something could not be produced to sell on the open market, it was not considered valuable. Pinchot dismissed recreation as "quite incidental" to the ultimate purpose of the forest (although today it is second in priority only to logging). He had no appreciation for plain and simple scenic preservation. So unattuned was Pinchot to the national park idea that he became a champion of the Hetch Hetchy project in Yosemite National Park, and every park bill that came up before Congress was disputed by the Forest Service. Finally, Pinchot and Muir, who had gotten along very well while traveling with the 1896 Forestry Commission, broke off their friendship because of vastly different expectations of the natural world. In his autobiography, Pinchot tells the story of the time he was hiking with Muir in the Grand Canyon when they came across a tarantula. Pinchot was ready to shoot it, but Muir stopped him. "He wouldn't let me kill it," Pinchot wrote. "He said it had as much right there as we did." Pinchot was amazed.

While the word "conservation" is most often associated these days with the advocates of John Muir's worldview, it was Pinchot's word at the start. He coined it, not long after discovering what it meant. The meaning of conservation came to Pinchot on a gloomy day in February 1907, while he was riding through Rock Creek Park in Washington, D.C. It suddenly struck him that the "wise use" of all natural resources was "the key to the safety and prosperity of the American people, and all the people of the world, for all time to come." Together with a fellow forester, Pinchot derived the word "conservation" from the forest conservancies of British-ruled India. Later, while riding with Roosevelt, Pinchot described his philosophy and told Roosevelt what he called it. Roosevelt "understood, accepted, and adopted it without the smallest hesitation," wrote Pinchot. "It was directly in line with everything he had been thinking and doing." The concept of conservation had been at the heart of Roosevelt's administration all along. And now there was a word to keep it there, forever.

## THE BIG STEAL

Even before the 43 million acres of forest reserves were transferred from Interior to Agriculture, Pinchot worried about the fate of the remaining unreserved forestlands on the public domain, most of them scattered through the Rocky Mountain region. Without federal protection, they would be open to the same ravages evident to a large degree elsewhere. Timber in the Rocky Mountain West grew in rough terrain, and its species of Engelmann spruce and ponderosa and lodgepole pine were considered commercially inferior to the Douglas fir and Sitka spruce of the Northwest. As a result, except in mining regions, the Rockies had not been raided as thoroughly as other parts of the country. Pinchot did not believe this could last, and he convinced Roosevelt that surveys had to be made before the inevitable assault. During 1903 and 1904—even before creation of the Forest Service—Pinchot had fifteen men fresh out of forestry schools making field investigations to determine the proper boundaries of future reserves.

He had other reasons as well. Under the terms of the "lieu-lands" clause of the 1897 Organic Act, owners of property enclosed within a forest reserve could exchange that property for land anywhere outside the confines of the reserve. However much lumber companies detested forest reserves, few were reluctant to take advantage of this clause, trading land they had already harvested for virgin territory elsewhere. Millions of acres of previously untouched forest had gone into private hands in this manner; the Weyerhaeuser company alone acquired more than 900,000 acres of new land in exchange for its cut-over property.

Understandably, Pinchot detested the lieu-lands clause, and his surveyors were instructed to draw reserve boundaries in such a way as to exclude large private landholdings wherever possible. His men complied readily, even with a certain arrogance. "The boundary men were a corps d'elite," asserted Coert duBois in his memoirs (published in *Forest History*). "We strutted around and lorded it over the working plan boys and would scarce deign to spit at a tree planter." During his first summer, duBois was assigned to Colorado: "The area that each examiner was to cover was painted with Pommeroy's yellow drawing ink on General Land Office state maps on a scale of half an inch to the township," duBois wrote in his memoirs. "When [supervisor] Allen handed me the map indicating my first season's job I thought he had spilled the bottle of Pommeroy's ink all over southwest Colorado. It covered all the mountain country in the nine counties in the southeast corner of the state and slopped all over both sides of the Continental Divide." In two summers the boundary men walked and mapped about 150 million acres of potential reserve lands. When completed, the boundary men's work was to be put to a use as controversial as any in the annals of conservation.

Angered by Roosevelt's reserve-making tendencies, Western congressmen succeeded in having this executive power repealed in a rider to the 1907 agriculture funding bill. The bill with this stipulation passed, and although Roosevelt could easily have pocket-vetoed it as the closing act of his administration, Pinchot had a more dramatic exit in mind for the President. With Roosevelt's "enthusiastic consent," Pinchot and his staff drew up all the reserve proclamations for which the boundary men had already done the legwork. "We set every available man at work drawing proclamations for the national forests in six states," wrote Pinchot. "We knew precisely what we wanted . . . our office worked straight through, some of them working thirty-six and forty-eight hours on end to finish the job." When the work was done, Roosevelt signed into existence another twenty-one new national forests totaling 16 million acres. Then, and only then, did he sign the agricultural bill denying every President after him the privilege of doing what he had just done. During the course of his presidency, Roosevelt had set aside about 80 million acres of national forests.

The West, as predicted, exploded when it learned what Roosevelt and Pinchot had done. Pinchot, according to Washington's governor at the time, "has done more to retard the growth and development of the Northwest than any other man." The editor of the *Seattle Post-Intelligencer* avowed that "the recent abuses of power have grown to the point that there will be bitter revolt against the entire policy of forest reserves and an appeal to Congress to repeal all laws on the subject." Roosevelt perhaps described the situation best when he said, gleefully, that "the opponents of the Forest Service turned handsprings in their wrath, and dire were the threats against the executive, but the threats could not be carried out, and were really a tribute to the efficiency of our action."

Out of his respect for Roosevelt, William Howard Taft retained Pinchot in 1909 as his "administration's conscience" but drastically curtailed his rabble-rousing. Taft, who did not share Roosevelt's preoccupation with conservation, though he felt strongly about it, thought Pinchot was "a good deal of a radical and a good deal of a crank." After Pinchot publicly insinuated that Interior Secretary Richard Ballinger had committed improprieties regarding the leasing of Alaskan coal lands and triggered a Senate investigation into the matter, Taft, in 1910, fired his chief forester for insubordination. Such cross fire between departments, particularly when it was a lower official sniping at a higher one, could not be tolerated. Pinchot eventually returned to Pennsylvania, entered politics, became governor, considered running for President, and remained a potent force in conservation and forestry until his death in 1948. "I have since been a governor, every now and then," he was heard to say on more than one occasion. "But I am a forester all the time—have been, and shall be, all my working life."

## RESCUE IN THE EAST

Pinchot's unceremonious departure from the Forest Service did not injure the agency at all. It continued to gain strength in its enforcement policies and earned the respect even of those who detested governmental interference. Henry Solon Graves, dean of the Yale Forestry School, replaced Pinchot, becoming one of the few chief foresters who did not work his way up through the ranks as a career man. One thing that troubled Graves and his successors was the fact that the Forest Service returned so little income to the U.S. Treasury from the sale of timber. Not more than 5 percent of the nation's supply came from the national forests in any year, and all timber sales were restricted to those needed for forest custodial reasons. But Graves hoped the Forest Service could one day be self-sufficient. To challenging legislators he explained why it was not already. Forests had values other than those associated with sawn timber, Graves said. If the Forest Service stopped all noncustodial timber operations and ignored the importance of watershed protection "the forests could easily be made to show a net profit." He quickly added, however, that forests were never to be looked at as a source of short-term income. They were a long-term investment. Also, the Forest Service understanding with private timber operators was that government land would not compete with private land. Chief Forester Greeley, who followed Graves, asserted that the agency would never be allowed to "sacrifice the intrinsic value" of public property by a "bargain-day policy" of dumping timber on the market (a policy that did not survive into modern times, as we shall see).

Conflicts with Stephen Mather's new National Park Service also occupied forestry officials. With almost every new national park that came along, some national forestland was transferred from Agriculture's "multiple use" department—the Forest Service—to Interior's "preservation" department—the Park Service. Possibly as a way to stanch the outflow of its lands, the Forest Service began to promote the national forests' recreational opportunities. In 1929 the agency began to designate parts of national forests as primitive, which meant they were left alone as much as possible (see chapter 5).

From the standpoint of environmental protection, which is to say watershed and timber protection, the National Forest System in the West was so successful that Eastern states began to agitate for similar help. This was harder to accomplish, since there was little public domain left east of the Mississippi; most had passed into private hands almost a century before. In 1901, Agriculture Secretary Wilson recommended the establishment of a forest reserve in the Southern Appalachians, but there was no federal money for the necessary purchases, and efforts to attract it failed. Support for the idea was growing in the East, however, where the cycle of fire, floods, and erosion had been particularly severe. "During March 1907, heavy rains brought flood waters down the Monongahela River," wrote C. R. McKim in his history of the area. "The trees and other healthy vegetation were no longer there to regulate the rainwater's flow. It devastated all the agricultural land in the basin of the Monongahela River, causing some $100 million in damages—a gigantic sum for those times—then descended in all its fury upon the helpless city of Pittsburgh, causing there additional damages of $8 million, drowning people and ruining homes."

This disaster was enough to make the West Virginia legislature ask Congress to purchase the despoiled lands for reforestation. In 1911 the passage of the Weeks Act authorized these purchases, as well as those of similar cut-over lands in other Eastern states. This act, named for Massachusetts congressman John W. Weeks, appropriated $9 million to buy 5 million acres in the Southern Appalachians and another million acres in the White Mountains of New Hampshire. It provided for the acquisition of "forested, cut-over or denuded lands within the watersheds of navigable streams. . . ." The emphasis on stream protection was necessary, for it appeared to be the only way Congress could constitutionally buy land, using its power to regulate interstate commerce by maintaining navigable streams. The "production of timber" was added to navigable stream protection in 1924 when the Clarke-McNary Act was passed. Clarke-McNary also introduced the notion of "cooperation to inspire voluntary action" and offered incentives to private landowners to improve the condition of their forests and manage their land more soundly. Finally, the act required that states put up funds matching those of the federal government for fire protection.

The Pisgah National Forest in North Carolina was the first established in the East, in 1916, near the Biltmore estate where Pinchot had done his forestry apprenticeship. Acquisition of forestlands gained momentum during the 1920s, and again during the 1930s, when twenty-six new forests were established. The Great Depression was a boom time for Eastern national forests, because people were desperate to sell their land, and nobody but the federal government was in a position to buy it. Most of the land purchased for Eastern forests cost less than five dollars an acre. "Nearly all were lands that had been abused, poorly protected or ignored, whose owners were happy to unload on the federal government," one commentator of the era noted. Federal investment in reforestation, fire protection, and timber-stand improvement, mostly through the Civilian Conservation Corps, returned the lands to their original heavily forested condition. A comparatively mild climate and abundant rainfall allowed the reforestation work to take hold sooner than most people expected.

Reforestation everywhere was given a boost by the passage of the Knutsen-Vanderberg Act in 1930, which required that money received from the sale of federal timber be set aside for reseeding and planting, in addition to what Congress could be convinced to appropriate every year. By Chief Forester Greeley's count, the high tide of denuded forestlands in the nation had been 81 million acres; much of this had now been given new life.

### POINTS OF CONTENTION

The comfortable, almost symbiotic relationship between the Forest Service and the timber industry that had developed during the first three decades of the system got a rude jolt in 1933. That was the year of the Service's Copeland Report, which urged the federal government to buy a good deal more forestland for the national forest system and exert tighter controls over logging on private lands. "The period of voluntary private forestry is over," declared Robert Marshall, one of the young Turks in the agency, who also advocated, in a book called *The People's Forests*, the outright nationalization of all forests. It was just such pronouncements that soon made loggers cast the agency in an ominous shade of red and sparked a letter-writing campaign between timber executives and agency officials regarding "the tremendous impetus given socialism." Fear of creeping socialism finally forced the Copeland recommendations out of the realm of consideration, and the report disappeared into the maw of the bureaucracy.

Pinchot, watching from the wings, had said he was pleased that a bit of a wedge had been driven into the logger-forester relationship. Things between the regulators and the regulated had gotten too cozy even for his taste; in 1928, for example, Chief Forester Greeley had quit the Service to manage the West Coast Lumbermen's Association, thus setting in motion what later critics came to call the Service's "revolving door" tradition of employee exchanges between the government agency and private industry. But when President Franklin D. Roosevelt appointed Ferdinand A. Silcox, a forester who had spent most of his time working in labor relations, to the position of chief forester, Pinchot was relieved. He said that once again his Forest Service might become "the aggressive agent and advocate of the public good, and not the humble little brother of the lumbermen."

In this second Roosevelt the Forest Service acquired another fond admirer; it seemed to run in the family. As a child, Franklin Roosevelt had developed a deep affection for trees on his Hyde Park estate. There, he raised them as a cash crop and as a way to reclaim the land. By 1944 Roosevelt, who listed his occupation as "tree grower" when he went to vote, had supervised the planting of half a million trees on his land. He transferred his "gospel of conservation" to many of his New Deal programs—at least those having to do with making land and water available for planned and regulated human use. (Parks and wilderness and refuges, on the other hand, were not quite so high on his list of priorities.) While Roosevelt was campaigning for the presidency, someone remarked that he seemed to dwell on the importance of land, trees, and water as the solution for perhaps too many of America's most pressing concerns. "I fear that I must plead guilty to that charge," he replied.

Under Roosevelt it was not always easy to tell a Forest Service friend from a Forest Service foe, because in Harold Ickes, Secretary of the Interior, they were one and the same. Not long after taking office, Ickes conceived the notion of turning the Department of the Interior into what he called a "true" Department of Conservation. It probably was New Deal "brain truster" Rexford G. Tugwell who first proposed this to Ickes, along with suggesting that the Forest Service would be a natural part of such an agency. In any case, Ickes soon made the idea his own. The possibility of transfer had arisen before. In 1886, Fernow had thought that the division of forestry belonged in the Interior Department, since that was where all the other federal land responsibilities were housed. During the Graves administration, the states had tried several times to have national forests turned over to them, and during Greeley's tenure Interior Secretary Albert Fall had tried to recover the forests Pinchot had taken. Fall might even have succeeded, had he not been interrupted by the Teapot Dome scandal and suddenly found his hands quite full.

Ickes, who called himself "as hard-boiled and enthusiastic a conservationist as there is in the country," was a more serious challenger than Fall. "I'm going to get the Forest Service," he announced, and for nearly ten years he tried. Roosevelt encouraged him, but never went so far as to use his personal influence on Congress; there were too many other things he wanted done and he feared overextending himself. Moreover, Ickes was opposed vigorously by Agriculture Secretary Henry A. Wallace, who looked upon the Ickes attempts at a raid with no enthusiasm whatever. Neither did Pinchot, who reminded everyone within earshot of the sorry record of the Interior Department before Ickes's arrival there and implied that it could well revert to old habits once Ickes was gone. "Ickes is sincere and honest," Pinchot said, "but he cannot live forever." In the end, although he did get the U.S. Biological Survey and the Bureau of Fisheries in the Reorganization Act of 1939 (see chapter 4), Ickes never did get his Conservation Department—or the forests.

Following World War II, a serious attempt was made not merely to transfer the national forests but to dismantle them. This scheme, beginning in 1946, was forged by a handful of powerful Western ranchers who had always been rebellious against federal intervention, and against paying the grazing fees instituted in 1906. What triggered this particular attack was the Forest Service decree that livestock on national forest ranges would have to be cut back to give the land time to recover from the overgrazing permitted during the war. Stockmen had never developed the camaraderie with the Forest Service that loggers enjoyed. And rangers were accused of not liking stockmen any more than stockmen liked them, a point made clear in Norman Maclean's story "USFS 1919: The Ranger, the Cook and a Hole in the Sky" in *A River Runs Through It*: "Bill Bell was the toughest [guy] in the Bitterroot Valley, and we thought he was the best ranger in the Forest Service. We were strengthened in this belief by the rumor that Bill had killed a sheepherder. We were a little disappointed that he had been acquitted of the charges, but nobody held it against him, for we all knew that being acquitted of killing a sheepherder in Montana isn't the same as being innocent."

And so stockmen gathered in Salt Lake City in the summer of 1946 and began to think about how they might acquire 80 million acres of national forest range—and, while they were at it, the 142 million acres of Taylor Act grazing lands as well (more on this in chapter 3). The states in which the lands were located, they decided, would serve as a conduit, taking possession of the ranges until a select group of ranchers could buy them, at nine cents an acre, and keep them for their exclusive use. Western politicians, traditionally under powerful obligation to the livestock industry, went along cheerfully. Then the historian and social critic Bernard DeVoto got wind of the idea and spread it before the nation in the pages of *Harper's*. He called it "one of the biggest landgrabs in history," and accused the stock business of wanting "to shovel most of the West into its rivers." According to DeVoto, overgrazing had done more damage to the West than anything else. He kept the heat on the ranchers until there was no hope of success. They retaliated by calling for congressional field hearings into Forest Service grazing policies. Congressman Frank A. Barrett, a Wyoming rancher, served as chairman as the hearings traveled to Western cities. For their lack of decorum the whole series was dubbed "Barrett's Wild West Show," as audiences packed with angry ranchers "yelled, stamped and applauded" every time a charge was leveled against the Forest Service.

It was all very much in keeping with the sentiments expressed by one J. Elmer Brock, a Wyoming stockman who repudiated DeVoto's outrage with some of his own. "The users of grazing lands must conform to the whims of numerous federal bureaus," he wrote in a guest column in the *Denver Post*. These bureaus were "all predacious and most of them tinged with pink or even deeper hue." Federal ownership and management of land, Brock asserted, was nothing other than a "form of communism." Charges of socialism failed to arouse the public's sympathy for ranchers; their plan to acquire the national forest ranges in the name of free enterprise failed completely. The forests would stay put in the Department of Agriculture, and, for the time being, continue under government protection.

## ROADS-FOR-TIMBER-FOR-ROADS-FOR . . .

At the start, the U.S. Forest Service was understood to be a caretaker agency, for the most part. Trees were cut largely for custodial reasons rather than for commercial ones, and the annual harvest from national forests remained below 2 percent of the national total annually until World War II. From the beginning, in fact, lumber industry executives constantly had sought assurances that national forest timber would not compete with that taken from their own forests. Almost 75 percent of the woodlands in the country belonged to private landowners or the lumber industry. Since these lands had originally been selected for their superior productivity and accessibility, it was generally agreed that with the application of wise forestry, private and commercial forests could meet the needs of the nation almost indefinitely. Much of the Forest Service's early work, after all, had concentrated on teaching the right management techniques to the private forestry sector. (The agency still does this through its State and Private Forestry Division, dwarfed though it is by other Forest Service programs.) The national forests were to be saved for the Future, a shadowy time that might one day arrive, like the Apocalypse, beyond dispute. When the right time came, the national forests would be there, in prime condition to render their share of timber.

By Forest Service and timber industry reckoning, the right time coincided with the end of World War II. The pace of logging had gained momentum during the war, but it was not to be temporary. Soldiers became civilians with pent-up purchasing power and a keen desire for houses. War-torn Europe needed to be rebuilt, and a great deal of American lumber was exported for that purpose. Faced with depletion on its own lands, the timber industry began looking toward the national forests to furnish what its own forests could not. Under this pressure, cutting in the national forests accelerated until, as Forest Service historian Harold K. Steen put it, "timber management had ceased to be largely custodial, and good logging practices were no longer to be advocated on private lands alone."

In 1952, Assistant Chief Forester Christopher Granger wrote an article in *American Forest* announcing that national forest harvests would continue to increase significantly. The increase was due not only to heavier industrial demand for the wood, but also to "the initiative of the Forest Service men going out and getting business." Granger, among others, expressed delight in the prospect of expanded logging in the national forests because it looked as though the agency might be able to realize one of its most elusive dreams: the operation of the entire forest system "in the black," as though it were a business and not a long-term investment. The major obstacle to this goal was the lack of roads into merchantable stands. For years the Forest Service had complained about both the number and the condition of its roads, but Congress had not appropriated enough money to improve the situation, according to agency officials. With the press of timber demands, funds could no longer be denied, particularly in light of the argument that greater harvests would help the national forests pay their own way, as well as cover the cost of road construction. It was not long before a roads-for-timber-for-roads mentality began to take root, producing ever-greater amounts of both. Between 1950 and 1969 the amount of timber cut from the national forests jumped from 5.6 billion to 12.8 billion board feet. The roadbuilding budget soared, and the hiring of civil engineers became a priority. Today more than 350,000 miles of roads run through the national forests, making it the most extensive road system in the world, and civil engineers, the next largest professional group after foresters, number about 3,500 (among them Chief Forester Max Peterson). The accelerated cutting did not improve the Service's bottom line at first (and, as we shall see, in some areas it never did), largely because of the increased roading costs; the Service began to attribute more benefits to logging

89

roads than might ordinarily pass inspection—such as the somewhat tortuous claim that logging itself was a multiple-use tool, since it made roads possible, and roads, after the trees had been hauled out over them, served many other uses.

One of these uses, the Service admitted, was recreation, although a bias against this activity had reemerged by now, almost as if foresters once again viewed it through Pinchot's eyes as "quite incidental." It wasn't. From a fairly constant prewar level of 10 million visitors a year, recreation visits in the national forests leaped to 190 million a year in just three decades. As early as the 1950s, recreationists were beginning to compete seriously with the timber industry for choice lands—lands that the Service and the industry wanted to log and recreationists wanted to enjoy. The two desires were not compatible. To those who ventured into the national forests for something other than a flatbed of timber, "it seemed that the agency was adopting the very methods it had held up for so many years as examples of bad land management," wrote Steen. It did not look as though the Forest Service was protecting the forest from "rampaging, greedy lumbermen," as the public had been told all these years. And a crisis of confidence was in the making.

### HOW MULTIPLE IS MULTIPLE USE?
In his 1955 annual report, Chief Forester Richard E. McArdle had written that the "needs for water, timber, and forage, for recreation, wilderness areas, and for hunting and fishing, mount constantly. This places our multiple-use principle of management under severe strain and tests our skill in both resource management and human relations." Caught between the demands of the timber industry and the nature-seeking public, the Forest Service decided it was time to go back to basics, to a reaffirmation of multiple use, and to a clearer statement of precisely what the term meant. The Forest Service turned to Congress in the late 1950s to codify the words it had tried to live by for half a century under its own administrative edict. It would not seem that legislative adoption of something as democratic-sounding and as historically significant as multiple use could generate controversy. But it did. Comments within the agency ranged from "It's about time" to a puzzled "We've been practicing this all along." Outside of the

Forest Service, some people were even more wary of a multiple-use law. The National Lumber Manufacturers Association opposed multiple use because its leaders felt it diluted the intent of the 1897 Organic Act specifying the need for national forests for watershed protection and for a continuous supply of timber. One spokesman for the lumbermen's association told Chief Forester McArdle that multiple use held no advantage for the lumbermen; they already had what they needed. "By making all uses equal in priority the forest manager will probably act on the basis of public pressure," industry spokesman Ralph Hodges explained. "This doesn't give protection to the lumber industry."

The Sierra Club (the only conservation organization to do so) also opposed what finally emerged in 1959 as the Multiple Use–Sustained Yield Bill (sustained yield being the historic operating principle that timber harvesting must ensure a continuous supply of timber into the future; simply put, you must not cut more than you can grow). As far as the Sierra Club was concerned, the foresters were not trained to choose between such uses as lumber and scenery. Rather than place all uses on an equal footing with timber, the club's leaders worried, the bill would instead sanction existing agency attitudes toward logging. "The Forest Service is not as well equipped administratively as it needs to be to deal with the problems of conflict in land use which it must face in the years to come," warned an article in the Sierra Club *Bulletin*. The club did not drop its opposition until sponsors of the bill agreed to a clause stipulating that wilderness preservation qualified as a legitimate use under the umbrella of recreation, and in that form the bill was passed and signed into law by President Dwight D. Eisenhower on June 12, 1960.

For the first time in national forest history, five major uses, listed alphabetically to avoid the appearance of favoritism, were accorded equal billing in one law: outdoor recreation, range, timber, watershed, and wildlife and fish habitat. As some had feared, however, the law did not slow the growth of logging, nor was there any substantial shift in favor of the other prescribed uses. According to a growing number of conservationists, multiple-use planning had not achieved the "preeminent stature" they had hoped for. Many claim it still has not. Barry Flamm, a forester now in the employ of The Wilderness Society, testified in 1985 in regard to the Reagan administration's proposed 1986 budget and outlined the problem: "The basic laws guiding the management of the National Forests are founded on the principle of multiple-use conservation," he said. He then pointed out that the proposed 1986 Forest Service budget simply undercut the whole idea of multiple use: "The resource development and exploitation line items (e.g., timber sales, minerals, grazing) total approximately $600 million. In contrast, the resource stewardship programs (e.g., soil and water, wildlife and fish, recreation and trails, and land acquisition) are allocated one-fourth this amount—$170 million."

## A CLEAR-CUT CONTROVERSY

The Forest Service defended itself vigorously against the critics of its multiple-use policies from the beginning—but not always successfully, or sometimes even logically. In 1971, for example, Chief Forester Edward Cliff asserted that thanks to the Forest Service's interpretation of the multiple-use principle, "the national forests are producing more goods and services for the use and enjoyment of the American people, and in greater variety than ever before." This was not the sort of defense to engender confidence in the agency among those who were its severest critics, particularly when in plain view was the Forest Service's increasing reliance on clear-cutting as a way to fulfill such multiple uses as proposed by Chief Forester Cliff. Clear-cutting, in which all trees were removed from large expanses of forest in a single operation, was, after all, the single most dramatic and visible manifestation of logging's impact. To most people who happened upon a clear-cut site, the stumpy land looked no different from the way it might have looked in the generation of the scoundrel loggers who cut and ran.

Once shunned by the Forest Service, clear-cutting had become normal procedure. By 1969, 61 percent of the harvest from the Western national forests was clear-cut, while about 50 percent of the Eastern national forest harvest was obtained this way. Before clear-cutting became so common, foresters had practiced various types of selective cutting, being careful to leave enough trees in a patch to regenerate the stand, with or without artificial reseeding. The Forest Service maintained that clear-cutting was cheaper and faster and for insect-infested stands, it claimed that this was sometimes the only way to contain the damage. Mostly, however, foresters expressed a sharp interest in raising trees of commercial value, and believed that many of these species would not regenerate in the shade provided by trees left standing after selective cutting. Douglas fir, for example, needed broad, open light as a seedling, and clear-cutting was the only way to ensure its return. Clear-cutting prepared the ground for even-aged stands and so maximized the yield of more desirable species.

But clear-cutting on a grand scale also had significant ecological consequences. It accelerated the rate of erosion and water runoff, which sapped nutrients from the soil, and allowed too much sediment in too short a time to enter streams, destroying natural stream vegetation and organisms. (Excessive sedimentation buried newly laid fish eggs or smothered hatchlings.) In addition, stream temperatures were raised by three or four degrees while flowing through unshaded clear-cut areas, and the higher water temperatures were lethal to salmon and trout. Finally, the municipal water treatment plants downstream of a clear-cut area had a more difficult time removing abnormal amounts of siltation from the water supply, and required additional investments from local governments to expand their silt-removal capacity. Dredging of community reservoirs also would have been needed more frequently if sedimentation were not controlled at the entry point. Nor could the fact that a clear-cut area is an ugly area be dismissed, since many towns near national forests relied on natural beauty for tourism.

The case against clear-cutting was perhaps made most tellingly in regard to Bitterroot National Forest in Montana and the Monongahela National Forest in West Virginia during the 1960s and 1970s. Residents of the towns closest to the afflicted forests were the first to protest. A logger from Darby, Montana, charged that "the Forest Service is knocking down and burying and burning the next 150 years of future in our area. They're destroying our forest and our livelihood." G. M. Brandborg, who had worked as forest supervisor on the Bitterroot between 1935 and 1955, told a reporter fourteen years later that "forestry practices today are entirely different from those applied when I was associated with the Forest Service." To Brandborg, it seemed modern foresters had "lost feeling for the good earth."

The verdict of a task force appointed by the Forest Service itself

93

to consider clear-cutting on the Bitterroot was not much better. In 1969 the committee criticized the agency for its "preoccupation with timber management objectives." A second damning report, this one in 1970, came from a committee chaired by Arnold Bolle, dean of the University of Montana's forestry school. "Multiple-use management in fact does not exist as the governing principle of the Bitterroot National Forest," the Bolle report concluded. The rate and method of cutting could be defended only "on a purely technical basis." On environmental and long-term economic grounds, however, the technology was insupportable.

Similar disagreements with the Forest Service were meanwhile developing about the Monongahela National Forest in West Virginia. In 1964 the Forest Service switched from an all-age management program of the hardwood forest to an even-aged management program, which required extensive clear-cutting in a forest largely supported by recreational users. Local residents and the state legislature protested because clear-cutting would undermine the region's considerable tourism business, which depended almost entirely on good hunting and fishing and the rolling beauty found in the national forest. The West Virginia division of the Izaak Walton League filed a suit against the Forest Service on the grounds that the agency was ignoring the 1897 instruction to "mark and designate" individual trees before cutting them. A 1975 court of appeals decision upheld the league's argument, and the Forest Service finally declared a system-wide moratorium on clear-cutting.

In the meantime, Senator Frank Church of Idaho, chairman of the Senate Subcommittee on Public Lands, conducted hearings on the subject both in the field and in Washington, D.C., in which his committee heard damning testimony on every hand and sifted through piles of corroborating evidence. In the end, the committee issued a series of suggested guidelines to the Forest Service in regard to clear-cutting abuses; perhaps the most significant of these was a stipulation that no clear-cutting should be undertaken unless it could be proved that the area in question could be restored to full growth within five years—an almost impossible goal in many areas (which the committee probably knew full well), thus effectively taking them out of production.

## FORESTS AND THE FUTURE

Throughout this long process of questioning Forest Service practices, a movement grew in support of congressional legislation to spell out management policies in a far more precise manner than that reflected in the Organic Act of 1897. Even the timber industry, frustrated by a confusion of policy, backed such an idea, and conservationists rallied behind it as a means of bringing up for public consideration the environmental soundness of all standard forestry practices. Congress responded in 1976 with the National Forest Management Act (NFMA), the single most far-reaching piece of legislation for the national forests since their inception more than eighty years before.

The NFMA did not ban clear-cutting outright, but by adopting the so-called Church guidelines it did limit its applications severely. Furthermore, the NFMA stated that the sale of timber from each forest had to be limited to a quantity equal to or less than that which the forest could replace on a sustained-yield basis, provided all multiple-use objectives were met. The Forest Service also was instructed to maintain species diversity and not just maximize the growth of trees that were commercially sought. Finally, all uses of the forest were to be laid out in detailed fifty-year plans, which were to be completed in 1985, one plan to a forest, and subject to public review.

Probably the act's most significant provision was to mandate the public's role in reviewing and formulating forest plans. Nothing so formal as a comprehensive plan had ever existed before, but if one had, public contributions to its preparation would certainly not have been sought by the Forest Service, an agency understandably jealous of its long tradition of autonomy. Before World War II, ordinary Americans never questioned the wisdom of the Forest Service on such matters as timber-cutting and environmental protection. In two of the very few lawsuits ever filed against the Service in regard to management practices in its first fifty years, the courts emphasized in their decisions that it was the agency's responsibility to "fill in the details"; it had grown accustomed to functioning with no one looking over its shoulder. With the passage of the NFMA, this changed. Scrutiny, rather than blind trust, would characterize the relationship of the public—and Congress—to the Forest Service from now on.

Forestry analyst and professor of natural law Charles Wilkinson, for one, considered this a good thing. "Within just fifteen years," he wrote in a 1984 law review article, "we have seen, if not a near-revolution, at the very least a deep and fundamental change in Forest Service law and policy." The nation's "oldest and proudest conservation agency" no longer stood outside the law. It was just as well, for in Wilkinson's opinion it had become "too inward-looking, too large (with more than thirty thousand permanent employees), and too fixed in its traditions; consequently it had "refused to respond to profound national forces." Congress acted because it seemed the only way to force the agency to accommodate the times, as Pinchot had urged it to do so many years before. But laws and Forest Service traditions still remained new to each other in 1984, Wilkinson added, and "the relationship is not remotely a comfortable one."

## THE BRIGHT RED BOTTOM LINE

The relationship did not grow notably more comfortable in the months that followed Wilkinson's assessment. The issue of clear-cutting had been, if hardly resolved, at least clarified and ameliorated by passage of the NFMA. The issue of wilderness preservation, a subject discussed in greater detail in chapter 5, had paralleled that of clear-cutting in its intensity during the 1960s and 1970s, and while it remained a live one in 1985, a combination of public pressure and congressional action had at least managed to overcome the foot-dragging reluctance of the Service sufficiently to designate an additional 8.6 million acres to the National Wilderness Preservation System in 1984. By then, another issue had come to the fore, one that spoke perhaps even more directly than any other to the management capabilities of the Forest Service.

This was the question of money—specifically, that which was lost every year in what were called "below-cost" timber sales. There was nothing new about this except the amounts involved. The selling of some timber at prices below the cost of administration had been a traditional part of Forest Service policy for years. While it had troubled Forest Service leaders, from Henry Graves on, that each and every national forest could not be made to pay its own way, they became accustomed to reminding bottom-line-minded congressmen that the national forest system was never meant to be operated like a business. It was an investment in the nation's distant resource future. But before World War II, when the Forest Service was much more particular about where and how it allowed timber to be cut, below-cost sales were kept to a minimum. They occurred and were tolerated, but never encouraged.

But by the 1980s, when as much as one-fourth of all the nation's timber was being taken off national forestland, below-cost timber sales were becoming far more routine—and infinitely more expensive. The problem began with the system of pricing used by the Forest Service. First, a forester examined a stand of timber being offered for sale through open bidding, then calculated what its likely value would be in milled form; he then deducted from that calculation the estimated costs to a timber operator of cutting it down, hauling it out, and selling it; finally, he threw in an estimate of what a "fair" profit margin to the company would be. The remainder was the "stumpage rate," below which no bids would be accepted.

On the face of it, this was a perfectly workable system, except for one thing: at no point did the "stumpage rate" take into consideration the costs to the government for administration, reforestation, timber-stand improvement, mitigation (reducing or repairing environmental damage), or—and here was the core of the problem—roadbuilding. In the view of many, all of these costs in effect amounted to an outright subsidy to the lumber industry, and in the case of road-building the subsidy could be a sizable one indeed. In some of the more rugged areas—such as Alaska's Tongass National Forest or Colorado's San Juan—it could cost as much as $250,000 a mile to run in a logging road. These kinds of costs were only compounded, of course, when roads were thrust into areas that had not even been put up for bidding yet, a practice common in the first few years of the Reagan administration. John Crowell, Assistant Secretary of Agriculture in charge of the forests in these years, maintained that having the roads in place would encourage bidding on timber and help him meet his announced goal of doubling the annual cut on the national forests by the year 2000 (in the 1980s, it was running between 10 and 12 billion board feet a year). Many conservationists argued that it was merely a convenient way to destroy forever a region's eligibility for inclusion in the National Wilderness Preservation System.

In any case, it was all costing money—more money than the Forest Service was making public, more money than even Congress suspected, even though conservationists with an economic bent had been raising the issue with increasing urgency for some time. Their claims were dramatically corroborated in June 1984, when the General Accounting Office published a study that laid before Congress the extent of below-cost sales. The GAO analyzed more than three thousand timber sales in four Western regions and found that, in 1981, 27 percent of the sales did not cover Forest Service costs to administer them, and in 1982 below-costs soared to 42 percent of the sales, accounting for a loss of more than $156 million in those two years. In two of the regions studied, "over 88 percent of the sales were below cost in 1981 and over 96 percent were below cost in 1982," the GAO report stated. The GAO cited the Forest Service's policy of selling low-quality timber in steep, remote terrain as the chief contributor to its elevated costs. In such places environmental damage is harder to mitigate, and greater expenditures are incurred from "involved high road engineering."

"On the basis of sale economics alone," the GAO report continued, "one could conclude that some national forest lands should not be managed for timber production." The Forest Service had not been able to reach the same conclusion on economic grounds because it had never identified the cost of individual timber sales. Having conducted an investigation similar to that of the GAO, economists at The Wilderness Society concluded that "over the last decade, if below-cost timber sales had been eliminated in both good and bad years, the federal treasury would have netted at least $2 billion more." It was not just a matter of reducing taxpayer losses, the economists wrote in a *Wall Street Journal* guest editorial, but one of curtailing the private sector's timber contribution as well: "The Forest Industry Council estimated in 1980 that domestic timber demand in the year 2030 could be supplied by private forests alone, using intensive timber management practices, if landowners could realize a 10 percent annual return on investment. Unfortunately, the continuation of below-cost timber sales in the national forests retard this development."

In an age in which the national deficit was growing at an alarming rate—and was growing in the public consciousness at a rate commensurate with its size—the loss of hundreds of millions of dollars annually in below-cost timber sales by a government agency swiftly became an issue embraced by the conservation community. Among other things, conservationists pointed out that in many areas what it all came down to was that it was costing the taxpayers millions of dollars to destroy the beauty and ecological significance of potential wilderness—hardly an outcome the public would have endorsed, had it been given any real say in the matter. This concern provided a significant intensity to the perusal of the fifty-year management plans mandated by the NFMA, as the first of them began to be issued. The Wilderness Society, for one, announced early in 1985 that it would be devoting a large share of its energy and resources to the painstaking analysis of the plans as they emerged; and in April of that year The Society filed lawsuits challenging the plans issued for San Juan and Grand Mesa national forests in Colorado. By the end of the summer of 1985, so many conservationists and other concerned citizens had challenged the conclusions of so many draft management plans that on several occasions the planners had been forced back to their drawing boards.

The Forest Service was learning, if it had not learned already, that the benign image of Smokey the Bear was no longer enough—the age of public scrutiny was well under way.

## AN AGENDA FOR THE NATIONAL FORESTS

The forest and the idea of the forest, to borrow from Joseph Wood Krutch, has largely shaped us as a nation, has given us a sense of adventure, of possibility, of the mysterious about to be made known. It has colored our imaginations, become a part of our cultural heritage. A little of Natty Bumppo resides in all of us, and Daniel Boone still walks at the back of our minds. Along the way, it has also sustained us as an engine of life—giving us much of the air we breathe, the water we drink. Such is the way of forests.

We have given little enough back in the way of care. Indeed, for generations we ripped at our forests in a frenzy of ignorance until, appalled by what we had accomplished, we fumbled toward a concept we chose to call "wise use." We fumble still, and it is time now to clarify in no uncertain terms the means whereby we finally can achieve a working combination of utility and ethics in the management of our national forests.

The problems facing us can realistically be placed under a single rubric: insufficient dedication to the principles of multiple use. A confusion of values lies at the heart of the matter. Multiple use as it is now practiced by no means guarantees equality among uses in our national forests; the great weight of policy governing the management of these lands has usually been placed on the exploitive, extractive end of the scales, most often to the detriment of such other uses as wilderness, watershed, recreation, and wildlife. The recommendations The Wilderness Society offers here are based on the conviction that the concept of balanced multiple use should finally be factored solidly into our system of values and used as the tool it was designed to be if we are to face squarely the needs of the immediate future and the more distant future.

For our concern goes beyond the immediate. This nation's abundant forests are among our most enduring resources, and we are in the enviable position of being able to plan now for the management of that resource for an age in which the very concept of multiple use may come to mean highly restricted, selective use to satisfy the needs of a world that will demand quality quite as much as quantity— *quality* of watersheds, *quality* of recreation, *quality* of timber. This is the context in which we should begin to formulate change.

Two areas of immediate concern have to do, first, with strengthening the multiple-use stipulations of the National Forest Management Act of 1976 so that the objective of *balance* is made paramount as a management goal, and, second, with redefining the idea of multiple use as it is applied to wilderness areas in order to facilitate a necessary expansion of the National Wilderness Preservation System. We believe both concerns should be addressed by:

*The exercise of strict congressional oversight.* NFMA mandates a balanced multiple-use program. The term "multiple use" appears repeatedly in the language of the act. Forest management, it says, for example, must be accomplished with "coordination of multiple-use and sustained-yield opportunities," must be "consistent with the principles of sustained yield and multiple use," must "secure the most effective mix of multiple-use benefits," must "provide for multiple use and sustained yield . . . and, in particular, include coordination of outdoor recreation, range, timber, watershed, wildlife and fish, and wilderness. . . ." There is little ambiguity here, but in practice, as noted, commodity uses such as timber extraction too often are allowed to overbalance all other uses. We urge Congress to exercise stringently its oversight function to ensure that the Forest Service adheres firmly to the multiple-use strictures of the law. If all else fails, it may be necessary to make NFMA's language even more precise and detailed to prevent continued distortion of the multiple-use principle, and if so, the act should be amended to that effect.

*The broad recognition of wilderness as a multiple-use resource.* The Wilderness Act clearly established wilderness as a legitimate use and land-management category of the national forests. Underlying this, however, was the understanding that wilderness itself encompasses a broad and varied array of resource values. Outdoor recreation, widely seen as the foremost reason for maintaining wilderness environments, is really only one of many reasons, some of which have even more importance. At a time when scientists tell us that the availability of pure water will be one of the gravest problems of the twenty-first century, wilderness stands unsurpassed as a means of maintaining the quality and integrity of forest watersheds. (Of particular importance in this regard is the fact that 50 percent of all the water in the West flows out of the watersheds of the national forests—certainly a "use" whose significance cannot be denied.)

And wilderness embraces another "use" that received long-overdue recognition in NFMA: preservation of biological diversity. The diverse habitats represented in the National Wilderness Preservation System enrich the great gene pool that contains the future of all life. As the biologist Edward O. Wilson has written, in the long view that use may well be paramount: "The one process ongoing in the 1980s that will take millions of years to correct is the loss of genetic and species

101

diversity by the destruction of natural habitats. This is the folly our descendants are least likely to forgive us." (For more on this, see chapter 5.)

Clearly, wilderness itself is a multiple-use entity, and this fact should be categorically recognized in future law, regulations, and management plans. And, as a vitally important multiple-use resource, the wilderness system should be expanded. Only 81 of the nation's 233 basic ecosystems are adequately represented today in the National Wilderness Preservation System. We should add more, a good deal more, much of it from the national forest system—more "old-growth" climax forest, more desert, more rain forest, more wetland—to round out the system and establish a representative balance. This is not a process that should end with the current Roadless Area Review and Evaluation program. Surveying national forestland for its wilderness potential—and adding appropriate areas to the National Wilderness Preservation System when and where appropriate—should be accomplished on a continuing basis in the decades ahead. The goal would be to create a "landbank" of wilderness sufficiently large to sustain the projected needs of at least the next century.

Recreation is still a tremendous and rapidly growing public use of the national forests. Hiking, backpacking, family camping, fishing, hunting, swimming, boating—all are needs that already have reached impressive dimensions. Americans annually spend 235 million days of recreational use in national forests compared to 100 million days in national parks, and since World War II visits to national forest roadless areas have increased fifteenfold. These numbers are likely to expand geometrically as we approach the twenty-first century, particularly in the Sunbelt states and the densely populated Northeast. The needs of this recreational explosion and the natural values that inspire it can be met with proper vision and planning. In addition to substantially increasing the dimensions of the National Wilderness Preservation System, as outlined above, we should:

*Restructure individual units in forests close to major urban areas so that they are managed predominantly for resource protection and rec-*

*reation*. In areas of particularly intensive recreational need, this may mean significant reduction of planned commodity development, including timber management. In many areas, the economic impact of such a reduction would be minor; only about 4 percent of the commercial forestland in the Southeast, for example, is in the national forests. This option would be especially applicable to the eastern third of the nation, where recreational use already is approaching the saturation point—174 million people live within a day's drive of one Eastern national forest or another.

*Institute a major program of rehabilitation and possible relocation of some recreational facilities*. One particularly startling need is the trail system of the national forests. The system now encompasses nearly 100,000 miles of trails—the bulk of the entire federal trail system. Yet nearly a third of this is in desperate need of rebuilding and repair. And to further enhance the quality of the forest experience, some *types* of recreation should be emphasized over others. Dispersed recreational use of the national forests has grown by 68 percent over the past two decades, nearly four times the growth in developed recreational use during the same period. Budget and management emphasis should be focused on providing the facilities, and the environment, for such clearly preferred recreational activities. Such developed-site activities as automobile campgrounds and ski resorts can often best be served by private entrepreneurs on private lands.

*Accelerate and expand the forest acquisition program established by the Weeks Act of 1911*. First, we should gradually incorporate into the forest system a significant portion of the 39.1 million acres now held within the unit boundaries of many national forests by state, local, and private ownership. Many such forests of mixed ownership are close to major urban areas and vulnerable to significant recreational pressure—a situation made particularly difficult by a confusion of management policies and practices that ultimately degrades the quality of such forests as a whole.

Second, we should gradually complete the acquisition of forestlands outside the boundaries of federal forests. More than two million acres have been identified by the Forest Service for acquisition under its "purchase unit" program in twenty-seven individual areas, but only 284,000 of these acres have actually been added to the forest system. Many purchase units, such as the 687,000-acre Redbird of Kentucky or the 194,000-acre Yadkin of North Carolina, qualify in size as individual national forests.

Finally, we should enlarge the purchase unit program beyond its present goals. The Weeks Act was originally passed as a rescue effort to rehabilitate cut-over lands and to put Eastern forests into Forest Service management before nonfederal landholders degraded them beyond redemption. Without it, we would not have had such "success stories" as the White Mountain and Green Mountain national forests of New England or the Pisgah National Forest of North Carolina. There are hundreds and thousands of acres of abused and misused nonfederal forestland in need of similar reclamation.

The program briefly outlined above assumes the continued—and necessary—practice of resource development and utilization in the forests. Such development is demonstrably required for the nation's continued economic growth. It is equally obvious, however, that major changes should be undertaken if we are to maintain the health not only of the forests but of the economy itself, among them the following:

*The prohibition of timber sales that would result in a net economic loss to the government.* As emphasized earlier in this chapter, the government too often loses money on timber sales. It is not as if such losses cannot be anticipated in advance; they can, and are, but all too frequently they are then ignored by the Forest Service. Section 6(k), the relevant clause of the National Forest Management Act, is just vague enough to allow the Forest Service a loose interpretation when it is deemed convenient. This section of NFMA should be clarified to read, "In developing land management plans pursuant to this act, *the Secretary shall identify lands within the management area as not suited for timber production which have a negative benefit-cost ratio for timber production.*" Moreover, the law should require that cost-benefit analyses be displayed for public scrutiny before timber bidding sales begin.

*Revision of the pricing structure for grazing on national forestland.*
The high mountain meadows and grasslands of the national forest
system support 1.4 million cattle and 1.3 million sheep every year.
The average price charged for permits to graze these animals on the
public's land is $1.35 per animal-unit-month (AUM—the amount of
forage needed to support one cow or five sheep for one month). By
comparison, the average AUM price on privately owned land is $6.67.
The difference between the two prices amounts to a subsidy to the
livestock industry and an outright deficit for the Forest Service and
the American public. In 1982, for example, grazing fees brought in
only thirty-eight cents for every dollar spent on grazing management,
a loss that the Forest Service itself admits is "a reflection of reduced
grazing fees and not a reduction in grazing use." Cheap grazing fees
also lead to overgrazing by encouraging cattlemen and sheepmen to
run more animals on the land than it can reasonably absorb without
damage. Grazing fees should be adjusted upward toward a more
equitable return to the government, and use of these grasslands should
be strictly monitored to assure adherence to the principles of sustained
yield.

Both of the management changes suggested above can be mandated
by the creation of new law or the revision of present law, but more
is needed. The Forest Service, with more than fifty thousand employees and the responsibility for more than 191 million acres of
public land, is a bureaucratic entity of respectable dimensions. It
also is one of the oldest such agencies, and therefore too often resistant
to change and disproportionately loyal to a single constituency, namely
the timber industry. Both traditions should be challenged if the national forests of the future are to be managed according to the principles of a functioning Land Ethic, and two important proposals should
be adopted promptly:

*The creation of a Department of Natural Resources by combining the
land-management agencies of the Department of the Interior and the
Forest Service.* For many years, The Wilderness Society and several
other conservation organizations have called for the establishment of
a cabinet-level Department of Natural Resources that would assume

105

responsibility for the supervision of all land-managing agencies—including the Forest Service. We continue to call for the creation of such a department and the concomitant transfer of the Forest Service from the Department of Agriculture to the new agency. As well, we believe the position of chief of the Forest Service should be a presidential appointment subject to the advice and consent of the Senate.

There is every logical reason for such a change. The Department of Agriculture is essentially a regulatory and research body overseeing the production of foods on private lands. The Forest Service is a management agency supervising the multiple use of 191 million acres of public land. Its needs, functions, and priorities are separate from those of the agency that now controls it. With its head confirmed by the Senate and responsible only for forestry matters, the Forest Service would be more readily accountable to Congress and the public and would more likely be amenable to necessary change.

*An increase in public funding of forestry education and research to dilute the influence industry has exercised on both.* As foresters work their way up the rungs of the Forest Service ladder they carry with them a load of attitudes and priorities weighted heavily on the side of the industry's perceived needs and desires; in addition, much current research has a tendency to promote the growth of healthy, harvestable trees—not the preservation of healthy forests. Through carefully programmed major increases in public funding for public purposes over the years we could substantially diversify both research and the training of those within the Forest Service. Similarly, we should encourage the employment of people who have not been bound primarily to Forest Service educational traditions or the needs of industry—a broad force of zoologists, botanists, ecologists, geologists, hydrologists, wildlife managers, recreation specialists, and social scientists and humanists educated to counsel policymakers on the intangible as well as the economic needs of the American people in their forests.

To conclude, we should repeat that we are not talking here about short-term goals; we are considering the outlines of the next fifty years and beyond. Indeed, one of the fundamental problems of American resource management is the tendency to think and plan for the near-term. In a very real sense, we should begin thinking in spans of time that compare with the growth cycle of the trees themselves—and plan for requirements we can only begin to imagine today. For example, a century from now intelligent management may mean that most of the nation's softwood needs will continue to be met from forests on private lands and that timber production in the Eastern Appalachian national forests will be confined to the growth and harvesting of nothing but long-cycle hardwoods and in the West to harvesting all timber on a long-rotation basis. In other words, not necessarily *more* timber—rather, *better* timber. *Quality* rather than sheer productivity will be the hallmark of wisdom in the twenty-first century.

Anticipating the possibilities that lie ahead, we should take steps now to see that the treasures of the national forests are not squandered. While the forests can and should help serve the immediate commodity needs of American citizens, this should not be allowed to compromise those priceless assets that are becoming unique to the national forests—and are no less real than our economic demands for lumber and paper, oil and iron.

These needs will become paramount in the next century. The highest and best use of the national forests is to strive to meet those long-term requirements with products that cannot or will not be provided on other lands. This includes not only fish and wildlife habitat, undisturbed watersheds, habitat for endangered plant and animal species, and an environment for wilderness research and recreation, but trees capable of producing superb quality woods that are rapidly vanishing from the national forests and are essentially nonexistent on private lands.

In the broader sense, we are addressing ourselves to the enlightened stewardship of all the forests of the country—public and private alike—as well as those around the globe. As the National Forest Management Act makes clear, the Forest Service "has both a responsibility and an opportunity to be a leader in assuring that the nation maintains a natural resource conservation posture that will meet the requirements of our people in perpetuity. . . ." The Forest Service should administer its own lands in a manner that will make them nothing less than models of management to be looked to and imitated all over the country. And if the United States, the most conservation-minded country in the world, cannot demonstrate a proper concern for its forests, is it reasonable to assume that other countries will do any better?

LEFT: Theodore Roosevelt and the nation's first Chief Forester, Gifford Pinchot, aboard the steamer *Mississippi*, 1907. *U.S. Forest Service*
BELOW: A woodsman who did not spare that tree—a scene in the Santa Cruz Mountains, California, ca. 1880. *Bancroft Library, University of California, Berkeley*

ABOVE, LEFT: A clear-cut patch in Plumas National Forest, California, ca. 1965. *Philip Hyde*

ABOVE, RIGHT: The Idaho Primitive Area, as seen in 1940; it is now part of the Frank Church–River of No Return Wilderness. *U.S. Forest Service*

OPPOSITE, BOTTOM: Overlooking a clear-cut section in St. Joe National Forest, Idaho, 1966. *U.S. Forest Service*

ABOVE: View from Miner's Ridge, Wenatchee National Forest, Washington. *Philip Hyde*
BELOW: Looking west into the Snake River Canyon, Payette National Forest, Idaho. *U.S. Forest Service*

# 3

# THE LEFTOVER LEGACY

## The National Resource Lands of the BLM

Gertrude Stein, the sometime poet and playwright, was not ordinarily given to trenchant observations regarding the relationship of geography to history, but on one occasion she did give voice to such a thought: "In the United States," she wrote, "there is more space where nobody is than where anybody is. That is what makes America what it is." Poets seem to have liked this idea; Charles Olson, in Part One of *Call Me Ishmael*, his study of Herman Melville, says: "I take SPACE to be the central fact to man born in America. . . . I spell it large because it comes large here." Space, in the form of land, was indeed a major factor in shaping the character and institutions of America. It offered, among other things, a freedom of movement and opportunity denied to most other peoples, and in that freedom there was room for quite a lot of dreaming—2.1 billion acres, in the beginning.

Most of it is gone now. The lands under discussion in this chapter—some 341 million acres of them in the coterminous United States and Alaska—are all that remain of that original inheritance, after withdrawals for parks and forests, national grasslands and wildlife refuges, monuments, reservoir sites, and defense installations, after land grants to states, colleges, canal companies, veterans of domestic wars, and railroads, after creation of the Indian reservation system, after sale and disposal through hundreds of land laws over the past two centuries. They are sometimes called "the leftover lands," "the lands no one knows," or—a little harshly—"the lands nobody wanted." More

113

propitiously, they have officially been designated the National Resource Lands and placed under the administration of the Bureau of Land Management.

It is a complex and demanding inheritance the BLM monitors, "rich in a spectrum of resources," as one conservationist has described it, "from the wilderness that illuminates the spirit to the coal that lights a city." More than 174 million acres outside Alaska are contained in the eleven Western states—more than 48 million in Nevada alone (69 percent of the state's total acreage)—but odd lots crop up in a number of Eastern states: 589 acres in Wisconsin, 12 in Illinois, 3,962 in Louisiana, for example.

With so much land under its stewardship, the duties of the BLM are multitudinous. It is the chief administrator of public grazing lands, on which some 21,000 ranchers graze 7 million cattle, sheep, and goats. It controls the leasing program for oil, gas, coal, oil shale, and geothermal sites and the administration of claims for gold, silver, iron, copper, lead, molybdenum, and uranium mining on its own lands as well as those on another 370 million acres of national forests and other federal land units. It manages 7.9 million acres of commercial forest, from which it produces about 1.3 million board feet of timber each year, most of it from a 2.1-million-acre parcel in western Oregon once given to the Oregon and California Railroad and later taken back. Its domain includes 35 million acres of wetlands, 85,935 miles of fishable streams, and thousands of archaeological sites, petroglyphs, pictographs, and fossil remains—all reminders that the American continent was not always governed as it is now, and that civilization as we think we know it has lasted but a moment in the long stretch of human history and geologic time. Finally, by its own reckoning, the BLM administers some 25 million acres of land that are potential additions to the National Wilderness Preservation System.

An extraordinary legacy, these "leftover lands"—and perhaps the least understood and most underappreciated of all the nation's public lands. But then they always have been. In 1861, Daniel Webster gazed westward and perceived little but trash: "What do we want of that vast and worthless area, that region of savages and wild beasts, of wind, of dust, of cactus and prairie dogs? To what use could we ever hope to put those great deserts and those endless mountain ranges, impenetrable and covered to their base in eternal snow?" We know a little better now, but it has been a long journey to understanding the West, "a transition from fable to fact," as Wallace Stegner has described it. Its course follows the outline of the history of the unappropriated, unreserved public domain—which is what, at the beginning, the national resource lands were called.

## WHERE DID THEY COME FROM? WHERE DID THEY GO?

The idea of a national public domain owes its existence to the state of Maryland. In 1778 this tiny, landless state led a protest against states whose claims to western lands put them at an advantage. There was nothing modest about these claims. Under the royal charter that the colonies went to war to revoke, Virginia, for example, had been granted ownership to all the territory west to the Mississippi River and north into the Upper Peninsula of what would become Michigan, and still claimed this territory after the war. Massachusetts claimed enormous sections that now run through Michigan and Wisconsin. Maryland, not as blessed as such other states, threatened that it would not sign the Articles of Confederation until the landed states surrendered their claims to the newly formed central government. All lands, according to Maryland's statesmen, had been fought for by the "common blood and treasure" of the thirteen states, and therefore should be commonly owned.

On October 10, 1780, the Continental Congress agreed, and formally made the donation of these claims to the government a condition of equal membership in the federal union. Congress also resolved that "the unappropriated lands that may be ceded or relinquished to the United States, by any particular states . . . shall be disposed of for the common benefit of the United States, and be settled and formed into distinct Republican States, which shall become members of the Federal Union, and shall have the same rights of sovereignty, freedom and independence as other states."

In 1802 these transfers were completed and the infant government had become the landlord for more than 233 million acres. The following year the nation doubled its size when President Thomas Jefferson agreed to pay France $27 million for its Louisiana Territory, and over the next fifty-one years diplomacy, war, and purchase spread the sovereignty of the federal government to more than 1.4 billion acres.

The Northwest Ordinance of 1785 had spelled out the method by which such lands were to be surveyed and prepared for sale by auction to citizens moving westward. All lands were to be uniquely identified by the metes and bounds designated in what is called the rectilinear survey. They would be divided up into townships six miles to a side. These, in turn, would be subdivided into thirty-six numbered sections of one square mile each (640 acres). Whole townships as well as individual sections would be offered for sale—at a minimum bid of one dollar an acre—at public auctions to be held in each of the original thirteen states. Congress reserved to the federal government sections 8, 11, 26, and 29 in each township, and section 16 was to be set aside for the support of public schools. Later, in 1812, the General Land Office was established in the Treasury Department to handle all land sales.

From the beginning, there was a basic conflict between the philosophy held by such as Thomas Jefferson, who believed that land should be put into the hands of yeoman farmers ("the most precious part of the state," Jefferson called them), even if it came down to giving it away, and that held by Alexander Hamilton and his allies, who believed that land sales would remain the only sure source of income for the federal government and should therefore bring in the highest possible price. While this debate sputtered, the speculators and the squatters (who often were one and the same) moved in on the land itself. Corruption, bloated land booms, and consequent bankruptcies made a travesty of the orderly land sales program envisioned by the Ordinance of 1785. Land speculation, one Kentucky newspaper complained, was "the most portentous evil that ever existed in America," one that "threatened the dissolution of the union." For their part, pioneers subverted the stipulations of the ordinance by simply ignoring them. As Jefferson himself had predicted, the landless poor "would settle the lands in spite of everybody." They simply squatted on the land and would not be moved; by 1828, for example, two-thirds of the residents of Illinois lived on land that still belonged to the federal government.

116

As a result of all this, land sales never accounted for more than 10 percent of the government's operating revenue. Gradually, Congress accepted the inevitable and no longer looked upon the land as a great bank account. With the Preemption Act of 1841, it legitimized the squatter's impulse by allowing him to go out into the unsurveyed domain and stake a claim to a piece of it, at $1.25 an acre. The government also started giving land away to promote settlement and progress through a succession of gifts to wagon-road companies (3 million acres), land-grant colleges (77 million acres), swamp-reclamation projects (65 million acres), and railroads (94 million acres). But it was the Homestead Act of 1862 that demonstrated the final capitulation of the Hamiltonians.

Under the provisions of the Homestead Act, any citizen twenty-one years old or the head of a household could lay claim to 160 acres of government land; he could live on it for six months, then buy it for $1.25 an acre, or live on it for five continuous years and cultivate it, after which he would receive title for nothing more than the small filing fee. Here was the Jeffersonian impulse given full expression; between 1862 and 1882, 552,112 homestead entries were filed, and the term "land-office business" took on substance. In *The Northern Tier*, a contemporary account of Midwestern life, one E. Jeff Jenkins described a typical scene when the General Land Office opened its doors in Concordia, Kansas, on January 16, 1871:

The door opened—a shout—a rush—a scramble over each other—a confused shouting of the number of the range and township, as a half-dozen or more simultaneously presented their papers to the officers, who, in the tumult, could as well have told which animal was first taken into the ark, as to have designated which one of the settlers was prior in time with the presentation of his papers. . . . The following day was a repetition of the previous one and the rush continued for months. . . .

For all its noble intentions, the Homestead Act was based on experience learned in the humid and subhumid lands of the eastern third of the continent. The farther west the settlers scrambled to stake their claims, the greater the distance from reality. Beyond the 100th

117

Meridian, which bisects the country from a point a little east of Minot, North Dakota, to a point a little west of Laredo, Texas, aridity became the unifying geographic factor. Rainfall beyond this point averaged less than twenty inches a year. What had been true in one circumstance remained true in another; before the Civil War, the South's expansion of its cotton economy was checked in west Texas by what Daniel Webster called "the ordinance of nature, the will of God." Now, in the last quarter of the nineteenth century, what had stymied the South was killing the Western settler. "The possibilities of trouble, which increased in geometrical ratio beyond the 100th meridian, had a tendency to materialize in clusters," wrote Wallace Stegner in *Beyond the Hundredth Meridian*. Even if spring looked promising with green grass and blossoming wildflowers, later "the brassy sky of drouth might open to let across the fields winds like the breath of a blowtorch, or clouds of grasshoppers, or crawling armies of chinch bugs. Pests always seem to thrive best in drouth years. And if drouth and insect plagues did not appear there was always a chance of cyclones, cloudbursts, hail. It took a man to break and hold a homestead of 160 acres even in the subhumid zone. It took a superman to do it on the arid plains."

A lot of them tried, as Stegner notes, and a lot of them failed. Of those 552,112 claims filed in the first twenty years of the Homestead Act, only 35 percent ever "proved up" to full ownership. "The government," Senator William E. Borah noted cynically, "bets 160 acres against the filing fee that the settler can't live on the land for five years without starving to death."

Still, much of the land was gone—80 million acres of it by 1900—and not all of it to the benefit of the small family farmer it was meant to sustain. Fraud, usually through the medium of dummy entries, enabled already outsized ranching and farming operations to grow even larger with the gift of government land. The pattern continued with each of the land laws that followed, desperate efforts to reconcile the hope of land for the landless with the hard realities of the geography in which it was meant to flourish—chiefly the Timber Culture Act of 1873, which granted an additional 160 acres to homesteaders who promised to plant forty acres of the grant in trees, and the Desert Land Act of 1877, which made 640-acre tracts available at $1.25 an acre, providing the claimant could prove that he had "brought water" to his claim in an effort to irrigate it. Both of these offered sterling opportunities for anyone with gumption enough to evade the strict observance of law, and the General Land Office, understaffed and underpaid throughout its existence, could do little to monitor the situation. Millions of acres of public land were joined to private monopolies.

## THE ONE-ARMED REVOLUTIONARY

Even while giving it away in ever-increasing chunks, the government was investigating what it had in the public domain. In the years immediately following the Civil War, it had launched four major surveys of its Western lands: Ferdinand V. Hayden's Survey of Nebraska Territory, Clarence King's Survey of the 40th Parallel, Lieutenant George M. Wheeler's Survey of the Territory West of the 100th Meridian, and John Wesley Powell's Survey of the Plateau Province of the Colorado River. All of these expeditions enriched and enlarged the nation's knowledge of its patrimony (and Hayden's survey, as noted in chapter 1, led directly to the creation of Yellowstone National Park), but only Powell's gave birth to an idea—an idea that could have changed the history of the West.

The one-armed major (he gained the rank and lost his right arm during the Civil War) had achieved a measure of fame on an exploring expedition in 1869, when he and his men made the first recorded journey down the Colorado River through the Grand Canyon; his report of that journey, *Exploration of the Colorado River of the West and Its Tributaries*, published in 1875, came as close as any government document ever has to best-sellerdom. His next major publication, *Report on the Lands of the Arid Region of the United States, with a More Detailed Account of the Lands of Utah*, issued in 1879, was less well received—particularly by those who had a stake in the status quo as far as the administration of the public domain was concerned. For Powell was talking common sense and rational planning in a program designed to restructure the whole system; in other words, revolution.

First, he contradicted the claims of the boomers that the land west of the 100th Meridian was a garden waiting only for the plow and a

119

little water to make it blossom (and there were those who claimed that rain would *follow* the plow, according to the dictates of some never-explained physical law). Wrong, Powell said: Only part of the land was arable under any circumstances, and only part of that could be irrigated with the finite resource of water that was available. There were limits to this growth. Second, he pointed out that an irrigated farm of 160 acres was far too much for an ordinary family to handle; he recommended that the single-family farm be reduced to eighty acres. Conversely, the nature of pasturage in the West—which required anywhere from thirty to sixty acres to support each animal—meant that the 160 acres available under the Homestead Act or even the 640 acres available under the Desert Land Act were not enough to maintain a family ranch; pasturage land, he said, should be carved into tracts of 2,560 acres each. Third, he laid bare the fact that in this land of little rain, he who controlled the available water controlled the land around it—a condition that had already made land monopoly endemic in the West. He recommended that the system of rectilinear surveys be scrapped and that all eighty-acre family farm units and all 2,560-acre pasturage units be drawn so as to give each equal rights to available water.

There was more: he strongly recommended that all pasturage lands be held in common by Western communities, unfenced so as to make the most efficient use of the forage and to further ensure common access to water. Finally, since it was demonstrably impossible for individual families to finance irrigation projects for each family farm, he proposed that the federal government encourage the formation of cooperative irrigation districts whose common financing could build the necessary distribution systems.

An accommodating soul, the major included in his report sample legislation designed to meet these goals. These prototype bills, like the rest of the report, were quietly applauded by a few brave members of Congress, loudly condemned by a few others, and studiously ignored by most. Congress was not yet ready to accept limitations to growth, or even commonsense planning—especially planning that included proposals that smacked suspiciously of socialism. In the meantime, the National Academy of Sciences (on whose deliberations Powell exerted some considerable influence) recommended to Congress that the four Western surveys be consolidated into one, that the century-old rectilinear survey system be revised, and that a public land commission be established to examine all existing land laws with an eye toward revising or eliminating them. At the request of Interior Secretary Carl Schurz, Powell drafted legislation on all three recommendations. These were introduced in Congress and two of the proposals got passed; the surveys were put under the aegis of a new agency, the U.S. Geological Survey (Clarence King was named its first director), and a Public Lands Commission was created, with the major as a member. (In addition to all of this, Powell slipped through legislation creating a Bureau of American Ethnology, which he would direct until his death, in 1902.)

The Public Lands Commission issued its report in 1880. It included the first codification of the nearly three thousand land laws and regulations that had been applied to the public domain since 1785, as well as a number of arguments reminiscent of Powell's thinking, among them the statement that the West's most important characteristic was its heterogeneity: "One region is exclusively valuable for mining, another solely for timber, a third for nothing but pasturage, and a fourth serves no useful purpose whatever. . . . Hence it has come to pass that the homestead and preemption laws are not suited for securing the settlement of more than an insignificant portion of the country." It, too, recommended that the traditional survey be scrapped and the lands classified instead according to their mineral, grazing, timber, and irrigation resources.

The report was ignored. In 1881, Powell replaced King as director of the U.S. Geological Survey and began the project of mapping the entire country, quadrant by quadrant (the task is still unfinished). In 1888 he joined in an unlikely alliance with Senator William D. "Big Bill" Stewart of Nevada, one of the leading boomers of the West, to engineer a joint resolution in Congress that ordered the Geological Survey to examine the public domain and identify all irrigable lands and potential reservoir sites. Stewart, of course, wanted to stimulate growth, and was furious when a rider was attached to the resolution that would remove all lands "susceptible to irrigation" from settlement under the various land laws; he got this amended to include a provision allowing the President to reopen such lands at his discretion, though only under the stipulations of the Homestead Act.

Powell methodically began work on the irrigation survey. Too me-

121

thodically, by Stewart's lights. Months passed, then a year, then two years, and still there was no report from Powell. In the meantime the land was closed to settlement. Stewart lost patience. In 1890 he got Powell's budget trimmed from $720,000 to $162,500 and persuaded his colleagues to cancel the withdrawal of the lands under study. Two years later the budget was cut another $90,000 and sixteen staff positions were eliminated, and two years after that, Powell gave up; he resigned as director of the U.S. Geological Survey.

Ironically, in that same year of 1894, Congress passed the first of two pieces of legislation that reflected, at least in part, Powell's arguments in his *Arid Region* report of 1879: the Carey Act, which authorized the transfer of as much as one million acres of the public domain to individual states, providing those states then turned around and sold it cheaply to irrigation companies, who, in their turn, would sell it to individual farmers, with attached water rights, in order to finance irrigation works. The second piece of legislation was the Reclamation (or Newlands) Act of 1902, which created the Reclamation Service (later renamed the Bureau of Reclamation), whose function it would be to build federal dams and irrigation works in the West. The major almost certainly would have approved one stipulation of this act: water derived from federal irrigation works would be made available only to farm units of 160 acres (or 320 acres, in the case of a man and wife) and only to those who would live on and work the land. The major would not have approved of the fact that at no time in the next eighty years, during which period more than $11 billion in taxpayers' money went to dam most of the major rivers in the West, would the 160-acre limitation be enforced with any consistency at all—and in 1982 would be removed entirely by another act of Congress.

## USING IT UP

While the vision of John Wesley Powell was being formulated (then casually dismissed), the exploitation of the public domain proceeded at an alarming rate—sometimes with consequences Powell could have foretold. Except for those reservations involved in the beginning of the national park and national forest systems (see chapters 1 and 2), the land was vulnerable, governed by laws too easily subverted and in any case, as we have seen, inadequate to the task of protection.

Among the first of those to venture into the farthest reaches of this domain were the miners, and it is instructive to remember that every single major mining strike in the history of the West was made on public land—gold in California in 1849, gold in Colorado in 1859, silver in Nevada in 1859, gold in Montana in 1862, silver in Idaho in 1864. In these and half a hundred other early mining developments, the treasure was claimed and extracted from land owned by the federal government. It was not until 1872 that Congress got around to imposing federal law on the extraction of federal treasure from federal land—and this General Mining Law, as it was called, was less than draconian. Under its provisions, a mining patent could be obtained by making a "valid" mineral discovery, paying for a boundary survey, applying to a land office for the land included in such a survey, paying $2.50 an acre for placer (surface) mining and five dollars an acre for lode (underground) mining, and investing one hundred dollars a year in improvements for five consecutive years. That was it—that was the government's share of the estimated $20 billion in gold, silver, and other minerals taken from the public lands during the busiest decades of mining in the nineteenth-century West. The law is still with us, still active, and still being applied in national forests and the "leftover lands" of the Bureau of Land Management.

Broadly speaking, the extraction of gold, silver, and copper had minimal impact on the whole sweep of the public domain. Not as much can be said of the other major Western industry of the nineteenth century. The grazing of cattle and sheep had a profound effect on the land from the beginning. When Powell suggested that livestock homesteads of 2,560 acres be established, congressmen from the East and Midwest were shocked by the amount of land he was suggesting was necessary to a grazier. Yet not even his amount was sufficient, and in practice stockmen were in possession of far greater areas. One Mormon cattle enterprise ruled 2 million acres, or about 3,500 square miles of open range. While this was larger than most, it was not uncommon to find other stock operations of similarly impressive proportions.

The American stock industry grew out of Texas after the Civil War, when the demand for beef in the North and East encouraged the raising of larger and larger herds. The animals were driven straight north to railheads like Abilene, Kansas, for shipment to Chicago, or even farther north to fatten on the sweet grass of the High Plains. Within ten years after the Civil War the herds had spread over the grasslands of Kansas, Nebraska, the Dakotas, Colorado, Wyoming, Montana, and Utah, consuming the fine, free grass of the public domain before being shipped to market. Operating expenses on the range were irresistibly low. It might cost four dollars to buy a single calf. To feed the calf cost nothing, since it fed itself on the range. In a year the animal would bring forty dollars in the northern markets. The business began to attract investors from the East and from as far away as Canada, England, and Scotland.

In less than fifteen years the northern range was stocked to capacity. Running out of water and grass, ranchers began squabbling among themselves, resorting to gang wars on occasion in the competitive struggle. There was unity, however, in their shared contempt for the homesteader, a benighted soul who often fenced the open range in patches of 160 acres (making sure to enclose the water, if there was any), depriving the cattle of free movement. "Now there is so much land taken up and fenced in that the trail for most of the way is little better than a crooked land," grumbled one trail hand in 1874, the year barbed wire was invented and made its appearance on the plains. "These fellows from Ohio, Indiana and other northern and eastern states—the 'bone and sinew of the country,' as politicians call them— have made farms, enclosed pastures and fenced water holes until you can't rest; and I say, Damn such bone and sinew! They are the ruin of the country, and have everlastingly, eternally now and forever, destroyed the best grazing-land in the world."

In retaliation—and quite illegally in many cases—ranchers began fencing in vast areas to keep homesteaders out. The scene was set for the enactment of what the biologist Garrett Hardin would call "the tragedy of the commons": limited resources, when subjected to un- limited use, reduced the welfare of all.

As Theodore Roosevelt learned during his brief tenure as a Dakota rancher, "overstocking [the range] may cause little or no harm for two or three years, but sooner or later there comes a winter which means ruin to the ranches that have too many cattle on them. It is merely a question of time as to when a winter will come that will understock the ranges by the summary process of killing off about half of all the cattle throughout the Northwest."

In 1886 the northern range was stocked well beyond its carrying capacity. Drought that spring and summer reduced the available forage, leaving hundreds of thousands (no one knows precisely how many) of cattle undernourished. Winter came early and stayed long. Snow drifted so deep throughout the West that cattle and people were buried alive in it. Temperatures stayed well below zero for weeks, and the wind whipped the plains. Cattle piled up like driftwood in all the fenced-in corners of the range. When the snowdrifts melted away, the damage was tallied. About three-fourths of all the herds in the West had been killed off. Roosevelt, who came back to survey the catastrophe, recalled riding through the Dakota country for three days without seeing a live animal. It was, he said, "a perfect smashup."

A smashup for the land, too; millions of acres had been stripped as clean as a billiard table by the combination of drought and too many cattle, and it would be decades before recovery. Some areas never did recover, and the consequent erosion left true wastelands where once the grass had grown belly-high to a horse.

## A DAWNING REALITY

Reform of the sweeping nature called for in Powell's *Arid Region* report was beyond the capabilities of a Congress and a federal bureaucracy resistant to change under the best of circumstances, but by the turn of the century it was clear that the nation's stewardship of the public domain was a travesty. Something had to be done, and something was—reluctantly and cautiously, at first, but with increasing scope in the first decade of the twentieth century.

In 1891 the General Revision Act repealed the Preemption Act of 1841, the Timber Culture Act of 1873, and the auction sale of land; it also reduced the land obtainable under the Desert Land Act from 640 acres to 320—and, as noted in chapter 2, the act's "Forest Reserve" clause empowered the President to make withdrawals of any forest areas the Secretary of the Interior deemed necessary for watershed protection and timber preservation. In 1897 these forest reserves were placed under the control of the General Land Office, and when that agency proved too amenable to corruption, an act of 1901 moved the reserves from the Department of the Interior to the Department of Agriculture.

In 1902, Theodore Roosevelt's first Secretary of the Interior, Ethan Allen Hitchcock, launched an investigation of land frauds that ultimately returned more than one million acres to the public domain. In 1904, Congress passed the Kincaid Homestead Act, which allowed entries of 640 acres in the Sand Hills region of Nebraska; it proved so successful that a demand rose for its extension to the rest of the public domain. In 1905 an executive order put a moratorium on entries under the provisions of the Timber and Stone Act of 1878; this law, which allowed the negotiated sale of public lands unfit for cultivation, had been as cheerfully abused by timber companies as the Homestead and Desert Land acts had been by livestock companies.

Coal lands got special attention during the Roosevelt years. In 1873 an act modeled after the General Mining Law of 1872 allowed claims to be filed on 160 acres of coal-bearing lands, at a sale price of ten dollars an acre; the law stipulated that no more than four such claims could be owned by a single individual or corporation. Nearly 30 million acres had been disposed of by the turn of the century, and most of this, through dummy entries and prearranged agreements with the original purchasers, had ended up in the hands of a few companies. To prevent the spread of this kind of monopoly, in 1906 Roosevelt withdrew 66 million acres of coal lands, including a million in Alaska, where hundreds of mining claims were pending. It was the controversy over these claims during the administration of William Howard Taft that led to the dismissal of Chief Forester Gifford Pinchot in 1910 (as described in chapters 2 and 6).

The reformist movement began sputtering out during the Taft and Wilson administrations. An Enlarged Homestead Act of 1909 did increase the size of a homestead claim to 320 acres, but only on those lands not suitable for irrigation. The Pickett Act of 1910 authorized the President to make withdrawals for "any public purpose," but the lands so withdrawn were still open to mining for metalliferous minerals under the General Mining Law. The Stock-Raising Homestead Act of 1916, inspired by the imminence of World War I and the projected need for additional beef, did include stipulations that range improvements were mandatory, but the 640 acres obtainable simply made it easier for already huge ranching operations to grow bigger. The mandated improvements were largely ignored by those who began expanding their operations during the war and the boom years of the twenties, until the same kinds of mistakes that had brought the cattle industry down in the 1880s were being repeated—and would have even more spectacular consequences.

## THE TEAPOT DOME–ELK HILLS AFFAIR

Perhaps no single incident from the history of the public domain more accurately demonstrated its vulnerability to the excesses of greed and ignorance than the Teapot Dome–Elk Hills imbroglio of the 1920s. The public resource on the public lands here was oil, and for once the federal government developed an intelligent law for its extraction. The Mineral Leasing Act of 1920 allowed oil companies access to petroleum reserves on the public domain, national forests, and wildlife refuges by a leasing system. The leases were awarded through a competitive bidding process, and the government would receive a royalty on all oil extracted. (By folding coal lands into this same law, Congress also rationalized the extraction of this resource; natural gas, phosphate, and sodium were also covered in the legislation.) Later, the states in which the extraction took place would get a cut of the royalties.

Still off limits, however, were the petroleum reserves that had been withdrawn for the exclusive use of the navy. President Taft had established reserves for defense purposes in the Elk Hills and Buena Vista Hills of California. Similar reserves at the Teapot Dome formation in Wyoming and on the North Slope of Alaska were later added, all of which were closely guarded by Secretary of the Navy Josephus Daniels. His successor, Edwin Denby, was more lax. In 1920, Denby secretly agreed to transfer responsibilities for the naval reserves over to Interior Secretary Albert B. Fall, who had requested them. Just as secretly, President Warren G. Harding approved the transfer in 1921. Trouble began shortly thereafter, for Fall, a Kentucky gentleman transplanted to New Mexico, had plans for these reserves. In April 1922 he leased all of the Teapot Dome reserve to Harry F. Sinclair of Sinclair Oil, without the inconvenience of competitive bidding. A little over two weeks later, Fall turned over the Elk Hills Reserve to Edward L. Doheny of the Pan American Petroleum and Transport Company—also without the benefit of competitive bids. As well, he waived Doheny's royalty payment to the government, allowing Doheny to build storage tanks and other facilities for the navy at Pearl Harbor and San Pedro instead.

Fall's agreements with Sinclair and Doheny were never meant to become public knowledge, but word of them leaked out within weeks. An aroused resident of Wyoming wrote to Senator John B. Kendrick about the rumor concerning Teapot Dome. Kendrick in turn asked for an explanation from Secretary Fall. Finding no satisfaction there, Kendrick called for a Senate inquiry. Fall stonewalled the investigators, saying that the reserves had been transferred to his department for reasons of national security. He also explained to Senate questioners that he had used his discretionary powers to convey the privileged leases so that the country might have some of its oil reserves developed as quickly as possible.

The investigation could not proceed beyond that point; there was no evidence of wrongdoing, although Senator Thomas J. Walsh of Montana, who chaired the committee inquiry, remained suspicious of Fall's motives. In 1923, for reasons that Fall claimed had nothing to do with the stalled investigation, the Secretary resigned. He joined Sinclair's company as a negotiator for an oil-drilling contract on Russia's Sakhalin Island, taking himself to the ends of the earth to dodge Walsh's suspicions. The press sympathized with Fall, who had heroically weathered several personal tragedies. Walsh was denounced for hounding an innocent man as ruthlessly as Javert had pursued Jean Valjean in Victor Hugo's *Les Miserables*. Even Doheny's admission during the Senate inquiry that he expected to make $100 million from his preferential lease with Fall did not seem to offend the press.

So things might have remained, had it not been for the discovery of a sudden rise in Fall's buying power. He had never been rich. He had, in fact, pronounced himself "dead broke" in 1920. But in 1921 he paid ten years of back taxes on his Three Rivers Ranch in New

Mexico, and bought land adjacent to his ranch for $91,500. Home from Russia, Fall declined to testify before the Senate committee about the source of his extra income, on the grounds that he was ill. Finally he admitted that he had borrowed $100,000 from *Washington Post* owner Edward B. McLean. McLean admitted that Fall had asked him for such a loan and that he had gladly given it, but that Fall had later returned his check uncashed, saying that he had gotten the money he needed from someone else. Fall was back on the front pages, which prompted Edward Doheny to come forward and tell how he had lent Fall $100,000 in an unsecured loan ("a personal loan to a lifelong friend," Doheny called it), this at about the same time Fall handed Doheny the Elk Hills oil reserve. Doheny insisted he saw nothing peculiar in this. In the meantime, it seemed that Fall had also accepted at least $172,000 from Sinclair in exchange for the oil in the Teapot Dome reserve. Sinclair refused to answer questions from Senate investigators and was cited and later indicted for contempt. Doheny, angered by months of questioning at the hands of perfidious Democratic congressmen (during a Republican administration at that), finally turned on them all and provided the names of all those legislators who had been willing to sell him their votes. By the time Doheny was through, his account of influence-peddling implicated many of America's finest in Congress, on both sides of the aisle. Harding died of food poisoning in office before these scandals were exposed, but his administration went down in history as the nation's most corrupt. In October 1929, more than eight years after Fall's leasing arrangement had been made, he was convicted of accepting bribes and sentenced to jail. Fall earned the ignominious distinction of being the first and (until the Watergate debacle) only Cabinet member to go to prison.

Even before Fall's imprisonment, federal courts rescinded the Doheny and Sinclair leases and returned Teapot Dome and Elk Hills to the navy. Shortly after taking office in 1929, President Herbert Hoover announced that henceforth no federal oil lands would be leased unless Congress expressly requested it. The ban remained in force until 1932, by which time vast deposits of oil had been struck in east Texas and Oklahoma—all of it on private property. For the moment, the pressure to exploit the public reserves had cooled.

## CLOSING THE DOOR

Hoover's swift move to bar the oil reserves from exploitation was not an indication of his administration's deep regard for the public domain. What the Hoover administration, particularly Interior Secretary Lyman Wilbur, wanted to do, in fact, was get rid of it altogether. It was time, Wilbur told those attending the annual conference of governors in 1929, for the states to start taking care of their own internal affairs—including the public lands within their borders. He proposed to turn these lands over to the states.

Not all the lands, however; not the national parks or the national forests. And the federal government would retain rights to all subsurface minerals. The states looked askance at this gift and decided they did not want it. "The West doesn't care much about getting the lid without the bucket," observed an editorial in the *Billings* (Montana) *Gazette*. Governor George H. Dern of Utah agreed. "The states already own," he said, "in their school land grants, millions of acres of this same kind of land, which they can neither sell nor lease, and which is yielding no income. Why should they want more of this precious heritage of desert?"

Wilbur's plan died.

What may have been lurking in the back of Governor Dern's mind was the simple fact that his state and the rest of the Western states were not eager to assume responsibility for what was clearly a disaster in the making. Ever since the cattle boom of the prewar and war years, followed by the lush times of the 1920s, the Western range had been crowded with more and more animals, just as in the years preceding the "Big Die-Up" of 1886–87. Unlike grazing in the national forests, which was regulated to some degree (too much so, according to Western ranchers), that on the public domain remained almost entirely unregulated; the land was open to anyone who cared to put an animal there. It was brutally overgrazed, and by the early years of the Depression, wind erosion combined with drought to produce dust storms the size of half a state, blackening the skies from New Mexico to the Dakotas, sucking detritus into the upper atmosphere, where it drifted to bring twilight at noon to cities as far east as New York.

This was too much, even for a Western congressman. Even for

Representative Edward I. Taylor of Colorado, heretofore a vigorous foe of federal ownership of Western land. Shortly after President Franklin D. Roosevelt took office in 1933, Taylor introduced legislation designed to establish strict regulation of grazing on the public domain—the federal domain. As he later explained,

> I fought for the conservation of the public domain under federal leadership because the citizens were unable to cope with the situation under existing trends and circumstances. The job was too big and interwoven for even the states to handle with satisfactory coordination. On the Western Slope of Colorado and in nearby states I saw waste, competition, overuse, and abuse of valuable range lands and watersheds eating into the very heart of the Western economy. Farmers and ranchers everywhere in the range country were suffering. The basic economy of entire communities was threatened. There was terrific strife and bloodshed between the cattle and sheep men over the use of the range. Valuable irrigation projects stood in danger of ultimate deterioration. Erosion, yes, even human erosion, had taken root. The livestock industry, through circumstances beyond its control, was headed for self-strangulation.

The Taylor Grazing Act became law on June 28, 1934. Although it postdated the creation of the national forest system by almost fifty years, the act was billed as "the Magna Carta of conservation," for its conscientiousness and for its immediate scope. More than 80 million acres, later increased to 142 million, were closed to entry under any of the land laws, and New Deal economist Rexford Tugwell declared that "the day on which the President signed the Taylor Act, which virtually closed the public domain to further settlement, laid in its grave a land policy which had long since been dead and which walked abroad only as a troublesome ghost within the living world." Tugwell's glib analysis was a little premature.

### THE STOCKMEN TAKE CARE OF THEIR OWN

The Taylor Act created grazing districts, within which qualified (which is to say well-established and influential) local ranchers would be issued grazing permits every year for an allotted number of animals.

131

The Interior Secretary was authorized to set grazing fees, of which 25 percent was earmarked for range management and improvement. The act also established a Division of Grazing (later the Grazing Service), which would coordinate the program. Interior Secretary Harold L. Ickes selected Farrington R. Carpenter, a Colorado lawyer and rancher, to head the new agency. The Taylor Act was offered as a prime example of democracy in action, because it established "advisory committees" made up of local stockmen to cooperate with district managers. This, however, was the act's chief weakness, for the power these committees exercised was nearly absolute. District managers rarely went out of their way to antagonize men who were, after all, their neighbors, and even Service Director Carpenter sided so often with those he was supposed to be regulating that Interior Secretary Ickes reprimanded him on numerous occasions. Ickes was also upset with Carpenter's staffing—nine people had been hired to supervise the 80 million acres initially covered by the Taylor Grazing Act. "You have not developed sufficient personnel even to protect the government's interest, let alone develop adequate range conservation programs," Ickes scolded.

Even with all their power, stockmen were still unsatisfied. Possibly nothing angered them more than the fact that grazing fees had been instituted for something they had always taken at will. The first grazing fee set in 1936 was five cents per cow per month, a fraction of what private grazing lands cost to lease, but still, it rankled. Patrick A. McCarran of Nevada, who first won his Senate seat in 1934, heard his constituents' complaints and became an effective spokesman for their small cause. Senator McCarran, according to the historian E. Louise Peffer, "initiated what was to become the lengthiest, most concerted, and in some respects, the most successful attempt made in the twentieth century by one person to force a reinterpretation of land policy more in accordance with the wishes of the using interests." McCarran had been lukewarm toward the Taylor Grazing Act, and although he rose on several occasions to speak on public land issues, his comments did not attract much attention until 1940, after he became a member of the Senate Committee on Public Lands and Surveys. McCarran introduced his sentiments by reading Resolution 241, a nine-point program lambasting public land administration that closed with a demand for a Senate investigation into the Service's operations. "I do not propose to legislate the trailblazers of the West out of existence," McCarran said, referring to the cattlemen and sheepmen who had suddenly found themselves under the heel, timidly placed to be sure, of the federal government.

McCarran took issue with Secretary Ickes's stated intention of retaining all grazing lands; with the Grazing Service's attempt at range conservation; with federal interference with water rights; and with attempts to raise the pathetically low grazing fees. Despite the repeated requests of Grazing Service Director Clarence L. Forsling, formerly of the Forest Service, the five-cents-per-animal fee could not be budged for ten years. Forsling argued unsuccessfully that the raise was needed to pay for the cost of administering the range and improving it. Moreover, the federal range was in better condition than privately owned lands, and was therefore worth more.

The fee controversy broke wide open in 1946, when a House subcommittee chaired by Representative Jed Johnson of Oklahoma declared that the Interior Department had been too easy on the stockmen. To force the Grazing Service to get its "untidy, mismanaged house in order," Johnson and others recommended that congressional appropriations be slashed further so that the Interior Department would have no alternative but to make up the difference among the rancher permittees. The Grazing Service, continued Johnson, had practically turned over the Taylor Grazing Act lands to "the big cowman and the big sheepman of the West. Why, they even put them on the payroll . . . and it's common knowledge that they [stockmen] have been running the Grazing Service. They did not choose to assess grazing fees that were anywhere comparable to the fees other people pay. . . . They have made a joke out of the Grazing Service." Appropriations for the Service's budget in the following year were slashed from an already meager $1.7 million to about $500,000.

The stated purpose of the budget cuts was to force an increase in the grazing fees, but McCarran was able to keep them down—and he would have been justified in considering the whole affair a clear victory for the interests he represented.

There was another victory that year. Taking advantage of an executive reorganization bill introduced by the Truman administration,

McCarran and his allies in the Senate simply obliterated the Grazing Service by combining it with the old General Land Office to produce a brand-new agency—the Bureau of Land Management, which assumed the administration of all public lands. McCarran hoped that, under this new setup, grazing regulation, made just one part of the new agency's many responsibilities, would be lost in the shuffle of paperwork awaiting a harried and understaffed administration. Generally speaking, he was correct. With its wings pinned and its budget trimmed at the outset, the BLM would be in no position to extract itself from the powerful grip of the stockmen. It was little more than a "modern administrative structure for handling the Nation's public land," blandly observed the agency's first director, Fred W. Johnson. And, blandly, the structure administered.

The stockmen, feeling as though they were back in the saddle again, had called a meeting during that summer of 1946 in Salt Lake City to discuss other ways they might rid the West of the federal intruder. The meeting, with more than 150 in attendance, was notable in that it was composed of two groups that had actively hated each other for years, the cattlemen and the sheepmen, and representatives of the American National Livestock Association and the National Wool Growers Association. McCarran addressed the meeting briefly before the conferees turned their attention to a shared objective: the acquisition of all 142 million acres of Taylor Act lands, as well as the national forests (see chapter 2), national parks, and the rights to all minerals buried beneath this vast surface. The ranchers set their own prices for the public domain, starting at about nine cents an acre and going up to less than three dollars an acre. They also voted to limit the number of rightful owners of all this land to those in the room, and a few like-minded friends.

This grotesque proposal, unanimously approved by the convention, was translated into legislation by Senator Allan Robertson of Wyoming. Although its ultimate goal was the same as that of the stockmen, the Robertson bill was slightly more devious; it called for a massive transfer of all the lands to the thirteen Western states, to let the states decide the best course of action. There was little question about what that course of action would be. But historian and social commentator Bernard DeVoto had gotten wind of the bill and of the stockmen's meeting in Salt Lake City, and exposed it in the January 1947 issue of *Harper's*. DeVoto, a native of Utah, was furious. He wrote:

So, at the very moment when the West is blueprinting an economy which must be based on the sustained, permanent use of its natural resources, it is also conducting an assault on those resources with the simple objective of liquidating them. The dissociation of intelligence could go no farther, but there it is—and there is the West yesterday, today and forever. It is the Western mind stripped to the basic split. The West as its own worst enemy. The West committing suicide.

The public outcry raised by DeVoto quashed the takeover plan, and the stockmen retreated. For the moment, the Robertson bill was dead, and so was the movement.

## A CAPTIVE OF HISTORY

Today the Bureau of Land Management, "an unconvincing Goliath," in the words of law professor Sally Fairfax, remains a captive of its own history. So far it has almost no tradition of its own to pass on. The agency had no high-minded iconoclast in the mold of the Forest Service's Gifford Pinchot, no devoted idealist like the Park Service's Stephen Mather. Nor was the BLM spawned from the indefatigable legions that pressed for wilderness preservation and for the Alaska national interest lands. No President has come forward to champion the BLM's cause, as did President Theodore Roosevelt on behalf of wildlife refuges. Its directors have for the most part reveled in their low profiles, and often have been indistinguishable from those they supposedly regulate—a vestige of the McCarran era.

Livestock leaders rushed in to fill the vacuum created when the BLM was established. They started by insisting that the agency's director meet with their approval, but not all BLM directors were made in the permittees' own image. When Interior Secretary Julius Krug appointed Marion Clawson to the top position in 1948, the stockmen accepted the appointment because Clawson, a Nevadan, formerly of the abolished Bureau of Agricultural Economics, seemed to share their interests. "It was difficult to attract a first-rate, top-

flight man to the job," recalled Clawson years later. "BLM was drift-
ing. So, somewhat in desperation, Krug offered me the job." Clawson
understood that the stockmen wielded power beyond their number,
but did not allow this to keep him from implementing new procedures.
Shortly after he became BLM's chief, Clawson wrote a booklet called
"Rebuilding the Federal Range," which was an affront to the stockmen. It included photographs, for comparative purposes, of overgrazed land and correctly grazed land, and sought significant reductions
in the number of animals permitted. Possibly the severest offense
against the stockmen was that the pamphlet used the word "privilege"
rather than "right" in describing the permittees' connection to the
federal range.

Nevertheless, Clawson, who served until 1963 and wrote many
valuable texts on the subject of federal land management, had inherited what has been called a "monopolitical structure." As palliative
as the Taylor Grazing Act was, it had established grazing as the
dominant use on much of the public domain. Adherence to the act
in its most basic form granted cattlemen and sheepmen an exclusive
interest in the land. Their use was framed as the highest, best, and—
in places—*only* use of rangeland. The only intervention tolerated
was by mineral and oil exploration outfits, since this did not seem
incompatible with grazing. As a result the federal range under Clawson and others was so closely identified with these two sectors that
cynics maintained the initials "BLM" stood for Bureau of Livestock
and Mining. The livestock interests had simply grown too proprietary
of the public land, and it was their best interests the BLM was
determined to serve.

### "GRAB!—GRAB!—GRAB!"

While stockmen consolidated their effective control of a harassed and
understaffed BLM, Congress made one more major push to rationalize
the nation's perception and use of its public domain. In 1964 it passed
two basic pieces of public land legislation that pointed the way: the
Classification and Multiple Use Act and the Public Land Law Review
Commission Act.

The Classification and Multiple Use Act instructed the BLM to
classify the public lands according to those that were suitable for

disposal and those that were suitable for retention and management by the federal government under the principles of multiple use and sustained yield. By 1969 the BLM had obediently classified some 180 million acres, and recommended that of these almost 150 million be retained and managed; another six parcels, amounting to 146,694 acres, were recommended for inclusion in the new National Wilderness Preservation System (see chapter 5); less than 5 million acres were recommended for disposal. The response throughout much of the West was predictable outrage—in some cases, near derangement. "Grab!—Grab!—Grab!" rancher-lawyer Clel Georgetta wailed in *Golden Fleece in Nevada*. "Nine million acres here, ten million acres there, and twenty million acres somewhere else will soon withdraw all the public domain from the possibility of ever becoming privately owned. Thus the Bureau of Land Management is spreading its permanent control over the face of the earth in true bureaucratic, self-perpetuation style."

The Public Land Law Review Commission (PLLRC) was established by its act to study "all existing statutes and regulations governing the retention, management and disposition of public lands," to "review policies and practices of federal agencies administering these laws," and to "determine present and future demands on public lands." Colorado Representative Wayne Aspinall, a strong advocate of disposal and development, was appointed chairman of the committee, which included six senators, six congressmen, six presidential appointees, and a pool of twenty-five advisers. Aspinall ruled the committee, and those who testified before the PLLRC found it nearly impossible to sway the deliberations away from discussions of the need for intense development and consideration of economic returns only. Aspinall was too shrewd to campaign hard for the decidedly unpopular quest for large land transfers to the states, but he made much of dominant use over multiple use, and often ignored recreational or wildlife considerations.

The commission's report, entitled *One Third of a Nation's Land*, was published in 1970, and listed 137 recommendations for improved federal management. It managed to satisfy almost no one. The report left both developers and conservationists feeling shortchanged and grumbling that the other side had made out better than they had.

Nevertheless, the PLLRC's report set forth one tenet that could not be ignored. Despite recommendations for small land sales to continue, the commissioners stated that "we urge reversal of the policy that the United States should dispose of the so-called unappropriated public domain lands." It was the first, clear, official, and straightforward recommendation for retention of the public domain that had ever been made. At its weakest the recommendation merely restated what all rational observers already accepted. At its strongest, it definitively charted a new course for the BLM and for the nation.

## AN ORGANIC SOLUTION

It was now established as public policy that the nation was going to retain and manage the great bulk of the public domain. But how manage—under what rules and regulations, with how much power? There were plenty of rules and regulations already, of course—principally those three thousand and more land laws that had accumulated over the course of the past two centuries. These were, as they always had been, a ghastly tangle of confusion. As for power, the BLM had precious little of it. Its authority was diffuse and confused, and for actual enforcement of federal law it was all but helpless. For example, if a BLM field man caught someone stealing a forbidden cactus or vandalizing a prehistoric petroglyph—both violations of federal law— his only recourse would be to hurry to the nearest town and contact the county sheriff and ask him to come out and arrest the culprit. Who would, of course, not be there.

The agency itself needed firm direction in a number of matters. Such as grazing. Although the condition of the range had improved markedly with passage of the Taylor Act, BLM researchers reported in 1975 that only 17 percent of the federal range was in good condition, 50 percent in fair condition, and the remaining 33 percent in poor condition. Despite its belated efforts and good intentions, the agency had not been aggressive enough in pursuing grazing cutbacks. Nor did it show much inclination to achieve them; to fulfill its responsibilities under the National Environmental Policy Act of 1970, BLM officials had decided to apply the broad brush to range considerations by lumping nearly 178 million acres of heterogeneous landscape into a single environmental impact statement on the effects of livestock grazing. In 1974 the Natural Resources Defense Council brought a suit to force the BLM to write individual impact statements for site-specific allotments, covering the impact of grazing on all resources—including wildlife and recreation. The NRDC won its point, and BLM officials agreed that 144 separate impact statements, reduced from 212, would be written by 1988.

For these and a number of other reasons, some of them outlined in *One Third of a Nation's Land*, it became increasingly clear to all concerned that the BLM needed its own organic act to facilitate the administration of its awesome responsibility of land—greater than that of any federal land-managing agency. "Despite the enormous responsibilities of the BLM," Interior Secretary Rogers C. B. Morton complained, "the definition of its mission and the authority to accomplish it have never been comprehensively enunciated by Congress." In 1976, Congress finally paid heed by passing the Federal Land Policy and Management Act (FLPMA), which placed the BLM on equal footing (on the face of it, at least) with the National Park Service and the Forest Service.

Among other things, the act repealed all public land laws (except the everlasting General Mining Law of 1872), and in its opening paragraph stated that the public lands were to be retained for the long-term use of the American people unless "it is determined that disposal of a particular parcel will serve the national interest." The lands were henceforth to be identified as the National Resource Lands, and the BLM was directed to pursue multiple-use, sustained-yield goals, with land-use planning as the cornerstone for management. The act also stipulated that the "United States receive fair market value of the use of the public lands and their resources," and that "areas of critical environmental concern" be designated to protect historic, cultural, and natural values. Although the BLM was allowed to retain its decentralized structure—a throwback to both the Taylor Act's advisory committees and the GLO's local land offices—appointment of the BLM's director was no longer left to the Interior Secretary. Instead, the director would be a presidential appointee subject to Senate approval. Finally, the FLPMA directed the BLM to study its lands for their wilderness qualities and to determine which of them ought to be included in the National Wilderness Preservation

System. The agency was given fifteen years to complete the task. (These wilderness study areas eventually included some 25 million acres.)

The Bureau of Land Management had finally been joined to the upper ranks of the administrative bureaucracy. It had no sooner achieved this exalted status, however, than a movement began to develop among its own constituency that would have obliterated it, given a choice.

## THE SAGEBRUSH REBELS

On June 4, 1979, the Nevada legislature passed a resolution proclaiming that "all public lands in Nevada and all minerals not previously appropriated are the property of the State of Nevada." This empty declaration was the symptom of one more Western revolt against the federal presence on federal land—or at least the federal presence on federal land in the West. The people who espoused the state ownership of federal lands called themselves the Sagebrush Rebels and mounted a campaign that seemed too vigorous to be merely symbolic. The rebels were well-financed and spread their message to the other public-land states. Legislature after legislature passed resolutions similar to Nevada's, and where a sagebrush resolution was defeated it did not go down without a struggle. Even Ronald Reagan, a presidential contender in 1980, got mileage out of the Westerners' cause. "Count me in as a rebel," he shouted to a Utah crowd, while campaigning. Reagan won votes and the rebellion glowed brightly in the national limelight. It was the Hoover plan of the 1930s and the DeVoto-denounced land grab of the 1940s repackaged and delivered to the 1980s. But to those who did not know better, the Sagebrush Rebellion's goal of ridding itself of federal land administration seemed like a good idea. Shortly after his election in 1980, Reagan, for example, admitted to being puzzled about why so much public land was in the West anyway, and promised to appoint a commission to look into the matter. Before the election he had promised to work for a "sagebrush solution," which meant that he wanted "the states to have an equitable share of public lands and their natural resources."

Once elected, however, President Reagan did not hand over the

West to those who demanded it. At least not literally. Instead, he opted for "privatization," or the sale of so-called surplus federal land. A 1982 executive order established the Property Review Board to identify properties that ought to be sold. Four million acres of BLM lands and about 6 million acres of national forests were targeted for sale, until the program encountered opposition among even the strongest administration allies. Nevertheless, Reagan had placated the Sagebrush Rebels by appointing Wyoming-born James Watt Secretary of the Interior. Watt was a Sagebrusher in steward's clothing, and made no secret of his distaste for federal conservation programs. As an attorney for the Denver-based Mountain States Legal Foundation before being named Interior Secretary, Watt had opposed Interior Department rulings on stricter strip-mining controls and had sued to speed up applications for oil and mineral exploration in wilderness areas. Just as environmentalists turned to litigation, so did Watt, declaring that he would "fight in the courts those bureaucrats and no-growth advocates who create a challenge to individual liberty and economic freedoms." As head of the department he had fought, he often seemed vaguely regretful that he could not simply turn over the public domain to the few states in the West, and assuaged his brothers with a promise that his department would be a "good neighbor."

The energy crisis gave him the perfect opportunity to step up private development of public resources. Indeed, since the Arab oil embargo in 1973, every President including Carter had made U.S. energy self-sufficiency a top priority. But whereas the Carter administration had pursued energy conservation measures and the development of alternative renewable energy sources, the Reagan administration concentrated on exploiting public reserves as quickly as possible. "Because of the actions taken by extremists to stop the orderly development of energy resources," Secretary Watt said, "the nation is likely to suffer energy shortages and thus severe economic hardship." He played upon the natural divisiveness between East and West by telling Westerners that if they listened too long to "environmental extremists," Easterners would gouge the West to extract the oil, gas, and coal needed to "light and heat the East and to maintain jobs in the Midwest and on the East Coast."

141

Watt's eagerness to exploit the energy resources in the BLM's domain got him into trouble almost immediately. In April 1982, in what was called by his office the "largest coal lease sale in history," the BLM awarded bids for a little over 1.1 billion tons of coal in the Powder River Basin of Montana and Wyoming. The bids brought in $43.5 million. Five additional lease sales were planned immediately. Before they could get under way, the General Accounting Office issued a report that the Powder River leases had been sold for $100 million less than fair market value. The House soon passed a resolution ordering a six-month moratorium on any further lease sales, and while the Senate would not concur, it did require Watt to set up an independent commission to study the integrity of such sales. In the meantime, another huge coal lease sale was allowed in the Fort Union District of North Dakota and Montana. When it was soon revealed that this sale, too, went for prices far below what the coal should have brought in, the House Interior Committee asked a federal court to invalidate the sale; the court accommodated the wish of the committee. The Senate changed its mind about a moratorium and, by an overwhelming bipartisan vote, joined with the House to declare one.

Secretary Watt was more successful in other aspects of his program. By the procedure of bypassing local BLM offices altogether, he managed to concentrate most decision-making in Washington, where he could keep an eye on things. "The power is concentrated in the Secretary's office," one BLM field man complained, and he was not alone. Between 1981 and 1983, Watt altered agency regulations for everything from geothermal leasing to wilderness management. In situations where public participation had been authorized, he eliminated it or reduced it so that it could not be meaningful. "Through budget cuts, Watt reinforced a historically strong preference in the Bureau for commodity programs like minerals extraction," wrote James Baker in the Winter 1983 issue of *Wilderness* magazine. A Sierra Club analysis of the BLM budget revealed "almost universal cuts between 1981 and 1984 in noncommodity programs: wildlife habitat, down 48 percent; wilderness, 41.8 percent; soil, air, and water management, 47.5 percent; land use planning, 25 percent." Yet the budget for mandatory archaeological inventories prior to clearances for mineral exploration soared to 426 percent in one year. In 1981 the Interior Department also fired two highly respected BLM state directors, and packed key advisory boards with those seeking rapid development of resources. To show its determination to get mineral exploration under way, the BLM, in keeping with Secretary Watt's goals, reduced the backlog of lease applications from 13,000 to fewer than 1,000 in less than a year. While such bureaucratic efficiency is often laudable, in this case it revealed devotion to one end rather than to the many mandated by the FLPMA, and led to unwarranted ecological impacts because of insufficient regulation.

The Secretary's distaste for the BLM's wilderness study responsibilities was especially pronounced. Not only were wilderness supervision and study reduced, the acres under consideration were also cut back. In 1982 Watt excluded 1.4 million acres of wilderness study areas from further consideration, and opened these to exploration and development. The Secretary claimed he had exercised his discretionary power in removing the wilderness study areas from BLM protection, but in 1983 the Sierra Club filed suit to have the lands restored, and in April 1985 a federal district judge ruled that "in large measure" Watt "failed to follow the law" when he allowed the lands to be opened for development. (By the summer of 1985 the BLM had restored the so-called Watt drops and had begun to include them in the study process.)

After Watt's departure, Interior officials persisted in their lack of appreciation for wilderness values. During BLM oversight hearings in 1984, for instance, Interior Secretary William P. Clarke referred to the BLM domain as the "land no one wanted," explaining in his curious syntax that the "adage becomes apparent the closer we got to the ground." Clarke said he was "surprised . . . that we have been able to find, frankly, 24 million acres of this stepchild acreage that we can even study" to fulfill the FLPMA's wilderness requirement.

The Sagebrush Rebels did not get the public domain—the national resource lands—placed in the hands of the Western states as they claimed they wanted. Not even "privatization" worked out to any significant degree. The Rebels are still encumbered by the federal presence on federal lands, and their noisy movement has generally died out. Until the next time. The National Wilderness Preservation System, however, did get some of the public domain; in 1984, some 300,000 acres of BLM land were added to the system, particularly a number of spectacularly beautiful areas of the "Arizona Strip" of northern Arizona and southern Utah. It was, conservationists hoped, only the beginning.

Nevertheless, the BLM has yet to achieve either the power or the prestige its responsibilities would seem to warrant, and the influence of the Western stockman, the Western miner, the Western developer, and the Western politician still obstructs the agency's exercise of what power it does possess. Appropriations and staffing are a good guide to the BLM's status at the official level. In 1985, the BLM received $2.14 per acre to manage its 340 million acres, while the Forest Service received $9.85 for each of its 191 million acres; the BLM had one field person for every 30,500 acres, the Forest Service one person for every 4,800 acres. This, it seems clear, is far short of enough to enable the BLM to shake off the weight of history and begin to shape the future of the country's largest part of its national inheritance of land.

## AN AGENDA FOR THE NATIONAL RESOURCE LANDS

The National Resource Lands of the Bureau of Land Management are unique among the various national public land systems. Not only do they constitute the largest single unit of those systems, they embody within them many of the same natural qualities that distinguish our national parks, national monuments, historic sites, cultural sites, wilderness areas, wildlife refuges, even national forests, and contain important deposits of such extractive resources as coal, oil, gas, and other energy materials.

That very diversity—and the user conflicts that derive from it—has confounded us in our attempts to manage these lands intelligently. That we have done so badly in the past the most generous narrative of our history could not deny, and even passage of the Federal Land Policy and Management Act of 1976 was no guarantee that the future would see revolutionary change, however necessary.

The story consistently has been one of a confusion of values, but time no longer gives us the latitude for mistakes of a dimension similar to those of the past. It is one of the axioms of modern history that the events and issues that affect our lives are both accelerated and compressed as we approach the end of the century; we repeatedly find ourselves caught up in circumstances over which we too often appear to have little or no control and consequently rush headlong into error.

One telling demonstration of this is what has happened to the BLM's wilderness review process over the past three years. When Congress in 1976 decided upon 1991 as the deadline for completion of the study process for BLM wilderness study areas, it clearly recognized that fifteen years was not too long a time to make a careful assessment of the lands involved—25 million acres of them, finally—before coming to an informed decision regarding what parts of them should be placed in the National Wilderness Preservation System and what parts allocated to commodity use and development. It was too important a decision, Congress realized, to be arrived at hurriedly. Former Interior Secretary James Watt apparently felt otherwise. In one of the major decisions of his administration, he moved the deadline up to 1984. This was not done, it should be pointed out, because the Secretary wanted to rush much of the land into wilderness protection; rather, it was a move deliberately and admittedly designed to release as much of it as possible, as soon as possible, to development. One of the consequences of this sudden policy shift was the swift elimination of 1.4 million acres from wilderness consideration (these were later reinstated, of course, once Watt was gone); another was the production of studies that were incomplete, inadequate, ill-informed, and weighted heavily on the side of release; and finally, development often was allowed to take place even during the study phase.

Obviously, one of the primary goals of the near future will be to reverse this policy and, by means of administrative action, legislation, or litigation, restore the study process to its former schedule. But the problem here is not merely the real or potential loss of wilderness, as important as that is. It is that these lands remain vulnerable, in spite of new law designed to protect them, to the whipsaw traditions of the past.

We must free the lands of that legacy. It is time to put forth a

145

major new effort to assure that this last and largest "resource bank" left to the United States is managed in such a way as to assure the sustained and balanced use of its resources by the American people in perpetuity—as the FLPMA intended.

To achieve this goal, there are any number of things that could and should be done in the near term that in aggregate would have significant long-range effects. In addition to reversing current policy in the wilderness review process, as mentioned above, we should raise the funding and staffing levels of the BLM to something approaching parity with those of the Forest Service (which, after all, manages only a little over half as much land). We should overhaul the entire grazing management system, including the function and membership of advisory boards and district councils and the fee structure and administration of the grazing permit system. We should most definitely repeal the Mining Law of 1872. For more than a century, this "giveaway" law has allowed hardrock mining on the public lands with virtually no recompense to the American people and no control over the damage it can inflict on the land. New law must be devised that will establish a leasing and royalty system; will require that detailed mining plans be submitted for approval before any development work is allowed to begin, with such plans meeting strict environmental standards and criteria; and will further require land reclamation to repair any damage from the mining process.

More such actions could be taken, but, however necessary, they would by no means be enough to initiate the kind of sweeping change required to meet the needs of the next century and beyond. This kind of change will demand a major break with the past. Planning, obviously, is the key here. But what kind of planning—and how organized? The FLPMA throws considerable weight behind the concept of planning, including resource inventory. Indeed, the act declares at the outset that "the national interest will be best realized if the public lands and their resources are periodically and systematically inventoried and their present and future use is projected through a land use planning process. . . ."

Yet the planning system that has evolved lacks the necessary coherence and firm direction to do the job properly. Furthermore, this inadequate planning is being undertaken at the same time that much of the land already is being used for various purposes or is at least open to such use—a condition that further complicates an already demanding task.

It might be instructive here to recall the work of John Wesley Powell. In his seminal 1879 *Report on the Lands of the Arid Region of the United States*, Powell argued that the traditional system of rectangular cadastral surveys was an arbitrary device that imposed purely political boundaries on the land of the West, with no attention to geographical realities. He maintained that the lands should be surveyed instead according to land types: timberland, mineral land, irrigable land, and pastureland. All such unappropriated land, he said, should be closed to settlement or development until such surveys had been completed, the boundaries carefully drawn, and the units classified as to type. They should then be opened only according to strict rules laid down to guide the proper use of each land type.

The political realities of his time defeated Powell, and Congress largely ignored his recommendations, but after a century of the kind of waste and misuse that his ideas might have prevented, it is perhaps necessary for us to revive at least some of his concepts and do with them what we can to institute a modern program designed to revolutionize our future utilization of the public lands.

The passage of the FLPMA was a good step in this direction. Clearly, it was only the first step and in itself not sufficient to ensure the creation and performance of a long-range management program. Congress should move swiftly to engineer new legislation—perhaps as a major amendment to the FLPMA or to the Natural Resources Planning Act of 1974—that will ensure that the intentions expressed in the FLPMA are indeed carried out.

Such legislation should address itself to two major goals. First, inventory. Utilizing the mandate already established by the FLPMA, we should scrap the present system and institute a crash program to survey, map, and inventory these lands with an eye toward determining as precisely as possible the type and condition of all land forms in the system and the location and extent of all resources available—with primary emphasis placed upon the identification of noncommodity resources. To implement such a program, five separate resource surveys should be organized and firm deadlines established for their completion:

*A natural resources survey*. Probably the weakest element in the current BLM planning process is the determination of scientific, scenic, recreational, ecological, wildlife, historical, and archaeological values present in the lands. The FLPMA states that the lands shall be managed "in a manner that will protect" such values—but we cannot protect that which we do not know. At present, no comprehensive survey of such resources exists, and under the present system it is not likely that it ever would. And, although the act does call for the determination and setting aside of "areas of critical environmental concern" as a priority item, implementation has been inefficient and has fallen far short of any degree of completeness. This new survey would be organized specifically to examine all of the National Resource Lands to discover those that must be protected from any sort of commercial utilization.

*A soil and rangeland conservation survey*. Like the other surveys, this would seek to discover the quantity and condition of its designated resource responsibility. Unlike the others, it would also investigate lands already in use to determine the degree, if any, of soil damage and loss through overgrazing and consequent erosion and would be *instructed* to rescind or reduce, on an interim basis, permit-grazing use on any lands whose degradation has reached maximum levels of allowable resource damage. Such authority exists in the FLPMA, although it is at present exercised rarely, inconsistently, and purely at discretion.

*A Western water resources survey*. In a program to rationalize future water use in the West, including the needs of land and wildlife, this study would attempt to establish the precise quantity and quality of Western water resources and the overall ecological health of individual groundwater systems and watersheds; discover and clarify conflicts and present allocations among federal, state, local, Indian, and private rights; and determine which public-land water-development projects, planned or proposed, are justified on the basis of future available supplies and projected ecological impacts.

*A critical minerals survey.* This study would seek to determine domestic reserves of those strategic minerals—molybdenum, chromium, titanium, alunite, etc.—which are now or may in the future be in short supply and to establish for these minerals clearly defined Known Reserve Areas. Full environmental impact studies should be made a part of this survey to determine the effect of any future development.

*An energy resources survey.* This study would systematically establish the boundaries and estimated volumes of deposits of coal, oil, oil shale, and tar sands, as well as significantly productive geothermal sites, and place them in clearly demarcated preserves for future use— much as was done in creating the nation's naval petroleum reserves two generations ago. This survey, too, should include environmental impact studies.

Of even greater importance, concurrent with the creation of these ambitious surveys, the new legislation should mandate the organization of an equally coordinated, centralized, and coherent planning process to develop strict comprehensive guidelines governing the future use and development of each of the landforms and resources under investigation. To avoid the pitfalls of inconsistency inherent in the present planning structure, the law should establish overall standards and criteria to which all individual district management plans must adhere. Borrowing from the National Forest Management Act of 1976 (see chapter 2), the legislation also should stipulate that all plans developed would be subject to perpetual review and revision every ten years in order to ensure, first, that management is indeed taking place as it should and, second, that the plans are compatible with the nation's needs as they develop and change through the years. Finally, to ensure that the plans *are* completed, the new legislation should establish a firm deadline for their completion in the near future.

All of this, of course, would take both money and manpower. At the same time as it passes such new legislation, Congress should approve sufficient appropriations specifically earmarked to support the development and administration of the surveys and the planning process, and the BLM itself should undertake a wide-scale recruitment program to acquire personnel sufficient in numbers and expertise in a variety of disciplines to carry out the work of this complex blueprint for the future.

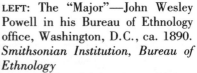

LEFT: The "Major"—John Wesley Powell in his Bureau of Ethnology office, Washington, D.C., ca. 1890. *Smithsonian Institution, Bureau of Ethnology*
BELOW: The Ocean Grove Mining Company at play in Colorado, ca. 1880. *Denver Public Library, Western History Department*

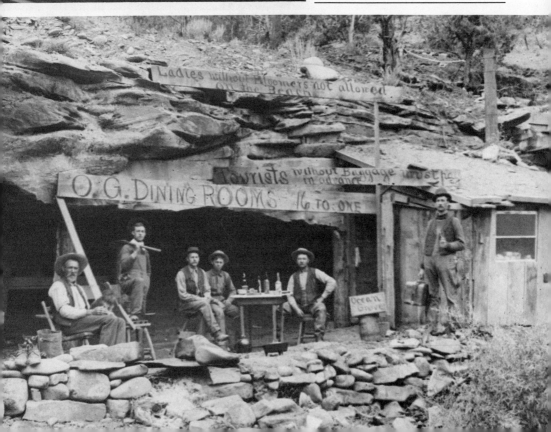

ABOVE: The Potosi Mountains in southwestern Nevada—another scene of BLM desert beauty. *U.S. Bureau of Land Management*
BELOW: Valley of the Gods, Utah—a typical stretch of incomparable BLM "wasteland." *Dale Schicketanz*

# 4

# ISLANDS OF LIFE

## The National Wildlife Refuge System

In the classic children's book *The Trumpet of the Swan*, by E. B. White, a father swan inspires his fledglings with a vision of their Promised Land:

> "Montana is a state of the union. And there, in a lovely valley surrounded by high mountains, are the Red Rock Lakes which nature has designed especially for swans. In the lakes you will enjoy warm winter, arising from hidden springs. Here, ice never forms, no matter how cold the nights. In the Red Rock Lakes you find other trumpeter swans, as well as the lesser waterfowl—the geese and ducks. There are few enemies. No gunners. Plenty of muskrat houses. Free grain. Games every day. What more can a swan ask, in the long, long cold of winter?"

What more indeed? And Red Rock Lakes was not just a place in a storybook. It was and is quite real—a 32,500-acre unit of the National Wildlife Refuge System, and a remarkable place. Remarkable, too, that it even exists, considering the precedence human desires take over those of other creatures nearly everywhere on the planet. There is simply no other entity in the world quite like America's National Wildlife Refuge System. Now 90 million acres, its size exceeds the national park system, although all but 13 million of its acres lie in Alaska. Of the 408 refuges outside Alaska, 65 percent are west of the Mississippi River. Over 90 percent of their lands were withdrawn from the public domain while Congress authorized the purchase of much of the rest, or accepted them as gifts to the nation from private donors. The system operates in seven different biomes, characterized by distinct communities of soil types, vegetation, and animals. An environmental impact statement prepared for the refuge system and released in 1976 described the refuges succinctly as "islands of habitat once widespread within each biome."

An "island" might be gigantic, as is the 19-million-acre Arctic National Wildlife Refuge, which stretches from the Arctic Circle north to the Arctic Ocean. Or it might be as small as a suburban backyard, as is the six-tenths-of-an-acre Mille Lacs Refuge in Minnesota. In Alaska the system preserves not just islands of life, but also their continental equivalent of unique ecosystems, where man has barely intruded. Not all refuges are remotely situated. The Great Swamp National Wildlife Refuge in New Jersey lies along a major commuting route well within Manhattan's sphere of influence. (Featuring the sort of landscape that people like to drain and fill and wood ducks like to nest in, the Great Swamp became a refuge only after conservationists fought to keep it from becoming an airport.)

The system is composed of 424 wildlife and waterfowl refuges, plus an assortment of related sites for waterfowl production. On these lands dwell at least 220 species of mammals and 260 species of amphibians and reptiles, 63 of which are endangered. More than 600 of the 813 bird species found in the United States spend at least one season within the refuge system. This is no accident, since about three-fourths of the refuges were set aside primarily for the benefit of waterfowl and migratory birds. Many of the bird refuges are along the four major north-south migratory routes, the Atlantic, Mississippi, Central, and Pacific flyways. Other refuges have been established to preserve the habitat primarily for an individual species, such as the elk at the National Elk Refuge in Jackson, Wyoming, or to reintroduce a species to an ancestral or otherwise suitable territory. In 1934 and 1935, for instance, thirty-one musk-ox from Greenland were released on Nunivak Island, part of Yukon Flats National Wildlife Refuge in Alaska. Now more than six hundred animals inhabit that refuge.

The refuge system has supported numerous near-miraculous wildlife recoveries. Tiny key deer numbered less than fifty in 1950, their population reduced by the conversion of their habitat into a resort development. Now there are hundreds of deer protected at the National Key Deer Refuge, in Florida. Perhaps the best known case of rejuvenation is occurring at the Aransas National Wildlife Refuge in Texas, where whooping cranes, mistakenly reported extinct in 1923 (they were only a few birds away), have made a limited recovery, with eighty-three birds accounted for in the 1984 census.

Refuge successes include the preservation of singular habitats of certain species, which, by virtue of their few but unalterable living requirements, have always been rare or endangered. The system also has recovered or aided many once-prolific, then drastically reduced species, such as the beaver, wood duck, sea otter, and dozens of shorebirds, which are once again very much in evidence in their native habitats.

Such success stories demonstrate the ideal for which the system was established. With the passage of the National Wildlife Refuge System Act in 1966, the Fish and Wildlife Service has earnestly set out to "provide, preserve, restore and manage a national network of lands and waters sufficient in size, diversity and location to meet society's needs for areas where the widest spectrum of benefits associated with wildlife and wildlands is enhanced and made available." This mission has spawned four key refuge goals. First, the refuges must preserve, restore, and enhance ecosystems of endangered species. Second, they must perpetuate migratory bird populations. Third, they must preserve natural diversity and abundance of all animals and nonmigratory birds that are present on the refuges. And, finally, they must engender an understanding and an appreciation of fish and wildlife, and of man's role in protecting the environment. This last purpose sounds like something straight out of the mind of Aldo Leopold, who declared that the hope of the future lay not in curbing the influence of human occupancy (it was already too late for that, he asserted in 1931), but in "creating a better understanding of the extent of that influence and a new ethic of its governance."

By all rational measure, this is a noble system with a noble purpose, and there is good reason to have pride in its existence as one of the major legacies this nation has had the foresight to preserve. But, like Aldo Leopold's Land Ethic, it was a long time developing out of a complex welter of ideas and instincts—and again, like that ethic, it is still a long way from becoming all that it needs to be.

## TIPPING THE BALANCE

Eons before the current refuge system was devised, another system of wildlife perpetuation flourished. Cycles of animal reproduction, birth, and demise revolved around tides, or the length of days and nights, or the phases of the moon and other gravitational exhortations—just as they do now. The fundamental difference between the old and the new systems is the changing role of the human species. Aboriginal societies had developed "an intimate understanding of the habits and ecology of other species," according to William Cronon, whose book *Changes in the Land* explores New England's ecological history through colonization. Indian societies were characterized by dietary flexibility and residential impermanence, Cronon says, thereby ensuring that the impact of the human presence on a particular place was minimal. Indians of New England and elsewhere in precolonial America lived according to the seasons, moving to wherever food was most heavily concentrated in the ecosystem. Whole villages, which varied in population density as well as in shelter type, congregated by a river in spring when fish were spawning, or moved into low-lying forests to track deer through autumn and winter. They shifted to where subsistence was easiest, taking whatever species were plentiful, then moved on when game grew scarce, thus giving it time to recover. And, since Indians traveled on foot, with no other means to bring down their game than bows and arrows, or snares and pits, they were discouraged from taking more than they could quickly transport. Even to the south, where tribes subsisted largely on cultivated foods such as corn and legumes, land and wildlife had time to recover from intensive farming. Fields remained fertile for as long as ten years because of mixed plantings of beans and corn, which preserved nitrogen in the soil. Indians moved on when their fields were exhausted, giving the soil ample time to recover its nutrients.

This unconscious ecological balance was not universally achieved, of course. Primitive cultures could and did manipulate nature when it suited their purposes. But for the most part, the native American maintained himself in a symbiosis, by his tradition, his limitations, or his instinct, and thus perpetuated his own kind in a healthy manner.

The impact of Europeans on this relationship was profound and immediate. Sweeping changes in how aboriginal people affected wildlife populations began to occur as early as 1540 in the Southwest, as the Spanish forged their conqueror's path out of Mexico. Coronado apparently was the first to import livestock: 6,500 sheep and cattle from Spain to the New World. It was not only a cultural preference for domestic meat that encouraged these importations; they were also useful in converting nomadic, hunting tribes such as the Navajo to a pastoral life so that they might be more receptive to Catholicism. Sheep and cattle multiplied rapidly, devouring ancestral rangelands of the bighorn sheep, pronghorn antelope, elk, and deer. Domestic breeds often carried deadly parasites to wildlife that had never been exposed to them before.

White settlement along the East Coast did not begin to entrench itself for another eighty years or so, but brought predictable changes. Domestic herds were introduced, and forests were cleared permanently, since more wood was needed to build roads, fences, and houses, and for fuel. Trees were also girdled and burned to make space for agriculture. Despite the existence of abundant game during the first years, as many as half the settlers died of starvation only months after they arrived. Here was what Cronon calls the "paradox of want in a land of plenty," for these people had been mostly tradesmen and professionals in England, and did not know how to live off uncultivated land.

Those who survived either brought provisions to last a year or learned what to do from the Indians. At the same time, the Indians were eager to hunt meat for the settlers in exchange for glass beads, steel knives, metal pots, and wool blankets. Wildlife historian James Trefethen noted that "while it lasted, this was probably the most rewarding trading relationship in history. Each side thought it was taking advantage of the other and obtaining priceless commodities in exchange for practically nothing." The problem was that trade was not restricted to New World settlers and Indians. The North American continent had turned into a supermarket, capable of meeting all the wants of European society.

Fur trading became a prime occupation, instituted by the Dutch in the 1620s. Beaver pelts were in such high demand that by 1650 the animals had been trapped out of all streams from Maine to South Carolina. But the pursuit of wildlife for commerce was doomed from the start, for it first depleted the exploited animal populations and then bankrupted the commercial exploiter. No matter; in the early years there were so many resources to be converted into finished products that depletion of one stock was an incentive to generate markets in others. Once whites took to hunting, they typically killed more than they needed, for there was always a demand for fresh game in the burgeoning settlements. This practice of taking more than necessary and then selling it affected Indian hunting patterns as well. More people turned out to kill more animals more often.

Increasingly, habitat disappeared under the implacable assault of the westward-moving pioneers, and with it went the wildlife, retreating inland until there was no place left to go. The Eastern beavers vanished, as did Eastern wolves when predation of domestic livestock brought eradication down upon their heads. Salmon runs were blocked by dams for gristmills and sawmills. The million-winged flocks of passenger pigeons dwindled, then disappeared. The heath hen, the Labrador duck, the great auk, the Carolina paraquet, the eastern cougar, grasses, plants, wildflowers, trees . . . gone or so depleted as to border on extinction.

## BUFFALO RUN

Of all the life-forms put to the gun or driven out by a nation fulfilling its destiny, the fate of no creature so captured the imagination—and later the horror—of the country as did that of *Bison bison*—the American buffalo. In the beginning, buffalo herds had engulfed the land like a black sea, roaring and rolling in swells over the grasslands from the Canadian subarctic to as far south as central Mexico. Offshoots of the main herds spread as far west as the mountain valleys of Idaho and Montana and as far east as the banks of the Potomac. Aside from wolves, cougars, and grizzlies, the buffalo's only predators were Indians, particularly those Plains cultures that obtained their food, clothing, shelter, implements, and fuel from the herds that wandered into their territory. This required a great deal of effort

160

before the Spanish inadvertently introduced the horse in the sixteenth century. On horseback, Indians had an easier time hunting buffalo, but it was not until the white man discovered the sport that the slaughter really began.

Osborne Russell, a fur trapper who kept a journal of his life in the Rocky Mountains during the 1830s, reported the beginning of the end, and surmised that the insatiable demand for buffalo robes back East was contributing to the animal's destruction. In 1836, he noted, herds could be seen grazing almost every valley. Ten years later, Russell saw only their scattered bones, and remarked on how the wide swaths of earth that buffalo had worn bare during centuries of migration were becoming overgrown with weeds. To most people who saw them, the buffalo multitudes remained memorable for another fifty years. Herds were still large enough to feed the thousands of men laying down railroad track right through the heart of prime buffalo range. In 1867, Buffalo Bill Cody was hired by the Kansas Pacific Railway to provide fresh meat for the gandy dancers. In eighteen months he killed 4,280 animals. In a single day he slaughtered sixty-nine.

On May 10, 1869, the Central Pacific locomotive coasted to within handshaking distance of the Union Pacific's Number 119 locomotive at Promontory Point, Utah. East met West, making the country one, but cutting the last, best buffalo country in half. Now buffalo killing would begin in earnest, for the trains brought more people to the herds, which were confined to smaller and smaller ranges. Thanks to incentives created by the Civil War, ammunition for single-shot rifles such as the Remington and the Springfield, and for repeaters such as the Spencer, had been improved to the point that a hunter could get off twenty shots a minute with metallic cartridges, each packed with enough gunpowder to drop a buffalo. In less than a generation the millions of animals that had roamed Arizona, Colorado, Kansas, Oklahoma, and New Mexico had been processed into meat and hides.

Over time and under that country's blazing sun, the landscape became speckled with bright white buffalo ribs, femurs, and skulls. It made an impression, this graveyard of destiny, visible for miles and miles through the windows of the passing railroad cars—until the bones, too, were gone, picked up and sold to be ground into fertilizer. As is often the case, the engines of progress are simultaneously vehicles for resurrection as well as destruction, and the scenes to be witnessed from the passenger trains sparked enough public concern to make Congress consider the plight of the buffalo. In 1874 it passed a bill outlawing buffalo killing in the territories. President Grant, however, had been counseled by General William Tecumseh Sherman that annihilation of the buffalo was a sure way to incapacitate hostile Indian tribes who subsisted on them. Grant, an astute military logician in his own right, pocket-vetoed the bill. With the utter defeat of George Custer's troops at the hands of Sioux and Cheyenne warriors two years later, a bill for the protection of buffalo would never have a chance to pass. Killing buffalo, as well as Indians, became an act of patriotism.

## WHO OWNED THE WILDLIFE?

To its credit, Congress had at least tried to do something to save the buffalo. It is important to note, however, that it restricted its efforts to protecting the herds in the territories, since it was commonly accepted that the federal government had no business making decisions about wildlife within the states. Responsibility for wildlife at the federal level had not been expressly authorized by the Constitution, and therefore belonged to the states in which the animals were found. A Supreme Court decision reached in 1842 and written by Chief Justice Roger Taney reinforced that tradition. In *Martin v. Waddell*, a case regarding oyster-fishing rights in New Jersey, the Supreme Court ruled that "when the people of New Jersey took possession of the reins of government, and took into their own hands the powers of sovereignty, the prerogatives and regalities that belonged either to the crown or the parliament, became immediately and rightfully vested in the states." Wildlife law specialist Michael J. Bean notes that emphasis solely on this portion of Taney's ruling has always "ignored Taney's important qualifier that the powers assumed by the states were 'subject . . . to the rights since surrendered by the Constitution to the general government.' " No occasions arose on which Taney's decision could be read closely enough to consider this condition until the end of the century. Meanwhile, the doctrine of state

162

ownership of wildlife proceeded apace, while the idea of federal jurisdiction nearly shriveled up and blew away.

The states did make some progress toward establishing a framework of game management by restricting certain hunting practices. When the Revolutionary War began, twelve colonies had closed hunting seasons; in 1850 Massachusetts and New Hampshire appointed the first game wardens; in that same year Connecticut and New Jersey passed laws protecting nongame birds such as songbirds, and Iowa introduced the first bag limit of twenty-five prairie chickens per person per day. Arkansas, in 1875, was the first state to outlaw commercial hunting. By 1880 all states had game laws of one sort or another, their necessity becoming apparent as civilization advanced. But belief in the doctrine of state ownership of wildlife did not produce much in the way of effective regulation or enforcement. The position of game commissioner was often awarded to a political hack whose outstanding qualification was that he loved to hunt, out of season as well as in. Biological training for the job didn't exist, so the game commissioner's foremost concern was to ensure the rights of his fellow citizens to hunt as much as or more than the citizens of another state. Particularly where migratory waterfowl were concerned, it seemed a good state policy to set liberal bag limits, if any were set at all. This had the unwelcome effect of reducing the size of flocks continuing their migration through other states, where citizens expected to exercise comparable rights over the quarry.

After Justice Taney's decision, the test for upholding the doctrine of state ownership of wildlife did not occur until an 1896 Supreme Court ruling. A man named Geer had shot birds in Connecticut in accordance with that state's game law, but then tried to ship them out of state. The question that needed answering was whether Geer's intent to transport birds out of Connecticut interfered with Congress's power to regulate interstate commerce. Justice Edward White wrote the majority opinion and concluded that states had the right "to control and regulate the common property in game," a right to be exercised "as a trust for the benefit of the people." States could name whatever conditions were justified in taking game, and these conditions also applied after the game had been killed. White asserted that because of the "peculiar nature" of game and the state's ownership of it, it was doubtful whether interstate commerce was even created in the case. According to Michael Bean, Justice White's decision addressed the question too narrowly to rule out once and for all a federal role in wildlife matters.

Nevertheless, advocates for states took the extreme view, Bean says, that "the state ownership doctrine would render impossible the development of a body of federal wildlife law." States' rights advocates argued this way for years afterward. Still, the federal government could not stay entirely out of wildlife issues any more than it could have stayed out of commerce or agriculture, where it was deeply entrenched. In 1871 the Bureau of Fisheries was organized in the Department of Commerce to regulate ocean-based fishing operations, most taking place well beyond the borders of any state, often in international waters. And in 1885 a far-reaching bit of work was given to the Department of Agriculture, which involved the completion of a national survey of birdlife initiated by the American Ornithologists Union. The union had asked ornithologists and birdwatchers around the country to survey the birds in their locale. The response had been so great that Dr. C. Hart Merriam, chairman of the Ornithologists Union, was forced to seek government funding to complete the survey. He explained that information about birdlife would be useful to agriculture programs. On that representation, Congress appropriated $5,000 for the survey and handed the project over to the Agriculture Department, with Dr. Merriam at its head. In 1886, Dr. Merriam's organization became the Division of Economic Ornithology and Mammalogy. In 1906 it was renamed the Bureau of Biological Survey.

## SPORTSMEN TO THE RESCUE

Under constant pressure from agriculturists for "practical" information, the Bureau of Biological Survey eventually drifted away from mere survey efforts and toward more "useful" work. It conducted numerous experiments on how to destroy rodents and large predators. Its success in this undertaking was so marked that in 1917 the chief of the bureau boasted: "There is little question that in five years we can destroy most of the gray wolves and greatly reduce the numbers of other predatory animals. In New Mexico we have destroyed fifty percent of the gray wolves and expect to get the other fifty percent in the next two or three years."

Now here was federal intervention a farmer or stockman could appreciate, and as long as the government steered clear of hunting regulation, the states didn't mind the destruction either. Despite public concern over such examples as the buffalo, it was commonly accepted that the eradication of wild species was an inevitable part of the price of progress.

The only responsibility remaining, it seemed, was to catalogue and name every distinct animal form before it disappeared. This was the duty of the naturalists, and there was a sense of urgency attending their work because it was quite possible that a species could die out before a trained man could set eyes upon it. In 1875, for instance, the Labrador duck was eliminated from its territorial waters of northeastern Canada and the United States less than a year after its existence was dutifully recorded.

Ironically, the need to try to preserve wildlife was first recognized by those who most loved to kill it—the hunters. James Trefethen takes great pains to distinguish between two classes of hunters: sportsmen, who behaved honorably toward their quarry and enjoyed their interaction with nature whether they took down game or not, and market hunters, who killed for profit, using whatever means they could to bag the most game in the shortest time. This distinction is justified, although not always discernible, since many a good-hearted sportsman might kill more than he needed, certain he could dispose of it—if not profitably, then charitably. Nevertheless, few interest groups policed themselves as conscientiously as did sportsmen, for they divined that their avocation came a step closer to extinction with each species that was threatened. Conflicts between sportsmen and market hunters grew more severe as each favorite woodland or pond became gameless. Wealthy sportsmen formed groups to buy land that they alone could hunt, trying to preserve some places on the map from ambitious marketeers.

Some of the private reserves did not allow hunting of any kind, the grandest of these being the 12,000-acre Blooming Grove Park Association in Pennsylvania, created in 1871. The first state-designated sanctuary was created by the California legislature in 1870, eighteen years after a man-made lake in the city of Oakland had been expressly designed by Samuel Merritt for the protection of waterfowl. This tiny refuge attracted little public attention, and not much was done by the state to protect it. So the Merritt Lake sanctuary did not quite live up to its name.

Sportsmen, many of whom considered themselves the first conservationists, filled the void when it came to game law enforcement. The militant New York Sportsmen's Club was particularly strong in this regard. Organized in 1844, its wealthy and influential members pursued game violators on their own. Lawyers in the club sued poachers and restaurateurs who possessed game out of season. Colonial law had established the right of citizens to sue game violators, and often this was the only recourse left to official law enforcement, when state game wardens were either too scarce or too indifferent to uphold state regulations. Similarly disposed clubs sprang up in large cities, particularly after the Civil War, when hunting became leisure for the rich man rather than sustenance for the poor. The best known of these organizations was the Boone and Crockett Club, conceived by Theodore Roosevelt in 1887. The club sought to preserve large game animals and encouraged the "American hunting riflemen" to join its cause. One of Roosevelt's cofounders was George Bird Grinnell, an impressive spokesman for wildlife preservation on a national level. Grinnell was editor and publisher of *Forest and Stream* magazine, and he used it as a platform to denounce greedy hunters for their "sordid clutching after purses, gate money, entrance fees or prizes" in trophy competitions.

Grinnell, himself a hunter, was the son of a wealthy family in Brooklyn, New York. His father lost one fortune after the Civil War and made a second working for Commodore Vanderbilt. When Grinnell was eight years old, his family moved to an estate on the Hudson River near the home of John James Audubon's widow, Lucy. Under Lucy Audubon's tutelage the boy developed his love for natural subjects. One of Grinnell's fondest boyhood memories was of the passenger pigeons that flocked by the thousands near his house. By the time he was middle-aged, the pigeons were gone. The rapidity of their disappearance appalled Grinnell, who was also given to musing before two buffalo skulls that graced his hearth, thinking of the land they once commanded.

When careless readers of the magazine mistakenly sent him photographs of creatures they had shot, expecting praise for their bounty, Grinnell ran the pictures—above captions denouncing them by name for being "game hogs." He editorialized constantly for the creation of protective associations to halt the slaughter. The idea of such organizations appealed to Oliver Wendell Holmes, John Greenleaf Whittier, and other notables. It caught on quickly, and in honor of his childhood tutor, Grinnell in 1886 named the first association the Audubon Society—the first of many that spread throughout the country.

*Forest and Stream* launched attacks on every industry that abused game for profit. A favorite target was the fashion trade, which was then dictating that women wear colorful bird plumage and other bird parts in their hats. One of the magazine's first issues featured an essay by the poet Celia Thaxter, in which she attacked any woman who "goes her way, a charnel house of beaks, claws and bones and glass eyes upon her fatuous head." A major journalistic coup resulted in the passage of the Yellowstone Park Protection Act of 1894, which made it a crime to kill wildlife or remove it from the park. The act, which followed the creation of the park by twenty-two years, was the first federal law protecting wildlife and banned not only hunting, but any human activity that might upset the existence of wildlife.

Concerned by reports of epidemic poaching in the park, Grinnell had dispatched Emerson Hough, one of his top reporters, to Yellowstone to write a story on poaching. Hough's visit was fortuitous. He was on hand with a photographer the day Edgar Howell, the park's most infamous and uncaught poacher, was found skinning a buffalo. Five still-warm buffalo carcasses lay nearby. Moreover, Howell openly boasted to Hough regarding his killing exploits. Hough wrote it all up with a fine passion, and Grinnell added his own plea to readers to write their congressmen demanding some form of wildlife protection. The readers followed Grinnell's advice; within a year the Park Protection Act passed, making Yellowstone, and future parks, inviolate wildlife refuges.

In 1900 the federal government took a second step, albeit a tentative one, into the realm of wildlife regulation when Congress passed the Lacey Act. Based on congressional authority to regulate interstate commerce, the act prohibited the transportation of any wild animals or birds killed in violation of state law. Cautiously written, the act merely enlisted the aid of the federal government in enforcing state game laws. It also enhanced state prerogatives by allowing states to prohibit the export of game lawfully killed within their boundaries. This was an extension of the earlier *Geer* decision, although it differed in asserting that interstate commerce in wildlife did indeed exist. The Lacey Act authorized the Secretary of Agriculture to preserve, distribute, introduce, and restore game birds—subject, as always, to state laws.

## THE FIRST REFUGE SYSTEM

Like his longtime friend George Bird Grinnell, Theodore Roosevelt's affection for wild things was forged in childhood. As a boy of twelve his passion was taxidermy, a craft he had learned directly from the man who taught Audubon. It was not a particularly saving pursuit, but at that time the only thing that separated the scientist from the sportsman and the market hunter was what he did with the quarry's carcass. Being first a science-minded boy and second a sportsman, young Roosevelt donated his collection of "one bat, twelve mice, a turtle, the skull of a red squirrel, and four bird eggs" to the American Museum of Natural History, which his father had been instrumental in establishing. He killed and "stuffed" as much wildlife as his parents would allow. In the two months he spent floating down the Nile with his family, he shot and mounted about 200 birds—he lost count of exactly how many. The practice made him an excellent marksman.

In 1884, after the tragic deaths of his young wife and his mother within hours of each other, the twenty-five-year old lit out for the frontier. A Winchester rifle and a "very enduring and very hardy" horse named Manitou were his constant companions; with them he dropped his first buffalo, numerous antelope, bighorn sheep, and bear, including a few grizzlies. After months of riding and tracking game, Roosevelt headed for the Badlands, where he bought some land and cattle and became a rancher. The experience nearly bankrupted him, but it left him with a deep understanding of how easily land could be abused—including his own. He returned home in 1887 to "do something in a public, and political way." In the public way he helped found the Boone and Crockett Club, for he had come to realize that preserving big game was a challenge as great as stalking it. Subsequently he made his political way and became Vice-President and finally President of the United States, after William McKinley's assassination in 1901.

Two years later, Roosevelt created the first federal wildlife refuge. The American Ornithologists Union had been trying to acquire 3.5-acre Pelican Island off the coast of Florida to protect egrets, herons, and brown pelicans from plume hunters. The island, dense with black mangroves, was a nesting place for about five thousand birds. When the Ornithologists Union discovered that the island was federal property, it quickly requested federal protection by Roosevelt.

The President had little or no precedent to go by, but George Bird Grinnell urged him to invoke the 1891 Forest Reserve Act, citing the mangrove thickets on the island as qualifying forest. This was a dubious notion at best, but there was little visible opposition to the idea, and Roosevelt seized it and declared the island a forest reserve, with a special emphasis on the protection of the birds upon it.

Roosevelt's action bestirred Audubon Societies all over the country to locate other plots on federal lands appropriate for bird sanctuaries. But such sanctuaries, once created, did not receive any federal appropriations, although the Bureau of Biological Survey was instructed to care for them. Audubon Society members were often caretakers, or else they paid refuge guardians from their own funds. The word "refuge" was interpreted strictly, and areas so designated often were fenced off and posted with signs to ward off human trespassers. Consciously, the Audubon Society's measures were meant to exclude hunting. Subconsciously, they recognized the importance of habitat left in its natural state. Congress opened other possibilities for the refuge idea with passage of the Antiquities Act of 1906, reaffirming the Executive authority to withdraw lands for various purposes. Later that same year, Congress also declared it illegal to disturb birds on any federal lands "set aside as breeding grounds for birds by law, proclamation, or Executive Order."

Through such means, Roosevelt created fifty-one refuges before leaving office in 1909—the foundation of our present system. And not all of them were for birds. By the time Roosevelt became President, only twenty-three American buffalo remained in the wild, and these had been isolated in Yellowstone National Park. In 1904 the Boone and Crockett Club and the New York Zoological Society launched a joint restoration effort. First they chose 59,000 acres of native grasslands in the Wichita National Forest Reserve in Oklahoma and then persuaded Congress to reserve the area for buffalo breeding. The New York Zoological Society gave the government fifteen of its thirty-two captive animals in exchange for the government's promise to fence the area against predation and poaching. On January 24, 1905, Roosevelt signed into law a bill establishing the Wichita National Forest Reserve "for the protection of game animals and birds" and to be "recognized as a breeding place thereof." In reinforced cattle cars the buffalo arrived from the East.

The creation of the Wichita reserve inspired the formation of the American Bison Society, headed by William Temple Hornaday, a big-game hunter who had recanted his avocation and had turned virulently antihunting. Hornaday became prominent in 1896 when he was made head of the New York Zoological Society and helped to create one of the world's leading zoological parks. Many of Hornaday's views were controversial; while he denounced killing most animals for any reason, he excluded from his concern "noxious predatory animals" such as bears, mountain lions, wolves, and coyotes. He also listed "several species of birds that may at once be put under the sentence of death for their destructiveness of useful birds." Yet his commitment to bison was deep and abiding.

The American Bison Society scored its first victory in 1908, when Congress established the National Bison Range on the Flathead Indian Reservation in Montana. Through public subscription the society raised $10,000 to purchase thirty-four buffalo from private owners. Its efforts were so successful that eventually the American Bison Society disbanded, its job finished.

## JUSTICE HOLMES TAKES A HAND

The system was established by 1909, but wildlife was still in trouble. While the creation of refuges for plumed birds and the passage of the Lacey Act slowed the flow of supplies to milliners, populations of migratory waterfowl continued to decline sharply. Breeding grounds were plowed under for farm fields, and wetlands were absorbed by growing cities. Spring shooting, still legal in most states, devastated flocks, as did each state's insistence that its hunters be allowed to take all of the state's allotment of birds as the flocks passed through. The idea of protecting live birds seemed, even to the most avid of wildlife conservationists, too far removed from Congress's authority to regulate interstate commerce. Senator Elihu Root, who had served as President Roosevelt's Secretary of State and was a Nobel Laureate, at last devised an ingenious approach. He introduced a resolution authorizing the President of the United States to seek international agreements for the protection of migratory birds. Slowed by World War I, the agreements between the United States and Great Britain on behalf of Canada were finally ratified in 1916. Under the conditions of the migratory bird treaty, the United States had to uphold its end by protecting birds as long as they resided in U.S. territory.

States' rights advocates viewed the treaty as a ploy by the federal government to interfere with state wildlife regulation, and decided to test the pact's constitutionality. They lost. In a landmark case, *Missouri v. Holland,* Supreme Court Justice Oliver Wendell Holmes rendered this decision:

But for the treaty and the statute, there soon might be no birds for any powers to deal with. We see nothing in the Constitution that compels the government to sit by while a food supply is being cut off and the protectors of our forests and crops are destroyed. It is not sufficient to rely upon the States. The reliance is in vain, and were it otherwise, the question is whether the United States is forbidden to act. We are of the opinion that the treaty and statute must be upheld.

The Supreme Court having spoken, the Bureau of Biological Survey and its Canadian counterpart wrote regulations that restricted most of the destructive uses of migratory birds. The sale of game birds covered by the treaty was prohibited, spring shooting and night shooting were outlawed, and bag limits were reduced. Certain species, such as wood ducks and trumpeter swans, were off limits to all hunters, and the use of weapons of mass destruction was abolished. Considering all the opposition that had been mounted over the years against federal regulation of wildlife, all states eventually accepted the migratory bird treaty enthusiastically, promulgating their own regulations to toughen control.

As more was learned about flight patterns and nesting preferences of birds, treaties protecting other species were drawn between the United States and Mexico, Japan, and the Soviet Union. The vast territorial requirements of many birds dictated a global approach to their protection. Recognition of this fact was humbling, for wild things had long been considered the exclusive property of American states. Significantly, it was becoming more apparent that wildlife was not merely a special form of property, but an integral part of all life.

The conscientious enforcement of treaty restrictions on hunting and marketing dramatically increased migratory bird populations at the same time that habitat was disappearing at an alarming rate. More birds had fewer places to rest on their tiring north-south journey. This dilemma concerned visionaries among the game managers, who suspected that if the trend continued, the United States would not be able to uphold its end of the 1916 treaty with Great Britian. Most of the migratory bird refuges were in the West, where they had been carved out of public land. Unprotected was most of the Midwest, where wetlands and potholes had fallen into private hands and were being drained as quickly as possible for agricultural development. Birds would not deviate from their flyway patterns, so more refuges had to be created along the natural migration routes. This meant land would have to be bought, which seemed an unlikely prospect.

But as early as 1924, pressure from hunting groups and nonhunting groups alike finally persuaded Congress to appropriate $1.5 million to buy a ribbon of land along the Mississippi River—in all, 194,000 acres in four states were purchased to create the Upper Mississippi Wildlife and Fish Refuge, a 284-mile strip of riparian habitat. Much to the displeasure of the antihunting faction, however, this refuge allowed hunting; in fact, it was lauded as the first "public shooting ground." The accommodation of hunters seemed unavoidable. It spelled the difference between saving a key habitat and exploiting it for other purposes. As the need for more refuges along the Central and Mississippi flyways became apparent, Congress passed the Migratory Bird Conservation Act in 1929, which established a commission of Cabinet

172

members and congressional representatives to review and approve acquisitions of additional refuge lands. Unlike the Upper Mississippi project, these refuges were to be managed as "inviolate sanctuaries." All this was well and good except for the act's chief shortcoming: while it authorized the appropriation of funds necessary to buy the desperately needed lands, it did not specify *which* lands, and the early Depression years did not encourage Congress to hand money out. As a result, no new refuges were bought and the waterfowl situation deteriorated until the number of ducks in the fall migration sank to about 30 million from a previous population of 120 million.

## THE DARLING YEARS

With the coming of the first administration of Franklin D. Roosevelt and that patched-together system of emergency measures called the New Deal, the situation slowly began to change. These were the Dust Bowl years, when winds blew the fine grit of Kansas to Wall Street, and dust in Manhattan was so thick at times that cars drove with headlights on at noon. As bad as these years were for Americans everywhere, the peril they also posed for waterfowl could not be ignored. Under New Deal soil conservation programs and massive efforts to plant vegetation that would buffer wind and hold what topsoil remained, small mammals and insect-eating birds were enjoying a recovery. But refuges for waterfowl were still sorely lacking. In 1934, Roosevelt convened a committee to determine what to do about this. The committee consisted of wildlife biologist Aldo Leopold, magazine publisher Thomas Beck, and Pulitzer Prize–winning cartoonist J. N. "Ding" Darling, whose drawings in the *Des Moines Register* frequently pilloried the shortcomings of Roosevelt's wildlife policies. The committee discovered that about $50 million in new refuges was needed to save the waterfowl. The committee wielded considerable influence, and its recommendation that money be spent immediately reawakened an idea that had lain dormant for more than ten years. The idea was to require waterfowl hunters to buy a "duck stamp" each year, in much the same way Americans had been encouraged to purchase war savings stamps after World War I. Proceeds from stamp sales would be used to buy lands for refuges, thereby relieving Congress of the responsibility to appropriate funds for land purchases every year. The

173

Duck Stamp Act passed in 1934, although it was not to go into effect until 1935. In exchange for the right to hunt on non-refuge lands, hunters would pay one dollar for the stamp (the first one of which was illustrated by Darling himself). Proceeds would be used to purchase new refuge lands authorized in the 1929 Migratory Bird Act.

Hunters backed the stamp act because they believed the protected habitats would produce surplus game, and this would spill into adjacent shooting areas. (In practice this did not always happen, since many species develop an acute sense of what is safe habitat and what is not.) One of the far-reaching consequences of the Duck Stamp Act was that it encouraged hunters' support for refuges but did not similarly encourage nonhunter support. Since money talks—and loudly—nonhunters seldom had an equal say in the formation of refuge management policy.

Meanwhile, Roosevelt made the startling appointment of Darling as head of the Bureau of Biological Survey. It was a shrewd way of telling Darling that since he complained so much about the government's wildlife programs, he ought to do something constructive about them. Reluctantly, Darling accepted the challenge. "Darling was an extreme extrovert," one of his coworkers on the *Register* recalled. He was "awed by nobody, overflowing with self-confidence." With such leadership characteristics the bureau gained as powerful and able a director as the Park Service and Forest Service had first had. For the first time in the bureau's lusterless history it was devoted to refuge matters, and its director was committed to the bureau's own particular cause.

Darling, "a kind of visual Will Rogers," according to author Stephen Fox in *John Muir and His Legacy*, grew up in Iowa. He claimed his hobbies were "Roquefort cheese, dairy farming, rock gardening, black bass fishing, ornithology and duck shooting." Despite his passion for the last of these, he had been a close ally of Hornaday's in the 1920s. At one point conservationists accused Darling of knowing "nothing but ducks, if indeed he knows them," but he was a tireless advocate for more waterfowl refuges. Having served on the Leopold Committee, he knew he needed money before the Duck Stamp revenue would start flowing, so he took to the halls of the Agriculture Department, demanding funds to begin his purchases. By his own admission he used "a straw to suck funds from the other fellow's barrel," and explained to those he pressured that "ducks can't lay eggs on a picket fence."

His persistence paid off, for within a few months he had amassed $8.5 million for wildlife from drought relief funds, land retirement funds, and Work Projects Administration funds. Roosevelt teasingly accused Darling of robbing the U.S. Treasury—and getting away with it. He added that "the Federal Courts say that the United States Government has a perfect right to condemn millions of acres for the welfare, health and happiness of ducks, geese, sandpipers, owls and wrens, but has no constitutional right to condemn a few old tenements in the slums for the health and happiness of the little boys and girls who will be our citizens of the next generation! Nevertheless, more power to your arm!"

With the WPA money, Darling planned to buy worn-out agricultural land for wildlife habitat. The only problem was that all the WPA money he had sucked out with a straw had to be spent by April 1, 1935, which was less than a year away. To find suitable lands, Darling hired a young wildlife biologist named J. Clark Salyer, with whom he had worked on the Iowa State Conservation Commission. In his book, *Sign of the Flying Goose*, George Laycock describes how Salyer, determined to do more for waterfowl than anybody had ever done, crisscrossed the country for months in a battered black Pontiac that was also his home, office, and laboratory. He located 600,000 acres of new refuge lands, but as his March 31 deadline drew nigh, he was horrified to realize that he had committed—without authorization from Agriculture Secretary Henry Wallace—all but $250,000 of the millions of WPA dollars. Salyer drove back to Washington like a maniac, only to discover that the deadline for Wallace's authorization fell on a Sunday, and Wallace could not be reached until Monday. Seeing all his work inching closer to utter ruin, Salyer signed the authorizations for Wallace. "I could have gone to prison," Salyer recalled later. But he did not. Wallace heard Salyer's confession, then sent him back to his refuge-buying work.

With the joint effort of Darling and Salyer, refuges began to evolve into a respectable system. Salyer's time on the road led to the creation of fifty-five new refuges, and he was instrumental in the establishment

of some of the system's most impressive units: the Red Rock Lakes
Refuge for trumpeter swans in Montana, the Agassiz Refuge in Minnesota for the largest moose population in the lower forty-eight states,
and the Upper Souris Refuge in North Dakota, where great blue herons
and black-crowned night herons nested by the hundreds. As he had
promised from the outset, Darling stayed with the Biological Survey
less than two years. He was angered by the administration's refusal
to accept a $10 million endowment for wildlife protection in ex-
change for a repeal of the existing 10-percent excise tax on guns and
ammunition. "I know of no other way to accomplish the necessary
reversal from downhill slide to upward climb for wildlife resources,"
he said. In September 1935, Darling wrote to Wallace that "it now
seems the strategic moment to demand my resignation for insubordination, murder, incest and the good of the service." He left to head
the National Wildlife Federation and was replaced by Ira Gabrielson,
a biologist with the bureau since 1915.

COORDINATION, CONSOLIDATION, CONFLICT
While the Biological Survey pursued its goals, Congress was beginning to interject itself into questions of animal welfare. In 1934 it
passed the Fish and Wildlife Coordination Act, which required public
works administrators to assess the impact on wildlife of such projects
as dam-building and reclamation. In practice the requirement was
feebly met, since the only mandatory provisions were consultation
with the Bureau of Fisheries and impoundment of some water for fish
culture and migratory-bird resting sites. The consultation concentrated on whether fish ladders were necessary and "economically
practicable," narrowing the focus of fish and wildlife welfare measures
to less than meaningful assistance. A series of increasingly stringent
Endangered Species acts would have to be passed years later to make
up for the Coordination Act's shortcomings. Another important boost
for wildlife was the passage of the Pittman-Robertson Act of 1937,
which gave the states funds to establish their own refuges, and perpetuated the two-tiered approach to wildlife management. All told,
New Deal land conservation programs resulted in "the greatest up-
surge of the wildlife populations the nation had ever seen," historian
James Trefethen asserts.

Matters appeared to improve still more with the Reorganization Act of 1939, when the Bureau of Fisheries in the Department of Commerce and the Bureau of Biological Survey in the Department of Agriculture were consolidated into a single agency and transferred to the Department of the Interior. The new agency was called the United States Fish and Wildlife Service, and refuge administration was made one of its primary responsibilities. But the consolidation did not strengthen the position of refuges as was hoped. A new ethic evolved in which refuges were manipulated to yield more game species, often at the expense of other species. This overt favoritism led in 1949 to a Faustian bargain: Fish and Wildlife Service officials lobbied to raise the price of the Duck Stamp from one dollar to two, promising to open 25 percent of each refuge to hunting and later, in exchange for a three-dollar stamp, to open 40 percent to hunting. The policy, developed within the Service, signified a major turning point in the philosophy of the refuge concept.

Neither World War II nor the Truman and Eisenhower administrations that followed were strong on conservation measures. During the Eisenhower years, car dealer Douglas McKay was Interior Secretary, and morale at the Fish and Wildlife Service sank especially low. Among other things, McKay wanted to open refuges to oil and gas drilling to make them more economically attractive, and issued sixty-four permits for this work in three years. He often sided against his own agency in conflicts about the use of refuge lands. Cabeza Prieta Game Range in Arizona, for instance, a refuge for desert bighorn sheep, had been used during World War II for pilot and weapons testing. Fair enough, given wartime necessities—but when the war was over, the Air Force wanted to continue using it. McKay saw nothing wrong with this idea and promptly approved it, an act that appalled the Service.

In 1956, under a new Interior Secretary, the Service mutated again. Its name was changed to the Bureau of Sport Fisheries and Wildlife, and responsibility for commercial fishing was vested in the Bureau of Commercial Fishing. The two agencies were given equal billing *within* a third entity called the Fish and Wildlife Service, which many conservationists felt diluted the federal commitment to wildlife preservation. Meanwhile, the Bureau of Sport Fisheries and Wildlife

177

would have more aptly been named the Bureau of Sport Fisheries and *Sport* Wildlife, since emphasis in the refuges was definitely on increasing popular game species. A refuge's success was often measured by the number of huntable animals it hosted, an emphasis that sometimes produced unhappy consequences.

As a result of this policy, the number of huntable Canada geese at Horicon Marsh in Wisconsin, for example, grew from 2,000 in 1948 to about 208,000 in 1975. Through a vigorous program of artificial planting, the refuge had attracted most of the geese in the Mississippi Flyway, not only depriving other refuges in other states of their fair share, but creating tenement conditions at Horicon. Other waterfowl were driven out, and without enough food on the refuge to support the new population, flocks of geese dined in the grainfields of neighboring farms, stripping them bare. Only by adjusting Horicon's food and habitat could refuge managers force many geese farther south. The Horicon situation was a by-product of the circle in which refuge administration had been traveling, at least at the upper levels of management. (Many local managers sturdily fought the trend, to little avail.) Political support for the refuge system was strongest among hunters and fishermen; the system's primary concern was to produce the species these supporters preferred. Economic development via hunting was the chief measure of progress, and, while refuge officials were willing to go to bat against other economic developments such as logging or grazing, they would usually only do so for the benefit of hunters.

## A FLOCK OF LEGISLATION

Ironically, while the Fish and Wildlife Service during these early years (and later) never produced a nationally known leader to plead its cause or enhance its image—another Stephen Mather or Gifford Pinchot, say—it did, deep within its institutional structure, harbor perhaps the most influential environmentalist of the twentieth century. Her name was Rachel Carson, and she worked as an editor for the Service during the 1940s, becoming the first woman in the agency to hold a nonclerical position. Carson, who was born in 1907, was a writer and biologist who combined her talents exceedingly well. One of her chores at the Service was the production of a series of booklets under the general title "Conservation in Action," each of which examined the natural wildlife and habitat of a single refuge, and each of which was unabashedly devoted to the promotion of an ecological conscience. That interest and conviction, fostered and supported during her years with the Service, came to its fullest expression, of course, in her own 1962 book, *Silent Spring*—which many have called the single most important conservation manifesto since George Perkins Marsh's *Man and Nature* in 1867.

The alert raised by *Silent Spring* began a period in which ecological concern blossomed. Congress enlarged upon the federal role in environmental protection, passing legislation that mandated the cleanup of the country's air and water, recognized the value of wilderness, and expressed the intent that all species—birds, fish, reptiles, or mammals—would endure. This new national consciousness also held the promise of better days for the National Wildlife Refuge System. But hope and good intentions were consistently undermined by a combination of structural inadequacies within the Fish and Wildlife Service, a tortuous confusion of national priorities and public policy, and, in recent years, the influence of a presidential administration that often demonstrated either indifference or open antagonism toward the purposes for which the refuges were established.

To begin with, repeated legislative efforts designed to fix agreement on central issues turned out to dodge them neatly instead, resulting in many laws but little guidance. Preceding the publication of *Silent Spring* by one year was the Wetlands Loan Act, passed by Congress to speed acquisition of wetlands for the refuge system. The act authorized an advance appropriation of up to $105 million (later increased to $200 million) to buy essential wetlands over a seven-year period. (To encourage nonhunters to buy stamps also, the name of the Duck Stamp was ultimately changed to the Migratory Bird Hunting and Conservation Stamp.) Amazingly, the Wetlands Loan Act, given the interest-free use of money to buy land and have done with it in seven years, nevertheless has yet to reach the goal set twenty-four years ago. Only about half the land targeted for purchase has been acquired, while many acres have been lost to commercial development. Since it was the responsibility of the Fish and Wildlife Service to find the land and request the funding already authorized, it is obvious that other jobs rated a higher priority.

Another act designed to strengthen the refuge concept was the

Refuge Recreation Act, passed in 1962. The act stated that refuges were places of public recreation, so long as such activity was consistent with wildlife objectives. Out of this act arose the "dominant use" doctrine of the refuges. But the act's stipulations have not been clear enough to prevent types of recreation detrimental to wildlife. At the Ruby Lake Refuge in Nevada, for instance, the seven-thousand-acre lake had become a haven for some thirty thousand motorboats a year, with an alarming impact on the nesting sites of canvasback and redhead ducks, before a lawsuit resulted in court-ordered restrictions. In 1964 the passage of the Wilderness Act brought hope of a slight measure of relief, since it provided the means to gain an extra layer of protection for the small percentage of refuges qualifying for wilderness status. But the Wilderness Act is the only congressional guarantee that a fraction of refuge lands will be kept sacrosanct. Without it, technically any Interior Secretary could, if he or she wished, subject refuge lands to potentially degrading uses deemed "compatible" with the refuge purpose.

Refuges received another bit of ambiguous assistance when the Land and Water Conservation Fund Act was passed in 1964—but with a "catch." For the first twelve years the Service spent no LWCF money on new refuge lands because Congress insisted that the money be used for "incidental recreation purposes," which it defined as building something. Refuges left in an undeveloped condition did not qualify, and rather than turn them into parks, the Service accepted no money for their acquisition. Subsequent legislation made it clear that the agency could buy more refuge lands without altering them to attract recreationists, and the Fish and Wildlife Service finally spent more than half its allotment on the acquisition of lands for the protection of endangered and threatened species.

Another prime example of illogic in action is the fact that the internal organization of the Fish and Wildlife Service inevitably engenders conflicts between its refuge branch and its endangered species branch. Since 1966, when Congress passed the first Endangered Species Preservation Act, the two branches have been competing for funds. The problem that arises again and again is that the Service's duty to administer the act often usurps its commitment to the overall management of the refuge system, which does not seem quite as

180

urgent as protection of species on the verge of extinction. Yet it is obvious that the way to shorten the endangered species list is to protect species long before they are listed.

The Endangered Species Act, revised four times, was the basis for the National Wildlife Refuge System Administration Act of 1966—which may, on the face of it, sound like a much-needed organic act for the system, but is not. It provides only broad statutory guidance, while failing to define the basic purposes of the system or establish clear, strong measures for protection. In actuality, the Administration Act merely brought all types of wildlife areas and game ranges under one overreaching and weakly supported roof. Trouble arose because of the act's vagueness on how the lands were to be managed. Areas known as game ranges, for example, were managed jointly by the Bureau of Land Management and the Fish and Wildlife Service. The potential conflict inherent in such joint management was problem enough, but many conservationists were stunned when, in 1975, the Interior Secretary transferred three game ranges entirely over to the BLM. This was a precedent that conservationists did not like because it seemed impossible for the BLM, with its multiple-use mandate, to put the welfare of wildlife above all else. There was also the possibility that the Secretary could change other refuges into game ranges and take them out of Fish and Wildlife Service protection in the future. The Wilderness Society filed suit in the U.S. District Court for the District of Columbia to stop the transfer, and in *The Wilderness Society v. Hathaway*, the court ruled in The Society's favor, on the grounds that "The Secretary is required to exercise his discretion and authority with respect to the administration of game ranges and wildlife refuges through the Fish and Wildlife Service." In other words, the distinction between game ranges and wildlife refuges was artificial, and in either case lands should be managed primarily for wildlife. That decision was also adopted as a 1976 amendment to the Administration Act, and, as a result, all units are now consolidated under the Fish and Wildlife Service alone.

## THE WATT INTERLUDE

There are still "windows of vulnerability" in the Refuge Administration Act. It grants broad discretionary authority to the Interior Secretary to "permit the use of any area within the System for any purpose, including, but not limited to hunting, fishing, public recreation and accommodations, and access whenever he determines that such use is compatible with the major purposes for which such areas were established." Although standards of compatibility did not and still do not exist, many felt that the Secretary's freedom of movement was of no real concern. As Service Director Lynn Greenwalt explained in 1978, "The process which must be followed by the Secretary to permit the use of federally owned oil and gas resources in refuges is sufficiently rigorous and subject to public scrutiny to assure that no real hazard to fish or wildlife will result." And so it seemed—until 1981. Shortly after President Reagan appointed James Watt as Secretary of the Interior, Watt asked that all refuge managers identify potential commercial operations on their lands.

"After this request was summarily ignored, a second one was issued on July 27, 1982, calling the response to the first one 'unsatisfactory,' " say Nathaniel P. Reed and Dennis Drabell in *The Fish and Wildlife Service,* a recent analysis of the agency. The second time around, some suggestions were made, resulting in a memo from the director of the Service, saying he hoped to increase commercial receipts from $6 million to $8 million a year. The increase seemed insignificant, considering the extra strain it would create. "Moreover," claim Reed and Drabell, "such revenues do not benefit the refuges themselves but are used to make payments to states and local communities for the deletion of refuge lands from their tax rolls." Watt also attempted to accelerate oil and gas leasing on the refuges, using his discretionary power under the act. This power was vigorously exercised by the development-minded Watt—to the point that he tried to give away a portion of the Alaska Maritime National Wildlife Refuge in a swap for other land interests. About four thousand acres of St. Matthew Island, the site of one of the largest seabird nesting populations in North America, and one of the few known nesting grounds for McKay's bunting, was destined by this scheme to be turned over to the Atlantic Richfield Company for an airfield, seaport, and support base for their oil and gas exploration and development operations. The fact that the island was a refuge and a designated wilderness area did not stop the land exchange—although an Alaska district court decision succeeded in doing so in December 1984, by declaring Watt's act a "misapplication of the law."

Structural weakness is also the cause of another situation that has been controversial for more than ten years involving the management of Matagorda Island, off the Gulf Coast of Texas. The 50,000-acre barrier island was partly owned by the Army Corps of Engineers until 1971 and used for Air Force target practice. Since 1971, it has been divided into three parts: the southern tip is in private hands; the northern portion is divided between the state of Texas's wetlands and the United States' higher lands on the Gulf side. The Fish and Wildlife Service has managed its portion as a part of the Aransas National Wildlife Refuge, through a permanent agreement with the Air Force. The Service had tried to acquire the state-owned wetlands, since these are the most critical habitat for the refuge's whooping cranes, seven other endangered species, and thousands of migratory birds. At the same time, Texas wanted the federal land for a park. Until 1981, neither side could acquire the portion it wanted. Then Secretary Watt reversed the policies of his four predecessors and proposed to transfer the entire federal portion to Texas. To the National Audubon Society the transfer looked like the end of protected wetlands in the area, and it threatened to sue to stop the transfer. After negotiations among officials of the Audubon Society, Texas, and the Interior Department, an elaborate compromise was struck whereby management of wildlife would be shared by state and federal authorities. To some, the compromise still looks as though the Fish and Wildlife Service surrendered its authority, and the entire matter illustrates that there is not enough guidance in wildlife refuge law if ad hoc measures must be used.

## THE CONUNDRUM OF COMPATIBILITY

While administrative anomalies and policy confusions are legion throughout the system, in some areas *people* pose the biggest problem. Refuges record more than 30 million visits a year; spread out over the entire system, this might not seem like much. But nearly 80 percent of visitation takes place on only forty of the existing 424 refuges. Chincoteague National Wildlife Refuge in Maryland and Virginia, for example, receives about one million visitors a year, while Bear River Migratory Bird Refuge in northern Utah (before floods destroyed it in 1983 and 1984) rarely saw more than 25,000.

And where crowds are a problem, they are a *large* problem. Until off-road access was barred and a permit system established at Back Bay National Wildlife Refuge in Virginia, proper administration of the refuge had reached the point of impossibility, according to Dennis Holland, refuge manager at the time. "In the summertime the [refuge] was packed with people pouring onto the beach. In that first north mile of beach, we had swimming, surfing, fishing, sunbathing, plus a constant flow of bumper-to-bumper traffic. With all of these uses and children wading in the water and running up and down the beach, it was just a frightening experience to feel that I had the responsibility for their safety," said Holland. "And my conservation upbringing to that point told me that this was a refuge and, by golly, you're not supposed to be doing all these things. . . . We were not wild-life enforcement officers, hell, we were city policemen. That's all we did. . . . It was something that we just weren't prepared to handle."

Nonhunters still have trouble understanding that hunting is permitted on more than half the refuges. The Fish and Wildlife Service justifiably argues that it manages wildlife populations, not individual animals. Hunting has replaced natural predation on many refuges, and to have neither could lead to habitat destruction and populations too large to be supported on the ground allotted. "Nature habitually maintains a wide margin of overproduction," explains wildlife biologist Durwood Allen. "She kills off a huge surplus of animals whether we take our harvest or not." The Fish and Wildlife Service does not merely tolerate hunting seasons as a way to limit animal numbers, but views the sport as "an acceptable, traditional and legitimate form of wildlife-oriented recreation." If hunting is considered on other than moral grounds, it must be recognized that "since the development of modern wildlife management in the 1930s, no American wildlife has been exterminated by sport hunting," according to a conclusion reached by the U.S. Council on Environmental Quality in 1974. Nor has hunting caused any species to be placed on the endangered list for North America. Finally, hunting is permitted only on refuges where, in the words of the *Refuge Manual*, "it contributes to, or

184

is not incompatible with the management objectives of the refuge."

Compatibility is the key word here, for incompatibility means, more often than not, that genuine harm is being done, and by more than hunting. Threats to a refuge's integrity are posed by a number of allowable uses, such as haying, grazing, timber-cutting, farming, oil and gas leasing, and—on claims established before an area was given refuge status—mining. Poorly administered, these uses pose real threats that are exacerbated by air pollution, urban sprawl, and land reclamation. This is perhaps most dramatically illustrated by the fate of the Kesterson National Wildlife Refuge in California's San Joaquin Valley, where the dumping of chemical-laden agricultural waste water has killed thousands of birds and aquatic creatures and deformed and aborted thousands more—conditions so brutal that refuge personnel have taken to wearing protective masks and clothing and now discourage birds from taking refuge in the refuge by shooting off loud "popguns" to frighten them away.

Kesterson is significant mainly in the degree of harm done there; the potential for harm exists to a greater or lesser degree on many other refuges. The Fish and Wildlife Service knows this. In 1981 it was ordered to investigate threats and conflicts facing the system. The agency's August 1982 draft report listed 7,717 internal and external threats facing the system. "These threats," the report warned, "will continue to degrade certain fish and wildlife resources until such time as mitigation measures are implemented. In some cases, this degradation or loss of resource is irreversible. It represents a sacrifice by a public that, for the most part, is unaware that such a price is being paid."

## AN ADMINISTRATIVE NO-MAN'S-LAND

It is sad and ironic that all the newspaper and television coverage of the dreadful state of affairs at Kesterson marks one of the few times when the National Wildlife Refuge System or any of its parts have been brought to the national consciousness. For all its scope, for all its impressive and saving accomplishments, the National Wildlife Refuge System is largely a stranger to the general public. Lynn Greenwalt, once director of the Fish and Wildlife Service, painfully noticed this while reviewing public comments of a refuge task force report, months in the making. "If there is any part of this very productive exercise about which I am disappointed," wrote Greenwalt at the conclusion of the task force's recommendations, "it is in the sense that there was so little broad public reaction." More than two thousand responses were received, which sounds acceptable until one recalls the enormous public input triggered by the preparation a few years ago of Yosemite National Park's master plan; more than sixty thousand people involved themselves in planning the future of this single park.

Wildlife biologist Robert Giles, who has worked closely with refuges, calls the system "the most underdeveloped public wildlife resource in the nation." It is, he wrote, "an administrative no-man's-land—a prime example of how failure to consolidate a system and to provide consistent leadership can prevent a system from achieving its potential." In addition, "the Fish and Wildlife Service has tended to treat refuges as unwanted responsibilities rather than build them into a land management agency fully as productive of public benefits as the national forests and national parks."

Giles, like many critics of the refuge system, is particularly distressed by the Fish and Wildlife Service itself, which author John Mitchell has observed "pays peculiar inattention to image and panache." The administration of the refuge system, considered the backbone of the entire service, bears no resemblance to forest, park, and National Resource Land counterparts, where whole agencies devote themselves to the lands that are their foundation. Refuge administration lies buried beneath bureaucratic sediments within the Fish and Wildlife Service, and has no direct link to the Interior Secretary, as does the park system. Until 1984 there was not even a line on the national budget revealing how much money was spent on refuges. The number, now extractable, is small: for fiscal 1984 the nation spent $90 million for on-site care of the whole system, or roughly one dollar an acre. By comparison, national park operations approach $600 million out of a $1 billion budget. The Fish and Wildlife Service employs 5,200 people, 1,500 of whom work on refuges—or are supposed to work on refuges. An informal survey taken by an agency administrator in 1984 revealed that only about 960 people were actually stationed on the refuges, despite the fact that more had been authorized. Many refuges do not even have on-site managers, but are managed as a group. Some refuges are one-man operations, while others might have a staff of six.

The Fish and Wildlife Service has much to occupy it besides refuges. It runs the national fish hatcheries, conducts law-enforcement programs, administers the Endangered Species Act along with more than 150 other acts of Congress (or portions of them), oversees animal damage control, conducts wildlife research, manages migratory birds in association with international treaties, evaluates the impacts of public works projects on wildlife, administers grant programs for state wildlife agencies, and provides technical assistance on wildlife matters to nearly anyone who asks for it. Refuges themselves are considered a function, not a program, explain Reed and Drabell. Refuges are not viewed as ends in themselves, "but means to achieving programmatic goals, such as restoring endangered ecosystems and species, perpetuating birds, preserving diverse ecosystems and providing wildlife-oriented recreation."

All of this makes it difficult to attract a broad, loyal constituency. As a result, the system's growth has been called opportunistic rather than planned, expanding where it could rather than where it should. Considering the concentration of refuges in some parts of the country and their notable scarcity in others, considering their emphasis on birds rather than all creatures, considering the seemingly contradictory allowance for hunting, and considering the system's bureaucratic fragmentation, the National Wildlife Refuge System brings to mind Voltaire's eighteenth-century evaluation of the Holy Roman Empire as being neither holy nor Roman nor an empire.

Amid such confusion, it might be well to recall the simpler vision expressed by a prestigious committee on wildlife refuges in 1969. The committee, headed by A. Starker Leopold, a zoology professor and son of Aldo Leopold, wrote in its report that the National Wildlife Refuge System ought to be viewed in the "old-fashioned sense of a bit of natural landscape where the full spectrum of native wildlife may find food, shelter, protection and a home. . . . It should be a 'wildlife display' in the most comprehensive sense." And finally, the committee issued a strong "plea for naturalism," where wildlife ecology holds sway over agricultural engineering and other high-tech

187

advances that raise man's estimation of his own cleverness but do little or nothing for the creatures he has, this once, stooped to serve.

## AN AGENDA FOR THE NATIONAL WILDLIFE REFUGES

Any rational system of planning for the future of the National Wildlife Refuge System must first assume the necessity of dealing not merely with the near future, or even with the next few decades; we must plan in terms of entire lifetimes. The stakes are as high here as in any other environmental issue, for in the face of increasing habitat loss and environmental degradation, refuges stand alone as the only federal lands devoted chiefly to preserving and enhancing wildlife and wildlife habitats. The refuge system represents every major biome in the country. It includes thousands of plant, animal, and insect species, among them 600 species of birds, 220 species of mammals, and 63 federally listed endangered species.

The proper mission of the refuge system is perhaps best stated in the current *Refuge Manual* issued by the Fish and Wildlife Service. That mission is, the manual states, "to provide, preserve, restore, and manage a national network of lands and waters sufficient in size, diversity, and location to meet society's needs for areas where the widest possible spectrum of benefits associated with wildlife and wildlands is enhanced and made available." More specifically, the various goals and objectives of this diverse land management system are:

1. to preserve, restore, and enhance in their natural ecosystems all species of animals and plants that are threatened or endangered

2. to perpetuate the migratory bird resource for the benefit of people

3. to preserve natural diversity and abundance of mammals and nonmigratory birds

4. to provide an understanding and appreciation of fish and wildlife ecology and man's proper role in his environment

5. to provide high-quality recreational experiences oriented toward wildlife

188

As "Islands of Life" makes clear, the implementation of the mission for the National Wildlife Refuge System is seriously hampered on a number of levels. As an entity within the Fish and Wildlife Service, its management priorities are confused by the lack of a clear bureaucratic identity and self-sufficiency. Federal funding and personnel are inadequate to carry out proper scientific research, law enforcement, planning, habitat preservation and expansion, employee training, and on-site wildlife educational programs necessary to the development of a supportive public constituency. Serious abuses have arisen from a too-careless accommodation to commercial and recreational uses at the expense of wildlife and habitat values, and more abuses appear to be imminent.

Many of the problems now affecting the refuge system have reached the level of urgency; others have the potential for future degradation of the resource. Problems in both categories, however, should be addressed promptly. And of all the recommendations The Wilderness Society offers here, none is more important or inclusive than the call for passage of an "organic" act designed specifically for the National Wildlife Refuge System—a single, comprehensive piece of legislation that, for the first time, would provide overall statutory guidance for the present and future management and use of refuge lands.

By far one of the most pressing immediate needs, which also has major significance in the long run, is expansion of the system. The 90 million acres now included (only 13 million of them outside Alaska) are not enough to sustain the needs of the near future, much less those of the next century. Habitats for many species are under great pressures from urban, industrial, and agricultural expansion, recreational use, and economic development. Furthermore, the acquisition of lands for many existing refuges remains to be completed; such units should be "rounded out" in order to more closely resemble functional ecosystems and more thoroughly provide for the purposes for which they were created. To satisfy both short-term and long-term acquisition and expansion needs, we should:

*Appropriate—and spend—enough money to support an immediate and aggressive purchasing program.* For fiscal year 1983, the adminis-

189

tration requested only $1.6 million for refuge acquisition from the Land and Water Conservation Fund (most of it obtained from oil and gas leases on the outer continental shelf). Congress appropriated $27.2 million. For fiscal years 1984, 1985, 1986, and 1987, the administration requested no funds for acquisition at all. Congress should appropriate no less—and preferably more—than $40 million for the next several years—particularly with the aim of acquiring habitat critical to migratory birds and federally listed threatened and endangered species.

*Emphasize the immediate acquisition of critical wetland habitat.* There is no more urgent need today than the protection and preservation of the country's fast-disappearing wetland habitat, of which 300,000 acres are lost every year. Between 1955 and 1975, by Fish and Wildlife Service estimates, more than 15,000 acres of estuarine sub-tidal habitats were lost in the Atlantic Flyway because of urban development; 1.5 million acres of forested wetland habitat were lost in the Mississippi Flyway, mostly because of agriculture; and in the Central Flyway, 10,000 acres of estuarine habitat were lost from the coast of Texas and hundreds of thousands of acres of prairie wetlands were lost in the interior states. At present rates, there will be almost no waterfowl breeding habitat left in the lower forty-eight states in another century. An emergency program of acquisition should be initiated with funding from such existing sources as the Land and Water Conservation Fund and the Migratory Bird Account, as well as by any other means—legislative or administrative—that may be deemed necessary and appropriate.

*Immediately initiate an inventory of all appropriate federal land that might qualify for refuge classification.* More than 97 percent of the existing National Wildlife Refuge System was originally created from land in federal ownership. Many of the millions of acres still in such ownership could appropriately be transferred to the refuge system. These lands could include much that is now administered by the Department of Defense, the U.S. Forest Service, and the Bureau of Land Management—particularly any land considered "excess" by any federal land management agency. No better or cheaper method

190

exists to expand the system quickly to meet the present and future needs of all forms of wildlife.

*Authorize and justify system expansion by means of a long-range acquisition plan subject to public review.* During the Carter administration, the Fish and Wildlife Service authorized the drafting of a ten-year acquisition plan. The target date for completion of the plan was February 6, 1981. It was neither completed nor released for public scrutiny. Such an acquisition plan should immediately be revived and updated by the Fish and Wildlife Service and its scope broadened from ten to at least twenty years. Further, the acquisition process should be more thoroughly incorporated into refuge programming and master planning; the size of the refuge system should always be considered open-ended and subject to growth as future requirements dictate. Many attractive possibilities currently exist for the creation of new refuges, such as the Birds of Prey area of Idaho, the Copper River Delta of Alaska, a portion of the National Petroleum Reserve of Alaska, the Currituck Outer Banks of North Carolina, and the Canaan Valley of West Virginia.

As individual units of the refuge system are completed and the system as a whole is expanded with new units, it should be kept in mind that many refuge lands are or will be prime candidates for inclusion in the National Wilderness Preservation System. Pursuant to the Wilderness Act of 1964, 652,000 acres—or 5 percent of the total refuge acreage in the lower forty-eight states—have been designated wilderness, but 3,387,199 acres of additional Fish and Wildlife Service recommendations in the lower forty-eight—some of them dating back nearly fifteen years—remain undesignated. We will need these areas and more, for future generations will see an increasing necessity for the protection of watersheds, wildlife, recreational opportunities, educational, scientific, and aesthetic values, and species diversity that only wilderness designation can provide. Refuge lands offer some of the best opportunities available not only to expand the existing National Wilderness Preservation System, but to create within the complex of refuges a unique system of wilderness that encompasses an unparalleled range of diverse habitats. We believe this goal can best be achieved by:

*Acting swiftly on existing fish and wildlife recommendations*. As noted above, the Fish and Wildlife Service has recommended for wilderness designation nearly 3.4 million acres of refuge lands in the lower forty-eight states above and beyond the 652,000 acres already designated. From a low of six-tenths of an acre in Mille Lacs National Wildlife Refuge, Minnesota, to a high of 1,588,779 acres in Desert National Wildlife Refuge, Nevada, the twenty-six areas involved cover a broad and valuable spectrum of habitat types, including coastal, river, and lake wetlands, Sonoran and Great Basin deserts, and High Plains grasslands. These recommendations have remained dormant for much too long and should be approved promptly by Congress. Several might be folded into state wilderness bills now in preparation or currently under consideration by Congress in the Roadless Area Review and Evaluation II process. Those which are not should quickly be designated wilderness either individually or as part of an omnibus refuge wilderness bill.

*Carefully monitoring the development of wilderness recommendations in the Alaskan refuges*. The Alaska National Interest Lands Conservation Act (ANILCA) of 1980 created sixteen Alaskan refuges that total 76 million acres. Section 1317 of ANILCA stipulated that these lands be studied for potential inclusion in the National Wilderness Preservation System, and a deadline of 1985 was established for wilderness recommendations. This deadline has now come and gone, and no recommendations have been forthcoming. These are extremely important lands—not only as the single largest portion out of which future wilderness areas are likely to be created, but as highly sensitive ecosystems requiring wilderness classification to ensure their future productivity. Damage inflicted here can remain for generations, and in such refuges as those in the extreme north, dominated by delicate tundra ecosystems, the land may never recover. Some Alaskan refuges, such as Kenai in the south, already have felt serious impacts from heavy recreational use, road and settlement construction, and the exploration and development of oil and gas resources. Such refuge lands are in particularly urgent need of wilderness protection, and Congress should see to it that the Fish and Wildlife Service adheres faithfully to the study and recommendation process established by ANILCA.

*Establishing an ongoing wilderness review process for the refuge system.* Even if all the wilderness recommendations and potential recommendations touched upon here were acted on by Congress, it would not mean that the refuge wilderness system had been completed. Just as the creation of new refuge areas should be viewed as an open-ended process, so should the creation of new wilderness areas within a growing refuge system. We recommend, therefore, that wilderness review of all refuge lands (including those in Alaska) be mandated by law to take place at least once every twenty years, and that appropriate additional areas be nominated for wilderness designation on a regularly scheduled basis. That law should be made a specific part of any future organic act governing the management of the refuges.

Of all the difficulties attending the National Wildlife Refuge System today, none is more onerous than the lack of any single overall guiding body of law for its administration. It is the only major federal public land entity that does not have such a law. The National Park System acquired its direction with passage of the Organic Act of 1916; the National Wilderness Preservation System was *created* by its law, the Wilderness Act of 1964; the national forests received the National Forest Management Act of 1976; and the Bureau of Land Management's National Resource Lands were given the Federal Land Policy and Management Act of 1976. By comparison, the 90-million-acre refuge system basically operates under the administration of a loose amalgam of individual laws and legal authorities: the Fish and Wildlife Act of 1956, which created the present Fish and Wildlife Service; the Wetlands Loan Act of 1961, designed to accelerate a wetlands acquisition program; the Refuge Recreation Act of 1962, which authorized the recreational use of refuges so long as such use is secondary to the system's primary purpose of habitat protection and preservation; and the National Wildlife Refuge System Administration

Act of 1966, an incomplete and unsuccessful attempt to rationalize refuge management goals and operations. Administration has been further confused by separate instructions contained in many of the executive orders that created individual refuges.

The Wilderness Society believes that these separate laws and executive orders do not endow the National Wildlife Refuge System with the legislative strength adequate to ensure consistent protective management. We propose that an organic act be formulated and introduced as soon as possible, and that the Interior Department and the administration give it their vigorous support.

As a general point of policy, any such act should state clearly and unequivocally that the National Wildlife Refuge System will be administered to ensure that the various units of the system are managed so as to retain or restore natural ecosystems for wildlife habitat, ecological study, interpretation, and other appropriate uses; that no native species of plant, fish, or animal life shall become rare, endangered, or extinct because of a lack of proper habitat; and that the *primary* purpose of the refuge system is the protection and preservation of all aspects of individual ecosystems.

Without dwelling on the specific details of such an act, we believe that it should address itself to three areas of major importance:

*Retention of refuge system lands.* The transfer of the management of a major part of Matagorda Island National Wildlife Refuge to the state of Texas, the transfer of St. Matthew Island National Wildlife Refuge to three Alaska native corporations for subsequent leasing to ARCO, and other such transfers and disposals seriously undermine the integrity of the National Wildlife Refuge System as a whole. The language of any organic act should specifically uphold the paramount role of the federal government in the task of wildlife conservation on refuge lands. Accordingly, it should state that the administration of the nation's refuge lands should not be delegated to any state, local, or private agencies, or in any other way be disposed of, except by an act of Congress.

*A strict redefinition of "compatibility" standards.* The National Wildlife Refuge Administration Act of 1966 states that the Secretary of the

194

Interior may "permit any use of any area within the System for any purpose . . . whenever he determines that such use is compatible with the major purposes for which an area was established." Such broad secretarial discretion can lead to serious abuse. Commercial activities such as livestock-grazing, oil, gas, or mineral development, timber-harvesting, cooperative farming, and general recreation are not the primary purposes for which the refuge system exists. An organic act should declare that a refuge will be closed to such activities unless specifically opened, and will not be opened *until* a comprehensive refuge plan (with public input) has been completed and the activity has been found to be not only compatible with but enhancing to and necessary for wildlife and its habitat.

*Restructuring the Fish and Wildlife Service's Refuge Division as a separate, independent Wildlife Refuge Service*. This could best be accomplished by first merging all federal land management agencies into a single Cabinet-level Department of Natural Resources (as proposed in our Agenda for chapter 2) and placing the newly created Wildlife Refuge Service under its authority. Within this department, the Wildlife Refuge Service would have a separate, public identity, which would enhance the growth of a constituency of supporters; it would have its own director, appointed by the President with the advice and consent of the Senate; it would have its own internal structure and its own priorities, alleviating administrative confusion; it would have its own budget, adjusted internally to support its own priorities. Even without the creation of a Department of Natural Resources, the Refuge Division could still be removed from the Fish and Wildlife Service and re-created as an independent Wildlife Refuge Service with all the advantages noted above. In either case, the Fish and Wildlife Service would, of course, continue to function as a separate agency, performing those ongoing programs and duties not directly related to the active administration of the refuge system—including the cooperative identification, protection, and management of endangered species resources.

However far we may proceed in such a reorganization, at the very least an organic act should ensure, by one means or another, the creation of an entity—whether within the present agency or separate

195

from it—designed and structured to address itself to refuge matters and only to refuge matters.

We created the National Wildlife Refuge System because over millennia a profound change had taken place in the way in which the human animal perceived the wild creatures all around him. We learned that the concept of stewardship had implications far beyond simple human use for simple human needs. We learned that all forms of life have an individual integrity that should be respected and protected. We are learning still, and that is why the fate of the refuge system is a matter of such profound concern—and why the proposals we offer here are of paramount importance. For the islands of life that the refuge system includes are not merely separate parcels rescued from the past; they are touchstones for a future, the dimensions of which we can only surmise.

Back when duck shooters knew no limits. President Chester A. Arthur with the day's take, 1882. *Indiana Historical Society Library*

Rachel Carson, the Biological Survey writer who galvanized the modern conservation movement with the publication of *Silent Spring* in 1962. *Erich Hartmann/Magnum Photos*

President Theodore Roosevelt at rest (for a change) on Pelican Island, Florida—which he designated as the first wildlife refuge in 1903. *Theodore Roosevelt Collection, Harvard College Library*

ABOVE: Autumn marsh, Great Swamp National Wildlife Refuge, New Jersey. *David Muench*

OPPOSITE, TOP: Cypress boles, Okefenokee National Wildlife Refuge, Georgia. *David Muench*

OPPOSITE, BOTTOM: Ash Meadows National Wildlife Refuge, Nevada. *D. W. Sada/Courtesy of Defenders of Wildlife*

Prickly pear and mesquite, Santa Ana National Wildlife Refuge, Texas. *David Muench*

# 5

# THE FREEDOM OF
# THE WILDERNESS

## The National Wilderness Preservation System

In 1893, Frederick Jackson Turner, a young man recently out of graduate school, read his doctoral thesis to a gathering of the American Historical Association in Chicago. Turner, who was thirty-two at the time, told his audience that democracy flourished in America not in spite of the obstacles posed by its native landscape but because of them. He said that this landscape—or frontier—was nothing more than a wilderness that irradiated opportunity and encouraged freedom, mobility, and the development of free institutions. The frontier, he said in what became known as the Turner Thesis, was "the line of most rapid and effective Americanization." His interpretation was so convincing and extraordinary that it dictated the course of historical analysis for the next thirty years, and his thesis remains, after nearly a century, the most widely known historical essay explaining America to Americans. He wrote:

The wilderness masters the colonist. It finds him a European in dress, industries, tools, modes of travel, and thought. It takes him from the railroad car and puts him in the birch canoe. It strips off the garments of civilization and arrays him in the hunting shirt and the moccasin. . . . Little by little he transforms the wilderness, but the outcome is not the old Europe, not simply the development of Germanic germs. . . . Thus the advance of the frontier has meant a steady movement away from the influence of Europe, a steady growth of independence on American lines. And to study this advance, the men who grew up under these conditions, and the political, economic and social results of it, is to study the really American part of our history.

In his thesis, as in his subsequent writings, Turner's affection was for the frontier and its social institutions, and he mourned their passing—as described in the official 1890 Census, which declared that the "frontier line of settlement" had finally disappeared. For the wilderness itself he held little more regard than did most people of his time and place. Nevertheless, he had legitimized wilderness by writing about it and outlining what he believed its influence had been on the shaping of the American character. There were those after him who mourned not just the passing of the frontier but of the wild country that had given it form, and some of these—not many at first, but a recognizable vanguard—began to wonder if some wilderness could not be saved as a living reminder, so long as it endured, of the place from which the American civilization had emerged.

They stood firmly in a long tradition, those who thought about such things—one that stretched back through John Muir to Henry David Thoreau and beyond, one that held, as Thoreau had put it, that "a town is saved, not more by the men and women in it than by the woods and swamps that surround it." The final expression of that tradition is today's National Wilderness Preservation System, an administrative classification now placed on 88.6 million acres of national forest, national park, Bureau of Land Management, and wildlife refuge lands in the lower forty-eight states and Alaska—the Great Land holding more than any other state, with 56 million acres. It comes in all shapes and varieties—as alpine wilderness, desert wilderness, tundra wilderness, swampland wilderness, coastal wilderness, forest wilderness. It is there for its own sake and for ours, protected in perpetuity from all that there is in us that would destroy it. There is nothing in any country in the world to match it—and there are those who say it is not yet complete, may never be complete, even while they concede that this Wilderness Preservation System is already among this country's best accomplishments.

But before there was a system, there was an idea.

204

## TWO MEN AND A SINGLE STARTING POINT

One of the people who was beginning to do some serious thinking about wilderness and its preservation early on was a landscape architect named Arthur Carhart. In the summer of 1919, the Forest Service had hired him to work at its Region 2 headquarters in Denver. He had been turned down once before because he had no experience or education in building roads and dams, two activities in which agency officials had a large interest in those days. Between his first and second applications for a job, however, recreational use in the national forests had picked up considerably, thanks to the automobiles that visitors were now able to drive almost anywhere they dared. In many places, national forest scenery rivaled that of the national parks. Forest Service officials wanted this to become more widely known, and spread the word via posters and billboards that proclaimed the national forests as the "People's Playgrounds" (much to the irritation of Director Stephen Mather and other National Park Service people, who believed the nation's proper playgrounds were its parks). In 1915 the Secretary of Agriculture had issued special-use permits—at ten to twenty-five dollars a year—to anyone who wanted to build a cabin, store, or lodge in certain remote parts of the national forests. The response was so good that Carhart, calling himself a "beauty engineer," was hired to landscape new roads, disguise sanitation problems at ranger cabins, and plan for the development of summer communities.

Carhart was dispatched first to Trappers Lake in Colorado's San Isabel National Forest, about thirty miles from Glenwood Springs. He was told to design a through road that might show off the scenery to its best advantage, and to plan a vacation settlement on the lake. Carhart spent several days hiking around the three-hundred-acre lake. He marveled at the eleven-thousand-foot peaks tiered like wedding cakes, and thought about how a road might go through the area, how cabins could be arranged. After thinking, and thinking some more, he returned to Denver with a novel suggestion: squelch the entire project. Not far into his career with the Forest Service, then, Carhart had uncovered his own true feelings and spent the rest of the time bombarding his superiors with letters and long memoranda on the subject. He even began to write magazine articles about the need to

205

preserve natural areas. "Individuals naturally desire to help themselves to the best home sites they [can] obtain," he wrote in one of his Forest Service letters. "This very greed indirectly defeats our purpose." The time would come, Carhart prophesied, when "the scenic spots where nature has been allowed to remain unmarred will be some of the most highly prized scenic features in the country."

If the Forest Service encouraged the total exploitation of the forests for both recreational and commercial purposes, it would be severely criticized later, Carhart believed. Steadily he built a case for the retention of some areas "to which the lover of the outdoors can return without being confronted by a settlement, a country store, telephone pole, or other sights of civilization." Man-made improvements on backcountry lands had to stop—of this Carhart was sure. "How to do this, is perhaps the real question, rather than shall it be done," he wrote.

Carhart's persistent rejection of the vacation-home syndrome was so unusual at the Forest Service that it caught the attention of Aldo Leopold, at that time assistant district forester in Albuquerque. On his own, while surveying a remote ridge for "some fool road," Leopold had reached the same conclusion as Carhart. To Leopold it seemed that man's encroachment on the wildest places had reached the speeds traveled by motorized vehicles. He was beginning to see an insidious connection between roads and automobiles and the destruction of wildlife habitat in the national forests. "Who wants to stalk his buck to the music of a motor?" he asked. "Or track his turkey on the trail of a knobby tread? Who that is called to the high hills for a real *paseo* wants to wrangle his packs along a graveled highway? There's car sign in every canyon, car dust on every bush, a parking ground at every watering hole, and Fords on a thousand hills."

Leopold, an enthusiastic hunter who later would write the first treatise on game management, was born in Burlington, Iowa. His passion for wildlife developed from a boyhood spent along the Mississippi, prowling its banks for a closer look at birds and other creatures that concentrated there. Leopold went East to prep school, after which he enrolled in the Yale School of Forestry. He graduated in 1908 and joined the Forest Service the following year as a forest assistant in the Arizona Territory. It was here that the comprehensive meaning of wilderness first touched him. He and friends had been out "pumping lead" into a pack of wolves bounding down a mountainside, he later wrote. An old she-wolf went down, and in the dying green fire of the wolf's eyes Leopold saw something he had never seen before—"something known only to her and to the mountain." He spent the rest of his life, which ended in 1948 with a heart attack while he was fighting a fire on a neighbor's farm, trying to comprehend what the wolf and the mountain knew. In *A Sand County Almanac*, Leopold's last and best-known work, he put it all together:

> Ability to see the cultural value of wilderness boils down, in the last analysis, to a question of intellectual humility. The shallow-minded modern who has lost his rootage in the land assumes that he has already discovered what is important; it is such who prate of empires, political or economic, that will last a thousand years. It is only the scholar who appreciates that all history consists of successive excursions from a single starting-point, to which man returns again and again to organize yet another search for a durable scale of values. It is only the scholar who understands why the raw wilderness gives definition and meaning to the human enterprise.

These ideas were still germinating when Leopold went to Denver on a winter day in 1919 to meet Arthur Carhart, who had been prating himself—in government memoranda, no less—about the same sort of things. Their meeting must have been productive; Carhart immediately dashed off a "Memo to Mr. Leopold," in which he restated their shared views regarding permanent alterations in wild places. In 1920 the Forest Service accepted Carhart's Trappers Lake recommendation, the first time the Service had ever denied a project because of the threat it posed to an area's natural integrity. In his short tenure with the Forest Service (he quit after four years because he did not like the direction it was taking in spite of his efforts), Carhart also influenced the denial of road funds for Superior National Forest in Minnesota. The forest consisted of more than one million acres of lakes and pine forests, and to Carhart keeping Superior in primitive condition was of prime importance; it was the only national forest in the nation where lakes dominated the landscape.

Meanwhile, Leopold had returned to his Southwest region determined to hold the line on encroachments. When he had first arrived, in 1909, there were six roadless areas, each of one million acres or more, in the national forests. In 1922 the only large tract that remained was in New Mexico's Gila National Forest, created in 1906. A 540,000-acre section at the headwaters of the Gila River contained a maze of red canyons that had thwarted railroads earlier and still presented problems to roadbuilders. Its stands of ponderosa pine, ancient juniper, piñon, and scrub oak were not considered commercially valuable. Leopold proposed that the area be preserved intact and designated as a special primitive area. State game protection associations and local stockmen saw preservation as a way to serve their own interests and supported the idea. Game protection advocates thought it would safeguard wildlife habitat, and stockmen figured that if the area remained roadless, tourists could not drive in and harass the sheep and cattle still allowed to graze there.

The Gila received its unique designation from the Forest Service in 1924. Two years later, L. F. Kniepp, chief of the division of lands and recreation, began to survey other national forests, looking for additional roadless areas to preserve along the lines set out by Leopold. Kniepp and his staff spent months squinting at quarter-inch topographical maps "upon which were recorded each forest supervisor's wildest flights of fancy as to the ultimate road and trail system for the forest." Through this scrim of dream-roads, Kniepp's survey identified seventy-four wilderness tracts unsuitable for roading, totaling 55 million acres, with the largest single unit covering 7 million acres. In 1929 this survey's findings led to an administrative regulation called L-20. It gave the chief of the Forest Service official authority to do what had already been done in the Gila—to establish "primitive areas" that were to remain primeval in their "environment, transportation, habitation and subsistence." Still, L-20 was not genuinely protective. Logging was still allowed, because it was believed that, if properly regulated, it would not be incompatible with the ultimate purpose of the reservation. Nor was L-20 strictly enforced. The fact is, most public land historians have viewed the L-20 regulation as merely a stalling measure to keep the most scenic lands within the national forests from being transferred to the national parks, which had often been the case.

## THE MAN WHO WALKED

The L-20 regulations fell short of satisfying the more wilderness-minded foresters like Leopold, who had transferred to a forest products laboratory in Madison, Wisconsin, in 1925. And they certainly did not satisfy a young man named Robert Marshall. Marshall, born into a wealthy family, was raised in New York City but spent his summers at Knollwood, his family's summer home on Saranac Lake in the Adirondacks. His father was Louis Marshall, a prominent attorney, civil libertarian, and wilderness advocate. The elder Marshall was one of those responsible for inclusion of a clause in the 1885 New York State constitution that "forever kept as wild" forestlands in the Adirondacks. Bob Marshall climbed his first Adirondack peak when he was fifteen, and he and his brother George climbed all forty-six together, becoming the first people ever to do so. By the time Bob was sixteen he knew he wanted to be a forester. "I love the woods and solitude," he wrote during his junior year in high school. "I like the various forms of scientific work a forester must do. I should hate to spend the greater part of my lifetime in a stuffy office or in a crowded city."

Ironically, many wilderness enthusiasts had been of the armchair variety—for them, simply knowing that wild places existed was stimulation enough. But Marshall felt incomplete anywhere but in the back of beyond, and would gladly expend all his energies getting there. When he was enrolled at the New York State College of Forestry in Syracuse, he decided to walk thirty miles in every state of the union, covering that distance in a single day in each state. He started in New York. A classmate remembers driving by Marshall and stopping to offer him a ride, which Marshall accepted, thinking he had walked his allotment. Studying the map as they rode together, Marshall realized he had fallen just short of the distance and leaped from the car to end the day properly. He was a powerful hiker. In college he once covered sixty-two miles in a day. Later, in Arizona, to break his own record, he walked for thirty-six hours and covered seventy miles. During forest tramps, friends who joined him fretted about getting their feet wet, but Marshall, always in sneakers for these occasions, started out by sloshing straight through the first puddle he came to.

After receiving his doctorate in plant pathology from Johns Hopkins

University in 1930, Marshall went to work for the Forest Service in the Wind River Mountains in Wyoming. Despite the L-20 regulations, he was disturbed by the rapid disappearance of wilderness from national forestlands and articulated his concern for the February 1930 issue of *Scientific Monthly* in an article that later came to be called the "Magna Carta of wilderness." Wilderness, he explained, was a region containing no permanent inhabitants, possessing "no possibility of conveyance by mechanical means and . . . sufficiently spacious that a person in crossing it must have the experience of sleeping out. The dominant attributes of such an area are: first, that it requires anyone who exists in it to depend exclusively on his own efforts for survival; and second, that it preserves as nearly as possible the primitive environment. This means all roads, power transportation and settlements are barred." Marshall's definition permitted the occasional temporary shelter, since this was common "long before the advent of the white race." He also softened his stance on wilderness purity by permitting fire-protection "infringements" such as telephone lines, trails, and lookout cabins.

To Marshall the wilderness offered the best chance to discover self-sufficiency. "Toting a fifty-pound pack over an abominable trail, snowshoeing across a blizzard-swept plateau, or scaling some jagged pinnacle which juts far above timber will develop a body distinguished by a soundness and stamina and élan unknown amid normal surroundings," he preached. He thought civilization's coddling gave nations the time to go to war: "People become so choked by the monotony of their lives that they are readily amenable to the suggestion of lurid diversions."

Sheer size had to be part of the wilderness spell. Marshall once compared wilderness to the Mona Lisa and said, "If you cut it up into little pieces one inch square and distribute them among the art galleries of the world so millions might see it where hundreds see it now, neither the millions nor the hundreds would get any genuine value."

Marshall's article called for the immediate identification and rescue of remaining wilderness, and for a thorough study of the country's future wilderness requirements, all of this to be carried out by those who firmly recognized the innate worth of land in its natural state.

210

"There is just one hope of repulsing the tyrannical ambition of civilization to conquer every niche on the whole earth," Marshall wrote. "That hope is the organization of spirited people who will fight for the freedom of the wilderness."

Within the Forest Service, Marshall had a reputation as an eccentric; he was not "of the family." His socialist convictions, among other things, made him stand out. Congressman Hamilton Fish of New York accused Marshall of being the single largest contributor to an unnamed "Communist veteran organization whose main purpose is to spread class hatred and propaganda for the destruction of American institutions." "I've been out in the woods and up in the arctic a good part of the past five years," Marshall responded. "It may be that the Bill of Rights was repealed without me hearing of it."

Yet, because he was bright and worked extremely hard, Marshall rose quickly in the ranks. And as he gained stature, so did his most fervent interests. As director of forestry for the Bureau of Indian Affairs in the Department of the Interior, Marshall created sixteen new wilderness areas on the reservations, with the full support of BIA chief John Collier and Interior Secretary Harold Ickes. Later, as head of the Division of Recreation and Lands in the Forest Service, Marshall restricted roads and development on 14 million acres. The work took him two years. During this time he personally financed out-of-pocket expenses for a new map inventorying remaining roadless areas larger than 300,000 acres. Doing the surveys himself, Marshall identified forty-six areas, thirty-two of which were in the Western national forests. He had in mind the eventual protection of nearly 45 million acres, constituting about 9 percent of the national forest system.

But there arose another impediment to the establishment of the fragile wilderness preservation system he was assembling. This time it was the generally progressive make-work industriousness of the Civilian Conservation Corps, in which a job often was created regardless of whether the work needed to be done. A good part of this work was roadbuilding. The CCC paid no special attention to administrative wilderness areas, so Marshall wrote to Ickes in 1934, pleading with the Secretary to keep the CCC highway work out of undeveloped areas in his jurisdiction, to "preserve a certain value of the timeless, mysterious, in a world overrun by split-second schedules, physical certainty and man-made superficiality." But President Roosevelt, ardent conservationist though he was, took special delight in being able to wheel his own specially equipped roadster through the countryside in spite of his paralysis. Through Ickes, he made it known that parkways would not be kept out of wilderness, and that was that.

## A WILDERNESS WAY

One of those parkways—intended for the wildest region of the Great Smokies—would have torn through portions of the two-thousand-mile-long Appalachian Trail. This possibility mobilized the trail's founder, Benton MacKaye, a forester who worked for the Tennessee Valley Authority, and his two friends, Harvey Broome and Harold Anderson. MacKaye had proposed the trail in 1921 to save a ribbon of wilderness between Maine and Georgia, calling the path "a wilderness way through civilization, not a civilized way through wilderness" (see chapter 7). The highway plans would have turned that around, MacKaye and his colleagues feared. Ironically, they had worked to bring the area of the proposed highway under the protection of the National Park Service, and it was now the Park Service that was suddenly pushing for construction of the new parkway. Anderson wrote to MacKaye that there had been enough rhetoric about the need for an organization of friends of the wilderness. The time had come to act. MacKaye met with Marshall, Broome, and Bernard Frank, another TVA forester, at a forestry convention in Knoxville in October 1934, and the four men drove out to look at a CCC camp. On the way they discussed—or rather, disagreed about—Marshall's version of a constitution for this "friends of the wilderness" group. The argument grew so heated that they pulled off the road, climbed an embankment, and haggled until they all agreed on what needed to be done to save wilderness, "that extremely minor fraction of outdoor America which yet remains free from mechanical sights and sounds and smells."

Selected others were asked to join them in a group that came to be known as The Wilderness Society. Additional charter members, in January 1935, were Aldo Leopold and Robert Sterling Yard, former publicity chief for Park Service Director Stephen Mather. At seventy-four, Yard remained a vigorous spokesman for wilderness and had become one of the Park Service's sternest critics. Months after The Wilderness Society's founding, Yard edited and distributed the first issue of The Society's magazine, *The Living Wilderness*. On the cover appeared Yard's "Summons to Save the Wilderness," a manifesto that described the organization's objectives:

> The Wilderness Society is born of an emergency in conservation which admits no delay. It consists of persons distressed by the exceedingly swift passing of the wilderness in a country which recently abounded in the richest and noblest wilderness forms, the primitive, and who purpose to do all they can to safeguard what is left of it. This is for transmission, a sacred charge, to its preservers of the future.

In closing, Yard denounced the "craze" to "build all the highways possible everywhere while billions may yet be borrowed from the unlucky future. The fashion is to barber and manicure wild America as smartly as the modern girl. Our duty is clear."

The Wilderness Society grew slowly at first, because its founders wanted no straddlers: "We want those who *already* think as we do," MacKaye told Marshall, "not those who have to be shown." Four years later, The Wilderness Society suffered a harsh personal blow. The kinetic Bob Marshall, just thirty-eight, died while traveling on a train from Washington to New York. For much of his life he had had a heart condition, and recently it had begun to show. On a hike in Oregon a month before he died, he had ended the day uncharacteristically breathless and exhausted. An autopsy found that he had succumbed to "thrombosis." But the Indian guides, foresters, fishermen, and park rangers who knew him from the mountains agreed that he had simply walked himself to death. Marshall left his personal fortune of $1.5 million to his favorite causes. To The Wilderness Society he bequeathed $400,000. The only bequest to a single person was $3,000 to his old Adirondack guide, Henry Clark.

In 1940 the Forest Service created the Bob Marshall Wilderness Area in Montana, in recognition of Marshall's many contributions to the preservation of wilderness. One of those contributions was the adoption of stricter regulations to replace the flimsy L-20 rules of 1929. The new regulations had been devised largely by Marshall and were promulgated by his successor and close friend John Sieker. This time they were called U Regulations, and defined three categories of wilderness. The first and largest of these were wilderness areas that consisted of tracts larger than 100,000 acres, designated for protection by the Secretary of Agriculture, based on Forest Service recommendations. Next in size were wild areas consisting of tracts between 5,000 and 10,000 acres. In the third category were roadless areas, to be managed primarily for recreation and left "substantially in their natural condition." Good enough, but still a little vague as to precisely what *kind* of land qualified as wilderness. Even within The Wilderness Society, members were having trouble agreeing on a universally acceptable definition. To straighten things out, The Society's Robert Sterling Yard wrote to the National Park Service for the agency's definition of wilderness, but was told that the one person who knew it was away, indefinitely. Some Wilderness Society members believed that a delineation of true wilderness could be achieved by subtracting all the roadless areas from the total area; one member believed that wilderness ought to be the national park for the poor; Aldo Leopold stressed that any wilderness designation should include "scientific research in ecology," along with programs in history, education, and recreation; Robert F. Griggs of the National Research Council insisted that wilderness must not be open to grazing because if it were, "there will be no wilderness areas"; and in a letter responding to Griggs's concern, wildlife biologist Olaus J. Murie allowed that grazing wasn't so bad, but road construction of any sort was the most serious threat and must be strictly prohibited. And so it went. With some reservations, Society leaders finally accepted the Forest Service definition that wilderness areas "provide the last frontier where the world of mechanization and of easy transportation has not yet penetrated. They have an important place historically, educationally and for recreation. The National Forests provide by far the greatest opportunity for wilderness areas. Suitable provision for them is an important part of the National Forest land use planning."

214

## UNTRAMMELING THE WILDERNESS

On the face of it, then, the Forest Service appeared ready to keep faith with Marshall's vision. In practice, this was not always the case. During World War II, when the exigencies of a nation at war gave increasing rein to industrial extraction and use of all natural resources, the utilitarian philosophy of forest use once again grew dominant within the Service. New wilderness designations nearly ceased, while other areas were withdrawn from protection and were roaded and logged. At times the agency seemed openly antagonistic toward the wilderness idea, causing Wilderness Society cofounder Bernard Frank to lament conditions in a letter to MacKaye in 1946: "Wilderness affairs are in serious shape. Just between us two, I don't think the Forest Service is really concerned." Postwar economic growth accelerated this shift through the Truman administration and on into that of Dwight D. Eisenhower. It was during the Eisenhower administration, it will be remembered (see chapter 1), that the utilitarian doctrine was given one of its most dramatic expressions with the Interior Department's support of a plan to build two major dams within the confines of Dinosaur National Monument. That unenlightened project was squelched by the coalition of conservation sentiment against it, but it stood as an ominous talisman for the future of wilderness preservation—whether on Forest Service lands or anywhere else.

The experience gave Howard Zahniser, executive secretary of The Wilderness Society and one of the most effective opponents of Dinosaur, pause for thought. Unless there was a strong national program of wilderness protection, Zahniser concluded, the conservation community would exhaust itself repulsing project after project. Worse, inevitably it would lose some of its battles. Zahniser was a bookish, polite, and, as it turned out, unflaggingly persistent man. Like Marshall, he had learned to love wild country during his long acquaintance with the Adirondacks. A journalist by training and an editor for the U.S. Biological Survey, he went to work for The Wilderness Society in 1945, became its editor and executive secretary, and eventually its executive director. Zahniser had always been impressed by the simplicity and power of the words in the New York constitution regarding the Adirondacks. The "forever wild" clause, as he called it, was all that stood between their grand beauty and their not-so-grand exploitation.

In 1956, a week after Dinosaur had been secured, Zahniser sat down to draft a bill to protect wilderness. "We must recognize that all our lands are destined to be put to some human use," he said. "If any of it is to be preserved in its natural condition it must be as the result of a deliberate setting aside of it for human use of it in a natural condition." By the end of May, his first draft of a wilderness bill was completed. The gist of the bill was that a federal umbrella of perpetual protection would be given to a small lot of federal lands that met approved standards of wilderness. Such designations would be made by executive order from recommendations of various land-managing agencies and a presidentially appointed citizens committee. Each agency would be responsible for managing the designated wilderness areas within its jurisdiction. Zahniser emphasized that no new bureaucracy was needed, nor would additional lands be purchased for inclusion in the system. The wilderness law, as he saw it, would only redefine the future of some lands already retained by the federal government. He outlined his idea first in a speech to the American Civic Planners Association, then gave Senator Hubert Humphrey a copy of the proposed legislation. Humphrey introduced it formally in 1957. As expected, opposition to the bill was loud and strong. Many commercial interests with political clout wanted to retain their "right" to enter and exploit any piece of public land. Both the National Park Service and the National Forest Service flatly opposed the bill. To the Park Service it was a slap in the face; was not the agency congressionally mandated to preserve wilderness from exploitation for profit? Forest Service officials rejected the proposal because participation by the citizens council would limit the range of their administrative judgments and keep them from making land-use decisions that, so they maintained, only Forest Service personnel were trained to make.

Finally, the Forest Service paraded its homegrown U Regulations to show that the agency was already doing something—that it had, in fact, pioneered the doing of something. Yet the record did not speak well for the Forest Service, and only supported Zahniser's conviction that a dose of something stronger was needed. Since 1939

216

the vaunted U Regulations had added only 350,000 acres to the administrative system—compared with the 14.2 million acres to which Bob Marshall alone had granted protection in the Bureau of Indian Affairs and the Forest Service from 1930 to 1937. A common complaint outside the Service was that permanent wilderness designation would "hamstring economic development in the West, leaving this vast area as a playground." So said, among others, Senator Arthur Watkins of Utah, one of the bill's most bitter antagonists. "Out our way millions of acres are already adequately preserved and reserved in the wilderness state," he asserted at a hearing in July 1958. They "probably always will be because nature has made it that way."

The battle over the wilderness bill divided along regional lines. The South and Northeast were generally for it, but the West, with its history of opposition to federal land management in any form, was generally against it. Oddly, even those who opposed wilderness legislation always explained that they had nothing against saving some wilderness per se. It was just a matter of how much, and where. "Wilderness has its place, but it mustn't destroy the economy," said W. D. Hagenstein, executive vice-president of the Industrial Forestry Association. "Conservationists want to build a wall with 'verboten' signs at 150-foot intervals completely around the wilderness system," he added. "This limits its use to the handful who have time, resources, and stamina to invade its depths by foot or on horseback." Hagenstein admitted that the idea of wilderness was appealing, "but so are three squares a day, money to pay monthly bills, with some left over to provide junior's education, and to have a cushion against catastrophe. We who are engaged in providing raw materials for our basic industries do not do so because we enjoy harvesting century-old trees, building roads up beautiful creeks, exploring the earth for its mineral and petroleum riches . . . but because the public demands it."

The wilderness bill was rewritten sixty-six times. The words in each version were mostly Zahniser's, and he fretted over each one. He did not like "bill language," and said he wished he could write legislation in iambic pentameter. Particularly troublesome to him was the bill's lack of a single word to convey the unique quality of wilderness. The words "undeveloped" and "undisturbed" were lusterless, he believed. One day Zahniser was talking with a friend who used the word "untrammeled" to describe what she loved about the seashore in Olympic National Park. It was exactly what he had been looking for, and he stuck by it. Zahniser steered each new version through eighteen public hearings in ten states, despite lung surgery and a heart problem. At times the struggle seemed so long and hopeless that Wilderness Society council members urged Zahniser to pour his declining energy into something else. But Zahniser would not let go. At every opportunity he drove home three main points: first, that wilderness was necessary for human health, welfare, knowledge, and happiness; second, that wilderness preservation concerned lands that were already largely unsuitable for economic exploitation; and third, that the wilderness system at its fullest would cover only about 60 million acres in the lower forty-eight states, or 2.5 percent of the total land area—this would be all the wilderness there could ever be on the American continent.

As time and Zahniser wore on, support for the wilderness bill grew in unexpected places. In the May 1961 *Journal of Forestry*, for example, one forester wrote that "there are a goodly number of us who like the forest exactly as Nature made it. We know we are a minority, like the Negroes and Jews, and I suppose we should naturally expect to some degree the same treatment." Testimony at the hearings ran into the thousands of pages, and speakers came forward by the hundreds. The proceedings were generally dull and predictable, but many of the most eloquent statements in favor of the bill were delivered by individuals who were not professional conservationists. During hearings in McCall, Idaho, a college student named Michael V. Mahoney, who had traveled from Portland, Oregon, addressed those who complained that any wilderness protection was a "lockup," that it was too nebulous and high-sounding, and that only a few people were able to partake in its pleasures anyway. Congress held the key to wilderness if it was needed in a national emergency, Mahoney reminded opponents, and continued:

As for the privileged few, this phrase represents a misconception of the way things are done in this country. What is privilege? Birth? Rank? Age? None of these. All you need to become "privileged" is

218

the desire for wilderness. The American way is not to distribute everything equally. We do not, for instance, distribute wealth equally. Instead, we distribute opportunity equally and let wealth be the reward for the successful endeavor. Similarly, there is nothing un-American about distributing wilderness experience only to those who seek it. For the opportunity is available to us all.

At last it seemed certain that there would be some sort of federal protection of wilderness. The final form of such a system was not clear, except that Zahniser's definition of what qualified for preservation stuck: "A wilderness," he had written, "in contrast with those areas where man and his own works dominate the landscape, is hereby recognized as an area where the earth and its community of life are untrammeled by man, where man himself is a visitor who does not remain." This language survived each legislative revision and emerged intact in the final version in 1964. Otherwise, that version was a collection of compromises. Among other changes from Zahniser's original, the citizens advisory committee had vanished, a concession to the Forest Service's territorial imperatives. Also gone was the President's power to create wilderness by executive fiat; instead, the land-managing agencies were directed to review their holdings and recommend those that qualified for wilderness designation, for which the President would request Congress to pass enabling legislation. (It was not until the passage of the Federal Land Policy and Management Act of 1976, however, that the more than 300 million acres of Bureau of Land Management lands would be placed in wilderness review—as discussed in chapter 3.) Moreover, Congress could now act independently to create new wilderness designations.

Many conservationists were not especially pleased with this aspect of the bill, fearing that it would delay the process. It did slow things down, but it also encouraged wider public participation in the designation process, and in the end probably contributed to the designation of more wilderness acreage than would have been established otherwise. But the most troubling compromise of all had to do with mining, prospecting, and oil and gas drilling. Exploration and possible development of all of these were permitted to continue until December 31, 1983, at the discretion of the Secretary of the Interior.

In previous drafts of the bill there had been no cutoff date at all for exploration, so in this twenty-year deadline conservationists at least gained a compromise of the compromise. Any mining claim established during this period, however, could be developed at any time in the future, as long as it was done in a manner vaguely defined as conforming to wilderness aesthetics.

On April 27, 1964, Zahniser testified for the last time in favor of the bill, confident now as he read his statement that it would pass.

> Civilization's ambition can encompass wilderness protection. And so sublimated, it can make preservation a prevailing purpose. We maintain the gallery of art, even though few use it. . . . The wilderness system that has come to us from the eternity of the past we have the boldness to project into the eternity of the future. It seems presumptuous for men and women who live only forty, fifty, sixty, seventy, or eighty years to dare to undertake a program for perpetuity, but that surely is our challenge.

When the Wilderness Act was signed into law by President Lyndon Johnson on September 3, 1964, Howard Zahniser did not attend the ceremony in the Rose Garden. He had died in his sleep a week after his last congressional testimony.

## THE BUREAUCRATIC BALK

At its signing, the Wilderness Act immediately designated as wilderness 9.1 million acres of national forest, national park, and wildlife refuge land. In the lower forty-eight states, the great bulk of land that might qualify for addition to this embryonic National Wilderness Preservation System lay under the administration of the Forest Service. To its credit, the Service diligently and constructively prepared regulations for the protection and management of areas already classified as wilderness under the provisions of the act. In the matter of studying and recommending additions to the system, however, it dragged its numerous feet. Between 1964 and 1973 it made not a single such recommendation. All proposals made during this period came from the swelling ranks of professional conservationists and

220

interested citizens. Steadfastly committed to the principles of multiple use—which, by agency interpretation, wilderness preservation defied—the Service was institutionally reluctant to move on wilderness designation and, many conservationists maintained, erected obstacles where there had been none.

One of these obstacles was an extremely narrow interpretation of the law regarding an area's suitability as wilderness. By agency standards, few places (if any, it seemed) were pristine or "untrammeled" enough to be classified as wilderness—at least as foresters were given to understand the word. If the ground showed evidence of any past alteration, such as an overgrown road or an abandoned mine shaft, chances were good that the entire tract would be eliminated for its lack of purity. Adhering to its high standards, the Forest Service declared it next to impossible to find wilderness areas east of the Front Range of the Rockies. Land in the East had been too long and too thoroughly disturbed by man and his commerce. Of 256 areas surveyed in the East, the Forest Service identified only three as potential wildernesses. To remedy this situation, Congress passed the Eastern Wilderness Act in 1973. The new law added sixteen parcels in thirteen states, for a total of 207,000 acres, and made it clear that in the opinion of Congress, if an area had recovered significantly from prior abuse—as was often the case in the fast-growing forests of the humid East—it was on its way back to a pristine condition and could be included in the National Wilderness Preservation System.

The agency showed similar disinclinations toward wilderness in the West. In 1968 the Gore Range Primitive Area in the White River National Forest in Colorado had been slated for inclusion in the wilderness system. Conservationists wanted the primitive area enlarged so that it would include forest cover and meadow as well as the "rocks and ice" that made up so much of wilderness acreage. But the area conservationists thought should be included in the eventual wilderness designation was also wanted by the Forest Service for timber-cutting. The Service had planned to sell 4.3 million board feet of the area's timber, and had dismissed its wilderness potential because an abandoned road less than a mile long marred a portion of the terrain.

Wilderness supporters ultimately sued the Forest Service in the U.S. District Court for the District of Colorado on the ground that if the agency went ahead with the logging, it would effectively remove the East Meadow Creek area from further wilderness consideration. In 1969, in a landmark decision, the court ruled against the Forest Service. In his opinion, Judge William E. Doyle wrote that the Forest Service action "thwart[ed] the purpose and spirit of the Act" because it prevented presidential or congressional involvement. "Decisions regarding the classification [of] areas which are predominantly of wilderness value must be left open through the presidential level," wrote Judge Doyle. The U.S. Court of Appeals for the Tenth Circuit later affirmed the lower court's decision.

The National Park Service was still finding the Wilderness Act difficult to digest. It had opposed passage of the act because it believed that the legislation was designed to duplicate or even supersede its own efforts. But while the Park Service had once been the unquestioned leader in natural preservation, its recreation development policies, especially after World War II, had weakened its claim to sovereignty in the eyes of many conservationists. In 1965 this view gained even more credence when some 400,000 acres of Great Smoky Mountains National Park came up for consideration as wilderness under the 1964 act. Almost simultaneously, national park officials announced plans for a new highway that would accommodate summer traffic jams, and fulfill an old Park Service promise to the town of Bryson City, Tennessee, to give it a new road.

When the officials unveiled their highway plans they noted that less than half of the park was recommended for inclusion in the wilderness preservation system, and the lands that were to be included had been broken up into chunks of from 5,000 to 110,000 acres each. Local businesses and the chamber of commerce heartily praised the new roadway. Scientists, conservationists, and concerned citizens opposed it just as heartily and in greater numbers. "The Park Service has put forward a roadbuilding project that transgresses the spirit of the Wilderness Act," moaned *The New York Times*. It would "bring heavy automobile traffic streaming through the very area that needs to be protected. The proposal for this trans-mountain road reflects weariness rather than foresight and clear thinking." Drawing constant

222

fire from such quarters, the road plan was finally shelved five years later in favor of a scenic loop highway around the perimeter of the park, as had been urged by citizen groups. (Wilderness classification, however, has not yet come to the park.)

Similar public pressure persuaded the Forest Service to launch a more ambitious survey of its "de facto" wildernesses—roadless areas that might be included in the National Wilderness Preservation System. In 1972, Chief Forester Edward Cliff announced an agency study of 56 million acres, known as the Roadless Area Review and Evaluation, or RARE. RARE's results two years later were disappointing because only 12.3 million acres, or 19 percent of the roadless areas surveyed, were recommended for wilderness protection. Conservation organizations ridiculed this recommendation, and the Sierra Club brought suit. The Forest Service quickly capitulated so far as to agree that it would comply with the stipulations requiring environmental impact statements mandated by the National Environmental Protection Act of 1969 before developing any roadless areas. Such compliance effectively slowed roadbuilding and timber-cutting, and in 1977 the Forest Service attempted another nationwide review.

This second review, called RARE II, was far more comprehensive than its predecessor. It identified almost three thousand potential wilderness areas in thirty-eight states, for a total of 62 million acres. But RARE II recommendations also raised conservationist protests. This time, only 15 million acres of national forest lands were to be set aside as wilderness, so little that, as one Sierra Club member put it, "the fact that timber operators complained was pro forma, for the record; they have been secretly delighted." A key part of the RARE II determinations were public hearings so that the Forest Service could be made aware of local and corporate sentiment regarding wilderness preservation in each locale. In the summer of 1977, remarks from 47,000 people were tabulated. Nevertheless, many foresters claimed that public participation was dominated by elitist professional conservationists, not ordinary citizens. "Those sought-after folks, the moms and pops who give their disinterested opinion on wilderness, are as mythical as unicorns," grumbled one forester in the *Journal of Forestry*. The magazine also carried the opinion that RARE II was "largely a political exercise masquerading as a professional study," and sarcastically referred to the whole wilderness designation system as a way to determine "where the hand of man never sets foot." Still, in 1980 the process resulted in statewide bills for Colorado, New Mexico, Missouri, Louisiana, and South Carolina, all passed by Congress.

In 1982 a federal court of appeals complicated the process by upholding a challenge to the validity of RARE II; in *California v. Block* the court ruled that the RARE II environmental impact statement covering several areas in the state—produced in compliance with the National Environmental Protection Act—was inadequate. This decision forced the Service to jettison RARE II. Assistant Secretary of Agriculture John Crowell announced that another study, "RARE III," would have to begin, but this time the study would be incorporated into the forest-by-forest management plans called for by the National Forest Management Act of 1976 (see chapter 2).

In the meantime, Congress continued to use the RARE II study as the basis for further state wilderness bills, and in 1984—twenty years after the passage of the Wilderness Act—the Ninety-eighth Congress designated 8.6 million acres of new wilderness in twenty-one states. It was the largest amount of acreage allotted to wilderness preservation since the Alaska National Interest Lands Conservation Act of 1980 (see chapter 7). But for those guided by the original estimates, it still was not enough. As the Ninety-ninth Congress got under way, lobbying began for the designation of more wilderness in such states as Nevada, Montana, Idaho, Kentucky, Michigan, Oklahoma, and Georgia. The struggle for—and against—wilderness would continue.

### GETTING AT THE NUMBERS

As Robert Marshall observed fifty years ago, one of the major problems facing those who advocate the designation of wilderness is that arguments *against* it can be made in undeniably simple, concrete terms, while arguments in favor of it are more amorphous, harder to pin down with facts and figures. Sigurd Olson, the Minnesota conservationist and veteran of many battles over economics and wilderness, once acknowledged the difficulty of justifying wilderness on economic grounds and refrained from doing so. Yet without such grounds, he said, "Someone will come up and hit you between the eyes. We will try to talk about wilderness values, and how they make people feel, and how unhappy we will be without them. They will look at you and realize that you must have spent all your life in the woods, because you don't really know the facts, and you don't know what makes the country go. They will be very polite, very kind, pat you on the back, and they will tell you it was a very fine statement you made but in fact it didn't mean a thing!"

But in the 1960s, conservationists decided to refute economics with economics—to learn the language and to speak it on behalf of their interests, including wilderness preservation. At the Sierra Club's Biennial Wilderness Conference in 1967, Lawrence G. Hines, professor of economics at Dartmouth, outlined arguments that might be useful to wilderness lobbyists. "The standard textbook tells us that if a resource has the capacity to satisfy a want and is scarce, it possesses economic value," he said. "Because the wilderness does satisfy a want and is scarce, it does have economic value; indeed, in the matter of scarcity, we might wish otherwise." But, said Hines, standard market economy includes no way in which to reflect many social and ethical considerations. Economic analyses were deficient in proving that public schools were worth the taxes spent on them, just as they obscured the economic return from the construction of newer and better highways. "Government projects become multipurpose to add to the benefit column in cost-benefit analysis," Hines said. "As such, a multipurpose project is likely to be a collection of individually unjustified undertakings. Reclamation projects provide a little bit of flood control after an exaggerated risk appraisal, a large amount of hydroelectric power, which is profitable business, and a smattering of recreation opportunities that may or may not be superior to those destroyed."

When confronted with economic arguments that allowed no room for wilderness in a particular area, Hines advised environmentalists not to conduct the same type of cost-benefit analysis used to justify a capital-improvement project. "It is not necessary to come up with an equally strong contrary economic argument in quantified terms," he said. "It is sufficient to demonstrate that the agency study is, at best, an incomplete measure of the economic validity of that kind of investment."

Nevertheless, some specific, nuts-and-bolts information did become necessary after 1981, when the Reagan administration took office and began to cast covetous glances westward. As noted earlier, the Wilderness Act had specified that designated wilderness areas would be open to leasing for oil, gas, and mineral exploration until December 31, 1983—at the discretion of the Secretary of the Interior. Out of respect for the idea manifest in the Wilderness Act, one Interior Secretary after another had declined to exercise this discretion. However, President Reagan's Secretary of the Interior, James Watt, had no such qualms, and even went so far as to claim that the act *obligated* him to begin leasing.

The Arab oil crisis in the 1970s had made the federal government eager to locate and develop substantial domestic sources of oil, and the discovery of new oil and gas deposits along the Overthrust Belt seemed to be the answer to a lot of prayers. The Overthrust Belt runs through Montana, Idaho, Utah, Wyoming, and Arizona, and cuts a swath one hundred miles wide. In the oil-drilling business the region was called "elephant country," because of the suspected gigantic size of the reserves. Many designated wilderness areas and proposed wilderness areas were situated on the edges of the Overthrust Belt; in LaBarge, Wyoming, four wildcat wells drilled between 1981 and 1983 revealed substantial deposits of natural gas on lands bordering wilderness study areas. In 1981 the Forest Service and the BLM were under great pressure to process the backlog of lease applications for exploring wilderness areas in the Overthrust region. Coincidentally, a 1980 U.S. district court decision on a lawsuit that Watt had brought several years before, when he was head of the Mountain States Legal Foundation in Denver, ordered the government to accept or dismiss industry applications. As Interior Secretary, Watt accelerated the processing of applications to abide by the court ruling he had prompted.

Seismic exploration commenced in several wilderness areas. Although the least intrusive part of oil and gas development, seismic exploration can have some notable impacts. First, there is dynamite, which must be exploded to ricochet shock waves off deep strata and give a reading, by the nature of the echo, of what might be buried there. In one seismic crew member's account of working near the Bob Marshall Wilderness Area, fifty pounds of dynamite were detonated every 220 feet, for a total of fifty to one hundred explosions a day.

226

Conservationists and their congressional allies, believing this clearly to be an incompatible use of wilderness, attempted to halt Watt's move, arguing that industry should explore other lands first. "There are only so many drill rigs available for exploration," said Andrew F. Wiessner, counsel to the House Interior Subcommittee on Public Lands and National Parks. "It will take years to explore the Overthrust Belt, so why not explore less fragile areas first?" In the meantime, The Wilderness Society commissioned a study by the economist Leonard L. Fischman that would determine the amounts of important minerals, oil, and natural gas within wilderness areas, designated as well as proposed. The study, issued early in 1982, and whose conclusions were later confirmed by the General Accounting Office, found that designated wilderness contained only about 1 percent of the nation's potentially producible onshore oil and gas reserves. The Fischman report also concluded that about 77 percent of the potential oil and 81 percent of the potential gas reserves were not on federal lands at all, but on private or state lands. Additionally, some 130 million acres of federal land outside the wilderness system already were leased for oil and gas exploration or development—with only a fraction of these ever having been seriously exploited.

Public disapproval of Secretary Watt's plans to speed up oil and gas exploration in wilderness ran so high that in 1982 the Secretary formulated what he called a compromise. He proposed a "Wilderness Protection Act," which critics quickly asserted might be more appropriately labeled a "Wilderness Destruction Act," since, they said, the bill would have made it more difficult to add lands to the wilderness system, would have made it easier to open existing wilderness to development, and would have removed protection altogether after the year 2000. The public was outraged again; The Wilderness Society, for one, counted more than three hundred newspaper editorials that appeared in response, most of which were dead against the bill.

Congress refused to take Watt's legislation seriously, and in August the House passed its own version, one that would have banned all oil and gas leasing immediately. The Senate did not go that far, but during a lame-duck session in December the two houses did tack an amendment to the Interior Appropriations Bill that prohibited the Forest Service from processing lease applications for wilderness during fiscal 1983. Finally, in July 1983, the administration capitulated. "That's it," said Garry Carruthers, then Assistant Secretary for Land and Water Resources. "We quit. What we wanted was exploration. But it has become so politically explosive that we determined that you can't jeopardize all our leasing programs on exploration in a limited number of areas." In October, James Watt resigned, a decision triggered most directly by his use of unbecoming public language one time too many. Congress renewed the leasing ban until the end of the year, during which time the December 31 deadline came and went with no further commotion.

## THE PITFALLS OF LOVE

The widespread degree of support for the continued sanctity of wilderness may have surprised James Watt and others in the Reagan administration; it may even have startled some conservation organizations. In any case, it seemed to call into question the validity of one of the oldest arguments against wilderness preservation—that it was a "single use" idea conceived by and meant for a small group of "elitists." It was a point raised often in the years preceding the Wilderness Act itself, and was raised again during the debate over the act's various incarnations, as attested to by the remarks in a joint statement by Senators Barry Goldwater, Henry Dworshak, J. J. Hickey, and Gordon Allott in 1961. The bill was "class legislation," they believed, since it proposed to set aside vast tracts of land "for the exclusive use of a small minority of well-endowed citizens, while excluding from its vaunted recreational delights the great number of citizens who, having completed their contributions to their country, now have time to travel and see the natural beauties of that country, but who have neither the physical stamina nor the rather considerable funds necessary to indulge in arduous, expensive pack trips." This sentiment was alive and well during the squabble over James Watt's wilderness policies. "Wildernesses," William Tucker informed readers of his 1982 book, *Progress and Privilege*, "are essentially parks for the upper middle class. They are vacation reserves for people who want to rough it—with the assurance that few other people will have the time, energy or means to follow them into the solitude."

*Someone*, however, was following them into the solitude. The one clear fact about wilderness use in the years following passage of the act was that it increased steadily—geometrically, even—until "the small minority of well-endowed citizens" took on the dimensions of a horde of "elitists" whose ages, backgrounds, abilities, and finances covered the spectrum of American life. But if this growing popularity heightened awareness of wilderness and contributed significantly to the support of measures designed to preserve it, it had its pitfalls, too. In *Wilderness and the American Mind*, the historian Roderick Nash summed up the problem: "The final irony in the history of the American wilderness is that increase in appreciation may ultimately prove its undoing. Having made remarkable gains in the public's estimation, wild country could well be loved out of existence."

Part of the intent behind wilderness recreation had been to perpetuate the explorer's birthright, to leave places where the awe that struck Lewis and Clark 183 years ago would make the senses quicken again and again. Referring to that adventuresome pair, Aldo Leopold wrote:

No traffic cop whistled them off the hidden rocks in the next rapids. No friendly roof kept them dry when they misguessed whether or not to pitch a tent. No guide showed them which camping spots offered a night-long breeze, which firewood made clear coals and which would smoke. The elemental simplicities of wilderness travel were thrills because they represented the freedom to make mistakes. The wilderness gave . . . those rewards and penalties for wise and foolish acts against which civilization has built a thousand buffers.

Wilderness management has tempered Leopold's version of wilderness recreation. For one thing, not all who venture into a designated wilderness area realize that it ought to be different from a national park or any other place where one might take a stroll in the woods. Improvements such as trail signs, wide, artificially hardened trails, and quaint log bridges help hikers out, but also have an ecological purpose—they protect wilderness from those who love it. The sheer number of hikers in some places drastically accelerates soil erosion; sloshing across streams tramples their soft banks; and detours taken to avoid mud kill fragile vegetation. Casual hikers penetrate farther into the landscape, never realizing that wilderness is not a park, or anything else they have known.

At times, the agencies themselves have promoted misconceptions. In some places high-density recreational facilities have been developed adjacent to wilderness areas. A case in point is the South Fork Meadows Trail in the San Gorgonio Wilderness Area in southern California. The trail used to be called "poopout hill" because its grade was so steep and its footing so difficult. Then the hill was paved, making it easier for more people to reach the top. In 1973, visitation to the area was so heavy that a permit system was introduced. So far, permit systems and rationing have been accepted well by the public everywhere they have been instituted, once the reasons are explained. "It appears that the public is more willing to yield their right to wildlife benefits than most managers realize," assert the authors of *Wilderness Management*, the Forest Service's chief reference on the subject. "By controlling the numbers, types and distribution of users at the entry point, the need for control within the area is minimized. . . . There is a point where the wilderness experience becomes so diluted by additional restrictions that it is in danger of being completely lost." Increasingly the management of existing areas, in addition to the classification of new ones, will decide whether or not the goals of the Wilderness Act are being met.

## THE GENETIC ARGUMENT

There is a final justification being offered these days for the perpetuation and growth of a wilderness preservation system, despite the complications it entails. In his essay "Walking," Henry David Thoreau had stated the argument in an age not ready to comprehend it as anything other than poetry: "In wildness is the preservation of the world." There are those who say it is high time we understood the full implications of Thoreau's simple statement. Writing in the Summer 1984 issue of *Wilderness* magazine, Edward O. Wilson, Baird Professor of Science at Harvard University, touches upon some of those implications as they apply to the destruction of wilderness: "In our own brief lifetime humanity will suffer an incomparable loss in aesthetic value, practical benefits from biological research, and worldwide biological stability. Deep mines of biological diversity will

230

have been dug out and carelessly discarded in the course of environmental exploitation, without our even knowing fully what they contained."

Wilderness, once reviled for its seeming lack of order, has become the standard against which to measure the condition of other lands. Aldo Leopold claimed that wilderness "is the most perfect norm of land health." Sound ecosystems are characteristic of wilderness. They consist of layer upon layer of life, each layer more complex than the one that supports it. Land is not merely soil. It is soil, insects, birds, rodents, larger mammals, and finally, most complicated of all, humans. The links between these groups form the food chain, from which comes the energy that maintains all life on earth. Species native to a specific area are compatible with other elements in the ecosystem. Introduced species may or may not be as compatible. Man-made changes are revolutionary rather than evolutionary because they happen fast, and their consequences are unpredictable and potentially more comprehensive. "Paleontology offers abundant evidence that wilderness maintained itself for immensely long periods; that its component species were rarely lost, neither did they get out of hand," Leopold wrote in *A Sand County Almanac*. Weather and water built soil as fast as, or faster than, natural calamity removed it. In damaged ecosystems this is not the case. Soil and nutrients disappear for the equivalent of forever; without the fullness of vegetation, water tables fall; climatic extremes are felt more harshly where land has been cleared; the presence of fewer plants reduces the amount of oxygen produced through photosynthesis; air and water, once cleansed of pollutants by weather and plant processes, harbor their filth; without other insects and birds to prey upon them, insects become pests.

The problem with being careless about habitat destruction is that one never knows what processes have been pathologically altered. All that is certain is that the loss of plants, insects, animals, or even bacteria debilitates the entire organism, much as a missing part, however tiny, hampers the operation of any machine.

If it is still difficult to accept the fact that every living thing is related to every other living thing biologically, there is another aspect of wilderness to consider. As always, the natural world holds abundant information and material that improves human life. Such riches as timber, minerals, grass, and water are obvious. But the future thrust of wilderness research might well be the analysis of the properties of many life-forms to determine their applications to medical science. Such research already has produced promising results. Over 40 percent of the prescription drugs sold in the United States contain substances derived from forty-one species of plants. Many of the plants in use come from tropical ecosystems, where biological diversity is unmatched. From the Amazon, for instance, comes the rosy periwinkle, used as standard treatment against leukemia, breast cancer, and Hodgkin's disease. Foxglove, imported from Europe, is converted into medications that treat congestive heart failure and circulatory ailments. In the United States the evening primrose is being studied for its gamma linoleic acid, otherwise found only in human breast milk. GLA is an essential fatty acid in cell functions, and its absence has been tied to arterial disintegration, arthritis, and eczema. There are sixty species of evening primrose in the United States; six are on the verge of extinction.

While the exploitation of nature in these varied forms raises additional ethical questions, few would consciously deprive society of the opportunity to answer them. But, as currently conceived, the wilderness preservation system can at best offer only a small representation of ecosystems. Of the 233 separate ecosystems identified in the United States, only eighty-one are within federally designated wilderness. Fifty of the nation's ecosystems will never be included because they are no longer found on federal lands. George Davis, a land and natural resource management consultant, who also served as national coordinator for the Forest Service's RARE II studies, nevertheless argues that the wilderness system still is the best hope for maintaining biological diversity. "Although Congress is moving ahead on some wilderness recommendations, ecosystem representation is a new concept and criterion for evaluating wilderness proposals," says Davis. "The notion of seeking to include as widespread as possible representations of ecosystems is not yet a driving force in the press to expand the wilderness system through the inclusion of areas such as Montana's Tongue River Breaks or Nebraska's Pine Ridge, both eastern ponderosa ecosystems." Davis mentions other areas required for ecosystem preservation, but they are not supported as candidates for wilderness designation because they are "less than spectacular" and "lack the dramatic high country appeal that has come to be associated with wilderness."

Davis also suggests that the Forest Service expand its involvement with the international Biosphere Research Program of UNESCO. Biosphere research was developed by the International Union for Conservation of Nature and Natural Resources in the hopes of eventually creating a network of protected areas representing major ecosystems throughout the world. Several wilderness areas in the United States have already been selected as biosphere research sites. "If we view wilderness as a legacy that will enable future generations to better understand their heritage, those future generations will need a legacy truly representative of the diverse landscapes and ecosystems we share with our fellow creatures," Davis says. "They will need some undeveloped areas that can be used to evaluate the true impacts of development and exploitation. They will need access to all of the possibilities still locked within today's diverse gene pools."

Such are the shifting dimensions of the wilderness system, now nearly 90 million acres in size—32.1 million of which are in the lower forty-eight states. It is a system extending far beyond Carhart's appreciative gaze across Trappers Lake, or Leopold's hope for the headwaters of the Gila; it would even have challenged Marshall's stamina, had he lived a normal span of years. The ultimate physical and philosophical dimensions of the wilderness system add weight to a dictum once laid down by historian Bernard DeVoto. He was not saying anything that those who had always esteemed wilderness did not already know, but he said it very well indeed. It was imperative, he wrote, "to maintain portions of the wilderness untouched, so that a tree will rot where it falls, a waterfall will pour its curves without generating electricity, a trumpeter swan may float on uncontaminated water—and moderns may at least see what their ancestors knew in their nerves and blood."

## AN AGENDA FOR
## THE WILDERNESS PRESERVATION SYSTEM

A key word in any discussion regarding the future of wilderness in this country is "system," and the very preamble of the Wilderness Act of 1964 spells it out plainly: ". . . there is hereby established a National Wilderness Preservation System. . . . " The point is important, for it emphasizes the intent of those who first conceived the idea: a broad and clearly articulated network that would put under permanent federal protection a major part of the American inheritance of wild country.

Twenty-two years later, as this book is published, that network includes 88.6 million acres, but by whatever means one measures it, the wilderness complex we have today is so far short of completion that to use the term "system" to describe it may be stretching the bounds of logic—particularly at a time when the recreational demand for wilderness experience is growing at a steadily increasing rate. The system is woefully incomplete, and the task of expanding it has been seriously impeded over the past four and a half years by a presidential administration that has exhibited a foot-dragging antagonism toward the whole idea of wilderness. It was in spite of such opposition, or because of it, that conservationists directed their energies from 1981 on toward fashioning wilderness legislation on a state-by-state basis, often bypassing the administrative agencies altogether to work closely with state congressional delegations and even with representatives of industry. The immediate upshot of this, of course, was the passage of legislation in 1984 designating 8.6 million acres of new wilderness areas.

That effort should continue unabated, with special emphasis over the next several years on wilderness classifications for a major portion of the 24 million acres of wilderness study area lands currently under consideration by the Bureau of Land Management for designation. With the designation of the Bisti and the De-na-zin wilderness areas in New Mexico and the inclusion of nearly 300,000 acres of BLM lands in the so-called Arizona Strip wilderness bill in 1984, some of these study areas finally made the list, but for the most part the BLM has been parsimonious in its recommendations. These recommendations need to be reviewed and, where necessary, revised upward by Congress. In the meantime, the BLM must be forced to effectively uphold the law's mandate to protect existing wilderness values until Congress makes a decision on which areas are to be designated.

Another important potential source of expansion is in the National Wildlife Refuge System. As mandated by the Wilderness Act, the Fish and Wildlife Service did review its lands and make wilderness recommendations, but it is important to note that no wilderness review has been made of any wildlife refuge added to the system *since* 1964, except in Alaska. That deficiency should be corrected, either by direct administrative action (the Fish and Wildlife Service has the authority to do so) or, if necessary, by congressional legislation in an Organic Act for the wildlife refuge system. In response to the same Wilderness Act mandate, the National Park Service contribution to wilderness expansion has been similarly inadequate, though for different reasons. Studies were completed and recommendations made (although some of these after the 1974 deadline established by the Wilderness Act), but many—totaling as much as 10 million acres—have since been stalled in a bureaucratic mire; these recommendations must be freed up and presented to Congress at the earliest possible date. Finally, all federal public lands in Alaska should be carefully reviewed for further potential additions to the National Wilderness Preservation System.

Setting aside wilderness is one thing; the question of how best to manage this preserved inheritance is quite another. The question may at first seem pointless—a wilderness, to remain a wilderness, should be left alone. But it is not that simple. Whatever the long-term ecological reasons for setting aside wilderness, however necessary this ethical gesture to the needs and priorities of a protected natural world, the fact is that wilderness is also for human use, however restricted, however transient. And the uses of human beings need to be managed.

As a general rule, the management stipulations in the Wilderness Act can be viewed as a kind of overlay on the present rules and regulations of the various agencies that administer wilderness within their larger responsibilities. The act itself generally lays down no

235

specific regulations for any given wilderness, but its intent is clear and its central principle unmistakable: the purpose of wilderness management is the maintenance and, if need be, the restoration of a dynamic equilibrium of natural forces; the fundamental purpose for designating and subsequently managing wilderness is the preservation of wilderness character in perpetuity.

That is the meaning of the law, but its application and enforcement are complicated by confusions and conflicts that can be overcome only by diligent effort. Consider, for example, just three areas of major management concern and what can and should be done about them:

*The "mining exception."* Since passage of the General Mining Law of 1872, tens of thousands of hardrock mining claims were established in areas all over the West that eventually became part of the National Wilderness Preservation System after the 1964 Wilderness Act. A "grandfather clause" in the 1964 act allowed the staking of further claims until December 31, 1983, after which date all validly established claims could be developed in perpetuity. As a result, some designated wilderness areas, such as the Absaroka-Beartooth of Montana, are positively riddled with both historic and modern mining claims whose development poses major threats to the watershed, wildlife habitat, and general wilderness characteristics of the affected regions. To ensure the minimum damage to the wilderness environment, the Forest Service and the BLM (which share the administration of mining claims) should not allow access or development without requiring clear and convincing evidence of a valid claim: proof of proper location and marking, proof of the presence of a valuable commercial mineral, and proof that the annual "assessment" work required by the Mining Law of 1872 has in fact been done. Second, the agencies should monitor development carefully and *strictly* enforce all environmental regulations that apply to mining. Third, when the development of a valid claim clearly will have unacceptable impact, the government should move to acquire the claim through outright purchase (as was done with a pumice claim in the Three Sisters Wilderness of Oregon in 1982); in some cases, it may become necessary to exercise eminent domain if there is no other way to protect the integrity of the wilderness environment.

*External threats.* Not all problems develop within wilderness areas. Nearby grazing, oil and gas drilling, logging, road construction, even urban development can have measurable impact on the primitive quality of a wilderness area, and such long-distance phenomena as smog and acid rain deposition have already severely damaged some areas. Low-level exercises in flight training by the Air Force have disrupted the aesthetic quality of wilderness in New Hampshire, and the Air Force has similar plans in mind for the Gila Wilderness in New Mexico. Individual wilderness managers can do little to control such impacts directly, of course; the individuals and agencies operating from the outside must be persuaded to respect the intent of the Wilderness Act just as rigidly as those who use wilderness directly. President Harry S Truman once banned all flights through the "air space" of the Boundary Waters Canoe Area even before the wilderness system was created; such controls might be called for in our own time.

*The recreation boom.* Projections of the future demand for wilderness or primitive-type recreation vary from area to area, but all point to a steady increase throughout the lower forty-eight states. In the Pacific Northwest, for example, it is estimated that even if all RARE II– recommended wilderness areas *and* all further planning areas were added to the wilderness system, demand for recreation use would still exceed the region's capacity by 50 percent by the year 2030. Such projections not only stand as a clear justification for the continued expansion of the system, but also point up the dimensions of a problem that already exists in many areas: the potential abuse of the land by too many people using it badly and without proper guidance by wilderness managers. Visitor freedom should be a management goal, and wilderness management must recognize "unconfined" recreation as one of the major appeals of wilderness. But user impacts should be closely monitored to prevent resource deterioration and maintain a high-quality wilderness experience. If and when some sort of visitor management becomes necessary, it should be designed to accomplish resource protection objectives with as little regulation of and interference with visitors as possible. To accomplish this goal, wilderness management training must be greatly accelerated at all levels. All agencies—the Forest Service, the National Park Service, the Fish and Wildlife Service, and the Bureau of Land Management—should be required, by congressional directive if necessary, to institute extensive training programs in wilderness management based on the practical application of the principles outlined above. Further, such training should go beyond the agencies themselves to the public at large; agencies should be encouraged (and given the necessary money and personnel) to develop major public educational programs.

As the discussion above illustrates, wilderness management problems are too varied and complex to lend themselves to any kind of simple, overall solution. Still, difficulty should be no excuse for careless administration. All agencies that administer wilderness should be required to prepare comprehensive guidelines for the management of individual areas; these must be reviewed and, when necessary, revised on a regular basis, with the opportunity for full public participation. Throughout the process, the intent of the Wilderness Act should be honored at all times and at all costs.

Finally, a system, if it is to be called a system at all, must have something more than size. It must have coherence, a distinct and calculated purpose that makes it more than the sum of its parts. For wilderness, one significant purpose—in addition to such traditional justifications as the protection of watersheds, wildlife habitat, scientific research, and scenic beauty—must be the protection of ecological integrity. And in that regard, the present system is particularly inadequate, as is made clear earlier in the chapter. Far too many ecosystems have not been included, largely because there never has been a systematic and coordinated effort by the various public land agencies to create a wilderness preservation network that represents *all* available systems. Such an effort must be initiated by all agencies involved as an ongoing part of the wilderness study process; it should be coordinated with a well-funded, centralized, and wide-scale biological research program in wilderness to expand significantly the isolated and scattered research presently under way.

238

Yet, even if this is done and even if Congress acts positively on all the wilderness legislation now before it or placed before it in the near or distant future, there still would be a significant shortfall in the number of ecosystems adequately represented. It may take a federal program of acquisition to add missing segments to the system, and where this is impossible, the federal government should at least accelerate cooperative programs with individual states that will encourage them to establish more state wilderness areas where none now exist. Only through such a major national commitment can we hope to preserve a realistic spectrum of wilderness ecosystems that will help ensure the continued diversity of plant and animal communities in this country.

Before this can be accomplished, we must also adopt a serious change in our perception of the National Wilderness Preservation System. Ever since passage of the Wilderness Act, there has been a tendency, particularly among opponents of wilderness designation, to think of the system in static terms: We will establish so much wilderness, and no more. This view has been most sharply represented in the debate resolved by Congress in the spring of 1984 regarding wilderness proposals coming out of the Forest Service's RARE II study. For several years, a major bone of contention had been over "hard release" versus "soft release" language in wilderness bills. "Hard release," favored by the Reagan administration and its supporters, meant that any areas not included in a Forest Service wilderness designation by Congress would be open to development and forever exempt from being considered again as wilderness. "Soft release," favored by conservationists, would have allowed nondesignated, or "de facto," wilderness to be developed as deemed necessary, but would have required that such areas also continue to be eligible for review as wilderness during the perpetual ten-to-fifteen-year management cycles mandated by the National Forest Management Act of 1976. The difference is significant, for "soft release" implies a perception of designated wilderness as an open-ended system, one subject to expansion wherever and whenever it is considered necessary and appropriate. The successful compromise worked out among congressional factions in 1984—in effect, a capitulation on the part of those favoring hard release—suggests that we may well be on the way toward establishing an open-ended view of wilderness designation as permanent national policy. Regular and continuing wilderness review must be made an integral part of the permanent planning process for *all* federal land-management agencies.

Only with such a perception can we hope to meet the demands of the future as populations shift and increase, as needs and priorities change and develop. In this view, the National Wilderness Preservation System can never truly be "completed"; it can only be improved. To paraphrase President Theodore Roosevelt, we should be building this system not for a day, but for the ages.

ABOVE: Aldo Leopold *(left)*, philosopher of the land and author of *Sand County Almanac*, was responsible for the first Forest Service primitive reserve, the Gila Wilderness; he is seen here with Wilderness Society President Olaus Murie, in 1946. *The Wilderness Society*

LEFT: Arthur C. Carhart, coauthor of the public wilderness concept, on a canoe trip in Minnesota, 1921. *U.S. Forest Service*

OPPOSITE: Arrowhead–Cramer Lakes Basin, Sawtooth Wilderness Area, Idaho. *Philip Hyde*

LEFT: Robert Marshall, walker extraordinaire and principal founder of The Wilderness Society, caught in an antic mood in Alaska, spring 1931. *The Wilderness Society*

BELOW: Howard Zahniser *(seated left)*, executive director of The Wilderness Society and author of the Wilderness Act, joined other members of the National Conservation Committee for a portrait in 1960; in the rear, left to right, Carl Gustafson, David Brower, Joseph Penfold; seated right, Ira Gabrielson. *The Wilderness Society*

OVERLEAF: The Minarets from above Lake Ediza, Ansel Adams Wilderness Area, California. *Philip Hyde*

ABOVE: Whitechurch Glacier, Glacier Peak Wilderness Area, Washington. *Philip Hyde*
BELOW: View of Mount Lester, Bridger Wilderness Area, Wyoming. *Philip Hyde*

# 6

# THE STATE OF
# NATURE

## The National Interest Lands of Alaska

Koyukon Natives of north central Alaska who have not broken with tradition consider it impolite to admire a mountain's size or a scene's beauty at the moment of observation. "Don't talk, your mouth is small," comes the hushed reprimand from an elder when a child misspeaks. Later, in less splendid surroundings, it is all right to show appreciation. In detail, then, the elder re-creates the scene, savoring the play of light and grandeur. Through such humble articulations, says anthropologist Richard K. Nelson, Koyukons, along with other Alaskan Eskimos, Indians, and Aleuts, express their devotion to lands that are, for humans, among the most inhospitable on earth. And among the most beautiful, with a sweep of variety, majesty, and richness matched nowhere else. It is perhaps for this reason that Native peoples speak carefully, reflectively, when attempting to describe what lies before them every day. It is perhaps for this reason that the Aleut people gave the place its name—Alaska, meaning, in their language, "Great Land."

When a map of the forty-ninth state is superimposed on a map of the coterminous United States, its southeastern tip reaches the Georgia coastline. The Aleutians meander into California. Alaska's northern edge runs through northern Wisconsin and Minnesota and its interior bulk throws a shadow across all of Illinois and Iowa, together with most of Nebraska, Indiana, Oklahoma, and Kansas. Its 35,000 miles of convoluted coastline is half that of the whole United States. From Alaska's western extremity you can see the Soviet Union, and

Japan lies within one thousand miles of its remotest Aleutian island. Author Joe McGinniss aptly titled his best-seller on Alaska *Going to Extremes*, with the climate being but one example. In summer, temperatures can hit one hundred degrees. In winter, readings plunge to seventy-five below zero, with temperatures remaining at about forty below zero for weeks of darkness. North of the Arctic Circle, the Kobuk sand dunes shift in the wind; farther south, glaciers, one bigger than the state of Rhode Island, calve into deep bays and inlets. Alaska's Mount McKinley is the highest mountain in North America, and its eighteen-thousand-foot rise from base to summit makes it one of the most impressive vistas in the world. Thousands of miles of rivers course through Alaska, and its lakes number in the tens of thousands, though much of the state is arid, receiving less than twenty inches of precipitation a year—except in the southeast panhandle, where precipitation is heavy enough to produce rain forests of giant Sitka spruce and hemlock.

Given such extremes, the diversity of wildlife is unexcelled. Alaska supports more than three hundred species of birds that come to nest or feed from six continents. Walruses and sea lions haul themselves up by the thousands on rocks worn smooth by the uncounted ancestors who were there before them. At least thirteen distinct herds of caribou roam Alaska's tundra; polar bears, grizzlies, moose, wolves, and Dall sheep are everywhere. At times certain rivers run red with salmon, and where salmon spawn and die, the sky clouds over with the bald eagles who come to feed on them. "Anybody who says the ecology is fragile is an ignoramus or liar," declared Joe Vogler, one of the most vociferous objectors to the Alaska National Interest Lands Conservation Act. Yet the teeming vigor of wildlife in Alaska is open to misinterpretation. Alaska is delicate precisely because it *still* holds the lives of so many creatures in the balance. They depend on Alaska for the survival of their kinds, which is the nature of any ecosystem that is intact.

The northern land, deprived of sun and moisture, vegetates slowly. Outside the rain forests, trees can take a century to grow as high as a man's knee; a campfire ring on the tundra remains visible for decades. The animal species that make their living here need space. A grizzly bear often requires one hundred square miles to sustain

248

# The Public Lands of Alaska

National Park System: 31.8 million acres
National Forest System: 22.9 million acres
National Resource Lands: 106.6 million acres
Wildlife Refuge System: 77.0 million acres
Wilderness Preservation System: 56 million acres
Wild and Scenic Rivers: 3,352 miles
National Trails: 2,037 miles

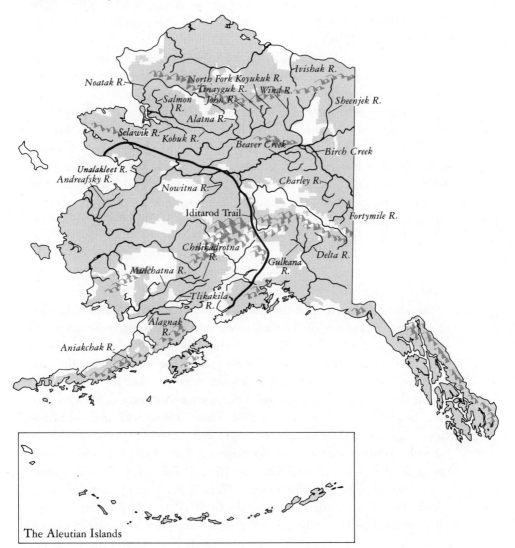

The Aleutian Islands

itself, and does not tolerate many intruders. Still, there are those who insist that Alaska needs no special looking after, that it can take care of itself. If anything, some would say, it is man who needs protection from the land. "The cold can kill you," said former Alaska governor Walter J. Hickel, in support of Alaska's resilience. "The beautiful sky can kill you. . . . It's a tough place up here. . . . This country can kill you."

Although Alaska's harshness has always been its best defense, human resolve to accomplish the impossible is often implacable; no sooner is a technology pronounced too costly or difficult to undertake than money and motivation conspire to undertake it. The greater challenge in the current age will be not how to engineer the subduing of Alaska, but how to save it from the weight of our whole history. This is the place, conservationists like to say, where we have the chance to do it right, to rise above and move beyond the misuse and ignorance that have so often governed our occupation of this continent. If so, we have a lot of tradition to overcome in this Great Land.

## "THE TSAR IS FAR AWAY"

Although rumors of its existence had been circulating for at least a generation, Alaska was not discovered until 1741, when a Danish sea captain named Vitus Bering, along with his Russian crew, glimpsed the peaks of the St. Elias Range. Bering, who never set foot on Alaska and died on an island named for him far to the west of its mainland, had no interest in exploring unknown new worlds. He represented Peter the Great of Russia, whose curiosity about his empire's eastern reaches triggered Bering's mission. First, Bering was ordered to determine once and for all whether Asia and America were land-joined, thereby settling a long-standing dispute. Next, Bering was instructed to explore Japan and map the western end of the American continent as far as Mexico. He did neither. Wracked by scurvy and short of food, Bering was anxious to return to St. Petersburg before winter. But he died in December, leaving his men to the long, frigid winter. The survivors sustained themselves on the meat and skins of sea otters. When spring came they headed back to civilization with great bundles of otter pelts—and became rich men. Alaska, or Russian

America as it was called, was soon a major source of furs for Russian royalty as well as for the sovereigns of Europe.

Aside from plundering Russian America for its furs, the Russians did some colonizing, although their numbers probably never exceeded twelve thousand throughout the territory. The colonizing effort entailed the massacre of resistant Aleut Indians and the establishment of about forty onion-domed Russian Orthodox churches. Guidance for colonial deportment in this backwash of a backward empire was summed up in the saying, "Heaven is high and the tsar is far away," according to historian Hector Chevigny. One Russian American governor had more devout intentions toward his realm, as indicated in the anthem he wrote: "The will of our hunters, the spirit of trade / On these far shores a new Muscovy made / In bleakness and hardship finding new wealth for fatherland and tsardom." The Russian presence in Alaska lasted 126 years. It was gently undermined by the vestiges of Manifest Destiny that a few American statesmen were clinging to. Chief among the holdouts was William Henry Seward, a powerful Secretary of State under President Lincoln, with presidential aspirations of his own. Seward did not accept the notion that Manifest Destiny had achieved its aims at the Pacific Coast. He thought American democracy quite suitable for numerous distant islands, as well as for the great mass of land on Canada's western border, Russian America. In 1860 he said:

Standing here and looking far off into the northwest, I see the Russian as he busily occupies himself by establishing seaports and towns and fortifications, on the verge of this continent, at the outposts of St. Petersburg, and I can say, "Go on, and build up your outposts all along the coast and up even to the Arctic Ocean—they will yet become the outposts of my own country—monuments to the civilization of the United States in the North West."

Seward's aspirations were not encouraged by his compatriots. He had lost much prestige by deciding to serve Andrew Johnson, whose enemies in Congress were plentiful enough to almost succeed in impeaching him. But the Russians took Seward more seriously. "The

United States are bound to spread over the whole of North America," predicted one Russian diplomat as early as 1853. "Sooner or later we shall have to surrender our North American possessions." Although America and Russia were on excellent terms at the time, the Russians feared that if they were not willing to surrender Alaska peaceably, they would one day have to go to war over it, judging from previous examples of American inclinations where land was concerned. Great Britain, with dominion over Canada, was the more obvious successor, but Russia and England were estranged during the Crimean War. In 1867, negotiations over Alaska proceeded despite enormous opposition. The treaty was negotiated secretly but still needed to be ratified by the Senate. The agreement, with its $7.5 million price tag, would have died in the Foreign Relations Committee but for the efforts of committee chairman Charles Sumner of Massachusetts, who, in a speech that lasted three hours, spoke movingly of the nation's duty to uplift the immense country that would otherwise remain "without form and without light." He based his argument for its purchase more on the need to keep Russia happy than on Alaska's worth to the United States. "Even if you doubt the value of these possessions," he said, "the treaty is a sign of amity. It is a new expression of that *entente cordiale* . . . which is a phenomenon of history." The Senate finally ratified the treaty by three votes, making it possible for the United States, which did not really want to buy Alaska, to acquire it from Russia, which did not really want to sell it. Ironically, after the sale, relations between the two nations worsened, and Russia had to wait more than eighteen months to be paid for its good intentions.

In the United States, Alaska was called many things: Walrussia, Icebergia, and—most enduringly—Seward's Folly. Despite the cost of about five cents an acre, Alaska was called a "swindle" and "utterly worthless." Alaska, declared Congressman Benjamin Loan of Missouri, was an "inhospitable and barren waste," and would "never add a dollar to the wealth of our country or furnish any homes to our people." Upon hearing that the United States had bought land on which every foot of soil was frozen, New York Congressman Dennis McCarthy observed that soon America would "hear that Greenland and Iceland are on the market." The ridicule did not abate. Government policy toward Alaska, what there was of it, became thoroughly ingrained with the belief that a region one-fourth the size of the lower forty-eight states was utterly, irrevocably worthless.

For the first seventeen years there was no government in Alaska, and therefore no law. Alaska was nothing more than a customs district. If a person moved to Alaska, he could not expect to be able to marry there, buy land, build a cabin, or draw up a will, since there were no laws permitting the execution of such routine matters. For ten years the navy ruled the district, overlooking drinking and Native-debauching sprees by the enlisted men stationed there.

Finally, in May 1884, Alaska was granted a greater semblance of government when Congress passed Senate Bill 153, sponsored by Indiana Senator Benjamin Harrison. The act gave Alaska a governor, a district judge, a district attorney, and a skeletal court system. Mining laws were put into effect, although general land laws were specifically excluded. Twenty-five thousand dollars was appropriated for the education of school-age children in the district, but there was no other revenue for government, aside from a fraction of the fees taken from seal hunting. Possibly the most significant provision of the 1884 act was its concern for Native Alaskans. Ironically, the campaign against Indians and their ancestral ways was still being brutally waged in the West when Congress generously stipulated that in Alaska, "Indians or other persons in said district shall not be disturbed in the possession of any lands actually in their use or occupation or now claimed by them, but the terms under which such persons may acquire title to such lands is reserved for future legislation." As long as Alaska seemed valueless to whites, such magnanimity posed no hardship to them.

## THE TOIL OF GIANTS

Spring came on once more, and at the end of all their wandering they found . . . a shallow placer in a broad valley where the gold showed like yellow butter across the bottom of the washing-pan. They sought no farther. Each day they worked earned them thousands of dollars in clean dust and nuggets, and they worked each day. The gold was sacked in moose-hide bags, fifty pounds to the bag, and piled like so much firewood outside the spruce-bough lodge. Like giants they toiled, days flashing on the heels of days like dreams as they heaped the treasure up.

It was the summer of 1897, and the discovery of gold near the junction of the Yukon and Klondike rivers stirred an international sensation. More than eighty thousand seekers streamed northward into Canada and Alaska, although few reaped the legendary bounty of John Thornton, Jack London's hero in his 1906 novel, *The Call of the Wild*, from which the excerpt above is taken. Alaska's gold rush was the last in which a poor man could become rich, or so it has been said, but only if he was first and could withstand brutal deprivation and loneliness. Most could not. The trail of optimism was littered with the log cribs of dreamers, in towns they named Arctic City or Beaver or Peavey or Jim Town. The wildness appealed to some and they stayed on. "We didn't have no time for prospecting," reminisced one German miner. "We was just running around wild, stampeding."

Injustices began to surface. Native Alaskans who joined the search for gold and who were lucky enough to find it were not entitled to stake their claims because they were not considered U.S. citizens. Worse, the infiltrators depleted native supplies of caribou, moose, and small game animals, putting settlements on the verge of starvation.

By 1906 the easy metal had been sifted from the creeks and rivers, leaving them silted and stocked with dead salmon. Gold extraction could no longer be left to the poor sourdough, loosely defined as any prospector who had been in Alaska long enough to see the Yukon's tributaries freeze up in fall and break up in spring. Hydraulic machinery owned by large mining concerns began to replace simple placer operations, powerful jets of water cutting away whole riverbanks and exposing the skeletons of prehistoric animals in the permafrost. But even the heavy-duty operators were forced to look for their wealth in less accessible regions, and the cost of discovery eventually became prohibitive.

Alaskan fish and wildlife suffered a frenzy of exploitation, and their depletion triggered some of the nation's first federal conservation measures. American ownership of Alaska had produced a flurry of sealing, trapping, and canning enterprises, and contributed hundreds of millions of dollars to the nation's wealth. Historian (and former Alaska governor and senator) Ernest Gruening measures the excessive attention by appropriations: in 1887 the entire budget for civil government in Alaska was $25,000, while Congress spent $43,000 on the supervision of such seal islands as the Pribilofs. Despite this attention, the fur seal population declined drastically, from more than 3 million at the time of Alaska's purchase to about 350,000 thirty years later. Walrus, whale, and otter were hunted nearly to extinction.

Salmon also declined precipitously, because of overfishing and illegal obstructions of streams and rivers. Canning soon became Alaska's first industry, and the number of canneries went from two in 1878 to thirty-seven ten years later. In that time their annual output climbed from eight thousand cases packed and shipped a year, to more than 700,000.

Fortunately the dramatic shrinkage in Alaska's fish and game populations coincided with the ascendance of wildlife preservation sentiment in the United States. Many felt that Alaska was a good place for the federal government to dabble in the conservation of species, notably the salmon. In the 1880s Livingstone Stone, head of fish hatcheries in California and Oregon, suggested that "national salmon parks and salmon reservations" be established in Alaska. "Not only is every contrivance employed that human ingenuity can devise to destroy the salmon of our West Coast rivers," he said, "but more surely destructive, more fatal than all is the slow but inexorable march of destroying agencies of human progress, before which the salmon must surely disappear, as did the buffalo of the plains and the Indian of California." Editor George Bird Grinnell took up Stone's idea and popularized it in his magazine *Forest and Stream*. On December 24, 1892, President Benjamin Harrison obliged the preservationists by proclaiming the Afognak Forest and Fish Culture Reserve on Afognak Island, off Alaska's southeast coast. Harrison's was the first cautious exercise of executive privilege granted when Congress passed the Forest Reserve Act ten months earlier. (The Forest Reserve Act also extended homestead laws into Alaska.)

The naturalist John Muir was the first to exalt Alaska's landscape for its own sake. He made his first trip there in 1879, when kind words about the district were virtually unrecorded. While sailing through the Inland Passage, Muir wrote along the way that "every view of islands and mountains [seemed] ever more and more beautiful; the one we chanced to have before us seeming the loveliest, the most surpassingly beautiful of all." Muir had probably seen more of America than anyone else of his day, but he declared he had never seen vistas "so hopelessly, overabundantly beautiful for description" as those of Alaska. Muir's articles helped change public opinion regarding Alaska, but its best promotion came in 1899 when Edward H. Harriman, owner of the Union Pacific Railroad, assembled scientists and artists for an appreciative cruise to Glacier Bay and other points on a 250-foot steamboat he had chartered. Muir was a member of the expedition, as was Henry Gannett, a surveyor of the Wyoming Territory in the 1870s and director of the U.S. Geological Survey. Gannett carried back with him a strong impression of where Alaska's enduring strengths could be found. "The Alaska coast is to become the showplace of the earth," he predicted in an essay in a 1901 issue of *National Geographic*. "Pilgrims, not only from the United States but from far beyond the seas, will throng in endless procession to see it." To Gannett, Alaska's economic good was grandeur, its worth "measured in direct returns in money received from tourists." Its scenery, he insisted, "is more valuable than the gold or the fish or the timber, for it will never be exhausted." He concluded his essay with advice that has been much quoted since: "If you are old, go by all means, but if you are young, stay away until you are older. The scenery of Alaska is so much grander than anything else of the kind in the world that, once beheld, all other scenery becomes flat and insipid. It is not well to dull one's capacity for such enjoyment by seeing the finest first."

## THE CONSERVATION FACTOR

In less than fifty years, Alaska went from being overlooked by the federal government to being over-federalized by it, with no pause in between for the orderly development of entrepreneurial freedom—at least, according to those who have always resented the government's presence there. By 1915 there were twenty-three separate Alaskan bureaus or offices of the Departments of Agriculture, Interior, Commerce, Navy, War, and Justice. Despite such "obstacles," fortunes had already been made in gold, copper, coal, salmon, seals, and timber—most by absentee corporations that contributed precious little to the welfare of Alaska or its citizens. Had it not been for the federal presence, particularly in the form of Theodore Roosevelt's gang of conservationists, much of the same kind of rampant exploitation that had brought ruin to so much Western land in the lower forty-eight states would have flourished in Alaska, too. In Alaska, foresight reared its intelligent head early on, and if it was not a permanent condition, it at least gave Alaska a better start in this direction than any other region of the country had enjoyed.

The establishment of Alaskan forest reserves, beginning with Afognak in 1892 and greatly increased during the Roosevelt years, is an obvious example of a priori protection. The cost of transportation discouraged wholesale logging for export, but President Theodore Roosevelt did not want to leave the continuance of this impediment to chance. First, he set aside the Alexander Archipelago and Tongass forest reserves on a chain of islands in the southeast. In 1907 he proclaimed the 4.9-million-acre Chugach National Forest, and a year later combined the Alexander Archipelago reserve with the Tongass reserve to form one entity of 6.7 million acres called Tongass National Forest. These reserves had been recommended by F. E. Olmsted, Chief Forester Gifford Pinchot's main inspector. Olmsted believed that if the reserves were not created there would soon be a scramble to acquire them from the public domain by Pacific Northwest lumbermen who were facing depletion closer to home. Also, Olmsted discovered, timber fetched higher prices when it was cut from forest reserves rather than from unreserved public-domain land. As usual, protests dogged Roosevelt's proclamations, some of them exceedingly strange. "It is well known that rainfall is attracted by large bodies of timber," explained a part-owner of a sawmill on Prince of Wales Island in the Alexander Archipelago. "The rainfall in southeastern Alaska is excessive. If the commercial timber on Prince of Wales Island were cut off, the miners would have wood they needed for their operations, the ground would be rid of its encumbering trees, the climate would become more livable, and prospecting would be easier."

The main problem faced by the Forest Service in Alaska, which for the first six years consisted of exactly one man, was in persuading people to accept the need for supervision. This was hardly different from the resistance met around forests of the West, though in some ways administration in Alaska was actually easier. Grazing, a major issue of conflict in the West, did not exist in Alaska. "Foxes are the only livestock on the reserve," reported Olmsted after a tour of the southeast. "They graze on salmon at the rate of four cents an acre. There is a trespassing mule somewhere in the Klawak region but he cannot be located." More embarrassing was the Forest Service's trouble with prostitutes and bootleggers who set up shop within Forest Service jurisdiction, since agents of the General Land Office occasionally allowed such types to file for land under the special Alaska Homestead Act, knowing full well how they meant to use it.

Dissension between Pinchot's Forest Service and the General Land Office broke out frequently around the country, but the rift over Alaska led to the sensational dismissal of Gifford Pinchot in 1910. While serving as land office commissioner under Roosevelt, Richard Ballinger, a quiet former mayor of Seattle and confidant of timbermen in the Pacific Northwest, had objected to the creation of the Tongass and Chugach national forests. To Ballinger, Alaskan forest reserves were unnecessary, and he saw in their establishment the influence of the empire-hungry Pinchot. Trouble between the two men led to Ballinger's resignation, but it began brewing again in 1909, when William Howard Taft appointed Ballinger Interior Secretary. Since 1907, rumors of questionable coal claims within the Chugach National Forest had been circulating among foresters. Even though the claims lay within Forest Service territory, the General Land Office was responsible for their administration. Meanwhile, between his term as General Land Office commissioner and his appointment as head of the Interior Department, Ballinger had returned to Seattle and served as attorney to the claimants of the clouded mining patents. Several years before, an Idaho miner named Clarence Cunningham had secretly been given the power to file claims on behalf of the Alaska Company, a syndicate controlled by the Morgan and Guggenheim banking interests. Such filing on behalf of absentee speculators was routine in Alaska and in remote regions of the lower forty-eight states, but syndicate control violated the stipulations of the Coal Mining Act of 1873, which limited the number of claims any one corporation could own. It was for this reason that Roosevelt had withdrawn 100,000 acres of coal-bearing lands in Alaska in 1906 (see chapter 3).

When Ballinger assumed his Interior post, he ordered that the Cunningham claims be allowed to go to final patent, without further investigation into their legitimacy. Louis Glavis, an unusually vigilant young land office agent in Seattle, became suspicious of Ballinger's eagerness to proceed with the claims and recommended a field examination. He wanted to pursue the rumor that the claims violated coal-mining laws, and that in truth the syndicate behind them was using mining laws to obtain not coal but marketable timber. Glavis went to Pinchot with his suspicions and was promptly dismissed for discussing the case with a rival department. Pinchot publicized his long-lived mistrust of Ballinger and land office procedures by publicly accusing the Secretary of conspiring with the syndicate, and of trying to cover up his association with it. President Taft fired Pinchot for gross insubordination, and a subsequent Senate investigation exonerated Ballinger—even though the suspected taint of corruption finally caused his second resignation. The highly visible case harmed the Forest Service's standing in Alaska, according to Tongass supervisor William A. Langille. Afterward, Langille noticed "a biased antagonism toward the Forest Service which is the outgrowth of the more or less radical anti-conservation movement in Alaska . . . conceived to be so radically unjust to Alaska and its development. . . ."

The national park system, limping along before the arrival of Stephen Mather in 1915, did not incorporate any Alaskan lands until 1910, when President Taft invoked the 1906 Antiquities Act to establish Sitka National Monument. Sitka, or New Archangel as the Russians had called it, was the first "capital" of Alaska. It was also the site of numerous Tlingit Indian relics and artifacts. The village of Old Kasaan was another obvious candidate for national monument designation. Although Old Kasaan was designated a monument in 1916, much of what had made it qualify for such recognition had been burned the summer before. In 1917, National Park Director Mather brought Mount McKinley National Park (now Denali National Park and Preserve) into the park system, largely as a result of naturalist Charles Sheldon's ten-year campaign to obtain national park

259

status for his beloved mountain and its wildlife. Sheldon, who had been a companion of Muir's on Alaskan treks, lived in a cabin through a winter at the base of Denali, Mount McKinley's Indian name. By 1927, Katmai and Glacier Bay national monuments were added to the park system.

It was to become customary for Alaskan lands to join the national park system by executive proclamation rather than by congressional act, though the areas were larger and surpassed in grandeur the parks in the lower forty-eight states. Although the National Park Service's presence in Alaska was quite meager, the antifederal sentiment pervading the territory was aroused by the monument proclamations. In 1924 the *Juneau Empire* labeled the establishment of the Glacier Bay reserve "a monstrous proposition." An editorial railed that "the suggestion that a reserve be established to protect a glacier that none could disturb if he wanted and none would want to disturb if he could, or to permit the study of plant and insect life is the quintessence of silliness. It leads one to wonder if Washington has gone crazy through catering to conservation faddists."

Since Director Mather and his successors devoted themselves to promoting the parks with the highest visibility, Alaska's parks functioned without guardians. Mount McKinley National Park, for example, did not record a park visit until 1922. Appropriations for visitor comforts were channeled to other park properties. It was, according to national park historian Frank Williss, "because of the remoteness of the areas and the relative lack of population and developmental pressures that administrative neglect of the Alaska parks and monuments was not as serious as it might have been. External factors, not design, served to buffer the areas from serious and irreversible encroachment."

The largest withdrawal of land from Alaska's public domain was made in 1923 by President Warren G. Harding. This time the area, which lay on the North Slope of the Brooks Range and was approximately the size of Indiana, was reserved for its oil potential and placed under the supervision of the Navy Department. Estimates of the recoverable reserves in Naval Petroleum No. 4, or Pet-4, ranged between 10 billion and 100 billion barrels. The navy, which supervised three other reserves including the infamous Teapot Dome in

Wyoming (see chapter 3), was constantly on guard to ensure that its emergency rights to the oil in the reserves were not abrogated. "I have been compelled to fight almost every day of my incumbency in office to prevent the dummy entrymen and illegal operators from taking the Naval Reserves," stated Josephus Daniels, Navy Secretary under President Woodrow Wilson. These reserves were "the only hope for the Navy when the all too rapid use of American oil will leave [the reserves] the only available supply." Particularly in Alaska, the major oil companies fought this arrangement for years, insisting that all exploration and extraction ought to be governed entirely by the needs of the private sector.

## THE PRESERVATIONISTS MUSH IN

In the summer of 1929, wilderness enthusiast Robert Marshall boarded a small plane and flew where no plane had ever landed before, to the town of Wiseman, population eighty-one, on the Middle Fork of the Yukon River near the Arctic Circle. Ostensibly, his reason for venturing into the Alaskan bush was to study Arctic plants. Aside from his desire to serve science, however, Marshall simply wanted to live among Eskimos and to explore country no white man had ever seen. He balanced restful periods in Wiseman with ambitious forays into the Central Brooks Range, the northernmost mountain chain in the world, extending six hundred miles across the Arctic. On his several trips by dogsled and on foot, he climbed twenty-eight peaks, many of them first ascents, and named a delicate valley bordered by steel-gray peaks decapitated by a low sky, calling it Gates of the Arctic. One of Marshall's expeditions was arranged simply to settle an argument about the source of the Clear River. "I had more work planned already than I could possibly ever accomplish, but the chance of following an unknown river to its source in mid-winter seemed more important than anything else," he wrote in his journal. Shortly before his death in 1939, Marshall devised a blueprint for Alaska's future that would come to bear on future legislation.

Because the unique recreational value of Alaska lies in its frontier character, it would seem desirable to establish a really sizeable area, free of roads and industries, where frontier conditions will be pre-

261

served. Fortunately, this is peculiarly possible in northern Alaska, for economic and social reasons. Economically, the population is so scattered that airplane transportation is the only feasible means of mechanical conveyance, and auto roads could not possibly justify their great cost. Sociologically, the country of northern Alaska is inhabited chiefly by native populations which would be much happier, if United States experience is any criterion, without either roads or industries.

During the 1930s, other travelers and scientists publicized the need to preserve vast parts of Alaska, for the sake of its wildlife as well as its people. It was an era when wildlife biologists were in ascendance and Alaska lay before them, a ripe field for scrutinizing. Writer-photographer John M. Holzworth produced his moving account of grizzlies and bald eagles on Admiralty Island and campaigned for its designation as a wildlife refuge or national park; Olaus Murie followed caribou through Arctic valleys and over mountains, in awe of the animals' "roaming freedom shared by no other creature"; his brother, Adolph Murie, wrote a precedent-setting monograph on Alaska's wolves, and promoted a deeper understanding of the synergism of species. Economic depression shrank Alaska's human population and industry. But scientific recognition of its incalculable worth had begun to rise.

## STATEHOOD AND THE CONSERVATION MOVEMENT

Until World War II, it was easy for many people inside and outside Alaska to ignore the territory's ties to the United States. Congress repeatedly refused entreaties by Alaskan boomers and boosters for admission to the Union on the grounds of its transient population (meaning its *white* population, the only one that counted politically). But then came the Japanese invasion of the Aleutian Islands in 1942, which strengthened the bonds with home as nothing else. During the spring of that year, 2,500 American soldiers died in combat on the islands of Attu and Kiska; it was the only time in the war that American soil in the Western Hemisphere was invaded and occupied by enemy troops. The task of defending this northwest corner of the United States introduced about 300,000 American soldiers to Alaska's beauty and resulted in the territory's first airfields, radio stations, sewers, schools—all those things Alaskan boomers had failed to get during peacetime.

After the war, the quest for statehood gained new momentum, though not without opposition from some politicians and not without giving concern to conservationists. Southerners were the foremost opponents of Alaska's admission—largely because of its nonwhite population, some critics said. In 1952, Senator John Stennis of Mississippi gave a more civic-minded explanation for his objections: "The county is the great training ground" for self-government, he said. "With all deference to the fine people of Alaska the main essential training element for American citizenship would be totally lacking," since Alaska had no counties. To Stennis, the fact that "only three-tenths of one percent of privately owned land" existed in Alaska was also a problem—the rest of it belonged to the federal government. In the growing clamor for statehood, that fact had not been lost on two agencies—the National Park Service and the Fish and Wildlife Service—which had been exploring the possibilities of preservation on a grand scale, once all the conditions of statehood had been decided. It was a nervous time for preservationists in and out of government, for the tone of Alaskan rhetoric, and its emphasis on unbridled development, did not further their own aims.

During the 1950s, George Collins and Lowell Sumner of the Park Service recommended that a substantial portion of the northeastern Arctic be protected as wilderness for "perpetual preservation as a scientific field laboratory and also for the education, enjoyment, and inspiration of outdoor-minded people." Olaus Murie and his wife, Margaret, who had lived off and on in Alaska since she was nine, pursued this recommendation for the establishment of the 9-million-acre Arctic National Wildlife Refuge. "There is a great gift to be won in places like the Arctic Wildlife Refuge," Mrs. Murie testified in one of many congressional hearings she attended for Alaska's sake. There was, she said, "the gift of personal satisfaction, the personal well-being, purchased by striving, by lifting and setting down legs, over and over, through the muskeg, up the slopes, gaining the summit— man using himself." Support for the designation of this refuge from the local statehood movement was one of the conditions Alaska's conservationists demanded in exchange for *their* support of statehood.

Both sides got their wish. In 1958, Alaska became a state, and in 1960 the refuge was designated. To make up for its "unique neglect" of Alaska for eighty-three years, Congress displayed unusual generosity in the statehood bill. First, the new state was allowed to choose, for its own use, 104.6 million acres from the public domain administered by the Bureau of Land Management, and was given twenty-five years to make its selections. This grant surpassed the total acreage of all federal lands transferred to seventeen Western states on their admission. Second, Alaska could retain 90 percent of the royalties generated from oil and mineral leases on the remaining public domain. In all other states, income from subsurface federal leases in their midst could not exceed 25 percent of the royalties earned.

Flushed with new hopes of growth, Alaskan boomers were now eager to extend American civilization into the farthest reaches of their state. The key project intended to do this was the construction of a dam about one hundred miles from Robert Marshall's beloved Wiseman. Rampart Dam, as proposed by the Army Corps of Engineers, would have flooded the Yukon flats with a body of water larger than Lake Erie—for hydroelectric power generation. "Search the whole world and it would be difficult to find an equivalent area with so little to be lost through flooding," claimed an assistant to Senator Ernest Gruening. The entire site being considered was larger than New Jersey and contained "not more than ten flush toilets," the assistant boasted, without bothering to add that it did not *need* ten flush toilets (a closer count revealed none). The Rampart Dam controversy erupted in the 1960s, with memories of the Echo Park and Split Mountain dam proposals for Dinosaur National Monument still vivid in the public's mind (see chapters 1 and 5). It was easy enough for the growing conservation community to become exercised about the Alaskan proposal—and defeat it.

As another sort of statehood gift, in 1958 the Atomic Energy Commission offered to demonstrate the civilian use of nuclear power by exploding a device to make a harbor at the western edge of the Brooks Range. This notion was called Project Chariot, and it appalled Native Alaskans, who feared that the blast would ruin their traditional hunting and ceremonial grounds, and thereby undermine their subsistence living. This project, too, was defeated.

The submission of such plans to promote an assumed prosperity caused more and more Alaskans to wonder whether they really wanted to create their state in the image of Los Angeles or Detroit. Somehow, the routine strivings of the rest of America did not seem to belong in Alaska. Quietly, the Park Service and the Bureau of Sport Fisheries, later known as the Fish and Wildlife Service, had been preparing alternative scenarios. The chief hope of Alaska wilderness preservationists lay with these two agencies, which, unlike the Forest Service and the BLM, did not, in theory at least, have to strike bargains and work trade-offs among eager multiple-users. Land and wildlife would remain their top concerns.

During the 1950s and 1960s the Park Service drew up a "wish list" of thirty-nine areas that might be added to the Alaskan park system. The Fish and Wildlife Service identified a comparable number for the refuge system.

In 1965, after traveling to Alaska in the company of top national park officials, Interior Secretary Stewart Udall became infected with their zeal for new parks there. The problem was how to get them. The state of Alaska was busily selecting its lands according to its charter, Natives were beginning to agitate for their fair share, and Congress was loath to step in and start preserving vast areas from the Arctic to the southeast and possibly thwart the whole state selection process. In 1968, Udall persuaded President Lyndon Johnson, who had shown little prior interest in Alaskan protection, to invoke the 1906 Antiquities Act and create a grand sweep of national monuments to rival even Theodore Roosevelt's dramatic withdrawals. At the same time Udall would establish two new wildlife refuges, each exceeding one million acres. The entire package would be billed the "President's Christmas conservation gift to the nation" and would send Johnson into history as the greatest conservation President since T. R. Christmas came and went, but the President's commitment was eroded by a brief illness and other executive business. Meanwhile, National Park Service officials had done their work. Necessary proclamations for a 4-million-acre Gates of the Arctic National Monument, a 2-million-acre addition to Mount McKinley National Park, and several

265

other key areas in Alaska and other states were drawn up for the President's signature. Johnson agreed to do all this, and even alluded to his intentions in his departing State of the Union Address in January 1969, but his consent was based on the assumption that Secretary Udall had informed House Interior Committee Chairman Wayne Aspinall of the presidential prerogative as a matter of courtesy. Udall, however, had not done this. He knew the Colorado congressman was vehemently against the freewheeling establishment of monuments by presidential proclamation because it circumvented congressional authority to create new parks. It was feared that if Aspinall was told too far in advance, he would marshal his considerable influence against the conservation package. As predicted, Aspinall was furious when he heard about it, and Johnson in turn flew into a rage at Udall—although he still agreed to go through with the proclamations. His signature on them seemed so certain that Park Service officials had already mailed out press releases announcing the new monuments.

Hours before Richard Nixon's inauguration, Johnson changed his mind and did not sign all the proclamations set out for him. In the end he added 94,000 acres to the existing Katmai National Monument, and agreed to let Udall go through with his new wildlife refuges. "Lyndon Johnson did the conservationists a favor," wrote journalist Robert Cahn, although at the time nobody saw it that way. "Johnson's negative action served to stimulate both Alaskan and national conservation groups to more vigorous activity." Had Johnson fulfilled all his intentions, chances are that the greater allotments of the future would have been impossible.

## THE NATIVE CONTINGENT

When Johnson left office, the state of Alaska had selected only about one-quarter of the lands to which it was entitled. State picks were largely oil and gas lands, for these were considered the highest revenue producers. But some of the lands wanted by the state were also wanted by Native Alaskans. In 1964 they formed the Alaskan Federation of Natives and began developing the political clout they had always lacked. At the request of the federation, Secretary Udall slapped a moratorium on state selections in 1966 so that all the overlapping claims could be straightened out. Udall's moratorium was still in effect two years later, when the Atlantic Richfield Company and the Humble Oil and Refining Company struck an immense pool of oil in Prudhoe Bay, north of the Arctic Circle, not far from Pet-4. The companies needed transportation corridors and rights-of-way before production could begin, but no one could say for certain who owned what land. Within a month of the discovery, a consortium of oil companies consisting of ARCO, Humble Oil, and British Petroleum announced plans to build an eight-hundred-mile pipeline from Prudhoe Bay to Valdez, a fishing village on Prince William Sound.

Suddenly the settlement of Native claims became urgent—to both the Natives and the oil companies. The odd alliance resulted, in 1971, in passage of the Alaska Native Claims Settlement Act (ANCSA). ANCSA awarded Alaska Natives—defined as any Alaskan-born persons at least one-quarter Eskimo, Aleut, or Indian—a land grant of 44 million acres plus a cash payment of $962 million for renouncing all claims to the rest of the state. The financial compensation was prorated so that half of it would be paid by oil royalties and the other half by the federal government. The Natives were required to form corporations for the ownership and management of the land and the administration of the money, which was to be viewed as corporate assets; only Natives could hold shares in these corporations and no shares could be sold or exchanged for a period of twenty years. All of this seemed fair enough, even generous, and most Natives signed up. Indeed, the settlement was so generous and arrived at so quickly that author John McPhee, in *Coming into the Country*, labeled it "the great, final and retributive payment for all of American history's Native claims—an attempt to extinguish something more than title. The settlement suggests not only principal but interest as well on twenty decades of national guilt."

Some Natives were more cynical about their good fortune. Joe Upicksoun, president of the North Slope Native Association, surmised that guilt had less to do with the arrangement than greed. "By accident of nature, right now the eyes of the nation and the world are centered on the North Slope," he said. "Without intending to belittle your land, the real reason for the entire settlement is oil, which by accident is on our land, not yours." Most non-Native Alaskans were downright jubilant. They truly believed the words of Governor Keith H. Miller, uttered back in September 1969: "Tomorrow we will reach our birthright. We will rendezvous with our dreams."

## SOMETHING FOR EVERYONE

The development of the Prudhoe Bay oil discovery and the construction of the pipeline to Valdez inspired an economic boom to rival that of the Gold Rush nearly eighty years before. Alyeska, as the pipeline consortium was called, employed more than twenty thousand people in 1975 and 1976, two years before the line's completion. At Prudhoe Bay, men were paid $2,000 a week plus room and board, and (according to Joe McGinniss, who witnessed the event) rioting reportedly broke out when employees were told that steak and lobster would no longer be served in the same meal, but only on alternating nights. Valdez's population bloated from four hundred to eight thousand. The city was so proud of its role in receiving the Arctic oil that the local newspaper urged that Valdez's main street be renamed "11:02 Boulevard," after the exact moment of the first oil's arrival eight years after pipeline construction had begun.

The discovery of mammoth oil reserves in Alaska carried with it something for everyone. The Natives secured their birthright (presumably), Alaskan boosters achieved their ultimate boom, and oil companies found something to sell. Conservationists found a way to save some land for the future, too. For, once the state and Natives had selected their lands, something had to be done with those that remained in the unreserved public domain. The solution to this third dilemma was drafted into ANCSA, under Section 17(d)(2). This section provided for the Interior Secretary to "withdraw from all forms of appropriation under the public land laws, including the mining and mineral leasing laws . . . up to, but not to exceed eighty million acres of unreserved public lands in the State of Alaska . . . which the Secretary deems are suitable [to study] for addition to or creation as units of the National Park, Forest, Wildlife Refuge, and Wild and Scenic River Systems. . . . " The act also stipulated that the Secretary would have two years to make his recommendations. If Congress did not ratify or otherwise act on them by the end of 1978, the

268

"d-2" lands would revert back to commercially exploitable public domain.

A few days after ANCSA was enacted, the Interior Department met with its agencies to brief them on the "d-2" lands. Theodor Swem, a National Park Service veteran and assistant director to Hartzog, was appointed head of the Park Service's planning effort. For Swem it was the career opportunity of a lifetime. As a boy growing up in Iowa, he had become enchanted with Alaska after he read John Holzworth's account of the grizzlies. Swem would retire from the Park Service in 1976, having made about forty visits to Alaska in fifteen years to study places he had previously seen only in his youthful imagination. There are two things Swem remembers about the initial ANCSA meeting at the Interior Department. "One was the real lack of knowledge as to what the law contained," he said. "The other was Under Secretary Bill Pecora's statement that Interior Secretary Rogers Morton saw in Alaska a great opportunity 'to do things right the first time.' " Swem and his colleagues would invoke those words many times over the next few years to ward off routine assaults on superb areas. At last, as Robert Cahn put it in *The Fight to Save Wild Alaska*, his account of the struggle, "The door to new parks, wildlife refuges, and wilderness in Alaska had been flung open." But constant vigilance was demanded to ensure that that door did not slam shut.

## THE ROAD TO ANILCA

Despite Secretary Morton's expressed commitment to the expansion of parks and refuges in Alaska, interdepartmental pressure built to keep as much land as possible in multiple-use classifications so that hunting, logging, and mining would be guaranteed. The National Park Service and Fish and Wildlife Service scrambled to identify all the areas where multiple use should not prevail. The first phase of study took two years. It was hobbled when the state of Alaska filed land selections on 72 million acres (including some "d-2" lands) and when it threatened to bring suit against the Department of the Interior for its 1966 moratorium. Forest Service demands for its share of the resource pie also proved a difficult obstacle. Agriculture Secretary Earl Butz had demanded that the Interior Department be generous to his agency. Specifically, he wanted 42 million acres of additional national forests, much of it in areas proposed for parks and refuges. At last Secretaries Morton and Butz compromised, and Morton offered 18.8 million acres to the Forest Service, most of it in central Alaska. Then he submitted his legislative recommendation for 83.6 million acres of parks, forests, refuges, and wild and scenic rivers.

Morton's proposal reached Congress at the end of 1973, a time when the country was becoming too preoccupied with President Nixon's Watergate indiscretions to pay attention to Alaskan conservation. Besides, according to ANCSA, Congress had until December 1978 to decide what to do with the public domain in the forty-ninth state. There was no rush. Not until Jimmy Carter was elected President in 1976 did the "d-2" lands begin to assume greater importance. The deadline for Congress to act on the recommendations was now less than two years away, and Carter had appointed numerous conservation-minded officials who saw in Alaska the chance for momentous decisions. Interior Secretary Cecil Andrus made his intentions clear at one of his first briefings on Alaska. Andrus remarked that since Republicans had recommended the preservation of about 80 million acres, Democrats would have to recommend more. He made good on his promise.

January 1977. Twenty-three months to go. The day Congress convened, Representative Morris Udall, the new chairman of the House Interior Committee, introduced H.R. 39, a bill for the protection of 110 million acres, cosigned by Ohio Representative John Seiberling, an ardent preservation advocate, and seventy-five other cosigners. Many of the House cosigners had been buttonholed by members of the Alaska Coalition, a grassroots citizens lobby that had picked up the fight for parks, wildernesses, and refuges where Interior Department officials left off. The coalition, chaired by Charles Clusen of the Sierra Club and later The Wilderness Society, was a consortium of fifty-five organizations that devoted itself to building broad public support for Alaska preservation. The future of Alaska, coalition leaders asserted, was a national issue, not a local one. The Alaska Coalition kept congressional hearings on Alaska well stocked with citizens from all over the country. The hearings, held at various sites around the country, were consistently packed. In Chicago, on a Saturday morning in May, three hundred people had come to speak on Alaska's behalf. In Atlanta the following week, two hundred people gave statements. "Those of us here in the great public land desert of the eastern United States know better than anyone what happens when the public domain is frittered away," said a woman who had come from Auburn, Alabama, to give her statement. "We need to communicate to Congress and to the people of Alaska what it is like to be living in a place a hundred and fifty or two hundred years after the public domain has been unloaded into private hands." In Denver, another three hundred people crowded the hearing room. In Alaska, one thousand residents of twenty towns and Native villages were heard, about half of whom were in favor of H.R. 39. This division disproved the assertion of Alaska's three congressmen that virtually all of their constituents opposed any preservation effort as dramatic as the one described in the Udall-Seiberling bill.

Although H.R. 39 substantially increased the acreage for the highest order of preservation, much of the land it encompassed had been classified as "preserves," which allowed for hunting and other activities that were typically anathema to parks. The "preserve" classification had been added to make the vast land designations more palatable to people who did not favor parks and wilderness. In addition to these concessions, when drawing all the boundaries for the national interest lands, great pains had been taken to exclude the areas with the highest estimated reserves of oil, gas, and minerals. Government documents indicated that only about 3 percent of lands with known oil reserves had been withdrawn by H.R. 39, and only 5 percent of those with various minerals. One geologist who testified for the preservation measure asserted that no more than a thirty-eight-day supply of oil lay beneath the Arctic Wildlife Refuge.

Nevertheless, antifederal feeling still ran high in Alaska, where many felt they were being deprived of their frontier heritage by meddlesome bureaucrats. In the late 1970s, for instance, when the Park Service temporarily increased its ranger power to administer new national monuments created by President Carter, outbreaks of violence were not uncommon. In some stores, rangers were refused service. One Park Service employee went to a dentist in Anchorage who refused to treat his impacted tooth because of the ranger's affiliation. Others received bomb threats at their lodgings, or death threats—

one accompanied by a spray of bullets into an office window. In Lake Clark, an arsonist burned an airplane that had been chartered by three rangers.

Back in Washington, Alaska Senators Mike Gravel and Ted Stevens were engaged in their own political sharpshooting to prevent what they saw as Alaska's "lockup." Senator Gravel repeatedly threatened to filibuster if H.R. 39 got as far as the Senate floor. It did. In April 1978, H.R. 39 passed the House by a vote of 277 to 31. Suddenly, in May, just seven months before the deadline set by ANCSA, Gravel changed his mind. In a letter to his fellow senator, Gravel stated that he had canvassed Alaskans in his area and found they were not strenuously opposed to the "d-2" legislation. He had decided to support it. This good news resulted in a negotiating session between jubilant House bill proponents and the Alaskan delegation, so that further agreements could be worked out. At the end of the long meeting, Udall stood up and began to leave. "Gentlemen," he said, "we've done something historic here today. Let's get it resolved on paper and go to the floor with it." Then Gravel spoke up, for the first time that day, though he had been present through the whole session. "Just a minute," he said. "I've got a few things I want to raise." His "few things" turned out to be serious. One of his demands was for five transportation corridors through the heart of several parks and refuges, which would have negated all efforts put into their preservation. No agreements could be reached before the Ninety-fifth Congress adjourned, and Gravel threatened to filibuster if anybody tried to submit a bill to extend the deadline for "d-2" consideration. The Senate adjourned, and Alaska's future again seemed uncertain.

The dissolution of H.R. 39 at the last minute prompted President Carter to keep a promise he had made. To ensure that the lands covered in H.R. 39 would not revert to unreserved public domain, he used the Antiquities Act to create 56 million acres of national monuments. Carter's proclamation, according to author David Rains Wallace, was "the most daring executive action for conservation since Theodore Roosevelt withdrew the national forests." Carter also directed Secretary Andrus to set aside 40 million acres of wildlife refuges, using authority granted in the 1976 Federal Land Policy and Management Act. "As the steward of these lands, I feel a responsibility to protect them until Congress legislates their future," Andrus said. The Alaska Coalition had not lost its momentum, despite the disheartening turn of events in May. To show its still-vigorous support for Alaskan protection, the coalition sent a telegram to the President that included the names of one thousand citizen groups with an aggregate membership of 10 million. The telegram overflowed onto the floor.

In the Ninety-sixth Congress, work began anew when Morris Udall introduced a new H.R. 39 to open the session. However, the opposition had gained some strength and, following a series of actions in committee, a substitute bill, which was a considerably diluted version, made it to the House floor in May 1980. It passed, 268 to 157. The Alaska delegation continued its delaying tactics in the Senate, hoping that time would give antipreservation lobbyists the opportunity to weaken the bill further. It did. The compromise bill that emerged from the Senate in July reduced the acreage designated as parks and refuges to 104.3 million. There were even worse elements in the bill, by the lights of the conservationists. Among these was the mandated annual "cut" of 450 million board feet of timber from Tongass National Forest. Other provisions stipulated that major parts of the recommended Yukon Flats National Wildlife Refuge continue under the jurisdiction of the Bureau of Land Management, not the Fish and Wildlife Service; eliminated the Copper River Delta as a potential wildlife refuge; allowed exploration for oil and gas in the Arctic National Wildlife Refuge; reduced the land corridor for Alaska's wild and scenic rivers from two miles on either side to half a mile; and severely cut wilderness classifications.

The Alaska Coalition prepared to win back what it had lost. Its determination, however, was overtaken by events. In November 1980, Ronald Reagan achieved a stunning upset over incumbent Carter, and conservationists correctly assumed that the chances for improved protection under a Reagan regime were slim. They decided to stick with what they had. On November 12, 1980, the Alaska National Interest Lands Conservation Act (ANILCA) was passed, and in one of the last acts of his administration, President Carter signed it into law. The greatest conservation act ever passed by any government had, at the last instant, become hostage to political expedience. "Our

273

sense of joy," remembered Theodor Swem, "was tempered by the uncertainty of what would come next."

## THE FRUITS OF COMPROMISE

During and after the battle to save pristine Alaska, one old Alaska hand was struck by how little credit the Interior Department and citizen conservation groups such as the Alaska Coalition were willing to give each other for ANILCA's realization. "Both sides worked for its passage, but they worked independently, and more often than not blamed each other for the act's shortcomings," he said. Interior Department field studies gave ANILCA its shape, long before conservation groups breathed national spirit into it. ANILCA, then, might be viewed as the result of a kind of alliance between citizens and federal administrators.

If so, the alliance came to a dead halt with the assumption of power of President Reagan and his colleagues. "The overall approach and attitude under the Reagan administration cannot have been made more clear," wrote Charles Clusen, former Alaska Coalition chairman, in a 1984 issue of *Wilderness* magazine. "The Interior Department has single-mindedly championed development interests in its interpretation of the law, repeatedly flouting clear congressional intent."

Two years earlier, Massachusetts Senator Paul Tsongas had sadly reported to his colleagues that Secretary James Watt was "in fact undoing the law." Tsongas explained that the Secretary employed three techniques to do this: "Through calculated use of the budget, selective enforcement of some provisions of the act but no enforcement of others, and by suspect interpretation of statutory authority—the Alaska National Interest Lands Conservation Act is being transformed into the Alaska National Interest Lands Development Act."

In Secretary Watt's case, not much investigation was needed to reveal his antagonism to ANILCA, however imperfect the act may have seemed to conservationists. He first revealed his intent just two months after being confirmed in his position. In a 1981 memo, he wrote:

In view of the continuing energy crisis and this administration's interest in becoming independent of reliance on foreign oil supplies, it is essential that we implement the [oil and gas leasing program] immediately . . . to identify at the earliest possible date areas in Alaska within the National Wildlife Refuge System . . . which could be leased for the exploration and development of oil and gas.

While such discretion is given to the Interior Secretary in the establishment of refuges, the underlying intent was that this discretion would be exercised only in the most extreme circumstances. Shortly thereafter, Watt took the responsibility of conducting fish and wildlife surveys on the Arctic National Wildlife Refuge away from the Fish and Wildlife Service and gave it to the U.S. Geological Survey, an agency with no experience in fish and wildlife matters. The surveys were required prior to issuance of permits for surface and seismic oil and mineral exploration. Secretary Watt cut the time needed for the wildlife survey by six months, giving the untrained Geological Survey not even a chance to fumble attempts at field studies in the refuge. A federal judge quickly overruled Watt's transfer of wildlife authority, ruling that "Secretary Watt's transfer . . . from the Fish and Wildlife Service to the U.S. Geological Survey of lead responsibility for approving exploration plans was a clear error of judgment beyond his statutory authority." In Alaska, other errors of judgment would surface before Secretary Watt's resignation in October 1983.

The lands of Alaska remain in a kind of limbo, imperfectly protected by ANILCA and still affected by the actions of Watt's brief tenure as chief steward of the Great Land. There is both a sadness and a hope to be found in the recent history of the state. The sadness lies in having missed the opportunity to "do it right" once and for all with ANILCA. The hope stems from the fact that it is not too late to change; the provisions of ANILCA are not implacable. Historian T. H. Watkins has written in regard to that hope:

Viewed from a sufficiently empyrean distance, much of our history can be read as a scenario of missed opportunities. For one appropriate example, had the federal government been farsighted enough to listen to such nineteenth-century conservationists as George Perkins Marsh or John Wesley Powell, a great deal of resource abuse would have been avoided—and we modern conservationists would have much less to complain about. Missed opportunities must have been at the forefront of his mind when F. Scott Fitzgerald remarked that "there are no second acts in American lives." He was wrong, of course— there are second acts, both in individual lives and in the national life, and one of the most dramatic of them all waits to be played out in the great fist of Alaska.

## AN AGENDA FOR
## THE NATIONAL INTEREST LANDS OF ALASKA

The Alaska National Interest Lands Conservation Act of 1980 is an extraordinary piece of legislation in many ways—not the least of which is the fact that it represents the first time in history that an attempt was made to lay out the land-use patterns for an area whose dimensions approach those of a subcontinent. It can be viewed as one of the great triumphs of the modern conservation movement. The document's sheer bulk is very much in keeping with the millions of acres of land it allocates, in many cases with detailed stipulations regarding its management; fifteen titles and 180 pages in the Statutes at Large, making it longer than some histories. Even so, at the eleventh hour, the results of a presidential election made it necessary to abandon the act's full potential. As a result, although it added 104.3 million acres to the various Alaska conservation systems, a figure not far off the 124.6 million that was considered desirable by conservationists, there were serious omissions and weaknesses.

The shifting of boundaries on maps in Washington, D.C., can create unimagined havoc on the ground in Alaska. Like everything else about that prodigious place, the effects can be colossal, spelling the difference between prosperity and decline for entire wildlife populations and ecosystems. And so, while it is true that the total acreage protected by ANILCA amounts to about 80 percent of the desirable figure, the numbers say nothing about the quality of the omissions.

That quality is considerable. Conservationists had identified pristine areas that had already been thoroughly studied and sought immediate wilderness designation for them via ANILCA. The version of the bill introduced in the House in January 1979 would have designated 85 million acres in three systems—national park, wildlife

276

refuge, and forest—as wilderness. As passed by the House in May of that year, the bill pared that figure to about 67 million. The Senate made further cuts, down to the 56 million acres given wilderness protection in the law as enacted. Among notable wilderness losses from the House-passed bill were about 3 million acres in Gates of the Arctic National Park and Preserve, Denali National Park and Preserve, and the Alaska Maritime National Wildlife Refuge. Most of these 29 million acres, already studied under the provisions of the Native Claims Act but excised from wilderness designation in ANILCA as enacted, should be placed in the National Wilderness Preservation System immediately.

Beyond these areas, there are significant additional portions of several Alaskan parks and refuges that should be added to the wilderness system under the provisions of ANILCA's Section 1317. This section specifically mandates a five-year wilderness review of all national park and wildlife refuge lands, with recommendations to be made to Congress when studies are completed. This wilderness review, however, is included in the park and refuge management plans, and because of insufficient personnel and funding, the plans and wilderness recommendations are currently as much as a year behind schedule. Areas such as the Yukon Flats Refuge of east central Alaska, one of the largest and most productive migratory waterfowl regions of the world, and other park and refuge lands of equal significance, should be given wilderness status swiftly.

Alaska's two national forests—Tongass and Chugach—offer similar opportunities to enlarge the wilderness preservation system in the state. Both the Prince William Sound wilderness study area and the Copper River Delta of Chugach National Forest, for instance, are prime examples of areas with clear wilderness character that should be recommended for wilderness through the Forest Service's planning process and designated as such by Congress.

Such actions would go a long way toward reinstating a properly broad preservation policy for Alaska's lands, but a great deal more needs to be done—and only a serious effort to correct and strengthen ANILCA itself can assure that it will be.

While there is some risk involved in reopening the Alaska debate, ANILCA as it stands cannot be accepted as a *fait accompli*, immune to improvement. The act remains too vulnerable to the kind of administrative mismanagement—by intent or simple misfeasance—that has been demonstrated during the more than six years since its passage. If we do not seek to improve the law and the way it is administered now, our failure to act will haunt us.

House Interior Committee Chairman Morris Udall succinctly remarked after the act's passage, "The first installment has been made. It's a beginning." Working to strengthen ANILCA, then, would be a way of compensating for its abrupt and difficult birth. The act should be specifically improved in ten major areas, as follows:

*Terminate oil and gas exploration in the Arctic National Wildlife Refuge by giving it wilderness status.* Title X of ANILCA, "Federal North Slope Lands Studies, Oil and Gas Leasing Program and Mineral Assessments," is one of the cardinal defects in the statute as enacted. In essence the title outlines the conditions for surface and seismic exploration of 1.4 million acres of the refuge's coastal plain. This is a fragile and unspoiled region that serves as calving ground for the Porcupine caribou herd; as denning ground for polar bears; and as habitat for grizzly bears, musk oxen, moose, wolves, arctic foxes, thousands of ducks, geese, swans, and loons, snowy owls, peregrine falcons, rough-legged hawks, golden eagles, and ten species of fish. Despite the panoply of wild creatures that depend on the area for survival, despite two votes by the full House to designate all of the refuge as wilderness, despite information from the U.S. Geological Survey showing that the area's total potential reserves would supply the nation with only thirty-eight days of fuel, despite Canada's interest in preserving its adjacent coastal region to form a splendid international wilderness zone—despite all these considerations, the Senate stripped the coastal plain of wilderness status and inserted the exploration provisions in the bill. Congress should repeal Title X, overlay the entire refuge with wilderness status, and direct the resumption of negotiations with Canada toward designating an international caribou refuge.

*Repeal Section 705 of ANILCA mandating an annual cut of 450 million board feet from Tongass National Forest.* One of the most destructive

278

compromises in ANILCA was engineered by a logging industry anxious to preserve its traditional privilege of harvesting timber from Tongass National Forest by hundreds of millions of board feet a year. The environmental damage inflicted in the 385,000 acres of the Tongass already logged has put the deer population of Alaska's southeast region in dire peril, has caused severe disruption of salmon spawning patterns—with a concomitant loss in fisheries revenue—has accelerated natural erosion throughout the region, and, if continued at present levels, will threaten the very existence of one of the world's few remaining temperate zone rain forests. Virtually all of the timber has been awarded to just two companies—Louisiana-Pacific's Ketchikan Pulp and the Japanese-owned Alaska Lumber and Pulp—under fifty-year Forest Service contracts, and, as a two-year study by The Wilderness Society has concluded, under a "below-cost" pricing structure that has cost the American taxpayers at least $200 million. This section of ANILCA should be repealed immediately.

The act should also be amended to extend wilderness protection to identified areas within the Tongass such as lands adjacent to the West Chichagof–Yakobi and Petersburg Creek–Duncan Salt Chuck wilderness areas, and Baker, Noyer, Lulu, and South Etolin islands. Additionally, all other lands within the Tongass should continue to be subject to the wilderness review process.

Parenthetically, it should be noted here that the Forest Service could and should take two actions outside the bounds of ANILCA itself that would immediately alleviate the problems in Tongass National Forest. First, it could—and it has the administrative authority to do so—abrogate the fifty-year cutting contracts with Louisiana Pacific's Ketchikan subsidiary and Alaska Lumber and Pulp; the antitrust violations of which both companies were charged and convicted in 1981 give clear justification for the Forest Service to cancel these contracts. Second, the agency should eliminate all "below-cost" operations so that the American taxpayers will not be losing money on every log sold.

*Establish the National Petroleum Reserve–Alaska as a unit of the National Wildlife Refuge System.* The most sizable missing element from the law as enacted is wildlife refuge status for National Petroleum

Reserve—Alaska, a 22.5-million-acre expanse that provides habitat for the Western Arctic caribou herd, millions of nesting waterfowl, the peregrine falcon, and many other wildlife species. Although the Alaska Reserve is not fully explored, it is thought to contain a number of medium-sized petroleum deposits. But it is unquestionably rich in wildlife values. Not only should this area be given wildlife refuge status where wildlife protection is given priority over oil and gas development, but certain areas should be included in the National Wilderness Preservation System.

*Restore wilderness status to the 150,000 acres deleted from Misty Fjords National Monument.* Fashioned out of Tongass National Forest land in southeastern Alaska, this new national monument is characterized by lofty waterfalls, mist-wreathed rain forests, and granite crags. The coastal region harbors a variety of marine mammals: sea lions, seals, killer whales, and porpoises. In ANILCA, Congress established the monument, designated all but about 143,000 of its 2,285,000 acres as wilderness, and guaranteed the issuance of a permit to construct a road through the deleted area regardless of environmental impacts. The exclusion was designed to accommodate the unpatented claims of U.S. Borax, a wholly-owned subsidiary of a British conglomerate, to molybdenum deposits within the excluded area. But the acreage left out is excessive—roughly ten times the amount that could possibly be needed for mining operations—and activities within the exclusion will disrupt or destroy salmon spawning grounds in three rivers, endanger black and brown bears that prey on the fish, and threaten the livelihoods of commercial fishermen. The act also endows the Secretary of Agriculture with broad authority to permit mining-related uses in that portion of Misty Fjords designated as wilderness if he considers them "necessary." ANILCA should be amended to allow the federal purchase of the mineral claims in Misty Fjords. At the very least, the exclusion from wilderness should be narrowed to the minimum necessary acreage, and the Secretary of Agriculture should be barred from permitting intrusive activities unless there is no feasible alternative means for developing the mineral deposits.

*Confer wildlife refuge or wilderness status to Steese National Conservation Area and White Mountains National Recreation Area.* These areas, which are adjacent to each other about eighty miles north of Fairbanks and comprise 2,220,000 acres, were part of the Yukon Flats National Wildlife Refuge in the House-passed bill. The Senate removed them from the refuge, redesignated them as above, and made the Bureau of Land Management responsible for their management under the principles of multiple use, by which all of its values—wilderness, recreation, wildlife, timber, minerals, and others—are pitted against one another and the managers are given discretion in balancing these uses. But both lie within the Yukon watershed, one of the most productive bird-breeding habitats on the continent, and deserve protection as refuge lands by incorporation of major watershed segments that qualify into the National Wilderness Preservation System.

*Eliminate the transportation corridor across Gates of the Arctic National Park and Preserve.* This is another case of the Senate whittling down the protection accorded by the House bill. Besides removing the park's "boot" section from wilderness, the law orders the Secretary of the Interior to allow access across that section to an undeveloped copper-mining area. Robert Marshall explored and named Gates of the Arctic, and many hikers rank it as the *ne plus ultra* of Alaskan backcountry. ANILCA should be amended to close the transportation corridor and restore the new park's wilderness integrity.

*Direct wilderness review for 76 million acres of BLM land.* Of the over 300 million acres of BLM land that once spanned Alaska, the great majority has been parceled out by ANILCA, the 1971 Alaska Native Claims Settlement Act, and Alaska's Statehood Act. Once the last conveyances have been made to Alaska Natives and the state, however, BLM will still have jurisdiction over up to 76 million acres. By the terms of BLM's managerial blueprint, the Federal Land Policy and Management Act of 1976 (FLPMA), this land would normally be studied in due course for possible additions to the National Wilderness Preservation System. But Section 1320 of ANILCA exempted these remaining BLM lands from FLPMA's mandatory wilderness review. ANILCA should be amended to repeal this exemption and direct wilderness review of all remaining public lands in the state.

*Restore full protection to areas deleted from park and wildlife refuge status in the Alaskan interior.* On the way to enactment, several areas in the Alaskan interior failed to receive adequate protection. For example, ANILCA did less than full justice to Denali National Park and Preserve; the act relegated the 1.3 million acres added to the old Mount McKinley National Park to the status of a national preserve, which translates into "sport hunting allowed." The same is true of 4.2 million acres of Wrangell–St. Elias National Park and Preserve. All such acreage should be given *full* protection within either the national park or wildlife refuge systems.

*Restore the width of Alaska's wild and scenic river corridors.* To reflect the large Alaskan scale, ANILCA as originally drafted set aside a wide corridor enveloping each of the bill's twenty-five additions to the National Wild and Scenic River System: two miles on each side of the river, where development that would derogate from scenic values is foreclosed, as opposed to the customary one-quarter mile on each side in the lower forty-eight states. In the final law, however, the protected zone shrank to one-half mile on each side. ANILCA should be amended to take advantage of the ample land available in Alaska and fully protect the wild character of the state's free-flowing rivers. ANILCA should also be amended to expand the Wild and Scenic Rivers System to include such outstanding rivers as the Porcupine, Squirrel, Sheenjeck, Situk, and Kisarikik.

*Revise Section 1302 regarding land exchange and Section 304 regarding cooperative management agreements.* Both of these sections of ANILCA have shown themselves vulnerable to administrative interpretations contrary to what the act intended. In the case of Section 1302, this enabled former Interior Secretary Watt to back initiatives for highly questionable land exchanges on St. Matthew Island and in Gates of the Arctic National Park and Preserve. Section 304 has been similarly misinterpreted to place virtually all control over wildlife in the Alaska refuges under the state Game and Fish Department. Both of these sections should be revised to tighten their language and impose restrictions that will prevent similar distortions of ANILCA's basic intent in the future.

The revision of ANILCA as outlined above has the advantage of being a specific program capable of implementation in the near term, but which at the same time has profound implications for the protection and carefully controlled development of Alaska's heritage over the next century and more. With the blueprint of improved and strengthened legislation at hand, we can plan for the proper balance of uses that the Great Land of Alaska has always offered us but that we have too often ignored, an opportunity to demonstrate dramatically our ability to learn from the failures of the past. "Over most of the United States," Robert Marshall wrote in 1937, "the prevalent attitude has been that the greater the development of natural resources, the greater the public welfare. . . . Many invaluable resources have been depleted disastrously. In Alaska the dominant development policies of the United States should be balanced by a policy of preservation."

This is as true today—and will be in the future—as it was in 1937. There is little now that we can do to reclaim the resources wasted in the lower forty-eight states or restore all the wilderness lost. But we *can* do something about Alaska.

LEFT: On the beach at Nome, Alaska, 1904; it was here that the last great gold rush in American history ended. *F. H. Nowell Collection, Bancroft Library, University of California, Berkeley*
ABOVE: One of the last of the *cheechakos*—the sourdough prospectors who brought civilization to Alaska at the turn of the century. *F. H. Nowell Collection, Bancroft Library, University of California, Berkeley*

OVERLEAF: Mount McKinley from Nugget Pond, Denali National Park and Preserve, Alaska. *Philip Hyde*

Alaska Range from Polychrome Pass, Denali National Park and Preserve.
*Philip Hyde*

Glacier Bay, Glacier Bay National Park and Preserve. *Philip Hyde*

Mount St. Elias, Wrangell–St. Elias National Park and Preserve. *National Park Service*

# 7

# INLAND PASSAGES

## The National Wild and Scenic Rivers and National Trails Systems

The 1960s were a time of turmoil and trouble in America, and it is sometimes too easily forgotten that this decade also was one of the most environmentally enlightened in our history. It saw, among other conservation highlights, publication of Rachel Carson's *Silent Spring*; passage of the Endangered Species Act, the Wilderness Act, the Clean Air and Clean Water acts, and the National Environmental Policy Act; the designation of Redwood National Park; and the creation of the Land and Water Conservation Fund, the Outdoor Recreation Resources Review Commission, the Environmental Protection Agency, and the President's Council on Environmental Quality—all of this capped off in 1970 by the nation's first Earth Day.

A busy and productive period, and near the end of it, on October 2, 1968, President Lyndon B. Johnson signed into law two bills particularly dear to him—one creating the National Wild and Scenic Rivers System, the other the National Trails System, linear variations of the National Wilderness Preservation System established four years earlier. Johnson, who wanted to originate the best ideas himself, or at least take credit for them, was so fond of the trails legislation that initially his administration delayed its progress so that it would come from his office rather than from that of its actual sponsor, Senator Gaylord Nelson, a Wisconsin Democrat.

The advocates for both of these systems cherished a grand design for them: they would span the continent. The Wild and Scenic Rivers

System, intended to preserve to varying degrees free-flowing water-ways, began with eight river segments totaling 789 miles, all part of the original legislation, but was anticipated to grow much larger. Another one hundred or so rivers were slated to be added to the system within ten years, But nearly twenty years later the system has scratched and clawed its way up to only sixty-six designated rivers and river segments, or about one-fifth of one percent of America's total, for a sum of 7,225 miles of water.

However short of its advocates' goals, the river system still en-compasses an impressive network of streams—from the Noatak, sweeping 330 miles along the southern base of the Brooks Range in Alaska, to the tiny (33 mile) stretch of the Little Beaver meandering through eastern Ohio; from the Allagash of Maine (95 miles) to the Eleven Point of Missouri (4.4 miles); from the Skagit, emptying into Puget Sound (157.5 miles), to the Rio Grande, discharging into the Gulf of Mexico (191.2 miles). These river segments, incorporating a wide variety of riverine ecosystems, are to be kept forever free of development—they are not to be canalized, dredged, filled, or dammed along their designated lengths. Except for some segments flowing through nonfederal lands, which are administered by the appropriate states, each designated river segment is administered by the federal agency responsible for the land that borders it—the National Park Service, the U.S. Forest Service, or the Bureau of Land Management.

The National Trails System, meanwhile, has come somewhat closer to realizing its potential—although it, too, is far from complete. The act of 1968 authorized the designation, after proper study, of scenic and recreation trails, and immediately designated the Appalachian Trail, running 2,000 miles through 12 states, from Springer Mountain in Georgia to Mount Katahdin in Maine, and the Pacific Crest Trail, running 2,350 miles from the Mexican border to the Canadian border through the states of California, Oregon, and Washington, as the first scenic trail. The act also named an additional fourteen trails as worthy of study for designation to the system and authorized the Secretaries of the Interior and Agriculture independently to designate recreation trails on land within their jurisdiction (all other trail designations could be made only through individual acts of Congress). A 1978 amendment established historic trails as an additional category.

To date, more than 23,650 miles of scenic and historic trails have been designated, the most recent of which—the 694-mile Natchez Trace Trail, the 704-mile Potomac Heritage Trail, and the 1,300-mile Florida Trail—were named as late as March 28, 1983. (For a complete list, see the Appendix.) In addition, the Interior and Agriculture departments have established 752 recreation trails comprising more than 8,000 miles. All but one of the thirteen existing scenic and historic trails—the Iditarod Trail of Alaska, administered by the Bureau of Land Management—are under the management of either the National Park Service or the U.S. Forest Service. Of the 752 National Recreation Trails, 499 are under federal management, 12 are jointly administered by federal, state, and local governments, 78 are administered by the states, 138 are administered by local governments, and 26 are managed by private organizations.

As the descriptions above suggest, one of the major problems shared by both the Wild and Scenic Rivers and the National Trails systems is a powerful confusion of responsibility. From creation to administration, both are tangled in a bureaucratic and political mix that has hampered their continued growth and proper management. In part, this is both understandable and inevitable; there has never before been anything remotely like either system, and the agencies involved are consequently without previous experience. Still, there has been a consistent lack of funding for both, and the current administration and its allies in Congress have demonstrated little more than calculated neglect—and, in some cases, downright antagonism. As a result, the anticipated expansion of the Wild and Scenic Rivers System has come to a nearly dead halt, and under present conditions there appears little hope that it will be revived in the near future. Similarly, the National Trails System remains incomplete—not only as a system, but in regard to the individual trails themselves, as the National Park Service noted in a March 19, 1985, report: "Except for the Appalachian and Pacific Crest Trails, which are usable for much of their lengths, the remaining trails are proposed routes and are not necessarily available at this time for long-distance, continuous trips. In some cases, the original route has been obliterated by commercial, industrial, residential, agricultural, and transportation development."

The confusion and incompleteness of both systems are regrettable, for any number of reasons, among them the fact that the demand for the recreational use of both is growing and can only increase even more markedly as the end of the century draws near, and the further fact that each system in its own way is capable of preserving significant portions of the national estate overlooked or impossible to administer by other conservation measures. Finally, no other conservation units in the country speak so eloquently or so directly to the narrative of our history.

## CONDUITS OF ADVENTURE

From the beginning, the rivers beckoned with promise. Along the river that would later bear his name, the English navigator Henry Hudson in 1609 reached into the country, did not find what he was looking for, turned his eighty-ton vessel *Half Moon* around, and sailed back out to sea. The waterway was not, as he had hoped, the legendary Northwest Passage through the continent to the Pacific—and from there to the riches of the Orient—and was therefore of no use. Still searching for the Northwest Passage 167 years later and three thousand miles to the west, Captain James Cook just missed the mouth of the Columbia River on the Northwest coast. He kept sailing north until he entered the Bering Strait, then pressed on to the Arctic Sea before turning back.

For these two and the dozens of similarly motivated explorers by land and sea who came and went in the years between, the rivers of America were a sore disappointment. But for those with smaller ambitions, who wished only to settle the new land and take what it had to give them, the rivers lacing down to the sea all along the Eastern Seaboard were a godsend and a necessity. They provided power for mills and, with them, the beginnings of industry. They were the first avenues of commerce, the best means at hand of moving people and goods from the interior to the coast and back again. Their valleys held soil so rich and moist a man could mold it in his fist. And with a little imagination, they could be made even more useful— or so it often was hoped. George Washington chose the site for the United States capital on a slough of the Potomac River largely because he anticipated that river's development as an avenue running deep into the Appalachian interior, and his own Potowmack Canal Company constructed canals to bypass the river's wild places and make it navigable by mule-drawn barge. The project—later called the Chesapeake and Ohio Canal—got as far as Cumberland, Maryland, falling far short of Washington's intended junction with the Ohio River, along which he had been promoting settlement on some land he happened to own there.

River country was plowed into farmscapes and citified, and as settlement spilled over the Appalachians into the valley of the Ohio (too late to do Washington any good), and then the broad, river-rich valley of the Mississippi from Canada to the Gulf of Mexico, it was the rivers again that both inspired and made possible the exploration of the trans-Mississippi West. The United States had hardly purchased the immense Louisiana Territory from France in 1803 when Jefferson, as President, ordered its exploration. He chose Captain Meriwether Lewis, a fellow Virginian who had served as his secretary, to head the expedition. Lewis chose Captain William Clark, also a Virginian, to share his command. "The object of your mission," Jefferson wrote to Lewis, "is to explore the Missouri River, & such principal stream of it, as by its course & communication with the waters of the Pacific Ocean, may offer the most direct and practicable water communication across this continent, for purposes of commerce." Again, the search for a shortcut, the old dream of a Northwest Passage.

On May 14, 1804, the thirty-five-member expedition launched its fifty-five-foot keelboat and two flat-bottomed boats called pirogues from their winter base just above St. Louis and began the ascent of the Missouri River—thus entering the "Big Muddy" in the list of what Bernard DeVoto called "the conduits of national adventure." This adventure could have, and even should have, ended tragically. Not only were the men heading into rough, uncharted country, but what they had expected to find—a short portage between the Missouri's eastward-flowing source and the next river's Pacific-bound source—did not exist. The Rocky Mountains stood in the way. If not for the help of a Shoshone Indian girl named Sacajawea who had joined the expedition at Fort Mandan in Montana, the party may have been doomed. Sacajawea had been captured from her tribe and taken

295

east by Minnetarees several years before, but she still remembered landmarks of her childhood, and correctly identified the Missouri's headwaters at the junction of three rivers, which the expedition named after Albert Gallatin, James Madison, and Thomas Jefferson. Her presence among the company also assured them safe passage through hostile Shoshone country, and she stayed with the expedition all the way to the mouth of the Columbia River.

Although the Lewis and Clark Expedition failed to substantiate the myth of an easy river passage across the continent, it did bring back a great deal of useful information about the country and its native inhabitants. Fur trappers and traders were the first to seize the opportunities laid open by Lewis and Clark. The Hudson's Bay Company, the Rocky Mountain Fur Company, and the American Fur Company all conducted operations on the watershed systems of the Missouri, Yellowstone, Columbia, and Colorado rivers, among others, for two decades. To go west before the 1840s was, in large part, to travel over water in the company of fur trappers. By the end of that period, however, the beaver—the primary item of the trade—had been trapped out of its ancestral waters, and rivers were invested with a new kind of romance.

Throughout the middle period of the nineteenth century—and to a lesser extent right up to the beginning of the twentieth—the heartland rivers of America were the great highways of the Industrial Revolution. The greatest of them all, of course, was the Mississippi. This was the home of Mark Twain's heart and the setting of his greatest books, *Huckleberry Finn* and *Life on the Mississippi*. In *Mark Twain's America*, Bernard DeVoto gave us the best capsule description of the river that called to Twain:

> There were barges, the broadhorns and the scows—the slow freight of the world moved by creatures of terror and romance. There were rafts of timber and of lumber floating from the forests to build the houses of democracy by the half-million. And the steamboats. Boats of the Cairo line and the Memphis line tied up daily at the wharf. So did boats from the Illinois River, the Red River, the White River, the Missouri, the upper Mississippi, the Ohio, the Monongahela, the Tennessee, the Cumberland, the Arkansas, the Yazoo.

And there were the travelers, the "traders, drovers, farmers, home-steaders, tinmen, miners, masons, shipwrights, actors, minstrels, mesmerists, phrenologists, bear leaders, circus men, gamblers, prostitutes and prophets." Duplicated in its parts—though nowhere on so grand a scale—this was river life in Victorian America.

In the years following the Civil War, this turmoil of life began to subside, increasingly affected by the rise of the railroad as the nation's principal transportation network. Which is not to say that we suddenly had no use for the rivers. We used them, right enough—used them badly, too many of them. Rivers had been and remained for a long time the open sewers of the nation. All the rubbish of industry and city life was dumped into them. The current, it was hoped, would simply carry the mess away. By the mid-nineteenth century, water pollution was a serious problem in Chicago and other major cities built along rivers. Between 1840 and 1860 the population of Illinois soared from 5,000 to nearly 110,000 and the Illinois River absorbed this growth poorly. Waterborne diseases, spread by the release of raw sewage into the source of drinking water, were rampant.

Near Chicago, wrote a researcher in 1911, the Illinois River reached its "lowest point of pollutional distress, becoming, when very hot weather coincides with a low stage of water, a thoroughly sick stream."

Its oxygen is nearly all gone; its carbon dioxide rises to the maximum; its sediments become substantially like the sludge of the septic tank; its surface bubbles with the gases of decomposition escaping from sludge banks on its bottom; its odor is offensive; and its color is gray with suspended specks and larger clusters of sewage orga-nisms. . . . On its surface are also floating masses of decaying debris, borne up by the gases developing within them, and covered and fringed with sewage fungus . . . the vegetation and drift at the edge of the stream are also everywhere slimy with these foul-water plants and minute, filth-loving animals.

Such sights and stenches were common to all rivers on whose banks cities and industry flourished; dead fish were a good sign of a successful papermill. Those who could afford to do so abandoned the stinking metropolises in summer and headed out to country estates, often to where a stretch of river flowed by, still cold, clear, and odorless.

### "TURNING OUR DARKNESS TO DAWN"

While the conservation of forests and wildlife was gaining influential adherents at the turn of the century, rivers in their wildest forms found few defenders. Even the intense battle over the flooding of Yosemite National Park's Hetch Hetchy Valley in 1913 was not so much a fight to keep the Tuolumne River running freely, as to preserve the integrity of the national park system. Rivers were understood not as organisms but as receptacles, to be filled or emptied as circumstances required. Waterways that seasonally flooded or dried up were of no use to people; in fact, they were a threat to health and prosperity. Hence, a conservationist in the Gifford Pinchot or Theodore Roosevelt tradition could agitate eloquently for the saving of forested land on the one hand and the calculated destruction of rivers on the other. There was no contradiction in these beliefs. Both were well-meaning. Rivers flowing freely for miles and miles through thirsty country were as wasteful, according to some, as cut-and-run logging methods. Water that could be put to immediate use but was not only wound up in the sea. Almost any way a person looked at it, a wild river was not considered as good a neighbor as a tamed one. Though the doctrine of utility was applied vigorously to forests, on the federal level perhaps its most ingenious expression was applied to rivers. Put plainly, the rivers were "engineered" from one end of the country to the other— dammed, turned into canals, dredged, burdened with flood-control works—much of this at the hands of the U.S. Bureau of Reclamation and the Army Corps of Engineers and almost all of it with the full and enthusiastic approval of the public. Engineered rivers have been among the proudest technological achievements of mankind. They have saved lives, spread electric power throughout the land, raised living standards, and reclaimed deserts. This was democracy in action. During the 1930s, when the Columbia River was being harnessed to generate the cheapest publicly owned electricity in the nation, Woody Guthrie could sing with a clear social conscience, "Roll on, Columbia, roll on. Your power is turning our darkness to dawn."

298

Between 1933 and 1963, ten dams were built on the Columbia, with large dams constructed on its major tributaries in that same period. And the Columbia was not the only river being restructured. All along the nation's major streams, massive projects were being undertaken for water storage, flood control, electric power generation, recreation, and irrigation. In 1933, Congress established the Tennessee Valley Authority to rejuvenate one of the most economically hard-pressed, river-ravaged regions of the country. The Tennessee River had always been destructive, periodically flooding Chattanooga and wiping out small towns located at its bottlenecks. The TVA engineered hope, and conservationists, believing in the authority's goals of land restoration, were proud to help. "What we are doing down there is taking a watershed with about 3.5 million in it, almost all of them rural, and we are trying to make a different type of citizen out of them," explained President Franklin Roosevelt. "TVA is primarily intended to change and improve the standards of living of the people in that Valley."

The TVA was comprehensive. Hills were reforested to check the massive erosion caused by the bad logging practices of the previous century. New farming techniques were introduced. The Tennessee's 652-mile main stem was made commercially navigable, and its flooding was checked. The river itself was reorganized into sixteen lakes covering more than 600,000 acres of land, forming links in a chain of water.

Far to the west, the Colorado River, beginning in the 1930s, was also being put to dramatic use. The 1922 interstate Colorado River Compact and later amendments apportioned the river's waters so that the dry states of Wyoming, Colorado, Utah, Nevada, Arizona, New Mexico, and California all received their share. The terms of that compact and other agreements have made the Colorado River "the most used, the most dramatic, the most highly litigated and politicized river in the nation, if not the world," according to Philip L. Fradkin in *A River No More*. Because of the demands placed on its changeable flow, the Colorado River is also the river that comes closest to having its last drop of water used; not for twenty years has the Colorado's water reached its natural outlet in the Gulf of California. To fulfill the demands on it, the Colorado was systematically dammed, beginning with Hoover Dam, which started backing up the river's waters along the Arizona-Nevada border in 1936, forming the serpentine Lake Mead. Thirty years and seven major dams later, the seven-hundred-foot-high Glen Canyon Dam at Lee's Ferry, Utah, was the Colorado River Storage Project's crowning glory. In 1963 it began impounding the Colorado's waters to form Lake Powell, the nation's largest man-made reservoir, named after the river's key nineteenth-century explorer—though it is not likely that he would have approved of the reservoir (see chapter 3). Lake Powell is a popular recreation site for thousands. Hundreds of feet beneath its surface, however, lie the canyons Powell himself had loved. Below the great dam, the river's level rises and falls with the flip of switches in the bowels of the dam, proving that even a river can be fully automated.

Perhaps many of the massive river projects undertaken during the first half of the twentieth century were worthwhile. Perhaps others were unavoidable. Perhaps they were even inspirational, for the way in which they pitted human wits against raw power. With the number of major dams now in excess of fifty thousand, and with several hundred thousand smaller ones, the job of remaking rivers had been tackled too zealously, and before all the consequences were understood. Examples of wretched excess abound. Take, for instance, the 1934 Pick-Sloan Plan, authorizing the construction of more than one hundred dams in the Missouri River's watershed, at a cost of $5 billion (in 1934 dollars). The plan was a compromise between the Army Corps of Engineers, which favored the Pick plan's dams for flood control and navigational purposes in one part of the river system, and the Bureau of Reclamation, which urged the Sloan plan's dams for irrigation and hydroelectric power in another. At the time it was passed, the Pick-Sloan Plan was described as a "loveless, shameless shotgun marriage of convenience" and the projected number of its dams nothing less than a gigantic boondoggle. Only a few—like the Garrison Dam in North Dakota—were in fact ever built.

The idea that there was no limit to the things one could and should do with a river was implanted as dogma. But for a lack of humor, some of the reasons given for damming, diverting, and dewatering began to sound almost like Dr. Seuss in their exuberance. *The Cat in the Hat* comes most readily to mind:

Look at me! Look at me! Look at me NOW! It is fun to have fun, but you have to know how. I can hold up the cup and the milk and the cake! I can hold up these books! And the fish and the rake! I can hold the toy ship and a little toy man! And look! With my tail I can hold a red fan! I can fan with the fan as I hop on the ball! But that is not all. Oh, no. That is not all. . . .

## AGAINST THE CURRENT

There are, as it turns out, a number of good reasons to question the propriety of water projects. Often the cost-benefit analysis written to justify impoundment or diversion ignores the fact that some of the benefits are already being supplied. Recreation, for example, does not require a lake. Free-flowing water offers even more chances for enjoyment than does placid water, and in one survey conducted in the West, public use of natural rivers was found to be twelve times greater than that of man-made lakes and reservoirs. The typical cost-benefit statement also fails to weigh the values inherent in the existing natural conditions; often it was assumed that there simply were not any. On thousands of rivers the alteration of the water's flow via dams or diversions has destroyed commercial as well as recreational fishing, and has thus resulted not in the addition of river-derived benefits, but in the displacement of long-established ones.

"Dams have no consideration for fish," says Verne Huser, a mediator in natural-resource disputes who specializes in water issues. Anadromous fish such as salmon, which must swim upriver to spawn, are cut off from their ancestral waters. Fish ladders can correct some of that problem, but dams and spillways confront fish with other perils. High flows through turbines are the prime killers of young fish, which may get caught in them or be suctioned against the fish screens designed to keep them out. Sudden changes in water temperature, in the form of thermal plumes at the points of water discharge, cause instant death, while temperature increases can delay fish migration, foster the growth of fungus and debilitating bacteria, and change the food situation. High nitrogen levels, which are found in the spillway portion of a dam, cause gas-bubble disease in salmon, also hindering their spawning. Young salmon require a strong current to push them out to sea, but a dam might hold back too much water at the wrong time, reducing the current so much that smolt are not able to reach their destination.

These are a few of the problems that dams cause for fish. The California planner for the Bureau of Reclamation who once remarked that "when the going gets tough, people will get the water, not fish," was no doubt correct, although it should be pointed out that dams can be a problem for people, too. Often they do not prevent floods, they merely move them someplace else—upstream, for example. And even along the most painstakingly controlled rivers, devastating floods have occurred, such as that on the lower Colorado in 1983, confirming Mark Twain's early skepticism about the value of making a river over again—"a job transcended in size only by the original job of creating it." (Speaking of the Mississippi River, Twain wrote that one who knows it "will promptly aver—not aloud but to himself—that ten thousand river commissions with the mines of the world at their back, cannot tame that lawless stream, cannot curb or confine it . . . cannot bar its path with an obstruction which it will not tear down, dance over and laugh at.")

The tendency to turn lawless streams into a chain of quiet lakes shortens by a millennium or so the waterway's natural lifespan. "The very nature of a lake is death," says Huser. "With their silt and vegetation lakes are the dying portions of water, and by creating more and more reservoirs we are increasing the number of dead parts." Indeed, siltation is a major and inescapable problem in all reservoirs. To postpone the inevitable, one dam must be built after another, as impoundments begin to fill with silt and are able to hold less water. Lake Powell, for instance, is expected to be completely filled with silt in less than three hundred years, while Arizona's Lake Mead is already well on its way to being incapacitated. Excessive salinity also plagues rivers where man's tinkering is apparent. Half of the Colorado River's burden of 11 million tons of salt each year is caused by evaporation from man-made reservoirs; evaporation leaves the naturally occurring salt behind, making the water progressively more salty. Waters used over and over again for irrigation also pick up salt from minerals in the ground. In some places the excessive salt has ruined the land for cultivation purposes.

For these reasons and others, major water projects, particularly

302

those involving dams, have become the symbol, for most conservationists, of all that is reprehensible about our technocratic society.
In the words of John McPhee, dams themselves represent "something
disproportionately and metaphysically sinister" to conservationists.
As McPhee wrote in his book *Encounters with the Archdruid*:

> The outermost circle of the Devil's world seems to be a moat filled
> mainly with DDT. Next to it is a moat of burning gasoline. Within
> that is a ring of pinheads each covered with a million people—and
> so on past phalanxed bulldozers and bicuspid chain saws, into the
> absolute epicenter of Hell on earth, where stands a dam. The impli-
> cations of the dam exceed its true level in the scale of environmental
> catastrophes. Conservationists who can hold themselves in reasonable
> check before new oil spills and fresh megalopolises mysteriously go
> insane at even the thought of a dam. The conservation movement is
> a mystical and religious force, and possibly the reaction to dams is
> so violent because rivers are the ultimate metaphors of existence, and
> dams destroy rivers.

This theory certainly would explain the intensity of the conservation
movement's reaction to the proposal to erect Echo Park Dam in
Dinosaur National Monument in the 1950s (see chapters 2 and 5), a
proposal defeated largely because it inspired the first major conservation coalition effort in our history. The victory sparked the wilderness preservation movement, and led almost nine years later to
the establishment of the National Wilderness Preservation System.
To a lesser extent it also bestirred a concern for all free-flowing rivers,
which, if the past was any indication, would continue to be viewed
by the government as little more than dam-building opportunities.
Separate opposition would have to be mounted on hundreds of separate
water projects. Driving that point home was the fact that while Dinosaur National Monument was saved, the exquisite Glen Canyon
was lost to another Colorado River Storage Project dam. It was only
as the floodgates closed that conservationists began to realize what
had been sacrificed by a momentary lapse in their vigilance. David
Brower of the Sierra Club, who had been the principal spokesman

against the Echo Park Dam, called the Glen Canyon Dam the greatest failure of his life.

Brower did not let down his guard again. That there are no dams within the Grand Canyon is largely his doing—and also his undoing. In the mid-1960s, the Bureau of Reclamation requested a portion of the Colorado River in the Grand Canyon for its use. Without authorization of the Sierra Club board, Brower spent funds to buy a full-page ad in *The New York Times* asking, "Should we also flood the Sistine Chapel so tourists can get nearer the ceiling?" That ad and similar applications of public pressure killed the plans. It also cost the Sierra Club its tax-exempt status, for the Internal Revenue Service had determined that its tactics smacked of lobbying. Shortly thereafter, Brower was dismissed as executive director but went on to found Friends of the Earth and continued his opposition to the dam-builders. In the course of John McPhee's long profile of him in *Encounters with the Archdruid*, Brower tells an audience that "I hate all dams, large and small."

"Why are you conservationists always against things?" came a question from the back of the room.

"If you are against something, you are for something," Brower replied. "If you are against a dam, you are for a river."


BEING FOR A RIVER

In 1960, while the furor over dam construction still ran high, National Park Service officials quietly recommended to the Senate Select Committee on National Water Resources that federal steps be taken to spare some of the nation's free-flowing rivers. Senate committee members accepted the notion. Support for national river preservation also filtered in from the Outdoor Recreation Resources Review Commission in 1962. The commission's final report proposed that "certain streams be preserved in their free-flowing condition because their natural scenic, scientific, aesthetic, and recreational values outweigh their value for water development and control purposes now and in the future." The commission suggested that those rivers deserving to be left alone be identified. For that purpose the Wild Rivers Committee, composed of people from the Departments of Interior and Agriculture, was formed. Twenty-two rivers were judged to be immediately worthy of federal protection, and it was agreed that a system be developed to encompass them.

The timing could hardly have been better. President Johnson supported the creation of such a system, for it fit in well with his stated commitment to the preservation of natural beauty. In 1965, Johnson told Congress that rivers "occupy a central place in myth and legend, folklore and literature. They are our first highways, and some remain among the most important. . . . We will continue to conserve their water and power for tomorrow's needs with well-planned reservoirs and power dams, but the time has come to identify and preserve free-flowing stretches of our great scenic rivers, before growth and development make the beauty of the unspoiled waterways a memory."

During congressional hearings to install a national river system, Interior Secretary Udall expanded on Johnson's theme. He reviewed the nation's largest river programs, specifically those for irrigation, championed by Theodore Roosevelt, and those for flood control and hydropower, pushed by Franklin Roosevelt. "We need to give further balance to these programs, and to systematically single out those rivers and segments of rivers that have not been developed. . . . We are not just talking about protecting our premier trout streams, as important as that is. We are not just talking about rivers to float. One of the things I would like to stress is what we will be doing for water quality and water conservation."

Despite the administration's strong backing of river-preservation bills, however, the first measure offered by the Wild Rivers Committee was deemed inadequate by conservationists. Pennsylvania Congressman John P. Saylor, who had served on the ORRRC, was particularly disappointed. "They must not have been listening to the President," he said during river hearings in 1967. "Or they were so fainthearted that they beached their canoe before they got to the water, because I can tell you that the bill they sent up left so much to be desired that some of us wondered whether or not those two secretaries were trying to support the President in his program of conservation." The bill Saylor was objecting to started the system with only seven designated rivers, and mentioned seventeen for further study. Saylor said he could think of at least sixteen rivers eligible for immediate protection, and could name another sixty-six candidates for study. Saylor and others began working up their own legislation.

One problem they faced was that many sections of river and land were not on public property. They would have to be acquired before protection could be assured. And, as popular as the concept of a national river-preservation system had grown, private landowners objected when it was their property being mentioned for acquisition. Federal jurisdiction where local control was long ensconced was "gall and wormwood" to many river frontage owners. Some felt that federal involvement was unnecessary, since they had willingly provided public access across their land. Past permission, however, was no guarantee of future access. There was no telling what would happen from one generation to the next. The federal agencies approached the issue of condemnations gingerly. "We don't come in here waving a flag, and say, 'Give us the power to condemn' " said Agriculture Secretary Orville Freeman. "We use it very charily, because it is always a bloody business, and we get hurt in the public image."

Nevertheless, the issue was so sensitive that many rivers had to be withdrawn from consideration. People who had lived along the Shenandoah River in West Virginia were particularly incensed by the proposed usurpation of their land, some of which had been in families for two hundred years. "I am truly appalled by the lack of safeguards afforded to innocent citizens whose only fault is being on land some other citizens covet," Dr. Barbara Moulton of Charles Town testified. "There is nothing the U.S. Government could give me that would make up for my losing that property if I lost it. And I don't think there is anything the rest of the country would gain from my losing it. Free citizens owning their own land, free to grow their own food, to enjoy the fruits of their labor—this is more a part of the American heritage than is a wilderness." Because of such persuasive opposition, the portion of the Shenandoah under consideration was cut.

Of course, many local groups also lobbied hard for the inclusion of their favorite rivers in a national system, because it was the only way to ensure their free-flowing existence. "The wild river concept in your bill is a great thing," declared Glenn Thompson, editor of the Dayton, Ohio, *Journal Herald*, who came to Washington to campaign for the preservation of the Little Miami River in his state. "I hope you capture them all. But the real urgency is on the hundred little rivers. The government owns the land along the dramatic western streams; the subdividers are after ours," he said. Federal protection was essential, Thompson asserted, because states and local governments "are not geared for this job. We are organized into counties which are big enough so you can drive to town in a wagon in one day. That is not big enough to manage a river."

When the Wild and Scenic Rivers Act finally passed, the Little Miami was not among those immediately preserved. Congress agreed instead to designate portions of the Middle Fork of the Clearwater and the Middle Fork of the Salmon in Idaho, the Eleven Point in Missouri, the Feather in California, the Rio Grande in New Mexico, the Rogue in Oregon, and the St. Croix and Wolf in Wisconsin, for protection. But the Little Miami and the hundreds of "little rivers" like it would at least have the opportunity to be considered for inclusion later. The act declared it to be "the policy of the United States that certain rivers, which, within their immediate environments possess outstandingly remarkable scenic, recreational, geological, fish and wildlife, historic, cultural, or other similar values, shall be preserved in a free-flowing condition, and that they and their immediate environments shall be protected for the benefit and enjoyment of present and future generations." The act stipulated that future rivers could be added either by Congress or by individual state legislation submitted for the Interior Secretary's approval, after study had been completed; during the study period of five years, no development was to be allowed. The responsibility for preservation was assigned to whichever federal land-managing agency happened to have the closest jurisdiction. The act, through negotiated purchase, condemnation, and various easements, also protected a half-mile corridor on both sides of the river. Depending on the degree of protection, rivers were defined as either recreational, which allowed the most development along the banks, or scenic and wild, for more pristine conditions. On these rivers the Army Corps of Engineers, the Bureau of Reclamation, and the Federal Power Commission (later the Federal Energy Regulatory Commission) were not allowed to perform their works.

As mentioned earlier, Congress expected the number of protected rivers to rise to one hundred within ten years. By 1990, another one hundred rivers and river segments were to be added. Instead, the river system has expanded at a snail's pace, adding only sixteen river segments by the end of the first decade. With the passage of the Alaska National Interest Lands Act in 1980, the system received its greatest boost—twenty-five rivers were added at once. Today, sixty-six protected portions flow through twenty-four states—a dismal showing, considering the enthusiasm and expectations originally invested in the system. How could the Wild and Scenic Rivers System fall so far short of its ambitions?

For one thing, self-limitation was built into the legislation. New rivers can be designated for protection only after a lengthy and convoluted process of proposal and study. It takes five or six years for a river to be added, from the moment local supporters rally around the idea, convince their congressional delegation to introduce the proposal, and see it through public hearings and congressional committees, which may or may not report it to the House and Senate for full consideration. The bill may then pass, or it may languish. If it passes and the President signs it, either the Department of Agriculture or the Department of the Interior studies the river and assesses the environmental impacts. The study recommendations are sent back to Congress, the President, and the Office of Management and Budget, which then arrive at a final decision.

And all this happens only if there is a local delegation committed enough to a river's salvation to carry it through. In practice, the designation of national rivers has remained very much a local matter. Local resistance to river preservation runs strong particularly in Colorado, which has had no rivers designated for wild and scenic protection, although eleven worthy candidates have been studied and recommended. "In the West, water is still a commodity to be hoarded and treasured," said Eric Olson, a staff member of the six-thousand-member American Rivers Conservation Council, the only national organization devoted exclusively to rivers. "People don't want to reduce their options. With that kind of sentiment, the congressman from such a district can be death on rivers." Political changes since the act's passage have also stymied its growth. Almost half the rivers now in the system were designated by President Carter—those twenty-five in Alaska and five in California that were granted protection the

308

day before Reagan came to office. And with Reagan's coming, new rivers did not have much of a chance.

Although many rivers were ready for designation when Reagan assumed the presidency, none was granted protection until 1983, when pressure for additions could no longer be ignored. In the meantime, funds for river study were cut to the bone, while appropriations for Bureau of Reclamation work increased. Shortly after becoming Secretary of the Interior, James Watt abolished the Heritage Conservation and Recreation Service, which had managed the wild and scenic rivers program at the national level. Secretary Watt shared his impressions of rivers with a group of national park concessioners after he rafted through the Grand Canyon. The first day, he said, was "thrilling." The second day was "a little tedious." By the fourth day, Watt said, he was "praying for helicopters" to rescue him. "I don't like to paddle and I don't like to walk," he explained.

When the Reagan administration at last submitted eight new river segments for protection, they were drastically reduced from what had been recommended by the Forest Service and others during the Carter years. Tacked onto the Reagan contribution to the rivers system were several potentially destructive amendments. Protection for rivers undergoing study was cut from five years to three, and state legislatures were given the opportunity to cancel protection of any wild and scenic rivers designated in their state. And, while Congress had appropriated $5 million for river acquisition, the Reagan administration was satisfied to request only $1.5 million. In 1983 and again in 1984, Minnesota Republican Senator Dave Durenberger introduced legislation designed to aid the expansion of the system at the state level. (Twenty-eight states currently have river preservation programs of their own, which all together have led to the protection of 317 river segments covering 11,404 miles. The degree of protection, of course, varies from state to state. Some are content merely to place a descriptive plaque by the water's edge; others, such as Minnesota, explicitly ban dams.) Durenberger's bill would have provided federal grants of as much as $5 million a year for state river conservation programs, banned federal water projects on any protected rivers if the state's governor submitted an objection, and clarified tax laws to ensure that donors of riverside land would receive appropriate tax breaks. The bill failed.

Durenberger's measure also would have provided a necessary degree of protection for at least some rivers outside the federal system. It was necessary, because two existing federal programs pose what many see as the single most consistent and far-reaching threat to free rivers. The first of these is the licensing powers of the Federal Energy Regulatory Commission (FERC), which controls all applications for the development of water power projects, large and small. The age of the megadams, some say, is over—they are simply too expensive and there are too few rivers left that are large enough to warrant them. But others see this as a new age of smaller, "low-head" hydropower projects developed at the local level, and the FERC has demonstrated its willingness to approve such efforts—hundreds of them all over the country. Moreover, the FERC also has the power to exempt from its major environmental provisions any project designed to deliver less than five megawatts of power; here, too, it has been generous, granting more than nine hundred such exemptions.

The second federal program posing a potential threat to the rivers is that established by the passage of the Public Utilities Regulatory Policies Act (PURPA) in 1978. This act, designed to enhance the nation's energy independence, requires public utilities to purchase power from small developers at a price equal to what it would cost the utilities to build their own facilities to produce the same amount of power. PURPA, too, has inspired a boom of applications, many for the reconstruction of now-unused hydropower projects—some of them decades old. In Washington, Oregon, and California, three states with an abundance of sites for such small projects, more than 1,300 applications have been made.

It does not necessarily follow—at least at present—that every appropriate unprotected river in the land is going to be stoppered. "The economics of this business are very shaky," one California developer maintains. "In California, the Corps of Engineers compiled a list of thousands of projects. Applications were filed on several hundred of those. More than ninety have made their way through the permitting and licensing process. How many do you see being built? Hardly any. This is a capital-intensive business. You're talking about borrowing a lot of money at high interest rates and getting a low rate of cash flow. In most cases, you plot out your investment and interest costs next to your anticipated cash flow and the two lines never meet. It's a case of slow, controlled bankruptcy."

So it is now, but in the Fall 1984 issue of *Wilderness* magazine, Marc Reisner suggested that things could change: "If two-thirds of the U.S. nuclear reactors—those of pressurized water design—enjoy a half-life instead of a full life because of unforeseen internal stress (as some consider likely), or if the Saudi oil fields are set afire by Iran . . . or if Canada shuts off its James Bay power unit until we do something about acid rain, the prospects for small-scale hydro-power might improve considerably."

Such possibilities, combined with continuing confusion on the part of a large portion of the public over what can and cannot be lost when a federal river is established, and the bland antagonism of the present administration, pose a troubled future for the expansion of the Wild and Scenic Rivers System. We have used our rivers and they have played an integral part in our growth as a civilization, but we still find it hard sometimes to love them and protect them, valuing them for those qualities described by former National Park Service planner John Kauffmann in his book *Flow East*: "Take a child to a river. Acquaint him with its wonder, its beauty, and its power; let him enter into the joy of running water, and it will not only be a playmate and playground but a teacher and classroom as well."

### A WALK IN THE COUNTRY

In the beginning, the trails were all business. The Indians put their feet where the animals had gone, and established a network that laced through the woodlands and mountains of the East for the purposes of hunting and trading. When the Europeans came, they put the same network to their own purposes, which included not only hunting and trading, but settlement, the footpaths gradually widening into horse trails, then wagon roads, interconnecting with the rivers to form a transportation system that serviced the needs of the loose coalition of colonies that became an adolescent nation between the Atlantic Coast and the banks of the Mississippi.

And then into the West, some trails blazed now instead of fol-

311

lowed—Lewis and Clark heading over the High Plains to the Rocky Mountains from their camp on the upper Missouri in 1804. Two decades later, the first trading caravans began rumbling southwest from St. Louis to the settlements in a foreign land called New Mexico, along the Santa Fe Trail, and from there north along the Taos Trail. In the 1830s and 1840s, the promise of rich land and richer opportunity in the Pacific Northwest and California called the wagons west from "jumping-off" points on the Mississippi and Missouri rivers, up the valley of the Platte River to Fort Laramie, through South Pass to Fort Bridger, then north up the valley of the Snake River, if you were bound for the Oregon country, or west by southwest across the Great Basin and the Sierra Nevada if you were bound for California. Depending upon where you were headed, it was called the Oregon Trail or the California Trail, and tens of thousands wore a tracery of ruts into both over the course of nearly thirty years. The Mormons, too, the definitive settlers, cutting off from the main stem in 1846 to the Great Salt Lake, then sending from there shoots of settlement all the way to San Bernardino in southern California, on what came to be known as the Mormon Trail.

The Natchez Trace, up from the Mississippi River through Mississippi and Tennessee, the Tamiami Trail across Florida, the Goodnight-Loving and Chisholm trails up through Texas to the cattle towns of Kansas, the Camino del Diablo west from Santa Fe to San Diego. We were a nation of trails that became roads, then highways, and even in some cases railroads, and over most of them was carried the baggage of our history. It was traffic with a purpose, most of it, but at an astonishingly early period there were those with little but the pleasure of a walk in the country in mind.

Up in the White Mountains of New Hampshire, in 1819, Abel Crawford and his son Ethan cut a trail to the top of Mount Washington. It was soon known as the Crawford Path, and it was the first route to the mountain's summit, where there seemed little reason to go, except for the pleasure of being there. Mount Washington was, after all, not only the highest peak in New England, but the windiest one in the world, with gusts later clocked at 235 miles an hour. No commerce or industry thrived there. Yet the Crawford family may have been the first in the nation to profit from those out for a mere hike in the hills.

Their taverns furnished food and warmth, while their knowledge of the mountains was sought by such illustrious visitors as Daniel Webster and Nathaniel Hawthorne. The Crawford Path, a portion of which is now used by the Appalachian Trail, is the oldest continuously used recreational footpath in North America.

In New England the tradition of taking to a path through the woods for the sheer pleasure of it runs deep, though educational benefits were not overlooked. In 1876 the Appalachian Mountain Club (AMC) was formed by a professor at the Massachusetts Institute of Technology "to explore the mountains of the Northeast and the adjacent regions, for both scientific and artistic purposes, and, in general, to cultivate an interest in geographic studies." Since then the group has built and maintained almost four hundred miles of trails through the White Mountains. By 1888, hiking in the Whites had become so popular that the club decided to build a hut in a high col for shelter, since many who ventured out were not prepared for the exigencies of mountain weather. The AMC eventually built seven more high huts along its trails, offering hot meals and beds to the stream of hikers—this in addition to maintaining another twenty shelters in New Hampshire and Maine. (The AMC is now not only the oldest mountain club in the United States, but the largest, with 35,000 members.) The trail tradition was picked up by James P. Taylor, associate principal of a boy's school in Vermont, who was disappointed by the lack of access to Vermont's Green Mountains. Following the AMC's example, Taylor formed the Green Mountain Club in 1910, and set its members to work cutting a 265-mile "footpath in the wilderness" between the Canadian border and the Massachusetts state line. They called it the Long Trail.

One man who had earlier visited the Green Mountains and decided the Long Trail was only the beginning was Benton MacKaye, son of the prominent dramatist Steele MacKaye. At the age of fourteen, MacKaye, descended from generations of New Englanders, decided that he would specialize in "geotechnics," which he defined as the "applied science of making the earth more habitable." He worked for the U.S. Forest Service from 1905 to 1916, then for the Labor Department for three years before turning to free-lance writing and consulting work. In 1923, he, Clarence Stein, Lewis Mumford, and

313

others formed the Regional Planning Association of America. At various times he served as a consultant in planning programs for the Commonwealth of Massachusetts, the Tennessee Valley Authority, the Bureau of Indian Affairs, and the Forest Service; became one of the principal founders (and later a president) of The Wilderness Society in 1935 (see chapter 5); and worked on the staff of the Rural Electrification Administration before his "retirement" after World War II. For the rest of his long life (he died in 1975 at the age of 96), he lived and worked in his hometown of Shirley Center, Massachusetts.

Precisely when the glimmer of the idea that became the Appalachian Trail first came to him MacKaye could never quite remember. "It may have been in 1891," he wrote in 1972, "while I was listening to bearded, one-armed Major John Wesley Powell recount to an enthralled audience in Washington City his historic trip through the Grand Canyon. . . . It may have been in 1897, in the White Mountains of New Hampshire, as Sturgis Pray and I struggled through a tangled blowdown. . . . Or it may have been in 1900 when I stood with another friend, Horace Hildreth, viewing the heights of the Green Mountains." Whenever its genesis, the idea simmered in him for a long time, until 1921, when he outlined it for Charles H. Whitaker, editor of the *Journal of the American Institute of Architects*. Whitaker asked for an article. "An Appalachian Trail: A Project in Regional Planning," which the journal published in October of that year, offered the blueprint for a hiking trail that eventually followed the crest of the Appalachian Mountains from Maine to Georgia, covering two thousand miles. As one of its justifications, MacKaye noted that

> we have neglected to improve the leisure which should be ours as a result of replacing stone and bronze with iron and steam. . . . The customary approach to the problem relates to work rather than play. Can we increase the efficiency of our *working* time? Can we solve the problem of labor? If so we can widen the opportunities for leisure. The new approach reverses this mental process. Can we increase the efficiency of our *spare* time? Can we develop opportunities for leisure as an aid in solving the problem of labor?

314

## A WILDERNESS WAY

In 1930, MacKaye offered some additional reflections on what his trail concept could mean. It presented, he said, "a wilderness way through civilization . . . not a civilized way through the wilderness. It is a real trail. A path and not a road . . . the foot replaces the wheel, the cabin replaces the hotel, the song replaces the radio, the campfire replaces the movie. It is the trail of the *new* pioneer, not the old pioneer." By then, a substantial number of people agreed with him. The work of building the Appalachian Trail began not long after his 1921 article, when volunteers from Georgia to Maine began cutting and marking it. Miles of existing sections of local trail systems established by such groups as the Dartmouth Outing Club, the Appalachian Mountain Club, and the Green Mountain Club were incorporated into the new trail. In seven years, five hundred miles of the trail had been established, and it was first completed for its entire length in 1937.

In 1925, MacKaye and a few of his compatriots founded the Appalachian Trail Conference (ATC) to act as a monitoring and coordinating body for volunteer efforts in the development and maintenance of the entire trail. Some such organization was necessary, for it was not long before this unique idea began to present some unique problems. Since most of the trail crossed private lands, its integrity depended upon the cooperation of various landholders, and a change of ownership could force the relocation of a section at any time. Worse, over the years, second-home real-estate development encroached upon the route. In 1938, at the urging of ATC leaders, the National Park Service and Forest Service agreed to establish a "recreation zone" wherever the trail entered federal lands, prohibiting any sort of development deemed incompatible with trail objectives. But not even the generally conservation-minded New Deal government could always be depended upon to preserve the trail's integrity. During the 1930s, as an anti-Depression measure, the Roosevelt administration gave approval for the construction of the Blue Ridge Parkway linking Great Smoky Mountains National Park and Shenandoah National Park—and cutting into the heart of pristine trail country. Benton MacKaye fought the proposal (it was one of the reasons he helped found The Wilderness Society), but to no avail.

During the ATC meeting of 1937, Edward B. Ballard of the National Park Service offered at least a partial solution to the vulnerability of the trail. He proposed that "trailway" agreements be made with federal and state agencies to secure inviolable rights-of-way. Myron Avery, chairman of the ATC, jumped at this idea and over the next several years negotiated agreements with the federal government that allowed for an inviolable right-of-way for a distance of one mile on either side of the trail through federal lands, and with state governments that established a similarly protected right-of-way one-half mile on either side through state-owned lands. Although a stipulation did allow logging to take place up to two hundred feet on each side of the trail on national forestlands, these government agreements at least established the concept that the trail's environment, wherever possible, should retain a wilderness character.

The trail way agreements did not, of course, alleviate the situation in regard to private lands, on which about half of the trail still remained vulnerable to development. In 1945, Avery persuaded Congressman Daniel Hoch of Pennsylvania to introduce an amendment to the Federal Highway Act of 1944 that would have mandated the creation of a nationwide federal system of foot trails, with provisions for the purchase of land and easements wherever necessary. The proposal died in committee, and it would be nearly two decades before the idea of federal protection could be revived. In 1963, during a meeting in Maine, ATC chairman Stanley A. Murray and a group discussed the possibility of legislation devoted to the protection of the Appalachian Trail specifically. At about the same time, at a cocktail party in Washington, D.C., an advocate of the trail mentioned his concern to Senator Gaylord Nelson, who had once proposed a 1,500-mile trail system for his home state of Wisconsin. Nelson had never set foot on the Appalachian Trail at that time, but, as he said in an interview years later, "I didn't have to be on it to know it was good!" and in 1964 he introduced the first of several bills for its protection.

## WHY NOT HERE?

By the time Gaylord Nelson's first bill for the protection of the Appalachian Trail entered the legislative process, a movement to establish similar trails all over the country had slowly gathered momentum. As early as 1932, the idea had leaped across the continent to emerge on the Pacific Coast, where Californian Clinton C. Clark proposed the establishment of an intermountain footpath running from Canada to Mexico across the Cascade and Sierra Nevada ranges. It was called the Pacific Crest Trail. Out in Wisconsin in the 1950s, Ray Zillmer, an attorney, began to promote the idea of a trail that would follow the traces of the great moraines that marked the deepest penetration of the last glaciers. This was called the Ice Age Trail. A few years later, citizens in Ohio conceived a trail running from Cleveland to Cincinnati, and later extended it northward to Toledo then back to Cleveland in a kind of great circle, 1,200 miles in length. They called it the Buckeye Trail. In upstate New York, in the Finger Lakes country, Wallace Wood and a few other enthusiasts began cutting a path from Allegheny State Park in western New York to the Catskills in the southeastern portion of the state—the Finger Lakes Trail.

After passage of the Wilderness Act of 1964, Benton MacKaye, well into his eighties by now, conceived of a "Cordilleran Trail" that would traverse the Rocky Mountains along the Continental Divide, linking one newly created wilderness with another. To him, both the trail and the areas served the common purpose of preserving wilderness in what he called the "French" strategy in a report for The Wilderness Society in 1966: "In order to hold the Mississippi Valley as part of *L'État Français*, the French established a series of forts held together by a winding river. In order to hold the Cordilleran Range as part of original America, let Americans establish a series of 'original' areas (wilderness areas) to be held together by a winding trail. As once a line of military posts defended the Great River, now a line of wilderness posts can defend the Great Divide."

These efforts and others found comfort in a 1962 report of the Outdoor Recreation Resources Review Commission, which lamented the fact that in this country very little had been done to encourage the healthful pastimes of walking and cycling, and a good deal had been done to discourage them. The commission stated:

We are spending billions for our new highways, but few of them being constructed or planned make any provision for safe walking and cy-

317

cling. Europe, which has even greater population densities, has much to teach us about building recreation into the environment. Holland is constructing a national network of bicycle trails. In Scotland, the right of the public to walk over the privately owned moors goes back centuries. In Scandinavia, buses going from the city to the countryside have pegs on their sides on which people can hang bicycles. Car ownership is rising all over Europe, but in the planning of their roads and the posting of them, Europeans make a special effort to provide for those who walk or cycle. Why not here?

Why not indeed? It was a question more and more people began to ask—including Senator Nelson, who in 1965 introduced another trails bill, which, going beyond protection for the Appalachian Trail alone, would add footpaths across the nation. The idea was suddenly so attractive that the Johnson administration seized it and began preparing legislation of its own out of the Department of the Interior. After three years of the kind of compromises and bickering typical of any sort of environmental legislation, a National Trails Act emerged from Congress in 1968 and was signed into law by President Johnson. It was the intent of Congress, the act stated, that "in order to provide for the ever-increasing outdoor recreation needs of an expanding population and in order to promote public access to, travel within, and enjoyment and appreciation of the open-air, outdoor areas of the Nation, trails should be established primarily, near the urban areas of the Nation, and secondarily, within established scenic areas more remotely located." As noted at the beginning of this chapter, the act immediately established the Appalachian Trail and the Pacific Crest Trail as the first components of the National Scenic Trails System, authorized the study of fourteen additional trails, and empowered the Secretaries of the Interior and of Agriculture to establish the shorter, urban-oriented recreation trails. It also established the category of Connecting and Side Trails (although no such routes have yet been designated). In 1978, because many of the trail studies were identifying extensive historic features and values on trails that did not quite qualify as "scenic," the Secretary of the Interior requested an amendment to the 1968 act that would establish Historic Trails as a separate category. In November, Congress complied with his re-

318

quest—and in the same amendment designated the Lewis and Clark, Mormon Pioneer, Oregon, and Iditarod as the first Historic Trails. In that same year, Congress also named the Continental Divide (MacKaye's "Cordilleran" concept) as the third Scenic Trail.

There now was, at least on paper, a National Trails System. But there were those in 1968 and later—as there are today—who questioned whether what we had could realistically be called a national system at all.

## DRAWING-BOARD DREAMS

Not a single designated Scenic or Historic Trail in the present system is complete. Even the Appalachian—the venerable AT—still needs the acquisition, through purchase or easements, of almost three hundred miles to finally make it the unbroken "footpath *of* the wilderness" dreamed of by Benton MacKaye. Furthermore, of the twenty-nine studies authorized by the act of 1968 and subsequent amendments, only ten of the trails involved have even been designated. Eight that were under study were found "not to qualify" for designation by the Park Service (although those who supported these trails would still be willing to offer arguments for their revival as candidates), and two—the 265-mile Long Trail of Vermont and the 1,000-mile Pacific Northwest Trail of Washington and Idaho—were "not recommended" for designation, a decision vague enough to leave room for hope. The nine remaining candidates are still under study.

Finally, as mentioned above, no Connecting or Side Trails have been designated, even though heavy recreational use on many trails—however incomplete—suggests a significant need for these. More than 4 million people use portions of the Appalachian Trail every year, for example. Designation of Vermont's Long Trail, extending from the Massachusetts border to the Canadian border, was seen as one way of relieving this pressure on the AT, while in Georgia, Tennessee, and North Carolina volunteers have been working for several years to construct the Benton MacKaye Trail, a 250-mile-long loop off the AT that would wind through scenic and remote portions of Great Smoky Mountains National Park and Cherokee, Nantahala, and Chattahoochee national forests. The Long Trail, as noted, was not recommended for designation by the Park Service, and the MacKaye

319

Trail has not yet been seriously considered, though it clearly is a very strong candidate.

At the heart of the problem is money, as it so often is. It was, in fact, ten years after the 1968 legislation before Congress appropriated *any* money specifically allotted for the administration of the trails system. A recent internal memorandum from an office in the National Park Service spells out the current situation precisely: "Inadequate funding for trails at all levels of government has made it impossible to meet the growing public demand for trail opportunities." The attitude of the Reagan administration toward the trails system is an echo of its policy in regard to other conservation programs—no support at all, if possible, and minimum support when absolutely forced to act. During the first three years of this administration, the Interior Department failed to ask for any acquisition money (available through the Land and Water Conservation Fund, among other budgetary sources) for the system, and while Congress appropriated some money in spite of this, most of it went to the needs of the AT alone. And when Interior Secretary James Watt abolished the Heritage Conservation and Recreation Service, he left the trails system without any federal agency primarily responsible for trails planning, development, or management; it, like the Wild and Scenic Rivers System, became a bureaucratic orphan.

In truth, however, the trails system has a low priority throughout the government, not just in the Executive branch. "The resulting lack of political support, inaction and nonresponsiveness," the internal memorandum cited earlier points out, "has contributed to an inadequate system." This sluggish attitude is compounded by the time-consuming and cumbersome process required on several levels of government to get trails developed, by a lack of proper communication, interest, and cooperation among individual agencies, by a confusion of regulations issued by various federal, state, and local entities—many of which often conflict and all of which require mounds of paperwork—and by a lack of public awareness of the needs and indeed the very existence of the National Trails System that sometimes borders on plain ignorance. There is little significant pressure placed on government from the private sector to improve the situation—and what there is tends to be fragmented and inadequate.

The largest single citizens group promoting and supporting the National Trails System remains the Appalachian Trail Conference. Its members now number about 18,000, although the combined membership of the independent hiking, camping, and trail clubs that are affiliated with the conference bring that total to somewhere between 70,000 and 80,000. It has long been the model for volunteer citizen involvement in long-distance trail development and management, and has been imitated—though never on so large a scale—by such groups as the Finger Lakes Trail Conference, the Buckeye Trail Association, the Ice Age Trail Council, the Benton MacKaye Trail Association, and the North Country Trail Association.

The government has nothing but praise for such citizen volunteers, and well it should—not only is their participation in the planning and management of trails mandated by the act of 1968, but without them there would not even be a trails system to manage. For the most part, private citizens, acting in groups of varying degrees of size and organization, have conceived, planned, maintained, and preserved the trails. But as yet they lack the national strength—the power of a single voice—necessary to force the government of the United States to invest the National Trails System, which it created, with a semblance of reality and the financial and bureaucratic support sufficient to make it something more than what most of it sadly is: dreams on a drawing-board.

## AN AGENDA FOR THE NATIONAL WILD AND SCENIC RIVERS AND THE NATIONAL TRAILS SYSTEMS

### THE RIVERS

Since its creation in 1968, the National Wild and Scenic Rivers system has taken on the character of a neglected stepchild. Only one river—the Tuolumne—has been added to the system since the Carter administration. The more than seven thousand miles of sixty-six rivers and tributaries currently represented in the system are but a fraction of those that could and should be included; at best, they constitute no more than the disarticulated skeleton of a system. Part of the reason behind this fitful and retarded growth lies in the inadequacies and confusions of the law that created the system, but an equally significant obstacle has been the absence of any clear, organized, and coherent constituency for its continued health and growth—a deficiency unfortunately true not only of the public at large, but of the conservation movement generally, the American Congress, and, most particularly, the current administration (whose interest in wild and scenic rivers, when demonstrated at all, has been plainly antagonistic). And, while the system lies in a state of arrested growth, the fate of hundreds of America's remaining free rivers—many of them prime candidates for preservation—is shadowed by the rapid development of small-scale hydropower technology whose potential impact may outstrip all the megadams and diversions of the past.

Clearly, this moribund situation cannot be allowed to continue if the system is to take its proper place in the full web of this country's legacy of public lands—resources whose future is vital to the future of the nation itself. It is equally clear that in order to change things significantly, it is the responsibility of the conservation community at large to begin to build the necessary base of widespread support. The piecemeal defense of individual rivers is not enough; local support of local rivers is not enough; state systems of protection are not enough. We must create national support on a national scale for a truly national system, just as we did for the National Wilderness Preservation System, just as we did for the national interest lands of Alaska. Achieving this may require the kind of formal cooperation among national conservation groups that was demonstrated so successfully by the Alaska Coalition of the 1970s. However such a community of effort is structured, it should be put into motion swiftly in full recognition of the dimensions and significance of the tasks that await it. We offer the following as the most important immediate goals:

*Passage of an omnibus wild and scenic rivers bill.* At present, there are 4,425 miles of rivers and tributaries on which studies have been completed, including the Priest of Idaho, the Youghiogheny of Pennsylvania, the Wisconsin of Wisconsin, the Dolores of Colorado, and many other segments. Yet these rivers are victims of political inertia, and there is no reason to expect that they will soon be placed in the federal system of protection if they are acted on one river at a time.

322

These rivers and river sections should be included in a single bill that will give them immediate designation with broad-based congressional consent. The passage of such a bill should be the first step in a continuing program aimed at accelerating and expanding the current study process (see below) and the designation by the year 2000 of at least fifty additional river segments on federal land and another fifty (through acquisition and easement) on nonfederal land.

*Completion of already authorized acquisitions and easements.* The incorporation of ridge-to-ridge "buffer zones" on either side of designated rivers flowing through private lands is a device essential to the protection of watershed and riverine habitat, and authorization for the purchase of this land through outright acquisition or easement procedures was included in the acts that designated each of the segments now in the system. Yet there is a large backlog of unacquired land (some of it on rivers designated as long ago as 1968). Sufficient Land and Water Conservation Fund money should be allocated for the completion of these unresolved purchases over the next five years.

*Initiation of a program of regular congressional oversight hearings.* Congress has been particularly dilatory in its responsibility to monitor the development of this important resource system. Since passage of the Wild and Scenic Rivers Act in 1968, there has not been a single oversight hearing on the rivers system by any committee or subcommittee in either branch, yet such hearings are the principal means Congress has of determining how any law it has created is being administered—whether the intent of Congress is being carried out faithfully, whether programs are being properly funded, whether interpretation and implementation need to be refined or substantially revised. The Wild and Scenic Rivers System is in serious need of such attention, and hearings should be scheduled as soon as possible— in the House, by the Subcommittee on Public Lands and National Parks; in the Senate, by the Subcommittee on Public Lands and Reserved Water.

Moving swiftly to accomplish the three goals listed above would go a long way toward putting the Wild and Scenic Rivers System on a better footing in the near future. But as we have emphasized in

323

each of these "agenda" statements, the management of America's public lands cannot be left hostage to the near-term syndrome; that very phenomenon is why the future of so much of the American land is in jeopardy today. In regard to the nation's rivers, then, as with all other units of the public lands, we must learn to think in the range of decades, indeed, of scores of years, if we are to properly maintain and even improve a legacy we have no right to neglect, and to that end we believe that three major long-range programs should be put into effect.

*Mandate a national rivers study program.* Under current procedures, an individual river is placed under study as a possible candidate for wild and scenic designation only after passage of a specific act of Congress. This ponderous approach is time-consuming and fraught with the possibility that many important rivers will not be seriously studied for inclusion before hydropower or other development renders them ineligible. Instead, we call for a nationwide study program for *all* currently eligible candidate rivers (a list that could easily be derived from the National Park Service's excellent "National Inventory of Rivers"); during a specified period of time for study (we recommend five years), no hydropower, real-estate, or any other kind of development that might affect the ecological integrity of a river or its wildlife or habitat would be allowed; after completion of the study, recommendations for individual rivers would then be passed on to Congress for designation where it is deemed appropriate. Such a program (similar in some respects to the National Forest Service's Roadless Area Review and Evaluation process) could be initiated by executive order, by separate legislation, or (as noted below) by amendment to the National Wild and Scenic Rivers Act of 1968.

*Establish a permanent administrative body for river policy and planning at the federal level.* At present, as many as fifteen government agencies at the federal, state, and local levels can be involved at one time or another in planning, policy, and management decisions affecting any given river. This is a confused and confusing business and must be simplified and clarified if we hope to produce any sort of long-range planning. Furthermore, the wild and scenic rivers need

324

a constituency of support *within* the federal government as well as outside it. The nearest thing to such a body was the Interior Department's Heritage Conservation and Recreation Service (before being abolished by James Watt), and even it had only six staff people in Washington, D.C., dealing with river programs. While day-to-day management decisions for any given river in the system should be left to the appropriate agencies—the U.S. Forest Service, the National Park Service, and the Bureau of Land Management—an Interior Department office of river planning should be created with adequate funds and staffing to take responsibility for the system as a whole in all matters of overall planning and policy—including the monitoring of a continuing study program and inventory, the supervision of all purchase procedures (including the allocation of funds), and technical assistance to individual states in the planning and development of their own wild and scenic rivers programs (a service now offered only by the National Park Service in a limited fashion). This Interior Department office should become the recognized government "voice" for American rivers.

*Encourage the development of meaningful state wild and scenic rivers programs.* Although the federal system of rivers is the best opportunity for preservation on a coherent national scale, this basic protection should be augmented by state programs to achieve the widest possible diversity and comprehensiveness. Only twenty-eight states now have river programs. A few of these—as in California—are comparable to the federal system in their scope and goals. Many others are little more than casual lists with little or no regulation or protection to give them weight. Through the agency described above, the federal government should vigorously promote the creation of substantive river programs in all fifty states. A major step in this direction would be swift passage of a bill similar to that introduced by Senator Dave Durenberger in 1984, the proposed State and Local Rivers Conservation bill. Such a measure would not only encourage states to designate rivers for special management, it would offer matching federal funds to help states develop river conservation efforts. Equally important, it would block the present autonomous power of the Federal Energy Regulatory Commission by declaring all state-designated rivers off-limits to hydropower development if the governor of a state so determines. Another measure introduced by Senator George Mitchell (D-Maine) in 1984 would have encouraged states to prepare comprehensive plans for their rivers to determine which should be available for hydropower development and which should be reserved for other purposes, such as recreation. The Federal Energy Regulatory Commission would be required to approve such comprehensive plans. Versions of both bills—or a combination of the two—should be acted upon by Congress as soon as possible.

The Wild and Scenic Rivers Act of 1968, like much conservation legislation, has revealed significant weaknesses and omissions over the years that were not sufficiently anticipated at the time of its passage. It needs to be refined and strengthened in a number of areas to aid and implement the kind of long-range proposals we have been discussing. First, as noted above, if it cannot be accomplished in any other manner, a nationwide study program for all eligible rivers on federal lands should be mandated by amendment of the act, eliminating the need for individual acts of Congress before any river or river segment can be placed under study. In addition, we recommend amendment of the act in three other areas:

*Management planning.* One of the greatest difficulties in properly administering the units of the rivers system as it now exists has been the lack of comprehensive management plans. To alleviate these problems in the future, the act should be amended to require each federal agency charged with the administration of each component of the system to prepare such a comprehensive management plan within three years after the component has been designated. In providing for the protection of river values, each plan should address the costs and effects of resource protection alternatives, the necessary development of lands and facilities, and appropriate user capacities, including provisions for the issuance of user permits, if deemed necessary. Further, this amendment should require similar plans to be drawn up by the appropriate agencies for those rivers already in the system.

*Acquisition.* Under the provisions of the present law, acquisition procedures through outright purchase or the purchase of easements are strictly limited to an area one-quarter mile from the ordinary high-water mark of both sides of a river. This rigid limitation does not properly take into account requirements for habitat protection that can vary considerably from river to river—and even portion to portion of any individual river. In addition, local landowners often desire to sell their entire property, rather than merely the portion that is contiguous to a river. For the purposes of intelligent planning, the act should be amended to allow the acquisition of land, where it is considered necessary to the purposes of the act, beyond the quarter-mile limits up to a maximum of one mile from the normal high-water mark. Further, this amendment should stipulate that such acquisition authority extends to those wild and scenic river systems that already have been designated, so that refinement and improvement of riverine habitat protection can be made where necessary during the continuing planning process.

*Nomenclature*. To further streamline the Wild and Scenic Rivers Act, we recommend the abolition of the "recreational" river category. A river can and should be classified either as wild (inaccessible except by boat) or as scenic (accessible by other means). There seems to be little reason for a third classification, which differs from "scenic" only in the *degree* of accessibility and frequently leads to needless confusion in management.

If they could be reduced to a single goal, the recommendations we make here are designed to provide the still-young National Wild and Scenic Rivers System with the stature and commitment long since given to such other units of the public lands as national parks and wilderness areas. Our rivers are no less important and should be treated with the same care so that they may play a full part in the future resource planning of the nation.

## THE TRAILS

As should be readily apparent, many of the problems—and hence, many of the solutions—that relate to the National Wild and Scenic Rivers System also have application to its "twin," the National Trails System. In some cases, the problems that afflict the trails system are more serious than those that now hamper the rivers system. Take, for example, the matter of a coherent public support network. The rivers at least have the American Rivers Conservation Council to speak for them at the national level. The trails of our country have not a single national organization equipped to do the same—and of all the major conservation organizations, only The Wilderness Society has ever had a continuing interest in the promotion and preservation of trails on any meaningful level (and it must be admitted that the press of other business in recent years has forced even The Wilderness Society to place its trails program low on the agenda). The chore of building a national constituency for the trails system, then, is significantly more difficult than establishing a similar consensus for the rivers. Nevertheless, such a coalition of support for the trails must be fashioned in the near future if the system is to survive even in its present crippled state. As with the rivers, this may require the formation of an interorganizational group similar to the Alaska Coalition—a conservation task force with the funding, resources, and expertise to study the system's needs and problems and formulate specific recommendations that can then be translated into administrative action or, where necessary, new legislation. The beginning of such a group effort exists in the recently formed National Trails Coalition—although member organizations so far include only the Sierra Club, the National Audubon Society, and The Wilderness Society. Membership should be broadened.

Certainly, one of the most immediate goals of any coalition effort should be to cut through the present condition of apathy that enwraps both Congress and the land-managing agencies of the federal government. Nowhere is this apathy—even antipathy—demonstrated more clearly than in the U.S. Forest Service, which has subjected its own system of national forest trails to neglect and degradation. A June 1985 report prepared for the National Trails Coalition outlined the situation succinctly:

The number of miles of trails in the National Forest System peaked in the 1940s at 144,000 miles. Since then the total number of trail miles being built, reconstructed, and maintained by the Forest Service has steadily declined. Between 1932 and 1950, 20 million acres were added to the National Forest System, but the number of trail miles decreased by 3,000 miles. In the next decade 23,000 miles of trails were lost. By 1974 the trail system mileage was only two-thirds what it had been forty years earlier. And by 1980, the last year the Forest Service reported systemwide figures for trail miles, only 101,000 miles remained.

More and more trail users are being crowded onto fewer and fewer trails. Since 1969, use of national forest trails has more than doubled. In the fourteen-year period between 1969 and 1983, the number of visitor days of trail use exploded from about 5.6 million to about 13 million. This is a systemwide increase of 132 percent. In 1960, there were nineteen visitor days of trail use recorded for each mile of trail in the system; by 1980, each remaining mile of trail was forced to support 126.5 visitor days of trail use.

To counter this kind of management philosophy, influence should be applied at all government levels to persuade policymakers that it is in the best interests of the nation to establish a truly realistic National Trails System that possesses both the prestige and the authority of other public land units; the system must be given weight within the government. The most effective immediate means to accomplish this would be to create an administrative body within the Interior Department whose only function would be to coordinate with other agencies and volunteer groups and generally administer the National Trails System—with the permanent staffing and funding necessary to do the job properly. The trails system has never had its own supervisory structure; it should be given one as soon as possible, and the new agency should move at once to outline, establish, and promote a trails program designed to meet the following immediate and long-term goals:

*A comprehensive survey of trail needs, now and in the future.* One of the tasks assumed by the Heritage Conservation and Recreation Service before it was abolished was to initiate a grassroots effort to assess the needs of the trails system throughout the nation. The objectives of this assessment were to define the scope and extent of the existing National Trails System and develop suitable amendments that would better implement the intent of the National Trails System Act of 1968;

to determine the number of trails now in use, their proximity and availability to users, and their deficiencies; and to report the concerns, perceptions, strengths, and recommendations of trail-user groups all over the country. After the Service was eliminated, that assignment was given to a tiny group within the National Park Service to complete. The resulting report, still in draft form at the end of 1985, was a noble effort but far short of the detailed and comprehensive document it should have been. An entirely new effort must be initiated, with sufficient funding and personnel—both in Washington, D.C., and in the field—to accomplish its goals properly. One other item should be added to this study's priorities: the production of a truly comprehensive and authoritative map of the system; the one currently available to the public was produced in 1979 and is excessively crude, inaccurate, out of date, and essentially useless.

*Completion of the present system within the next decade.* It will soon have been twenty years since passage of the 1968 act—and with the exception of the Appalachian and Pacific Crest trails, both of them now relatively near completion—virtually nothing has been done to fill in the gaps that have existed since the system was conceived. A classic example is the North Country Scenic Trail, designated in 1980. This unique trail, 3,200 miles in length, was planned to run from northeastern New York through a wide variety of environments in the states of Pennsylvania, Ohio, Michigan, Wisconsin (incorporating within it the present Ice Age Trail), Minnesota, and North Dakota before connecting with the Lewis and Clark Historic Trail. But except for much of the Ice Age segment, this exciting trail experience exists almost entirely on paper. It is not alone in this distinction. Congress must produce legislation designed to utilize Land and Water Conservation Fund monies to acquire the land necessary to complete and protect this and all other unfinished trails and, where negotiated purchase is impossible and condemnation proceedings are impractical, Congress must engineer appropriate easements and other agreements that may be required.

*Addition of new scenic trails to the system, with the objective of constructing a network of such trails throughout the country by the year 2000.* The emphasis here should be on Scenic Trails rather than

Historic Trails, for the paramount need in terms of providing a true sense of the nation's rich and various natural heritage is for hiking paths that offer the closest and most immediate contact with the environment. By their very nature, most Historic Trails are designations on a map that largely follow highways; just as in the past, these routes are used to get from one place to another. Only Scenic Trails can provide some idea of what it once was like to walk into new wilderness country. Three trails should be incorporated into the system immediately: the Pacific Northwest Trail, running more than one thousand miles from Glacier National Park in Montana across Idaho and northern Washington to the Olympic peninsula; the Long Trail, running through Vermont from a connection with the Appalachian Trail to the Canadian border; and the Benton MacKaye Trail, a much-needed 250-mile alternative route for the southern section of the AT. All three trails are basically in place and being used, but all three need federal recognition and protection if they are to be preserved. The Pacific Northwest and Long trails have both been studied and not recommended for designation by the National Park Service; those decisions should be reversed. The Benton MacKaye Trail, which is now being constructed by volunteers with the cooperation of the Forest Service and the National Park Service, should not even require study before its inclusion, since virtually all of its scenic route is presently under federal management. Those trails still under study—the Daniel Boone Trail through North Carolina, Tennessee, and Kentucky and the Nez Perce Trail through Oregon, Idaho, and Montana, for example—should be authorized as soon as possible. Furthermore, such other potential routes as the 2,000-mile Desert Trail from southwestern Arizona through Nevada and eastern Oregon or the Dominguez-Escalante Trail from Santa Fe through Arizona, Utah, and Colorado and back again to Santa Fe should be reconsidered for designation. And The Wilderness Society would like to recommend here for the first time another new national footpath: a Bob Marshall Trail through the Brooks Range of Alaska—not only to memorialize the first non-Native to explore the range to any significant extent, but to provide a unique hiking experience through the Arctic wilderness.

Another potentially important means of expanding the trails system lies in the conversion of railroad rights-of-way. Each year, more than

331

three thousand miles of railroad track are abandoned by companies as they discontinue service on various lines throughout the country. The Railroad Revitalization and Regulatory Reform Act of 1976 included a stipulation giving private citizen groups and local, state, and even federal park authorities the right to petition for the public use of any such abandoned railroad corridors. A 1983 amendment to the National Trails Act carried this idea even farther: in what is called a "railbank" system, the ownership of abandoned roadbeds can be retained and the rails and ties themselves sold by railroad companies; however, until such time as a company can demonstrate a need to reopen the abandoned line to rail service, it also can be managed as a public trail by any private group or government park agency, providing such groups maintain the trail, assume all liability for its use by the public, and pay any applicable taxes. Already, "rails-to-trails" conversions have been made successfully in Iowa, Wisconsin, Illinois, Virginia, California, Washington, and elsewhere, and late in 1985, the Rails-to-Trails Conservancy was founded in Washington, D.C., to promote this expansion program throughout the country.

Finally, the emphasis in the recommendations above has been on the government's role in the future of the National Trails System. This is only as it should be, for it is time that the federal government began to play a role commensurate with that performed by the private sector for nearly three-quarters of a century. The importance of the participation of such organizations as the Appalachian Trail Conference, as well as the public at large, is immeasurable, but if we allow the federal government to abdicate its responsibility—as it plainly has done over most of the past two decades—then we can never hope to achieve a lasting system of national trails that will enlarge the wilderness experience for the generations to come.

LEFT: Using one natural resource to exploit another, lumbermen float billions of board feet of rough-cut lumber taken from the forests of northern Wisconsin down the Wisconsin River; this shot of a "lumber-raft" was taken in 1886. *The H. H. Bennett Studio*

BELOW: Ripogerus Gorge on the West Branch of the Penobscot River, Maine. *Read D. Brugger*

ABOVE: Canyon on the Yampa River, Dinosaur National Monument, Colorado-Utah. *Philip Hyde*
OPPOSITE: A stretch of the Salt River of Arizona awaiting Wild and Scenic River status. *Dale Schicketanz*

View from Boarstone Mountain on the Appalachian Trail, Maine. *Read D. Brugger*

# APPENDIX

## The Public Lands and Major
## Public Land Legislation of the United States

### THE FEDERAL LAND-MANAGING AGENCIES

| | Established | Responsibility | FY 1985 Budget | FY 1985 Employees |
|---|---|---|---|---|
| National Park Service | 1916 | National Parks and Monuments | $ 954,345,000 | 11,000 permanent 12,000 seasonal |
| U.S. Forest Service | 1905 | National Forests and Grasslands | 1,971,569,000 | 47,944 permanent 13,556 seasonal |
| Bureau of Land Management | 1946 | National Resource Lands | 646,945,000 | 10,600 permanent |
| Fish & Wildlife Service | 1940 | Wildlife Refuges | 586,987,000 | 6,804 permanent |

### THE NATIONAL PARK SYSTEM

#### NATIONAL PARKS

| | State(s) | Acreage |
|---|---|---|
| Acadia | Maine | 38,523 |
| Arches | Utah | 73,378 |
| Badlands | South Dakota | 243,302 |

NATIONAL PARKS (*cont'd*)

| | State(s) | Acreage |
|---|---|---|
| Big Bend | Texas | 708,118 |
| Biscayne | Florida | 180,275 |
| Bryce Canyon | Utah | 35,835 |
| Canyonlands | Utah | 337,570 |
| Capitol Reef | Utah | 241,904 |
| Carlsbad Caverns | New Mexico | 46,755 |
| Channel Islands | California | 249,353 |
| Crater Lake | Oregon | 160,290 |
| Denali | Alaska | 4,698,583 |
| Everglades | Florida | 1,398,800 |
| Gates of the Arctic | Alaska | 7,498,066 |
| Glacier | Montana | 1,013,594 |
| Glacier Bay | Alaska | 3,220,396 |
| Grand Canyon | Arizona | 1,218,375 |
| Grand Teton | Wyoming | 310,515 |
| Great Smoky Mountains | North Carolina, Tennessee | 517,368 |
| Guadalupe Mountains | Texas | 76,293 |
| Haleakala | Hawaii | 28,655 |
| Hawaii Volcanoes | Hawaii | 229,177 |
| Hot Springs | Arkansas | 5,826 |
| Isle Royale | Michigan | 571,796 |
| Katmai | Alaska | 3,678,929 |
| Kenai Fjords | Alaska | 676,667 |
| Kings Canyon | California | 460,139 |
| Kobuk Valley | Alaska | 1,749,037 |
| Lake Clark | Alaska | 2,633,933 |
| Lassen Volcanic | California | 106,372 |
| Mammoth Cave | Kentucky | 52,128 |
| Mesa Verde | Colorado | 52,085 |
| Mount Rainier | Washington | 235,404 |
| North Cascades | Washington | 504,780 |
| Olympic | Washington | 908,720 |
| Petrified Forest | Arizona | 93,492 |
| Redwood | California | 109,225 |
| Rocky Mountain | Colorado | 263,790 |
| Sequoia | California | 403,023 |
| Shenandoah | Virginia | 194,801 |
| Theodore Roosevelt | North Dakota | 70,344 |

| | | |
|---|---|---|
| Virgin Islands | Virgin Islands | 14,708 |
| Voyageurs | Minnesota | 219,128 |
| Wind Cave | South Dakota | 28,292 |
| Wrangell–St. Elias | Alaska | 8,331,406 |
| Yellowstone | Idaho, Wyoming, Montana | 2,219,822 |
| Yosemite | California | 760,917 |
| Zion | Utah | 146,546 |

NATIONAL MONUMENTS

(of 20 acres or more in size)

| | | |
|---|---|---|
| Agate Fossil Beds | Nebraska | 3,055 |
| Alibates Flint Quarries | New Mexico, Texas | 1,332 |
| Aniakchak | Alaska | 136,955 |
| Aztec Ruins | New Mexico | 27 |
| Bandelier | New Mexico | 36,971 |
| Black Canyon of the Gunnison | Colorado | 13,672 |
| Buck Reef Island | Virgin Islands | 880 |
| Cabrilla | California | 143 |
| Canyon de Chelly | Arizona | 83,840 |
| Cape Krusenstern | Alaska | 636,685 |
| Capulin Mountains | New Mexico | 775 |
| Casa Grande Ruins | Arizona | 472 |
| Cedar Breaks | Utah | 6,154 |
| Chiricahua | Arizona | 11,088 |
| Colorado | Colorado | 20,449 |
| Congaree Swamp | South Carolina | 15,200 |
| Craters of the Moon | Idaho | 53 |
| Death Valley | California, Nevada | 2,067,627 |
| Devils Postpile | California | 798 |
| Devils Tower | Wyoming | 1,346 |
| Dinosaur | Colorado, Utah | 211,060 |
| Effigy Mounds | Iowa | 1,346 |
| El Morro | New Mexico | 1,278 |
| Florissant Fossil Beds | Colorado | 5,998 |
| Fossil Butte | Wyoming | 8,198 |
| Gila Cliff Dwellings | New Mexico | 553 |
| Grand Portage | Minnesota | 709 |
| Great Sand Dunes | Colorado | 38,951 |
| Hohokam Pima | Arizona | 1,690 |

NATIONAL MONUMENTS (*cont'd*)

|  | *State(s)* | *Acreage* |
|---|---|---|
| Homestead National Monument of America | Nebraska | 194 |
| Hovenweep | Colorado, Utah | 785 |
| Jewel Cave | South Dakota | 1,274 |
| John Day Fossil Beds | Oregon | 14,100 |
| Joshua Tree | California | 559,959 |
| Lava Beds | California | 46,821 |
| Lehman Caves | Nevada | 640 |
| Montezuma Castle | Arizona | 849 |
| Mound City Group | Ohio | 67 |
| Muir Woods | California | 553 |
| Natural Bridges | Utah | 7,779 |
| Navajo | Arizona | 360 |
| Ocmulgee | Georgia | 683 |
| Oregon Caves | Oregon | 473 |
| Organ Pipe Cactus | Arizona | 330,688 |
| Pecos | New Mexico | 364 |
| Pinnacles | California | 16,221 |
| Pipe Spring | Arizona | 40 |
| Pipestone | Minnesota | 281 |
| Rainbow Bridge | Utah | 160 |
| Russell Cave | Alabama | 310 |
| Saguaro | Arizona | 83,576 |
| Saint Croix Island | Maine | 35 |
| Salinas | New Mexico | 1,079 |
| Scotts Bluff | Nebraska | 2,987 |
| Sunset Crater | Arizona | 3,040 |
| Timpanogos Cave | Utah | 250 |
| Tonto | Arizona | 1,120 |
| Tuzigoot | Arizona | 848 |
| Walnut Canyon | Arizona | 2,249 |
| White Sands | New Mexico | 144,419 |
| Wupatki | Arizona | 35,253 |

## THE NATIONAL FOREST SYSTEM

FORESTS

|  | *State(s)* | *Acreage* |
|---|---|---|
| Allegheny | Pennsylvania | 510,406 |
| Angeles | California | 653,862 |
| Angelina | Texas | 154,244 |
| Apache | Arizona | 1,187,685 |
| Apalachicola | Florida | 558,737 |
| Arapaho | Colorado | 1,024,980 |
| Ashley | Utah, Wyoming | 1,384,699 |
| Beaverhead | Montana | 2,128,798 |
| Bienville | Mississippi | 179,394 |
| Bighorn | Wyoming | 1,107,670 |
| Bitterroot | Idaho, Montana | 1,578,330 |
| Black Hills | South Dakota, Wyoming | 1,235,411 |
| Boise | Idaho | 2,645,938 |
| Bridger | Wyoming | 1,733,555 |
| Cache | Idaho, Utah | 679,333 |
| Calaveras Bigtree | Arkansas | 380 |
| Caribou | Idaho, Utah, Wyoming | 987,187 |
| Carson | New Mexico | 1,391,355 |
| Challis | Idaho | 2,463,633 |
| Chattahoochee | Georgia | 748,663 |
| Chequamegon | Wisconsin | 847,954 |
| Cherokee | North Carolina, Tennessee | 625,606 |
| Chippewa | Minnesota | 661,218 |
| Choctawhatchee | Florida | 675 |
| Chugach | Alaska | 6,122,949 |
| Cibola | New Mexico | 1,635,510 |
| Clearwater | Idaho | 1,688,687 |
| Cleveland | California | 420,590 |
| Coconino | Arizona | 1,835,767 |
| Coeur d'Alene | Idaho | 722,571 |
| Colville | Washington | 945,120 |
| Conecuh | Alabama | 82,826 |
| Coronado | Arizona, New Mexico | 1,779,297 |
| Croatan | North Carolina | 157,054 |
| Custer | South Dakota, Montana | 2,173,506 |
| Daniel Boone | Kentucky | 529,121 |

341

FORESTS (*cont'd*)

| | State(s) | Acreage |
|---|---|---|
| Davy Crockett | Texas | 161,500 |
| Deerlodge | Montana | 1,196,547 |
| Delta | Mississippi | 59,518 |
| Deschutes | Oregon | 1,604,705 |
| DeSoto | Mississippi | 501,724 |
| Dixie | Utah | 1,883,736 |
| Eldorado | California, Nevada | 672,784 |
| Fishlake | Utah | 1,424,527 |
| Flathead | Montana | 2,350,439 |
| Francis Marion | South Carolina | 250,008 |
| Fremont | Oregon | 1,197,012 |
| Gallatin | Montana | 1,738,056 |
| George Washington | Virginia, West Virginia | 1,055,568 |
| Gifford Pinchot | Washington | 1,253,585 |
| Gila | New Mexico | 2,704,781 |
| Grand Mesa | Colorado | 346,219 |
| Green Mountain | New York, Vermont | 307,842 |
| Gunnison | Colorado | 1,662,839 |
| Helena | Montana | 975,088 |
| Hiawatha | Michigan | 879,593 |
| Holly Springs | Mississippi | 152,174 |
| Homochitto | Mississippi | 188,994 |
| Hoosier | Indiana | 187,523 |
| Humboldt | Nevada | 2,527,938 |
| Huron | Michigan | 428,669 |
| Inyo | California, Nevada | 1,861,540 |
| Jefferson | Kentucky, Virginia, West Virginia | 698,846 |
| Kaibab | Arizona | 1,556,432 |
| Kaniksu | Idaho, Montana, Washington | 1,616,201 |
| Kisatchie | Louisiana | 597,933 |
| Klamath | California, Oregon | 1,707,104 |
| Kootenai | Idaho, Montana | 2,224,717 |
| Lassen | California | 1,060,001 |
| Lewis and Clark | Montana | 1,843,587 |
| Lincoln | New Mexico | 1,103,490 |
| Lolo | Montana | 2,112,597 |
| Los Padres | California | 1,752,523 |

| | | |
|---|---|---|
| Malheur | Oregon | 1,459,422 |
| Manistee | Michigan | 522,167 |
| Manti–La Sal | Colorado, Utah | 1,265,254 |
| Mark Twain | Missouri | 1,453,743 |
| Medicine Bow | Wyoming | 1,093,667 |
| Mendocino | California | 884,231 |
| Modoc | California | 1,654,527 |
| Monongahela | West Virginia | 848,879 |
| Mount Baker | Washington | 1,280,972 |
| Mount Hood | Oregon | 1,060,092 |
| Nantahala | North Carolina | 515,287 |
| Nebraska | Nebraska | 141,553 |
| Nezperce | Idaho | 2,221,816 |
| Nicolet | Wisconsin | 656,248 |
| Ocala | Florida | 382,318 |
| Ochoco | Oregon | 843,721 |
| Oconee | Georgia | 114,248 |
| Okanogan | Washington | 1,499,462 |
| Olympic | Washington | 649,975 |
| Osceola | Florida | 157,379 |
| Ottawa | Michigan | 928,221 |
| Ouachita | Oklahoma | 248,965 |
| Ozark | Arkansas | 1,119,639 |
| Payette | Idaho | 2,314,379 |
| Pike | Colorado | 1,107,946 |
| Pisgah | North Carolina | 495,730 |
| Plumas | California | 1,154,610 |
| Prescott | Arizona | 1,237,061 |
| Rio Grande | Colorado | 1,851,296 |
| Rogue River | California, Oregon | 629,191 |
| Roosevelt | Colorado | 788,268 |
| Routt | Colorado | 1,127,291 |
| Sabine | Texas | 188,220 |
| St. Francis | Arkansas | 20,937 |
| St. Joe | Idaho | 866,500 |
| Salmon | Idaho | 1,771,180 |
| Sam Houston | Texas | 161,150 |
| Samuel R. McKelvie | Nebraska | 115,707 |
| San Bernardino | California | 657,975 |
| San Isabel | Colorado | 1,115,754 |
| San Juan | Colorado | 1,860,728 |

FORESTS (*cont'd*)

| | State(s) | Acreage |
|---|---|---|
| Santa Fe | New Mexico | 1,567,389 |
| Sawtooth | Utah, Idaho | 1,802,715 |
| Sequoia | California | 1,125,693 |
| Shasta | California | 1,133,519 |
| Shawnee | Illinois | 253,378 |
| Shoshone | Wyoming | 2,433,029 |
| Sierra | California | 1,303,032 |
| Siskiyou | California, Oregon | 1,083,488 |
| Sitgreaves | Arizona | 817,338 |
| Siuslaw | Oregon | 628,175 |
| Six Rivers | California | 987,920 |
| Snoqualmie | Washington | 1,225,748 |
| Stanislaus | California | 889,478 |
| Sumter | South Carolina | 359,648 |
| Superior | Minnesota | 2,054,022 |
| Tahoe | California | 391,970 |
| Talladega | Alabama | 371,850 |
| Targhee | Idaho, Wyoming | 1,642,755 |
| Toiyabe | California, Nevada | 3,195,400 |
| Tombigbee | Mississippi | 66,457 |
| Tongass | Alaska | 16,815,703 |
| Tonto | Arizona | 2,873,759 |
| Trinity | California | 1,045,441 |
| Tuskegee | Alabama | 10,925 |
| Uinta | Utah | 812,760 |
| Umatilla | Washington, Oregon | 1,402,500 |
| Umpqua | Oregon | 984,797 |
| Uncompahgre | Colorado | 943,894 |
| Uwharrie | North Carolina | 47,069 |
| Wallowa | Oregon | 985,980 |
| Wasatch | Utah, Idaho | 848,609 |
| Wayne | Ohio | 177,485 |
| Wenatchee | Washington | 1,620,031 |
| White Mountain | Maine, New Hampshire | 728,623 |
| White River | Colorado | 1,961,539 |
| Whitman | Oregon | 1,263,879 |
| William B. Bankhead | Alabama | 180,615 |
| Willamette | Oregon | 1,675,470 |
| Winema | Oregon | 1,034,915 |

## GRASSLANDS

| | | |
|---|---|---|
| Black Kettle | Oklahoma, Texas | 31,300 |
| Buffalo Gap | South Dakota | 591,700 |
| Caddo | Texas | 17,784 |
| Cedar River | North Dakota | 6,717 |
| Cimarron | Kansas | 108,177 |
| Comanche | Colorado | 418,870 |
| Crooked River | Oregon | 105,224 |
| Curlew | Idaho | 47,658 |
| Fort Pierre | South Dakota | 116,001 |
| Grand River | South Dakota | 155,170 |
| Kiowa | New Mexico | 136,412 |
| Little Missouri | North Dakota | 1,027,922 |
| Lyndon B. Johnson | Texas | 20,320 |
| McClelland Creek | Texas | 1,449 |
| Oglala | Nebraska | 94,332 |
| Pawnee | Colorado | 193,060 |
| Rita Blanca | Oklahoma, Texas | 92,989 |
| Thunder Basin | Wyoming | 571,885 |

## THE NATIONAL RESOURCE LANDS (BLM)

| State | Acreage | Wilderness Study Areas | WSA Acreage |
|---|---|---|---|
| Alabama | 3,100 | none | none |
| Alaska | 95,000* | none | none |
| Arizona | 12,283,541 | 62 | 1,521,000 |
| Arkansas | 1,820 | none | none |
| California | 17,158,098 | 185 | 6,829,000 |
| Colorado | 8,365,552 | 60 | 801,000 |
| Florida | 1,937 | none | none |
| Idaho | 11,906,806 | 61 | 1,913,000 |
| Illinois | 12 | none | none |
| Kansas | 728 | none | none |
| Louisiana | 3,962 | none | none |
| Michigan | 766 | none | none |

*Until completion of transfers to the state government under provisions of the Alaska Statehood Act and to Alaska Natives under provisions of the Alaska Native Claims Settlement Act. These should leave approximately 75 million acres under BLM management.

| State | Acreage | *Wilderness Study Areas* | WSA Acreage |
|---|---|---|---|
| Minnesota | 60,615 | none | none |
| Mississippi | 597 | none | none |
| Missouri | 400 | none | none |
| Montana | 8,093,612 | 42 | 437,000 |
| Nebraska | 8,002 | none | none |
| Nevada | 48,591,143 | 83 | 4,381,000 |
| New Mexico | 12,850,966 | 43 | 892,000 |
| North Dakota | 68,104 | none | none |
| Ohio | 120 | none | none |
| Oklahoma | 6,231 | none | none |
| Oregon | 15,694,891 | 85 | 2,312,000 |
| South Dakota | 274,599 | none | none |
| Utah | 22,166,755 | 81 | 3,139,000 |
| Washington | 312,451 | none | none |
| Wisconsin | 589 | none | none |
| Wyoming | 18,410,441 | 36 | 550,000 |

## THE NATIONAL WILDLIFE REFUGE SYSTEM

| | State(s) | Acreage |
|---|---|---|
| Agassiz | Minnesota | 61,052 |
| Alamosa | Colorado | 10,352 |
| Alaska Maritime | Alaska | 3,551,783 |
| Alaska Peninsula | Alaska | 3,500,000 |
| Alligator River | North Carolina | 120,000 |
| Amagansett | New York | 36 |
| Anaho Island | Nevada | 248 |
| Anahuac | Texas | 21,758 |
| Ankeny | Oregon | 2,796 |
| Antioch Dunes | California | 55 |
| Appert Lake | North Dakota | 908 |
| Aransas | Texas | 98,721 |
| Arapaho | Colorado | 17,654 |
| Arctic | Alaska | 19,046,382 |
| Ardoch | North Dakota | 2,696 |
| Arrowwood | North Dakota | 15,934 |
| Ash Meadows | Nevada | 11,173 |

| | | |
|---|---|---:|
| Attwater Prairie Chicken | Texas | 7,984 |
| Audubon | North Dakota | 14,736 |
| Back Bay | Virginia | 4,589 |
| Bamforth | Wyoming | 1,166 |
| Bandon Marsh | Oregon | 289 |
| Banks Lake | Georgia | 3,550 |
| Basket Slough | Oregon | 2,492 |
| Bear Butte | South Dakota | 374 |
| Bear Lake | Idaho | 17,605 |
| Bear River | Utah | 65,030 |
| Bear Valley | Oregon | 1,733 |
| Becharof | Alaska | 1,200,000 |
| Benton Lake | Montana | 12,383 |
| Big Boggy | Texas | 3,564 |
| Big Lake | Arkansas | 11,036 |
| Big Stone | Minnesota | 10,794 |
| Bitterlake | New Mexico | 23,350 |
| Blackbeard Island | Georgia | 5,618 |
| Black Coulee | Montana | 1,309 |
| Blackwater | Maryland | 14,263 |
| Block Island | Rhode Island | 29 |
| Blowing Wind Cave | Alabama | 264 |
| Blue Ridge | California | 897 |
| Bogue Chitto | Mississippi, Louisiana | 18,637 |
| Bombay Hook | Delaware | 15,122 |
| Bone Hill | North Dakota | 640 |
| Bonsecour | Alabama | 3,765 |
| Bosque del Apache | New Mexico | 57,191 |
| Bowdoin | Montana | 12,577 |
| Brazoria | Texas | 10,407 |
| Breton | Louisiana | 9,047 |
| Brown's Park | Colorado | 13,375 |
| Brumba | North Dakota | 1,977 |
| Buffalo Lake | Texas | 9,761 |
| Butte Sink | California | 1,490 |
| Cabeza Prieta | Arizona | 860,000 |
| Caloosahatchee | Florida | 40 |
| Camas | Indiana | 10,578 |
| Camp Lake | North Dakota | 585 |
| Canfield | North Dakota | 313 |
| Cape Charles | Virginia | 183 |

347

|  | *State(s)* | *Acreage* |
|---|---|---|
| Cape Mears | Oregon | 139 |
| Cape Romain | South Carolina | 34,229 |
| Carolina Sandhills | South Carolina | 45,591 |
| Castle Rock | California | 14 |
| Catahoula | Louisiana | 5,309 |
| Cedar Island | North Carolina | 12,526 |
| Cedar Keys | Florida | 721 |
| Cedar Point | Ohio | 2,445 |
| Charles M. Russell | Montana | 897,129 |
| Chase Lake | North Dakota | 4,385 |
| Chassahowitzka | Florida | 30,436 |
| Chautauqua | Illinois | 6,197 |
| Chincoteague | Virginia, Maryland | 9,931 |
| Choctaw | Alabama | 4,218 |
| Cibola | Arizona, California | 11,428 |
| Clarence Cannon | Mississippi | 3,737 |
| Clear Lake | California | 33,440 |
| Cold Springs | Oregon | 3,117 |
| Columbia | Washington | 28,952 |
| Columbian White-<br>Tailed Deer | Washington, Oregon | 4,757 |
| Colusa | California | 4,040 |
| Conboy Lake | Washington | 5,509 |
| Conscience Point | New York | 60 |
| Copalis | Washington | 61 |
| Cottonwood | North Dakota | 1,013 |
| Crab Orchard | Illinois | 43,550 |
| Creedman Coulee | Montana | 2,728 |
| Crescent Lake | Nebraska | 45,818 |
| Crocodile Lake | Florida | 1,466 |
| Cross Creeks | South Dakota | 8,862 |
| Cross Island | Maine | 1,355 |
| Crystal River | Florida | 33 |
| Currituck | North Carolina | 512 |
| Dakota Lake | North Dakota | 2,756 |
| D'Arbonne | Louisiana | 17,420 |
| Deer Flat | Idaho, Oregon | 11,410 |
| Delevan | California | 5,634 |
| Delta | Louisiana | 48,799 |

| | | |
|---|---|---|
| Desert | Nevada | 1,588,779 |
| Des Lacs | North Dakota | 19,544 |
| De Soto | Iowa, Nebraska | 7,823 |
| Dungeness | Washington | 756 |
| Eastern Neck | Maryland | 2,286 |
| Edwin B. Forsythe | New Jersey | 30,606 |
| Egmont Key | Florida | 328 |
| Elizabeth Morton | New York | 187 |
| Ellicott Slough | California | 126 |
| Ernie | Oregon | 7,994 |
| Eufaula | Alabama, Georgia | 11,160 |
| Fallon | Nevada | 17,902 |
| Farallon | California | 211 |
| Featherstone | Virginia | 164 |
| Felsenthal | Arkansas | 64,599 |
| Fern Cave | Alabama | 199 |
| Fisherman Island | Virginia | 1,025 |
| Fish Springs | Utah | 17,992 |
| Flattery Rocks | Washington | 125 |
| Flint Hills | Kansas | 18,463 |
| Florence Lake | North Dakota | 1,888 |
| Fort Niobrana | Nebraska | 18,667 |
| Fox River | Wisconsin | 641 |
| Franklin Island | Maine | 12 |
| Grasslands | California | 24,484 |
| Gravel Island | Wisconsin | 27 |
| Gray's Lake | Idaho | 16,153 |
| Great Dismal Swamp | North Carolina, Virgina | 101,873 |
| Great Meadows | Massachusetts | 2,878 |
| Great Swamp | New Jersey | 6,793 |
| Great White Heron | Florida | 7,404 |
| Green Bay | Wisconsin | 2 |
| Grulla | New Mexico, Texas | 3,236 |
| Hagerman | Texas | 11,320 |
| Hailstone | Montana | 920 |
| Halfbreed Lake | Montana, North Dakota | 3,257 |
| Hanalei | Hawaii | 917 |
| Harbor Island | Michigan | 695 |
| Harris Neck | Georgia | 2,687 |
| Hart Mountain | Oregon | 249,239 |
| Hatchie | Tennessee | 11,556 |

| | State(s) | Acreage |
|---|---|---|
| Havasu | Arizona, California | 45,851 |
| Hawaiian Islands | Hawaii | 254,418 |
| Hewitt Lake | Montana | 1,680 |
| Hiddenwood | North Dakota | 568 |
| Hillside | Mississippi | 15,406 |
| Hobart Lake | North Dakota | 2,076 |
| Hobe Sound | Florida | 969 |
| Holla Bend | Arkansas | 4,083 |
| Hopper Mountain | California | 1,871 |
| Horicon | Wisconsin | 20,976 |
| Huleia | Hawaii | 238 |
| Humboldt Bay | California | 559 |
| Huron | Michigan | 147 |
| Hutchinson Lake | North Dakota | 479 |
| Hutton Lake | Wyoming | 1,428 |
| Imperial | Arizona, California | 15,764 |
| Innoko | Alaska | 3,850,000 |
| Iroquois | New York | 10,818 |
| Island Bay | Florida | 20 |
| Izembek | Alaska | 320,893 |
| James C. Campbell | Hawaii | 145 |
| J. Clark Salyer | North Dakota | 58,693 |
| J. N. "Ding" Darling | Florida | 5,014 |
| Johnson Lake | North Dakota | 2,007 |
| Kakahaia | Hawaii | 45 |
| Kanuti | Alaska | 1,430,000 |
| Karl E. Mundt | Nebraska, South Dakota | 1,082 |
| Kelly's Slough | North Dakota | 1,270 |
| Kenai | Alaska | 1,970,000 |
| Kern | California | 10,618 |
| Kesterson | California | 5,900 |
| Key West | Florida | 2,019 |
| Kirtland Warbler | Michigan | 1,896 |
| Klamath Forest | Oregon | 16,377 |
| Kodiak | Alaska | 1,865,000 |
| Kofa | Arizona | 660,000 |
| Kootenai | Idaho | 2,764 |
| Koyukuk | Alaska | 3,550,000 |
| Lacassine | Louisiana | 31,776 |

| | | |
|---|---|---|
| Lacreek | South Dakota | 16,260 |
| Laguna Alascosca | Texas | 45,187 |
| Lake Alice | North Dakota | 10,954 |
| Lake Andes | South Dakota | 940 |
| Lake Elsie | North Dakota | 635 |
| Lake George | North Dakota | 3,119 |
| Lake Ilo | North Dakota | 4,033 |
| Lake Isom | South Dakota | 1,846 |
| Lake Mason | Montana | 16,968 |
| Lake Nettie | North Dakota | 2,895 |
| Lake Otis | North Dakota | 320 |
| Lake Thibadeau | Montana | 3,868 |
| Lake Woodruff | Florida | 18,506 |
| Lake Zahl | North Dakota | 3,823 |
| Lambs Lake | North Dakota | 1,207 |
| Lamesteer | Montana | 800 |
| Las Vegas | New Mexico | 8,672 |
| Lee Metcalf | Montana | 2,696 |
| Lewis and Clark | Oregon | 38,000 |
| Little Goose | North Dakota | 288 |
| Little Pend Oreille | Washington | 40,175 |
| Long Lake | North Dakota | 22,310 |
| Lords Lake | North Dakota | 1,915 |
| Lost Lake | North Dakota | 960 |
| Lostwood | North Dakota | 24,810 |
| Lower Hatchie | South Dakota | 2,628 |
| Lower Klamath | California | 40,295 |
| Lower Rio Grande Valley | Texas | 8,345 |
| Lower Suwannee | Florida | 22,821 |
| Loxahatchee | Florida | 145,635 |
| MacKay Island | North Carolina, Virginia | 7,056 |
| Malheur | Oregon | 183,964 |
| Maple River | North Dakota | 712 |
| Mark Twain | Illinois, Iowa | 25,768 |
| Martin | Maryland | 4,424 |
| Marumsco | Virginia | 63 |
| Mason Neck | Virginia | 1,935 |
| Massasoit | Massachusetts | 184 |
| Mathews Brake | Mississippi | 807 |
| Matlacha Pass | Florida | 231 |
| Mattamuskeet | North Carolina | 50,180 |

| | State(s) | Acreage |
|---|---|---|
| Maxwell | New Mexico | 3,699 |
| McFaddin | Texas | 42,956 |
| McKay Creek | Oregon | 1,837 |
| McLean | North Dakota | 760 |
| McNary | Washington | 3,629 |
| Medicine Lake | Montana | 22,824 |
| Merced | California | 2,562 |
| Meredosia | Illinois | 1,850 |
| Merritt Island | Michigan | 363 |
| Mille Lacs | Minnesota | .6 |
| Mingo | Mississippi | 21,676 |
| Minidoka | Idaho | 20,721 |
| Minnesota Valley | Minnesota | 4,878 |
| Missisquoi | Vermont | 5,839 |
| Mississippi River Cave | Illinois, Iowa, Wisconsin, Minnesota | 106,197 |
| Moapa Valley | Nevada | 33 |
| Modoc | California | 6,283 |
| Monomoy | Massachusetts | 2,702 |
| Monte Vista | Colorado | 14,189 |
| Montezuma | New York | 6,432 |
| Moody | Texas | 3,517 |
| Moosehorn | Maine | 22,745 |
| Morgan Brake | Mississippi | 1,465 |
| Muleshoe | Texas | 5,809 |
| Muscatatuck | Indiana | 7,724 |
| Nansemond | Virginia | 208 |
| Nantucket | Massachusetts | 40 |
| National Bison Range | Montana | 18,541 |
| National Elk | Wyoming | 24,247 |
| National Key Deer | Florida | 5,816 |
| Necedah | Wisconsin | 39,549 |
| Nine Pipe | Montana | 2,542 |
| Ninigret | Rhode Island | 408 |
| Nisqually | Washington | 2,824 |
| Nomans Land Island | Massachusetts | 620 |
| North Platte | Nebraska | 5,047 |
| Nowitna | Alaska | 1,560,000 |
| Noxubee | Mississippi | 46,324 |

| | | |
|---|---|---|
| Okefenokee | Florida, Georgia | 395,080 |
| Optima | Oklahoma | 4,333 |
| Oregon Islands | Oregon | 575 |
| Ottawa | Ohio | 5,794 |
| Ouray | Utah | 11,483 |
| Overflow | Arkansas | 6,790 |
| Oxbow | Massachusetts | 662 |
| Oyster Bay | New York | 3,204 |
| Pablo | Montana | 2,542 |
| Pahranagat | Nevada | 5,381 |
| Panther Swamp | Mississippi | 22,797 |
| Parker River | Massachusetts | 4,650 |
| Passage Key | Florida | 36 |
| Pathfinder | Wyoming | 16,807 |
| Patuxent | Maryland | 4,682 |
| Pea Island | North Carolina | 5,915 |
| Pearl Harbor | Hawaii | 61 |
| Pee Dee | North Carolina | 8,438 |
| Pelican Island | Florida | 4,396 |
| Petit Manan | Maine | 3,310 |
| Piedmont | Georgia | 34,863 |
| Pierce | Washington | 319 |
| Pinckney Island | South Carolina | 4,053 |
| Pine Island | Florida | 404 |
| Pinellas | Florida | 392 |
| Pixley | California | 5,187 |
| Pleasant Lake | North Dakota | 898 |
| Plum Tree Island | Virginia | 3,276 |
| Pocasse | South Dakota | 2,540 |
| Pond Island | Maine | 10 |
| Presquile | Virginia | 1,329 |
| Pretty Rock | North Dakota | 800 |
| Prime Hook | Delaware | 9,701 |
| Protection Land | Washington | 4 |
| Pungo | North Carolina | 12,380 |
| Quillayute Needles | Washington | 300 |
| Quivira | Kansas | 21,820 |
| Rabb Lake | North Dakota | 261 |
| Rachel Carson | Maine | 2,736 |
| Red Rock Lakes | Montana | 32,468 |
| Reelfoot | Kentucky | 10,428 |

| | *State(s)* | *Acreage* |
|---|---|---|
| Rice Lake | Minnesota | 16,516 |
| Ridgefield | Washington | 3,017 |
| Rock Lake | North Dakota | 5,507 |
| Rose Lake | North Dakota | 836 |
| Ruby Lake | Nevada | 37,632 |
| Sabine | Louisiana | 139,437 |
| Sachuest Point | Rhode Island | 228 |
| Sacramento | California | 10,783 |
| Saddle Mountain | Washington | 30,810 |
| St. Johns | Florida | 6,254 |
| St. Marks | Florida | 64,600 |
| St. Vincent | Florida | 12,490 |
| Salt Meadow | Connecticut | 183 |
| Salton Sea | California | 37,378 |
| Salt Plains | Oklahoma | 31,996 |
| San Andres | New Mexico | 57,215 |
| San Bernard | Texas | 24,454 |
| San Bernardino | Arizona | 2,309 |
| Sand Lake | South Dakota | 19,804 |
| San Francisco Bay | California | 17,218 |
| San Juan Island | Washington | 451 |
| San Luis | California | 7,430 |
| San Pablo Bay | California | 11,634 |
| Santa Ana | Texas | 2,088 |
| Santee | South Carolina | 43,636 |
| Savannah | South Carolina, Georgia | 26,584 |
| School Section Lake | North Dakota | 680 |
| Seal Beach | California | 911 |
| Seal Island | Maine | 65 |
| Seatuck | New York | 183 |
| Seedskadee | Wyoming | 14,842 |
| Selawik | Alaska | 2,150,000 |
| Seney | Michigan | 95,455 |
| Sequoyah | Oklahoma | 20,800 |
| Sevilleta | New Mexico | 228,134 |
| Sheldon | Nevada, Oregon | 571,048 |
| Shell Keys | Louisiana | 8 |
| Shell Lake | North Dakota | 1,835 |
| Sherburne | Minnesota | 29,583 |

| | | |
|---|---|---|
| Sheyenne Lake | North Dakota | 797 |
| Shiawassee | Michigan | 8,984 |
| Sibley Lake | North Dakota | 1,077 |
| Silver Lake | North Dakota | 3,348 |
| Slade | North Dakota | 3,000 |
| Snyder Lake | North Dakota | 1,500 |
| Springwater | North Dakota | 640 |
| Squaw Creek | Missouri | 5,919 |
| Stewart Lake | North Dakota | 2,230 |
| Stillwater | Nevada | 24,203 |
| Stoney Slough | North Dakota | 880 |
| Storm Lake | North Dakota | 686 |
| Stump Lake | North Dakota | 27 |
| Sullys Hill | North Carolina | 1,674 |
| Sunburst Lake | North Dakota | 328 |
| Supawna Meadows | New Jersey | 1,718 |
| Susquehanna | Maryland | 4 |
| Sutter | California | 2,591 |
| Swan Lake | Missouri | 10,669 |
| Swanquarter | North Carolina | 15,643 |
| Swan River | Montana | 1,569 |
| Tamarac | Minnesota | 35,191 |
| Target Rock | New York | 80 |
| Tennessee | Tennessee | 51,358 |
| Tetlin | Alaska | 700,000 |
| Tewaukon | North Dakota | 9,273 |
| Texas Point | Texas | 8,952 |
| Thacher Island | Massachusetts | 22 |
| Three Arch Rocks | Oregon | 15 |
| Tijuana Slough | California | 472 |
| Tinicum | Oregon | 898 |
| Tishomingo | Oklahoma | 16,464 |
| Togiak | Alaska | 4,105,000 |
| Tomahawk | North Dakota | 440 |
| Toppenish | Washington | 1,763 |
| Trempealeau | Wisconsin | 5,617 |
| Trustom Pond | Rhode Island | 579 |
| Tule Lake | California | 39,396 |
| Turnbull | Washington | 15,565 |
| Tybee | Georgia | 100 |
| Ul Bend | Montana | 55,489 |

| | State(s) | Acreage |
|---|---|---|
| Umatilla | Oregon, Washington | 22,885 |
| Union Slough | Iowa | 2,200 |
| Upper Klamath | Oregon | 12,457 |
| Upper Mississippi | Illinois, Iowa, Wisconsin, Minnesota | 88,900 |
| Upper Ouachita | Louisiana | 20,905 |
| Upper Souris | North Dakota | 32,092 |
| Valentine | Nebraska | 67,097 |
| Wallops Island | Virginia | 3,373 |
| Wapack | New Hampshire | 1,674 |
| Wapanocca | Arkansas | 5,484 |
| War Horse | Montana | 3,192 |
| Washita | Oklahoma | 8,084 |
| Wassaw | Georgia | 10,070 |
| Watercress Darter | Alabama | 7 |
| Waubay | South Dakota | 2,585 |
| Wertheim | New York | 2,395 |
| West Sister Island | Ohio | 77 |
| Wheeler | Alabama | 34,119 |
| White Lake | North Dakota | 1,040 |
| White River | Arkansas | 112,399 |
| Wichita Mountains | Oklahoma | 59,019 |
| Wild Rice Lake | North Dakota | 779 |
| Willapa | Washington | 14,297 |
| William L. Finley | Oregon | 5,325 |
| Willow Lake | North Dakota | 2,621 |
| Wintering River | North Dakota | 239 |
| Wolf Island | California | 5,126 |
| Wood Lake | North Dakota | 280 |
| Wyandotte | Michigan | 304 |
| Yazoo | Mississippi | 12,471 |
| Yukon Delta | Alaska | 19,624,458 |
| Yukon Flats | Alaska | 8,630,000 |

NOTE: Not included here are individual units of the Alaska Maritime National Wildlife Refuge System. These units, ranging from tiny offshore islets to full-sized islands like Attu in the Aleutians, comprise an additional 4.5 million acres.

## THE NATIONAL WILDERNESS PRESERVATION SYSTEM

The acreage figures given are totals. The first year designated for each wilderness is the year it was established; any subsequent year designated indicates when an addition was made.

| Wilderness | Agency | Acreage | Year Designated |
|---|---|---|---|
| **ALABAMA** | | | |
| Cheaha | USFS | 6,780 | 1975 |
| Sipsey | USFS | 12,646 | 1983 |
| | | State Total 19,426 | |
| **ALASKA** | | | |
| Admiralty Island National Monument | USFS | 937,396 | 1980 |
| Aleutian Islands | FWS | 1,300,000 | 1980 |
| Andreafsky | FWS | 1,300,000 | 1980 |
| Arctic | FWS | 8,000,000 | 1980 |
| Becharof | FWS | 400,000 | 1980 |
| Bering Sea | FWS | 81,340 | 1970 |
| Bogoslof | FWS | 175 | 1970 |
| Chamisso | FWS | 455 | 1975 |
| Coronation Island | USFS | 19,232 | 1980 |
| Denali | NPS | 1,900,000 | 1980 |
| Endicott River | USFS | 98,729 | 1980 |
| Forrester Island | FWS | 2,832 | 1970 |
| Gates of the Arctic | NPS | 7,052,000 | 1980 |
| Glacier Bay | NPS | 2,770,000 | 1980 |
| Hazy Islands | FWS | 32 | 1970 |
| Innoko | FWS | 1,240,000 | 1980 |
| Izembek | FWS | 300,000 | 1980 |
| Katmai | NPS | 3,473,000 | 1980 |
| Kenai | FWS | 1,350,000 | 1980 |
| Kobuk Valley | NPS | 190,000 | 1980 |
| Koyukuk | FWS | 400,000 | 1980 |
| Lake Clark | NPS | 2,470,000 | 1980 |
| Maurelle Islands | USFS | 4,937 | 1980 |
| Misty Fjords National Monument | USFS | 2,142,243 | 1980 |
| Noatak | NPS | 5,800,000 | 1980 |

357

| Wilderness | Agency | Acreage | Year Designated |
|---|---|---|---|
| ALASKA (cont'd) | | | |
| Nunivak | FWS | 600,000 | 1980 |
| Petersburg Creek– Duncan Salt Creek | USFS | 46,777 | 1980 |
| Russell Fjord | USFS | 348,701 | 1980 |
| St. Lazaria | FWS | 65 | 1980 |
| Selawik | FWS | 240,000 | 1980 |
| Semidi | FWS | 250,000 | 1980 |
| Simeonof | FWS | 25,855 | 1976 |
| South Baranof | USFS | 319,568 | 1976 |
| South Prince of Wales | USFS | 90,996 | 1980 |
| Stikine-LeConte | USFS | 448,841 | 1980 |
| Tebenkof | USFS | 66,839 | 1980 |
| Togiak | FWS | 2,270,000 | 1980 |
| Tracy-Arm-Ford- Terror | USFS | 653,179 | 1980 |
| Tuxedni | FWS | 5,566 | 1970 |
| Unimak | FWS | 910,000 | 1980 |
| Warren Island | USFS | 11,181 | 1980 |
| West Chichagof– Yakobi | USFS | 264,747 | 1980 |
| Wrangell–St. Elias | NPS | 8,700,000 | 1980 |
| State Total | | 56,484,686 | |
| | | | |
| ARIZONA | | | |
| Apache Creek | USFS | 5,420 | 1984 |
| Aravaipa Canyon | BLM | 6,670 | 1984 |
| Bear Wallow | USFS | 11,080 | 1984 |
| Beaver Dam Mountains | BLM | 19,600 | 1984 |
| Castle Creek | USFS | 26,030 | 1984 |
| Cedar Bench | USFS | 14,950 | 1984 |
| Chiricahua | USFS | 87,700 | 1964 1984 |
| | NPS | 9,440 | 1976 |

| | | | |
|---|---|---|---|
| Cottonwood Point | BLM | 6,500 | 1984 |
| Escudilla | USFS | 5,200 | 1984 |
| Fossil Springs | USFS | 11,550 | 1984 |
| Four Peaks | USFS | 53,500 | 1984 |
| Galiuro | USFS | 76,317 | 1964 |
| | | | 1984 |
| Grand Wash Cliffs | BLM | 36,300 | 1984 |
| Granite Mountain | USFS | 9,800 | 1984 |
| Hellsgate | USFS | 36,780 | 1984 |
| Juniper Mesa | USFS | 7,600 | 1984 |
| Kachina Peaks | USFS | 18,200 | 1984 |
| Kanab Creek | USFS | 68,250 | 1984 |
| | BLM | 8,850 | 1984 |
| Kendrich Mountain | USFS | 6,510 | 1984 |
| Mazatzal | USFS | 251,912 | 1964 |
| | | | 1984 |
| Miller Peak | USFS | 20,190 | 1984 |
| Mount Baldy | USFS | 7,079 | 1970 |
| Mount Logan | BLM | 14,600 | 1984 |
| Mount Trumbull | BLM | 7,900 | 1984 |
| Mount Wrightson | USFS | 25,260 | 1984 |
| Munds Mountain | USFS | 18,150 | 1984 |
| Organ Pipe Cactus | NPS | 312,600 | 1978 |
| Paiute | BLM | 84,700 | 1984 |
| Pajarita | USFS | 7,420 | 1984 |
| Paria Canyon– | | | |
|    Vermillion Cliff | BLM | 90,046 | 1984 |
| Petrified Forest | NPS | 50,260 | 1970 |
| Pine Mountain | USFS | 20,061 | 1972 |
| Pusch Ridge | USFS | 56,933 | 1978 |
| Red-Rock–Secret | | | |
|    Mountain | USFS | 43,950 | 1984 |
| Rincon Mountain | USFS | 38,590 | 1984 |
| Saddle Mountain | USFS | 40,600 | 1984 |
| Saguaro | NPS | 71,400 | 1976 |
| Salome | USFS | 18,950 | 1984 |
| Salt River Canyon | USFS | 32,800 | 1984 |
| Santa Teresa | USFS | 26,780 | 1984 |
| Sierra Ancha | USFS | 20,850 | 1964 |
| Strawberry Crater | USFS | 10,140 | 1984 |
| Superstition | USFS | 159,757 | 1964 |
| | | | 1984 |

| Wilderness | Agency | Acreage | Year Designated |
|---|---|---:|---:|
| ARIZONA (*cont'd*) | | | |
| Sycamore Canyon | USFS | 47,757 | 1972 |
| | | 8,180 | 1984 |
| West Clear Creek | USFS | 13,600 | 1984 |
| Wet Beaver | USFS | 6,700 | 1984 |
| Woodchute | USFS | 5,600 | 1984 |
| | State Total | 2,039,012 | |
| | | | |
| ARKANSAS | | | |
| Big Lake | FWS | 2,144 | 1976 |
| Black Fork Mountain | USFS | 7,568 | 1984 |
| Buffalo National River | NPS | 10,529 | 1978 |
| Caney Creek | USFS | 14,344 | 1984 |
| Dry Creek | USFS | 6,310 | 1984 |
| East Fork | USFS | 10,777 | 1984 |
| Flatside | USFS | 10,105 | 1984 |
| Hurricane Creek | USFS | 15,177 | 1984 |
| Leatherwood | USFS | 16,956 | 1984 |
| Poteau Mountain | USFS | 10,884 | 1984 |
| Richland Creek | USFS | 11,822 | 1984 |
| Upper Buffalo | USFS | 11,746 | 1974 |
| | | | 1984 |
| | State Total | 128,362 | |
| | | | |
| CALIFORNIA | | | |
| Ansel Adams | USFS | 228,669 | 1964 |
| | | | 1984 |
| | NPS | 665 | 1984 |
| Aqua Tibia | USFS | 15,933 | 1975 |
| Bucks Lake | USFS | 21,000 | 1984 |
| Caribou | USFS | 20,625 | 1964 |
| | | | 1984 |
| Carson-Iceberg | USFS | 160,000 | 1984 |
| Castle Craigs | USFS | 7,300 | 1984 |
| Chanchelvilla | USFS | 8,200 | 1984 |

| | | | |
|---|---|---|---|
| Cucamonga | USFS | 12,981 | 1964 |
| | | | 1984 |
| Desolation | USFS | 63,475 | 1969 |
| Dick Smith | USFS | 65,130 | 1984 |
| Dinkey Lakes | USFS | 30,000 | 1984 |
| Domeland | USFS | 94,686 | 1964 |
| | | | 1984 |
| Emigrant | USFS | 112,191 | 1975 |
| | | | 1984 |
| Farallon | FWS | 141 | 1974 |
| Golden Trout | USFS | 303,287 | 1978 |
| Granite Chief | USFS | 25,000 | 1984 |
| Hauser | USFS | 8,000 | 1984 |
| Hoover | USFS | 48,601 | 1964 |
| Ishi | USFS | 41,600 | 1984 |
| | BLM | 240 | 1984 |
| Jennie Lakes | USFS | 10,500 | 1984 |
| John Muir | USFS | 580,675 | 1964 |
| | | | 1984 |
| Joshua Tree | NPS | 429,690 | 1976 |
| Kaiser | USFS | 22,700 | 1976 |
| Lassen Volcanic | NPS | 78,982 | 1972 |
| Lava Beds | NPS | 28,460 | 1972 |
| Machesna Mountain | USFS | 19,880 | 1984 |
| | BLM | 120 | |
| Marble Mountain | USFS | 241,744 | 1964 |
| | | | 1984 |
| Mokelumne | USFS | 104,461 | 1964 |
| | | | 1984 |
| Monarch | USFS | 45,000 | 1984 |
| Mount Shasta | USFS | 37,000 | 1984 |
| North Fork | USFS | 8,100 | 1984 |
| Pine Creek | USFS | 13,100 | 1984 |
| Pinnacles | NPS | 12,952 | 1976 |
| Point Reyes | NPS | 25,370 | 1976 |
| | | | 1976 |
| | | | 1985 |
| Red Buttes | USFS | 16,150 | 1984 |
| Russian | USFS | 12,000 | 1984 |
| San Gabriel | USFS | 37,118 | 1968 |
| San Gorgonio | USFS | 56,722 | 1964 |
| | | | 1984 |

| Wilderness | Agency | Acreage | Year Designated |
|---|---|---|---|
| CALIFORNIA (*cont'd*) | | | |
| San Jacinto | USFS | 32,040 | 1964 |
| | | | 1984 |
| San Mateo Canyon | USFS | 39,540 | 1984 |
| San Rafael | USFS | 150,640 | 1968 |
| | | | 1984 |
| Santa Lucia | USFS | 18,679 | 1978 |
| | BLM | 1,733 | 1978 |
| Santa Rosa | USFS | 20,160 | 1984 |
| Sequoia–Kings Canyon | NPS | 736,980 | 1984 |
| Sheep Mountain | USFS | 43,600 | 1984 |
| Siskiyou | USFS | 153,000 | 1984 |
| Snow Mountain | USFS | 37,000 | 1984 |
| South Sierra | USFS | 63,000 | 1984 |
| South Warner | USFS | 70,385 | 1964 |
| | | | 1984 |
| Thousand Lakes | USFS | 16,335 | 1964 |
| Trinity Alps | USFS | 495,377 | 1984 |
| | BLM | 4,623 | 1984 |
| Ventana | USFS | 164,144 | 1969 |
| | | | 1978 |
| | | | 1984 |
| Yolla Bolly–Middle Eel | USFS | 145,404 | 1964 |
| | | | 1984 |
| | BLM | 8,500 | 1984 |
| Yosemite | NPS | 677,600 | 1984 |
| | | State Total 5,926,308 | |
| COLORADO | | | |
| Big Blue | USFS | 98,320 | 1980 |
| Black Canyon of the Gunnison | NPS | 11,180 | 1976 |
| Cache La Padre | USFS | 9,238 | 1980 |
| Collegiate Peaks | USFS | 166,654 | 1980 |
| Comanche Peak | USFS | 66,791 | 1980 |
| Eagles Nest | USFS | 133,325 | 1976 |
| Flat Tops | USFS | 235,035 | 1975 |

| | | | |
|---|---|---|---|
| Great Sand Dunes | NPS | 33,450 | 1976 |
| Holy Cross | USFS | 122,037 | 1980 |
| Hunter–Fryingpan | USFS | 74,250 | 1978 |
| Indian Peaks | USFS | 70,374 | 1978 |
| | | | 1980 |
| La Garita | USFS | 103,986 | 1964 |
| | | | 1980 |
| Lizard Head | USFS | 41,189 | 1980 |
| Lost Creek | USFS | 105,090 | 1980 |
| Maroon Bells–Snow | | | |
| Mass | USFS | 181,138 | 1980 |
| Mesa Verde | NPS | 8,100 | 1976 |
| Mount Evans | USFS | 74,401 | 1980 |
| Mount Massive | USFS | 27,980 | 1980 |
| | FWS | 2,560 | |
| Mount Sneffels | USFS | 16,505 | 1980 |
| Mount Zirkel | USFS | 139,818 | 1964 |
| | | | 1984 |
| Neota | USFS | 9,924 | 1980 |
| Never Summer | USFS | 13,702 | 1980 |
| Platte River | USFS | 770 | 1984 |
| Raggeds | USFS | 59,519 | 1980 |
| Rawah | USFS | 73,020 | 1964 |
| | | | 1980 |
| South San Juan | USFS | 127,690 | 1980 |
| Weminuche | USFS | 459,604 | 1975 |
| | | | 1980 |
| West Elk | USFS | | 1964 |
| | | 176,092 | 1980 |
| | State Total | 2,641,742 | |

FLORIDA

| | | | |
|---|---|---|---|
| Alexander Springs | USFS | 7,700 | 1984 |
| Big Gum Swamp | USFS | 13,600 | 1984 |
| Billies Bay | USFS | 3,120 | 1984 |
| Bradwell Bay | USFS | 24,602 | 1975 |
| | | | 1984 |
| Cedar Keys | FWS | 379 | 1972 |
| Chassahowitzka | FWS | 23,580 | 1976 |
| J.N. "Ding" Darling | FWS | 2,619 | 1976 |
| Everglades | NPS | 1,296,500 | 1978 |

363

| Wilderness | Agency | Acreage | Year Designated |
|---|---|---|---|
| **FLORIDA** (*cont'd*) | | | |
| Florida Keys | FWS | 6,197 | 1975 |
| | | | 1982 |
| Island Bay | FWS | 20 | 1970 |
| Juniper Prairie | USFS | 13,260 | 1984 |
| Lake Woodruff | FWS | 1,066 | 1976 |
| Little Lake George | USFS | 2,500 | 1984 |
| Mud Swamp/New River | USFS | 7,800 | 1984 |
| Passage Key | FWS | 36 | 1970 |
| Pelican Island | FWS | 6 | 1970 |
| St. Marks | FWS | 17,350 | 1975 |
| | State Total | 1,420,335 | |
| | | | |
| **GEORGIA** | | | |
| Big Frog | USFS | 83 | 1984 |
| Blackbeard Island | FWS | 3,000 | 1975 |
| Cohutta | USFS | 32,307 | 1974 |
| Cumberland Island | NPS | 8,840 | 1982 |
| Ellicott Rock | USFS | 2,181 | 1975 |
| | | | 1984 |
| Okefenokee | FWS | 353,981 | 1974 |
| Southern Nanahala | USFS | 12,439 | 1984 |
| Wolf Island | FWS | 5,126 | 1975 |
| | State Total | 417,957 | |
| | | | |
| **HAWAII** | | | |
| Haleakala | NPS | 19,270 | 1976 |
| Hawaii Volcanoes | NPS | 123,100 | 1978 |
| | State Total | 142,370 | |
| | | | |
| **IDAHO** | | | |
| Craters of the Moon | NPS | 43,243 | 1970 |
| Frank Church– River of No Return | USFS | 2,232,311 | 1964 |
| | BLM | 720 | 1980 |

| | | | | |
|---|---|---|---|---|
| Gospel Hump | USFS | | 205,900 | 1978 |
| Hells Canyon | USFS | | 83,800 | 1975 |
| Sawtooth | USFS | | 217,088 | 1972 |
| Selway-Bitterroot | USFS | | 1,089,017 | 1964 |
| | | | | 1980 |
| | | State Total | 3,872,079 | |

ILLINOIS

| | | | | |
|---|---|---|---|---|
| Crab Orchard | FWS | | 4,050 | 1976 |

INDIANA

| | | | | |
|---|---|---|---|---|
| Charles C. Dean | USFS | | 12,935 | 1982 |

KENTUCKY

| | | | | |
|---|---|---|---|---|
| Beaver Creek | USFS | | 4,756 | 1975 |

LOUISIANA

| | | | | |
|---|---|---|---|---|
| Breton | FWS | | 5,000 | 1975 |
| Kisatchie | USFS | | 8,700 | 1980 |
| Lacassine | FWS | | 3,346 | 1976 |
| | | State Total | 17,046 | |

MAINE

| | | | | |
|---|---|---|---|---|
| Moosehorn | FWS | | 7,386 | 1970 |
| | | | | 1975 |

MASSACHUSETTS

| | | | | |
|---|---|---|---|---|
| Monomoy | FWS | | 2,420 | 1970 |

MICHIGAN

| | | | | |
|---|---|---|---|---|
| Huron Islands | FWS | | 147 | 1970 |
| Isle Royal | NPS | | 131,880 | 1976 |
| Michigan Islands | FWS | | 12 | 1970 |
| Seney | FWS | | 25,150 | 1970 |
| | | State Total | 157,189 | |

| Wilderness | Agency | Acreage | Year Designated |
|---|---|---|---|
| **MINNESOTA** | | | |
| Agassiz | FWS | 4,000 | 1976 |
| Boundary Waters | | | 1964 |
|   Canoe Area | USFS | 798,309 | 1978 |
| Tamarac | FWS | 2,180 | 1976 |
| | | State Total 804,489 | |
| | | | |
| **MISSISSIPPI** | | | |
| Black Creek | USFS | 4,560 | 1984 |
| Gulf Islands | NPS | 1,800 | 1978 |
| Leaf | USFS | 940 | 1984 |
| | | State Total 7,300 | |
| | | | |
| **MISSOURI** | | | |
| Bell Mountain | USFS | 8,817 | 1980 |
| Devil's Backbone | USFS | 6,595 | 1980 |
| Hercules-Glades | USFS | 12,314 | 1976 |
| Irish | USFS | 16,500 | 1984 |
| Mingo | FWS | 7,730 | 1976 |
| Paddy Creek | USFS | 6,728 | 1983 |
| Piney Creek | USFS | 8,087 | 1980 |
| Rockpile Mountain | USFS | 4,089 | 1980 |
| | | State Total 70,860 | |
| | | | |
| **MONTANA** | | | |
| Absaroka-Beartooth | USFS | 920,310 | 1978 |
| | | | 1983 |
| Anaconda-Pintler | USFS | 157,874 | 1964 |
| Bob Marshall | USFS | 1,009,356 | 1964 |
| | | | 1978 |
| Cabinet Mountains | USFS | 94,272 | 1964 |
| Gates of the | | | |
|   Mountains | USFS | 28,562 | 1964 |
| Great Bear | USFS | 286,700 | 1978 |
| Lee Metcalf | USFS | 248,944 | 1983 |
| | BLM | 6,000 | 1983 |
| Medicine Lake | FWS | 11,366 | 1976 |

| | | | |
|---|---|---:|---|
| Mission Mountains | USFS | 73,877 | 1975 |
| Rattlesnake | USFS | 29,824 | 1980 |
| Red Rock Lakes | FWS | 32,350 | 1976 |
| Scapegoat | USFS | 239,296 | 1972 |
| Selway-Bitterroot | USFS | 248,893 | 1964 |
| Ul Bend | FWS | 20,819 | 1976 |
| | | | 1983 |
| Welcome Creek | USFS | 28,135 | 1978 |
| | State Total | 3,436,578 | |

NEBRASKA

| | | | |
|---|---|---:|---|
| Fort Niobrara | FWS | 4,635 | 1976 |

NEVADA

| | | | |
|---|---|---:|---|
| Jarbidge | USFS | 64,667 | 1964 |

NEW HAMPSHIRE

| | | | |
|---|---|---:|---|
| Great Gulf | USFS | 5,552 | 1964 |
| Pemigewasset | USFS | 45,000 | 1984 |
| Presidential Range– Dry River | USFS | 27,380 | 1975 1984 |
| Sandwich Range | USFS | 25,000 | 1984 |
| | State Total | 102,932 | |

NEW JERSEY

| | | | |
|---|---|---:|---|
| Brigantine | FWS | 6,681 | 1975 |
| Great Swamp | FWS | 3,660 | 1968 |
| | State Total | 10,341 | |

NEW MEXICO

| | | | |
|---|---|---:|---|
| Aldo Leopold | USFS | 201,966 | 1980 |
| Apache Kid | USFS | 44,650 | 1980 |
| Bandelier | NPS | 23,267 | 1976 |
| Bisti | BLM | 3,968 | 1984 |
| Blue Range | USFS | 30,000 | 1980 |
| Bosque del Apache | FWS | 30,287 | 1975 |
| Capitan Mountains | USFS | 34,513 | 1980 |
| Carlsbad Mountains | NPS | 33,125 | 1978 |

| Wilderness | Agency | Acreage | Year Designated |
|---|---|---:|---|
| NEW MEXICO (cont'd) | | | |
| Chama River Canyon | USFS | 50,260 | 1978 |
| Cruces Basin | USFS | 18,000 | 1980 |
| De-na-zin | BLM | 23,872 | 1984 |
| Dome | USFS | 5,200 | 1980 |
| Gila | USFS | 557,819 | 1964 |
| | | | 1980 |
| Latir Peak | USFS | 20,000 | 1980 |
| Manzano Mountain | USFS | 36,650 | 1978 |
| Pecos | USFS | 233,333 | 1964 |
| | | | 1980 |
| Salt Creek | FWS | 9,621 | 1970 |
| Sandia Mountain | USFS | 37,028 | 1978 |
| | | | 1980 |
| | | | 1984 |
| San Pedro Parks | USFS | 41,132 | 1964 |
| Wheeler Peak | USFS | 19,661 | 1964 |
| | | | 1980 |
| White Mountain | USFS | 48,366 | 1964 |
| | | | 1980 |
| Withington | USFS | 18,869 | 1980 |
| State Total | | 1,521,587 | |
| NEW YORK | | | |
| Fire Island | NPS | 1,363 | 1980 |
| NORTH CAROLINA | | | |
| Birkhead Mountains | USFS | 4,790 | 1984 |
| Catfish Lake South | USFS | 7,600 | 1984 |
| Ellicott Rock | USFS | 4,022 | 1975 |
| | | | 1984 |
| Joyce Kilmer | USFS | 13,181 | 1975 |
| | | | 1984 |
| Linville Gorge | USFS | 10,975 | 1964 |
| | | | 1984 |
| Middle Prong | USFS | 7,900 | 1984 |
| Pond Pine | USFS | 1,860 | 1984 |

| | | | | |
|---|---|---|---:|---|
| Popcosin | USFS | | 11,000 | 1984 |
| Sheep Ridge | USFS | | 9,540 | 1984 |
| Shining Rock | USFS | | 18,450 | 1964 |
| | | | | 1984 |
| Southern Nantahala | USFS | | 10,900 | 1984 |
| Swanquarter | FWS | | 8,785 | 1976 |
| | | State Total | 109,003 | |

NORTH DAKOTA

| | | | | |
|---|---|---|---:|---|
| Chase Lake | FWS | | 4,155 | 1975 |
| Lostwood | FWS | | 5,577 | 1975 |
| Theodore Roosevelt | NPS | | 29,920 | 1978 |
| | | State Total | 39,652 | |

OHIO

| | | | | |
|---|---|---|---:|---|
| West Sister Island | FWS | | 77 | 1975 |

OKLAHOMA

| | | | | |
|---|---|---|---:|---|
| Wichita Mountains | FWS | | 8,570 | 1970 |

OREGON

| | | | | |
|---|---|---|---:|---|
| Badger Creek | USFS | | 24,000 | 1984 |
| Black Canyon | USFS | | 13,400 | 1984 |
| Boulder Creek | USFS | | 19,100 | 1984 |
| Bridge Creek | USFS | | 5,400 | 1984 |
| Bull of the Woods | USFS | | 34,900 | 1984 |
| Columbia | USFS | | 39,000 | 1984 |
| Cummins Creek | USFS | | 9,300 | 1984 |
| Diamond Peak | USFS | | 52,337 | 1964 |
| | | | | 1984 |
| Drift Creek | USFS | | 5,800 | 1984 |
| Eagle Cap | USFS | | 358,461 | 1964 |
| | | | | 1972 |
| | | | | 1984 |
| Gearhart Mountain | USFS | | 22,809 | 1964 |
| | | | | 1984 |
| Grassy Knob | USFS | | 17,200 | 1984 |
| Hells Canyon | USFS | | 130,095 | 1975 |
| | BLM | | 1,038 | 1984 |
| Kalmiopsis | USFS | | 179,700 | 1964 |
| | | | | 1978 |

| Wilderness | Agency | Acreage | Year Designated |
|---|---|---:|---|
| OREGON (cont'd) | | | |
| Menagerie | USFS | 4,725 | 1984 |
| Middle Santiam | USFS | 7,500 | 1984 |
| Mill Creek | USFS | 17,400 | 1984 |
| Monument Rock | USFS | 19,800 | 1984 |
| Mountain Lake | USFS | 23,071 | 1964 |
| Mount Hood | USFS | 46,520 | 1964 |
| | | | 1978 |
| Mount Jefferson | USFS | 107,008 | 1968 |
| | | | 1984 |
| Mount Thielsen | USFS | 55,100 | 1984 |
| Mount Washington | USFS | 52,516 | 1964 |
| | | | 1984 |
| North Fork John Day | USFS | 121,400 | 1984 |
| North Fork Umatilla | USFS | 20,200 | 1984 |
| Oregon Islands | BLM | 5 | 1978 |
| | FWS | 480 | 1970 |
| | | | 1978 |
| Red Buttes | USFS | 3,750 | 1984 |
| | | | 1984 |
| Rock Creek | USFS | 7,400 | 1984 |
| Rogue-Umpqua Divide | USFS | 33,200 | 1984 |
| Salmon Huckleberry | USFS | 44,560 | 1984 |
| Skylake | USFS | 116,300 | 1984 |
| Strawberry Mountain | USFS | 68,303 | 1964 |
| | | | 1984 |
| Table Rock | BLM | 5,500 | 1984 |
| Three Arch Rocks | FWS | 15 | 1970 |
| Three Sisters | USFS | 285,202 | 1964 |
| | | | 1978 |
| | | | 1984 |
| Waldo Lake | USFS | 39,200 | 1984 |
| Wenaha-Tucannon | USFS | 66,375 | 1978 |
| Wild Rogue | USFS | 25,658 | 1978 |
| | BLM | 10,160 | 1978 |
| | State Total | 2,093,888 | |

**PENNSYLVANIA**

| | | | | |
|---|---|---|---|---|
| Allegheny Islands | USFS | | 368 | 1984 |
| Hickory Creek | USFS | | 9,337 | 1984 |
| | | State Total | 9,705 | |

**SOUTH CAROLINA**

| | | | | |
|---|---|---|---|---|
| Cape Romain | FWS | | 29,000 | 1975 |
| Ellicott Rock | USFS | | 2,809 | 1974 |
| Hell Hole Bay | USFS | | 1,980 | 1980 |
| Little Wambaw Swamp | USFS | | 5,000 | 1980 |
| Wambaw Creek | USFS | | 1,640 | 1980 |
| Wambaw Swamp | USFS | | 5,100 | 1980 |
| | | State Total | 45,529 | |

**SOUTH DAKOTA**

| | | | | |
|---|---|---|---|---|
| Badlands | NPS | | 64,250 | 1976 |
| Black Elk | USFS | | 9,824 | 1980 |
| | | State Total | 74,074 | |

**TENNESSEE**

| | | | | |
|---|---|---|---|---|
| Bald River Gorge | USFS | | 3,887 | 1984 |
| Big Frog | USFS | | 4,972 | 1984 |
| Citico Creek | USFS | | 16,000 | 1984 |
| Cohutta | USFS | | 1,795 | 1975 |
| Gee Creek | USFS | | 2,493 | 1975 |
| Joyce Kilmer–Slickrock | USFS | | 3,832 | 1974 |
| | | State Total | 32,979 | |

**TEXAS**

| | | | | |
|---|---|---|---|---|
| Big Slough | USFS | | 3,000 | 1984 |
| Guadalupe Mountains | NPS | | 46,850 | 1978 |
| Indian Mounds | USFS | | 9,946 | 1984 |
| Little Lake Creek | USFS | | 4,000 | 1984 |
| Turkey Hill | USFS | | 5,400 | 1984 |

371

| Wilderness | Agency | Acreage | Year Designated |
|---|---|---|---|
| TEXAS (*cont'd*) | | | |
| Upland Island | USFS | 12,000 | 1984 |
| | | State Total 81,196 | |
| | | | |
| UTAH | | | |
| Ashdown Gorge | USFS | 7,000 | 1984 |
| Beaver Dam Mountains | BLM | 2,597 | 1984 |
| Box-Death Hollow | USFS | 26,000 | 1984 |
| Dark Canyon | USFS | 45,000 | 1984 |
| Deseret Peak | USFS | 25,500 | 1984 |
| High Uintas | USFS | 460,000 | 1984 |
| Lone Peak | USFS | 30,088 | 1978 |
| Mount Naomi | USFS | 44,350 | 1984 |
| Mount Nebo | USFS | 28,000 | 1984 |
| Mount Olympus | USFS | 16,000 | 1984 |
| Mount Timpanogos | USFS | 10,750 | 1984 |
| Paria Canyon– Vermillion Cliffs | BLM | 19,954 | 1984 |
| Pine Valley Mountain | USFS | 50,000 | 1984 |
| Twin Peaks | USFS | 13,100 | 1984 |
| Wellsville Mountain | USFS | 23,850 | 1984 |
| | | State Total 802,189 | |
| | | | |
| VERMONT | | | |
| Big Branch | USFS | 6,720 | 1984 |
| Breadloaf | USFS | 21,480 | 1984 |
| Bristol Cliffs | USFS | 3,738 | 1975 1976 |
| George D. Aiken | USFS | 5,060 | 1984 |
| Lye Brook | USFS | 14,621 | 1975 1984 |
| Peru Peak | USFS | 6,920 | 1984 |
| | | State Total 58,539 | |

## VIRGINIA

| | | | |
|---|---|---|---|
| Beartown | USFS | 6,375 | 1984 |
| James River Face | USFS | 8,903 | 1975 |
| | | | 1984 |
| Kimberling Creek | USFS | 5,580 | 1984 |
| Lewis Fork | USFS | 5,730 | 1984 |
| Little Dry Run | USFS | 3,400 | 1984 |
| Little Wilson Creek | USFS | 3,855 | 1984 |
| Mountain Lake | USFS | 8,253 | 1984 |
| Peters Mountain | USFS | 3,326 | 1984 |
| Ramsey's Draft | USFS | 6,725 | 1984 |
| Saint Mary's | USFS | 10,090 | 1984 |
| Shenandoah | NPS | 79,579 | 1976 |
| Thunder Ridge | USFS | 2,450 | 1984 |
| | State Total | 144,266 | |

## WASHINGTON

| | | | |
|---|---|---|---|
| Alpine Lakes | USFS | 305,407 | 1976 |
| Boulder River | USFS | 49,000 | 1984 |
| Buckhorn | USFS | 45,601 | 1984 |
| Clearwater | USFS | 14,300 | 1984 |
| Colonel Bob | USFS | 12,120 | 1984 |
| Glacier Peak | USFS | 576,648 | 1964 |
| | | | 1968 |
| | | | 1984 |
| Glacier View | USFS | 3,050 | 1984 |
| Goat Rocks | USFS | 105,023 | 1964 |
| | | | 1984 |
| Henry M. Jackson | USFS | 102,671 | 1984 |
| Indian Heaven | USFS | 20,650 | 1984 |
| Juniper Dunes | BLM | 7,140 | 1984 |
| Lake Chelan– Sawtooth | USFS | 150,704 | 1984 |
| Mount Adams | USFS | 46,776 | 1964 |
| | | | 1984 |
| Mount Baker | USFS | 117,900 | 1984 |
| Mount Skokomish | USFS | 15,686 | 1984 |
| Noisy-Diobsud | USFS | 14,300 | 1984 |
| Norse Peak | USFS | 50,902 | 1984 |
| Pasayten | USFS | 529,850 | 1968 |
| | | | 1984 |

| Wilderness | Agency | Acreage | | Year Designated |
|---|---|---|---|---|
| WASHINGTON (cont'd) | | | | |
| Salmo-Priest | USFS | | 41,335 | 1984 |
| San Juan Islands | FWS | | 353 | 1976 |
| Tatoosh | USFS | | 15,720 | 1984 |
| The Brothers | USFS | | 17,239 | 1984 |
| Trapper Creek | USFS | | 6,050 | 1984 |
| Washington Islands | FWS | | 485 | 1970 |
| Wenaha-Tucannon | USFS | | 111,048 | 1978 |
| William O. Douglas | USFS | | 166,603 | 1984 |
| Wonder Mountain | USFS | | 2,320 | 1984 |
| | | State Total | 2,528,561 | |
| WEST VIRGINIA | | | | |
| Cranberry | USFS | | 35,864 | 1983 |
| Dolly Sods | USFS | | 10,215 | 1974 |
| Laurel Fork North | USFS | | 6,055 | 1982 |
| Laurel Fork South | USFS | | 5,997 | 1982 |
| Otter Creek | USFS | | 20,000 | 1974 |
| | | State Total | 78,131 | |
| WISCONSIN | | | | |
| Blackjack Springs | USFS | | 5,886 | 1978 |
| Headwater | USFS | | 19,950 | 1984 |
| Porcupine Lake | USFS | | 4,195 | 1984 |
| Rainbow Lake | USFS | | 6,583 | 1975 |
| Whisker Lake | USFS | | 7,343 | 1978 |
| Wisconsin Islands | FWS | | 29 | 1970 |
| | | State Total | 43,988 | |
| WYOMING | | | | |
| Absaroka-Beartooth | USFS | | 23,750 | 1984 |
| Bridger | USFS | | 428,169 | 1964 |
| | | | | 1984 |
| Cloud Peak | USFS | | 195,500 | 1984 |
| Encampment River | USFS | | 10,400 | 1984 |
| Fitzpatrick | USFS | | 198,838 | 1976 |
| | | | | 1984 |

| | | | | |
|---|---|---|---:|---|
| Gros Ventre | USFS | | 287,000 | 1984 |
| Huston Park | USFS | | 31,300 | 1984 |
| Jedediah Smith | USFS | | 116,535 | 1984 |
| North Absaroka | USFS | | 350,538 | 1964 |
| Platte River | USFS | | 22,230 | 1984 |
| Popo Agie | USFS | | 101,991 | 1984 |
| Savage Run | USFS | | 14,940 | 1978 |
| Teton | USFS | | 585,468 | 1964 |
| | | | | 1984 |
| Washakie | USFS | | 703,981 | 1964 |
| | | | | 1972 |
| | | | | 1984 |
| Winegar Hole | USFS | | 14,000 | 1984 |
| | | State Total | 3,084,640 | |

## THE WILD AND SCENIC RIVERS SYSTEM

| | State(s) | Miles |
|---|---|---:|
| Alagnak | Alaska | 67 |
| Alatna | Alaska | 83 |
| Allagash Wilderness Waterway | Maine | 95 |
| American (Lower) | California | 23 |
| American (North Fork) | California | 38.3 |
| Andreafsky | Alaska | 262 |
| Aniakchak | Alaska | 63 |
| Au Sable | Michigan | 23 |
| Beaver Creek | Alaska | 127 |
| Birch Creek | Alaska | 126 |
| Charley | Alaska | 208 |
| Chattooga | North Carolina, South Carolina, Georgia | 56.9 |
| Chilikadrotna | Alaska | 11 |
| Delaware Middle | New York, Pennsylvania, New Jersey | 35 |
| Delaware Upper | New York, Pennsylvania | 75.4 |
| Delta | Alaska | 62 |
| Eel | California | 364 |

| | State(s) | Miles |
|---|---|---|
| Eleven Point | Missouri | 44.4 |
| Feather | California | 77.6 |
| Flathead | Montana | 219 |
| Fortymile | Alaska | 392 |
| Gulkana | Alaska | 181 |
| Illinois | Oregon | 50.4 |
| Ivishak | Alaska | 80 |
| John | Alaska | 52 |
| Klamath | California | 286 |
| Kobuk | Alaska | 110 |
| Koyukuk (North Fork) | Alaska | 102 |
| Little Beaver | Ohio | 33 |
| Little Miami | Ohio | 66 |
| Little Miami | Ohio | 28 |
| Middle Fork Clearwater | Idaho | 185 |
| Middle Fork Salmon | Idaho | 104 |
| Missouri | Montana | 149 |
| Missouri | Nebraska, South Dakota | 59 |
| Mulchatna | Alaska | 24 |
| New | North Carolina | 26.5 |
| Noatak | Alaska | 330 |
| Nowitna | Alaska | 225 |
| Obed | Tennessee | 45.2 |
| Owyhee | Oregon | 112 |
| Pere Marquette | Michigan | 66.4 |
| Rapid | Idaho | 26.8 |
| Rio Grande | New Mexico | 52.75 |
| Rio Grande | Texas | 191.2 |
| Rogue | Oregon | 84.5 |
| St. Croix | Minnesota, Wisconsin | 200 |
| St. Croix (Lower) | Minnesota, Wisconsin | 27 |
| St. Croix (Lower) | Minnesota, Wisconsin | 25 |
| St. Joe | Idaho | 67.3 |
| Salmon | Alaska | 70 |
| Salmon | Idaho | 125 |
| Selawik | Alaska | 160 |
| Sheenjek | Alaska | 160 |
| Skagit | Washington | 157.5 |
| Smith | California | 340 |
| Snake | Idaho, Oregon | 66.9 |

| | | |
|---|---|---|
| Tinayguk | Alaska | 44 |
| Tlikakila | Alaska | 51 |
| Trinity | California | 203 |
| Tuolumne | California | 83 |
| Unalakleet | Alaska | 80 |
| Verde | Arizona | 40.5 |
| Wind | Alaska | 140 |
| Wolf | Wisconsin | 25 |

## THE NATIONAL TRAILS SYSTEM

### SCENIC TRAILS

| | State(s) | Miles |
|---|---|---|
| Appalachian | Georgia, North Carolina, Virginia, Maryland, Pennsylvania, New Jersey, New York, Connecticut, Massachusetts, Vermont, New Hampshire, Maine | 2,000 |
| Continental Divide | Montana, Wyoming, Colorado, New Mexico | 3,100 |
| Florida | Florida | 1,300 |
| Ice Age | Wisconsin | 1,000 |
| Natchez Trace | Mississippi, Tennessee | 694 |
| North Country | North Dakota, Minnesota, Wisconsin, Michigan, Ohio, Pennsylvania | 3,200 |
| Pacific Crest | Washington, Oregon, California | 2,350 |
| Potomac Heritage | Virginia, Maryland, West Virginia | 704 |

### HISTORIC TRAILS

| | | |
|---|---|---|
| Iditarod | Alaska | 2,037 |
| Lewis and Clark | Washington, Montana, North Dakota, South Dakota, Nebraska, Iowa, Missouri | 3,700 |
| Mormon Pioneer | Utah, Wyoming, Nebraska, Iowa | 1,300 |
| Oregon | Oregon, Idaho, Wyoming, Nebraska, Kansas, Missouri | 2,000 |
| Overmountain | | |
| Victory | South Carolina | 272 |

## MAJOR PUBLIC LAND LEGISLATION

|  | *Date Passed* | *Application* |
|---|---|---|
| Preemption Act | 1841 | Sale and disposal of public lands. |
| Homestead Act | 1862 | Unrestricted settlement on public lands to all settlers, requiring only the residence, improvement, and cultivation of a tract of 160 acres. |
| General Mining Law | 1872 | Opened all public lands to private prospecting and development. |
| Desert Land Act | 1877 | Authorized the purchase of 640 acres of public land at $1.25 an acre, providing that the settler irrigated the tract within three years. |
| General Revision Act | 1891 | Repealed the Preemption Act, reduced the acreage limitation under the Desert Land Act from 640 to 320 acres, and put limits on the auction sale of land. Section 24 of the act, the "Forest Reserve Act," authorized the President of the United States to withdraw from settlement or exploitation any forest area of the public domain that, in the opinion of the Secretary of the Interior, required watershed protection and timber preservation. |
| Forest "Organic Act" | 1897 | Declared that forest reserves were established to "improve and protect the forest within the boundaries for the purpose of securing favorable conditions of water flow, and to furnish a continuous supply of |

|  |  |  |
|---|---|---|
|  |  | timber for the use and necessities of citizens of the United States." Placed reserves under the administration of the General Land Office of the Department of the Interior. |
| Newlands (Reclamation) Act | 1902 | Authorized the financing and construction of federal irrigation projects on public lands in the West, with restrictions on the private use of public water; amended in 1982 to relieve those restrictions. |
| Reorganization Act | 1905 | Transferred forest reserves to the Department of Agriculture and created the U.S. Forest Service. |
| Weeks Act | 1911 | Appropriated $9 million for the purchase of private land in order to establish national forests in the eastern United States. |
| National Park "Organic Act" | 1916 | Established the National Park Service under the Department of the Interior; established guidelines for the management of the national park system. |
| Mineral Leasing Act | 1920 | Authorized the federal government to lease public lands for the private extraction of oil, gas, coal, phosphates, sodium, and other minerals. |
| Taylor Grazing Act | 1934 | Closed to indiscriminate settlement and use all remaining unreserved and unappropriated public-domain land in nine Western states and the Territory of Alaska; placed 142 million acres into grazing dis- |

| | *Date Passed* | *Application* |
|---|---|---|
| | | tricts and created the Grazing Service to administer them. |
| Reorganization Act | 1946 | Created the Bureau of Land Management within the Department of the Interior, merging the Grazing Service with the General Land Office. |
| Outdoor Recreation Resources Review Commission Act | 1958 | Established commission to study present and future recreation needs on all federal land systems. |
| Multiple Use and Sustained Yield Act | 1960 | Redefined the purposes of the national forests to include recreation, soil, range, timber, watershed, wildlife, fishing, hunting, and mining on a "most judicious use" basis. |
| Public Land Law Review Commission Act | 1961 | Created a body to investigate all existing statutes and regulations governing the retention, management, and disposal of public lands and to determine present and future demands on the public domain. |
| Classification and Multiple Use Act | 1964 | Directed the Bureau of Land Management to classify public lands, determining which were suitable for disposal and which were suitable for retention and management by the government. |
| Wilderness Act | 1964 | Established the National Wilderness Preservation System to be composed of portions of national parks, forests, and wildlife refuges designated by |

| | | Congress as "Wilderness Areas." |
|---|---|---|
| Land and Water Conservation Fund Act | 1964 | Provided funds for and authorized federal assistance to the states in planning, acquisition, and development of needed land and water areas and facilities; and provided funds for the federal acquisition and development of lands for national parks, wildlife refuges, wild and scenic rivers, and other federal conservation programs. |
| National Wild and Scenic Rivers Act | 1968 | Provided for the establishment of a system of river segments to be preserved as free-flowing streams accessible for public use and enjoyment. |
| National Trails System Act | 1968 | Authorized National Scenic Trails for public enjoyment and appreciation of open-air outdoor areas of the nation; later amended to include Historic Trails. |
| National Environmental Policy Act | 1969 | Required public involvement and development of environmental impact statements in the formulation and adoption of all federal land management plans. |
| Forest and Rangeland Renewal Resource Planning Act | 1974 | Established planning process for comprehensive long-range and continuous inventory of all forest and rangeland resources under federal, state, local, and private ownership. |
| Eastern Wilderness Act | 1974 | Added sixteen designated areas in the East to the Na- |

| | *Date Passed* | *Application* |
|---|---|---|
| | | tional Wilderness Preservation System. |
| National Forest Management Act | 1976 | Mandated the development of fifty-year unit-by-unit management plans for all U.S. Forest Service lands—planning to include economic, wildlife, wilderness, and recreation uses. |
| Federal Land Policy and Management Act | 1976 | Established public land policy guidelines for the administration, protection, and development of all national resource lands of the Bureau of Land Management. |
| Omnibus Parks Act | 1978 | Established a number of new park units, including Golden Gate, Santa Monica, and Gateway national recreation areas in California and New York, and formulated guidelines for the creation of additional parks, wilderness areas, trails, and wild and scenic rivers. |
| Alaska National Interest Lands Conservation Act | 1980 | Provided for the designation and conservation of certain public lands in the state of Alaska, including the designation of units of the national park system, National Wildlife Refuges, national forests, National Wild and Scenic Rivers, and National Wilderness Preservation System. |

# SELECTED BIBLIOGRAPHY

The list of secondary sources below is by no means exhaustive. It is meant only to highlight the publications that were most valuable to me in the preparation of this book. I have concentrated on listing books, since the government documents, magazines, newspapers, and unpublished agency reports I consulted for this book are too numerous to mention. Nevertheless, I think the entries indicate the breadth of material available on the subject of public lands, and cover all aspects of their historical, political, social, economic, ecological, and, yes, even spiritual significance. They are a good place to start for anyone wishing to study the matter further.     —D.Z.

### GENERAL REFERENCES

Arrandale, Thomas. *The Battle for Natural Resources*. Washington, D.C.: Congressional Quarterly, 1983.

Coggins, George Cameron, and Charles F. Wilkinson. *Federal Public Land and Resource Law*. University Casebook Law Series. Mineola, N.Y.: Foundation Press, 1981.

Cronon, William. *Changes in the Land*. New York: Hill & Wang, 1983.

Dana, Samuel Trask. *Forest and Range Policy*. New York: McGraw-Hill, 1956.

Fox, Stephen. *John Muir and His Legacy: The American Conservation Movement*. Boston: Little, Brown, 1981.

Gates, Paul W. *The History of Public Land Law Development*. Washington, D.C.: Public Land Law Review Commission, 1968.

Hays, Samuel P. *Conservation and the Gospel of Efficiency: The Progressive Conservation Movement, 1890–1920*. Cambridge: Harvard University Press, 1959.

Nash, Roderick. *Wilderness and the American Mind*. New Haven: Yale University Press, 1982.

Robbins, Roy. *Our Landed Heritage: The Public Domain 1776–1970*. Lincoln: University of Nebraska Press, 1976.

*Wilderness* (magazine). Special issues: Spring, Summer, Fall, Winter 1983; Spring, Summer, Fall 1984.

Wyant, William K. *Westward in Eden*. Berkeley: University of California Press, 1982.

## 1. THE PLEASURING GROUNDS

Abbey, Edward. *Desert Solitaire*. New York: Ballantine Books, 1968.

Darling, F. Frazer, and Noel D. Eichhorn. *Man and Nature in the National Parks*. Washington, D.C.: The Conservation Foundation, 1971.

Everhart, William C. *The National Park Service*. Boulder: Westview Press, 1985.

Foresta, Ronald A. *America's National Parks and Their Keepers*. Washington, D.C.: Resources for the Future, 1984.

Hampton, H. Duane. *How the U.S. Cavalry Saved Our National Parks*. Bloomington: Indiana University Press, 1971.

Ise, John. *Our National Park Policy, a Critical History*. Baltimore: Johns Hopkins University Press, 1961.

Lee, Ronald F. *The Family Tree of the National Park System*. Philadelphia: Eastern National Parks and Monuments Association, 1972.

Runte, Alfred. *The National Parks: An American Experience*. Lincoln: University of Nebraska Press, 1979.

Sax, Joseph L. *Mountains Without Handrails: Reflections on the National Parks*. Ann Arbor: University of Michigan Press, 1981.

Shankland, Robert. *Steve Mather of the National Parks*. New York: Alfred A. Knopf, 1951.

Tilden, Freeman. *The National Parks*. New York: Alfred A. Knopf, 1983.

## 2. A HEART OF WOOD

Catton, Bruce. *Waiting for the Morning Train*. New York: Doubleday, 1972.

Clawson, Marion. *Forests for Whom and for What?* Baltimore: Resources for the Future, 1975.

DeVoto, Bernard. *The Easy Chair*. Boston: Houghton Mifflin, 1955.

Frome, Michael. *Whose Woods These Are: The Story of the National Forests*. Garden City, N.Y.: Doubleday, 1962.

Ise, John. *The United States Forest Policy*. New Haven: Yale University Press, 1920.

Lillard, Richard G. *The Great Forest*. New York: Da Capo, 1947.

Maclean, Norman. *A River Runs Through It and Other Stories*. Chicago: University of Chicago Press, 1976.

Marsh, George Perkins. *Man and Nature*. Cambridge: Harvard University Press, 1965.

Pinchot, Gifford, *Breaking New Ground*. New York: Harcourt Brace and Co., 1946.

Platt, Rutherford. *The Great American Forest*. Englewood Cliffs, N.J.: Prentice-Hall, 1971.

Robinson, Glen O. *The Forest Service: A Study in Public Land Management*. Baltimore: Resources for the Future, 1977.

Shands, William E., and Robert G. Healy. *The Lands Nobody Wanted*. Washington, D.C.: The Conservation Foundation, 1977.

Steen, Harold K. *The U.S. Forest Service: A History*. Seattle: University of Washington Press, 1976.

Stegner, Wallace. *The Uneasy Chair: A Biography of Bernard DeVoto*. Garden City, N.Y.: Doubleday, 1974.

Tichi, Cecelia. *New World, New Earth*. New Haven: Yale University Press, 1979.

## 3. THE LEFTOVER LEGACY

Clawson, Marion. *The Land System of the United States: An Introduction to the History and Practice of Land Use and Land Tenure*. Lincoln: University of Nebraska Press, 1972.

————. *Uncle Sam's Acres*. New York: Dodd, Mead, 1951.

Foss, Philip. *Politics and Grass: The Administration of Grazing on the Public Domain*. New York: Greenwood Press, 1960.

Peffer, E. Louise. *The Closing of the Public Domain: Disposal and Reservation Policies 1900–1950*. Stanford, Calif.: Stanford University Press, 1951.

Stegner, Wallace. *Angle of Repose*. New York: Doubleday, 1971.

————. *Beyond the Hundredth Meridian: John Wesley Powell and the Second Opening of the West*. Lincoln: University of Nebraska Press, 1982.

Voigt, William, Jr. *Public Grazing Lands: Use and Misuse by Industry and Government*. New Brunswick, N.J.: Rutgers University Press, 1976.

Watkins, T. H., and Charles S. Watson, Jr. *The Lands No One Knows*. San Francisco: Sierra Club Books, 1975.

Webb, Walter Prescott. *The Great Plains*. Lincoln: University of Nebraska Press, 1981.

Zaslowsky, Dyan. "Does the West Have a Death Wish?" *American Heritage*, Spring/Summer 1982.


4. ISLANDS OF LIFE

Allen, Durwood L. *Our Wildlife Legacy*. New York: Funk & Wagnalls, 1954.

Bean, Michael J. *The Evolution of National Wildlife Law*. Revised and expanded edition. New York: Praeger, 1983.

Brooks, Paul. *Speaking for Nature: How Literary Naturalists from Henry Thoreau to Rachel Carson Have Shaped America*. Boston: Houghton Mifflin, 1980.

Defenders of Wildlife. *A Report on the National Wildlife Refuge System*. Washington, D.C.: Defenders of Wildlife, 1977.

Doherty, Jim. "An Audubon Report: America's Incomparable, Troubled National Wildlife Refuges System." *Audubon*, July 1983.

Giles, Robert H., Jr. *Wildlife Management*. San Francisco: W. H. Freeman, 1978.

Graham, Edward H. *The Land and Wildlife*. New York: Oxford University Press, 1947.

Laycock, George. *The Sign of the Flying Goose: A Guide to the National Wildlife Refuges*. Garden City, N.Y.: Doubleday/Natural History Press, 1965.

Leopold, Aldo. *Game Management*. New York: Scribner's, 1933.

McCullough, David. *Mornings on Horseback*. New York: Simon & Schuster, 1981.

Reed, Nathaniel P., and Dennis Drabell. *The U.S. Fish and Wildlife Service*. Boulder: Westview Press, 1984.

Reiger, John F. *American Sportsmen and the Origins of Conservation*. Lincoln: University of Nebraska Press, 1975.

Riley, Laura and William. *Guide to the National Wildlife Refuges*. Garden City, N.Y.: Doubleday, 1979.

U.S. Department of the Interior. Fish and Wildlife Service. *The Final Environmental Statement on the Operation of the National Wildlife Refuge System*. Washington, D.C., 1979.

## 5. THE FREEDOM OF THE WILDERNESS

Dubos, René. *The Wooing of Earth*. New York: Scribner's, 1980.

Frome, Michael. *Battle for the Wilderness*. New York: Praeger, 1974.

Hendee, John C., George H. Stankey, and Robert C. Lucas. *Wilderness Management*. Publication of the U.S. Department of Agriculture. Washington, D.C., 1978.

Leopold, Aldo. *A Sand County Almanac*. New York: Ballantine Books, 1978.

Marshall, Robert. "The Problems of Wilderness." *Scientific Monthly*, Spring 1930.

McCloskey, Maxine E., and James P. Gilligan, eds. *Wilderness and the Quality of Life*. San Francisco: Sierra Club Books, 1969.

Thoreau, Henry David. *Walden: Or, Life in the Woods*. New York: Signet, 1960.

Turner, Frederick. *Beyond Geography: The Western Spirit Against the Wilderness*. New York: Viking, 1981.

———. *Rediscovering America: John Muir in His Time and Ours*. New York: Viking, 1985.

Turner, Frederick Jackson. "The Significance of the Frontier in American History." In *Problems in American Civilization*, edited by George Rogers Taylor. Boston: D. C. Heath and Co., 1956.

Watkins, T. H. *John Muir's America*. Portland, Ore.: Graphic Arts Center Publishing Company, 1976.


## 6. THE STATE OF NATURE

Cahn, Robert. *The Fight to Save Wild Alaska*. New York: National Audubon Society, 1982.

Chevigny, Hector. *Russian America: The Great Alaskan Venture 1741–1867*. New York: Ballantine Books, 1973.

Gruening, Ernest. *The State of Alaska*. New York: Random House, 1968.

Hanrahan, John, and Peter Gruenstein. *Lost Frontier: The Marketing of Alaska*. New York: W. W. Norton, 1977.

London, Jack. *The Call of the Wild*. New York: Grosset & Dunlap, 1931.

Marshall, Robert. *Alaska Wilderness*. Berkeley: University of California Press, 1970.

———. *Arctic Village*. New York: Random House, 1933.

McGinniss, Joe. *Going to Extremes*. New York: Alfred A. Knopf, 1980.

McPhee, John. *Coming into the Country*. New York: Farrar, Straus and Giroux, 1977.

Murie, Margaret E. *Two in the Far North*. Anchorage: Alaska Northwest Publishing Company, 1957.

Nelson, Richard K., Kathleen Mautner, and G. Ray Bane. *Tracks in the Wild: A Portrayal of Koyukon and Nunamiut Subsistence*. Fairbanks: University of Alaska, 1982.

Norton, Boyd. *Alaska: Wilderness Frontier*. New York: Reader's Digest Press, 1977.

Rakestraw, Lawrence W. *A History of the United States Forest Service in Alaska*. Anchorage: Alaska Historical Commission, 1981.

Williss, G. Frank. *Do It Right the First Time: The National Park Service and the Alaska National Interest Lands Conservation Act of 1980*. Publication of the U.S. Department of the Interior. Washington, D.C., 1986.

### 7. INLAND PASSAGES

Appalachian Mountain Club. *The A.M.C. White Mountain Guide*. Boston: Appalachian Mountain Club, 1979.

DeVoto, Bernard. *Across the Wide Missouri*. Boston: Houghton Mifflin, 1947.

———. *Mark Twain's America*. New York: Chautauqua Institution, 1933.

———, ed. *The Journals of Lewis and Clark*. Boston: Houghton Mifflin, 1953.

Ford, Daniel. *The Country Northward*. Somersworth: New Hampshire Publishing Company, 1976.

Fradkin, Philip L. *A River No More: The Colorado River and the West*. New York: Alfred A. Knopf, 1981.

Huser, Verne. "Wild and Scenic Rivers: Alive But Not Well." *American Forests*, November 1982.

Kauffmann, John, M. *Flow East*. New York: McGraw-Hill, 1973.

McPhee, John. *Encounters with the Archdruid*. New York: Farrar, Straus and Giroux, 1982.

Nichols, John. *The Milagro Beanfield War*. New York: Ballantine Books, 1974.

Palmer, Tim. *Stanislaus: The Struggle for a River*. Berkeley: University of California Press, 1982.

Robbins, Michael. *Along the Continental Divide*. Washington, D.C.: National Geographic Society, 1981.

Twain, Mark. *Life on the Mississippi*. New York: Penguin Books, 1984.

Waterman, Laura and Guy. *Backwoods Ethics: Environmental Concerns for Hikers and Campers*. Boston: Stone Wall Press, 1979.

# INDEX

389